Professional Landscape Management

David L. Hensley
University of Hawaii

ISBN 0-87563-521-0

Published by

STIPES PUBLISHING L.L.C.
204 W. University Ave.
Champaign, Illinois 61820

This book is dedicated to
my wife,
Glenda,
and to my children,
Erin, Joshua, Brooke, Jessica, and Noah.

PROFESSIONAL LANDSCAPE MANAGEMENT

David L. Hensley

Table of Contents

APPENDICES

Introduction

Landscape management has evolved from pick-up truck pseudoscience to a highly sophisticated, fully integrated business that embraces the most sophisticated technology and well trained employees. The 1980's spawned corporate and residential landscapes that demand (dictated) professional landscape management services. The industry grew at a more rapid pace than the educational materials necessary to undergird the art and science. Integrated information is scant and has never been available in a single, holistic reference.

Enter Dr. David Hensley, friend, horticultural colleague, teacher, researcher and contributing editor to Nursery Manager. Over the years, I read Dave's lively, entertaining and educational articles with great interest. His pen spoke clearly, with great knowledge and integrity. The Landscape Management field needed a broad encompassing reference and Dave agreed to the responsibility. He has spent the past five years researching, collating, writing, proofing and rewriting. From my personal experiences with book writing, I told Dave it was a love/hate affair. He crossed the fence many times during the book's development but stayed with the course. His literary journey has resulted in a reference and teaching text that has no parallel in the field.

Dave brought outside experts to bear on the final product, traveled extensively during sabbatical and reviewed thousands of landscape management and maintenance articles. The chapter on *specifications and contracts* provides superb guidance for the preparation of documents that translates to a successful or unsuccessful business. The *fertilization* chapter brings functional, pragmatic information to an area of landscape management that has been treated as voodoo horticulture. *Color in the landscape* is now an integrated part of professional grounds maintenance. Firms have hired full-time color coordinators to manage the design, layout and planting of the displays. Dave brings much needed, up-to-date information to this relatively new area.

Professional Landscape Management was written by a professional for professionals. The book is eminently readable and enjoyable because Dave injects his unique style of humor into the text. This reference will enjoy subsequent fruitful editions and become the standard in the field by which others are judged. Few books withstand the tests of scrutinization and time. Dr. David Hensley has produced such a reference.

Michael A. Dirr
University of Georgia
Department of Horticulture
Athens, GA 30602-7273

Acknowledgments

I must thank a number of people for their support, encouragement, and help with this book. First to my wife, I can never thank Glenda enough for her patience, understanding, and support. Without her, I would not have completed this project. She proofread these manuscripts many times, always without complaint. My children, Erin, Josh, Brooke, Jessica, and Noah provided their love, smiles, and encouragement.

I must also thank Dr. Michael Dirr for his time, enthusiasm, support, and for his editing skills. I learned a great deal from his comments and his help. I appreciate his assistance and friendship.

Many professional landscape managers provided their time and expertise that appear in these pages. I especially thank Mark Yahn and Tracy Morland, Grounds Control, Orlando, FL; Todd Tibbitts, Post Properties, Atlanta, GA; Brian Sichel, Rod Clinton, Karl Sims, and Harry Bell, Maintain, Inc., Dallas and Fort Worth, TX; Kevin Fateley, Kanscapes, Manhattan, KS; Kevin Kelly, Kelly Company, Kansas City, KS; Bill Gordon, Signature Landscape, Overland Park, KS; Mike Bratton, Los Colinas, Dallas, TX; Reg Robertson, Custom Lawn and Landscape, Olathe, KS; Hal Lawrence and Randy James, Hermes, Lenexa, KS; James Kuroiwa, Mahana Landscaping, Honolulu, HI; Joe Sweeny, Corporate Care, Kansas City, MO; Bob Suddarth and Wayne Lovelace, Forest Keeling Nursery, Elsberry, MO; The Morrill Group, Stone Mountain, GA; Cam Rees, Skinner Garden Store, Topeka, KS; Steve Nimz, The Tree People, Honolulu, HI; Jack Morgan, Hawaiian Earth Products, Honolulu, HI; Dave Suddarth, Mueller and Suddarth, Troy, MO; Larry Stouse, Olathe, KS; Karen Bento, LICH, Honolulu, HI; and Jim Welch, Manchester, MO. Many other landscape professionals and former students contributed information and ideas over the years. Thank you.

Former colleagues and forever friends Steve Wiest, Ed Hellman, Roch Gaussoin, Larry Leuthold, Frank Gibbons, Phil Carpenter, Bob McNiel, and Jim Robbins contributed more than they will ever realize.

I wish my parents, Geneva and Lawrence (Poke) Hensley, could have lived to see this effort. My mother passed her appreciation and love for plants to me. My father gave me an appreciation for hard work and a sense of humor.

David L. Hensley

Preface

Landscape management is the most challenging field of horticulture. The true *landscape manager* must appreciate landscape design, know plants and turfgrasses, identify and control pests of all sizes and forms, understand chemicals, soils, and plant nutrition, work with equipment, and know how to grow an ever expanding list of plants. Additionally, the landscape manager faces every day challenges in directing and supervising employees, managing a budget or keeping a business afloat, and dealing with owners, managers, sales representatives, customers, and clients. The landscape professional must also wade through the ever deepening mire of taxes, regulations, and government mandates. It is a tough job.

During the 12 years I have taught landscape management to landscape architecture and horticulture students at Kansas State University and at the University of Hawaii, I have tried to expose students to the diversity of landscape management as a profession, art, science, and as a business. My classes were about evenly divided between landscape architecture and horticulture students, with a sprinkling of park management, business, and other majors. I found no text that satisfied my needs. Many excellent books provided the nuts and bolts of maintaining plants or turf. None, however, treated landscape maintenance as a business.

Landscape architects must produce specifications and contracts. They must know something about maintaining plants before producing requirements for others to follow. Landscape managers must efficiently provide the highest quality care for the plants and everything else on and in the landscape. They must also budget and price work for a profit, if they are to remain in business. Too often texts and references deal only with discrete plant-oriented landscape units: turfgrass; trees; shrubs; or annuals. Landscape managers and landscape designers must deal with developing and maintaining the landscape as the sum of all of its parts. Each aspect of maintaining a landscape is interrelated with others. I have tried to develop a text that provides a survey of business, personnel, and profit oriented topics, as well as considering techniques and technology for properly managing landscape plants. No single edition, however, could adequately cover the depth and breadth of information that is landscape management.

During research for this book I had the opportunity to meet professionals across the country and visit many maintained landscapes. I spent a great deal of time reading journals, trade magazines, and books that had accumulated over the past few years. Writing this book is the most time consuming effort I have ever undertaken. I hope that I can provide some information or thoughts that will be worthwhile.

Chapter 1
Introduction to Landscape Management

Landscape management is the art, science, and skill employed by professionals who maintain all or any part of the exterior environment. The term management, rather than maintenance, is preferred by most professionals in the field. Management, in addition to having a more professional appeal, more correctly describes the responsibilities. Landscape managers are involved with much more than maintaining the plants in a landscape. They are responsible for everything within the site: plants, animals, and the inanimate. The true landscape supervisor is a manager of people, time, equipment, and money. He/she certainly does more than merely mow the grass and trim the "bushes." This text, and most in the profession, will use landscape management and landscape maintenance interchangeably. Either is meant to convey the vocation in the highest professional light.

Photo 1-1. Good landscape management improves the appearance, environment, and quality of public and private grounds. Quality management need not be expensive, but it does require knowledge, care, planning, appropriate design, and a budget appropriate for the needs and desires of the client. Photograph courtesy of James Robbins.

History

The management of landscapes has been conducted for as long as there have been gardens. During the dim reaches of history, gardens for the aristocracy were sometimes maintained by slaves. The landscape contractor, I suppose, was the slave driver. According to many, some things have not changed that much.

Private estates were and continue to be maintained by skilled gardeners. In the past, gardeners began as apprentices and, with time and skill, became head gardeners or superintendents. These *men* usually worked for the same estate their entire life. The position was often passed to their sons. The number of elaborate private gardens in the United States and Europe declined dramatically during the 1930s due to the Depression and inheritance taxes.

Nurseries and individuals have long offered their services to design, install, and maintain landscapes. Only the wealthy, however, could afford these landscape operations. Public and private grounds, including golf courses, sports fields, college campuses, parks, and others were maintained by their own employees. There was tremendous development in landscape design, contracting, and management after World War II. Improved wages and financing opportunities through the GI bill and government agencies made it possible for the number of "homeowners" to skyrocket.

Major growth in lawn and landscape management began in the 1960s. This was due to increases in income, leisure time, and recreational activities by the "masses." There was enhanced appreciation for the appearance of the home and landscape and for the environment. The importance and growth of television should also be mentioned. Consumers were able to experience gardens and maintained landscapes across the world without leaving home. A well-maintained lawn and landscape became an important status symbol with the growth of the suburbs and truly added value to the property.

These and a multitude of other reasons allowed energetic entrepreneurs to develop service-oriented companies that offered professional lawn and landscape maintenance to the public. They could care for the client's lawn better and often less expensively than he/she could do it alone. Some of these companies have grown to operate hundreds of individual franchises nationwide.

Attractive, functional surroundings for indoor and outdoor activities are highly desirable in the business and corporate world. Those who rent property to others—apartments, condominiums, homes, offices, or retail facilities—find and keep tenants more easily when the property is well landscaped and maintained. Attractive shopping centers and malls draw more customers and community approval. Retail managers strive to associate shopping with pleasant experiences: flowers, trees, fountains, and well-groomed landscapes. Motels compete for the traveler with conspicuous exteriors as well as the quality of their services. Private country clubs and golf courses are expected to be "manicured," pleasant, and attractive environments for their members and users.

Public tax dollars spent to beautify parks, playgrounds, schools, and highways contribute to the quality of life. A significant portion of the budget of most progressive cities and governmental organizations is used to maintain and improve the community landscape. Even the military spends millions of dollars per year for landscape development and maintenance by private contractors.

Growth in professional landscape and lawn management was also enhanced by technology. The introduction of reliable

Photo 1-2. Good maintenance of apartment and condominium landscapes is an important marketing tool. The landscape "humanizes" multiple family residences and makes each unit a home for the residents. Plants provide privacy, brighten public areas, and add quality to the property.

Photo 1-3. Well maintained public parks and grounds improve the quality of urban and suburban life. Unfortunately, maintenance is one of the first items to suffer from budget restraints.

automated equipment made it possible for one or two people to do the work of a large crew. Development of low-cost and effective herbicides, insecticides, fungicides, and other pesticides made it possible to realistically reduce biotic factors limiting lawn and landscape quality.

The importance of research and technology must be emphasized. In addition to university research, a significant number of national landscape management, chemical, and equipment corporations initiated and have continued *bona fide* research facilities. They serve their operators, franchises, and customers. Corporations, as well as professional associations, especially those oriented

Photo 1–4. Golf courses and other public or private recreational areas require specialized and intensive landscape management. The Green Industry is made up of many site and task specific parts. The overall goal, however, is improving and managing the environment.

to the turf industry, have been very generous in their continued support of university research programs. Most of the "break throughs" in landscape technology have come from private enterprise or through their financial support.

The Future

The future of lawn and landscape management is at best an educated guess. It can probably be best described by those famous words of the eminent (or notorious) philosopher, Willard Scott: "The outlook is sunny with a chance of showers." Landscape maintenance has and will continue to have the least capital intensive and simplest requirements for entry in all of horticulture. One must literally have a pickup, some tools, and a few customers. The ease of market entrance will decrease somewhat, but will not be an overwhelming obstacle. Competition will heighten and the market in many areas may become saturated.

The mixture of services offered has expanded with the length of time in business. Many firms that began as liquid lawn or turf care companies, for instance, have added mowing, woody plant care, annual color, irrigation, seeding, and a host of other maintenance-oriented activities. Non-management operations including landscape and irrigation design and installation have become part of once maintenance-only companies. Additional services are offered by landscape management firms with time, increased knowledge, and greater sophistication of the principals, expanded customer demand, and desire for increased market share. Companies will continue to evolve and growth will expand into non-horticultural areas, such as lighting, hard surface management, and janitorial services.

The techniques and materials used, especially in the lawn care industry, will certainly change as Americans re-discover concerns for the environment and their health. The population of chemicals on the market will decrease and change. New, safer, materials will replace stand-bys. Broad-spectrum materials will be replaced with pesticides affecting only specific target organisms.

Chemo phobia will reach an apex, and hopefully decline. New national and state pesticide and pesticide-handling legislation will result in a re-discovery of granular herbicides and pesticides.

3

Market research has indicated that consumers perceived dry products to be safer than liquids. Injection of materials into tree trunks will receive greater interest to avoid environmentally unsound spraying. The number of companies using or attempting *"organic"* landscape management will increase. *"Biorational"* will become a popular and probably overused buzz word.

Other environmental legislation limiting access to public landfills will certainly impact handling and costs for landscape and turf management. Mulching mowers will make a resurgence and to not bag clippings will become stylish. Prices and services offered will certainly be affected.

Legislation affecting employment, health care, workers' rights, immigration, and other business factors will impact the landscape manager. Several publications and experts are already talking about a reduction, in not only trained, but in general labor, shortly after the turn of the century. The Associated Landscape Contractors of America Crystal Ball Committee estimated that the landscape contracting industry could expand by 30,000 to 35,000 jobs a year. Labor is already becoming scarce and more expensive. On the positive side, the number of trained graduates from two- and four-year schools and universities will increase. Demand, however, will exceed supply.

Wages must increase to attract and retain employees. Large and small companies will be forced to offer benefit packages that compete with other employment areas. The economy, recession, the price of fuel, and wars in the Middle East will influence the mowing of turf, caring for trees and shrubs, and the general business climate.

Water shortages will increase. Irrigation scheduling and technology will affect prices, profits, and programs. Will your clients accept dormant turf in midsummer? Some may have to. Low water-demand landscape designs and plants will increase and irrigation scheduling and technology will improve.

A great deal of the future depends on the actions and reactions of the industry today. Professionalism in the landscape industry will grow. That in itself will stem many of the problems caused by unknowing and uncaring, "anything for a buck," "low bid mentality" green-pirates. Attitudes, image, and marketing must be positive. The reputation of the industry will improve as it polices itself. Landscape managers must develop and learn environmentally sound techniques. We will not be able to "solve" every problem in the landscape or lawn by spraying or fertilizing with something.

There will also be hard times for landscape managers. Landscape management is not immune to economic stress. As clients have hard times, they reduce the amount of commercial and residential services they purchase. Many present companies will not be able to weather the storm. Public landscape maintenance budgets will be further reduced. This can offer opportunities to privatize maintenance service in order to reduce costs by public agencies.

Good horticulturists must become good business people. The seasonal nature of the industry, under capitalization, profit margins, people and capital management, and business failure cannot be ignored. A survey of the lawn care industry showed business factors and costs were the greatest concerns facing the respondents.

The Industry

Landscape management is a vibrant and challenging profession and industry. Landscape service is an extremely diversified industry and very difficult to characterize. According to the experts, no one truly knows the extent of the landscape management industry, either in number of companies, number of employees, or in gross sales. While farm and nursery production statistics are collected by the Federal and state governments, no agency even estimates the economic contribution of the landscape service industries. It is fair to say that there are tens of thousands of companies, large and small, providing multi-billion dollars of services to millions of commercial and residential clients annually. The number of companies and clients grows daily.

The Crystal Ball Committee of ALCA examined the status of the industry, its growth, and its future in 1975 and again in 1989 [Anonymous, 1990, *Lawn & Landscape Maintenance*, 11(3):20]. Landscape maintenance has become a major profit center and the fastest growing part of the landscape contracting industry. The 1989 report estimated that there were over 15,000 landscape management/maintenance firms. This number did not include landscape contractors and other firms that operated exterior landscape management services as a minor discipline of the company. It also omitted specialized management, such as golf courses, athletic fields, parks, schools, universities, and similar organizations. Over 50,000 landscape management firms were considered as unidentifiable. These small one-person or part-time companies and private gardeners operate outside the recognized industry and reporting systems. The contribution of these firms must certainly be considered in the overall economic consideration of the industry.

Absolute characterization of the industry is impossible. There are many facets to the industry. One must consider the diversification of services and their variations, such as lawn service, liquid-lawn service, chemical lawn service, full-service maintenance, arboriculture, irrigation repair, and so on. There are also a myriad of specialized companies concentrating in turf aeration, annual color, chemical application, tree work, and so on. There is also segmentation by location of the work: golf courses, sports fields, public parks, arboretums, cemeteries, and so many others. Each of these groups, professions, areas, or subdivisions have different requirements, needs, professional associations, and concerns. Regardless, all are part of the landscape or Green Industry.

Educational opportunities and curriculum

The number of schools offering educational curricula in landscape management is increasing. These include more "hands-on" oriented two-year schools as well as four-year public and private colleges and universities. In many others, landscape management or maintenance may be an option within an ornamental or landscape horticulture major. Students in all curricula should receive a basic education in English, math, science, and the humanities. Literature courses may not make mowing a lawn easier, but they may make you a better person.

Photo 1–5. Internships provide important hands-on learning for students. Internships are available through many arboreta, public grounds, and private companies. If possible, students should find an internship outside of their home city or state to broaden their technical, horticultural, and geographic horizons.

Basic horticulture and affiliated course topics include, but are not limited to: plant materials, turf management, irrigation, plant science, pest management, equipment repair, soils, landscape

5

design and construction, and many others. A student should become a well-rounded horticulturist. Table 1–1 provides a more detailed curriculum.

Plant knowledge must be supplemented with business and management courses. If you make a horticultural mistake, you lose the crop; if you make a business mistake, you lose the farm. Include course work in: computers, marketing and sales, production management, personnel management, business law, and accounting. Too often students neglect business courses or take "pud" classes to merely fulfill their requirements. Most former students choosing this path of least resistance have expressed regret soon after experiencing the real world.

Opportunities for employment

Table 1–1. A Curriculum for the Landscape Management Industry
The Associated Landscape Contractors of America suggest combining landscape management, interiorscape management, ornamental horticulture, or landscape architecture with business training.

Basic professional-technical studies include, but are not limited to:

woody and herbaceous plant materials and their use	turfgrass management
irrigation	interior planting design
plant science	equipment use and care
soil science	landscape construction
landscape design	surveying
pest and pesticide management	landscape maintenance
soil fertility or plant nutrition	food production courses
	environmental studies

Business courses should include, but are not limited to:

computer applications	accounting
marketing and sales	business law
economics	finance
business management	business communications
advertising	personnel management
management operations	consumer psychology

All curricula must include a basic education of English, math, and the humanities. Classes should be written and oral communications intensive.

In addition, students should plan to participate in internship or cooperative education programs. Internships provide the basic job skills necessary and give hands-on experience in employee and business management operations.

Adapted with permission from *The Landscape Industry—Growing Careers for You!*, Associated Landscape Contractors of America, Reston, VA.

For the past several years there has been a tremendous demand for students trained in landscape management and all other areas of the "green industry." The requirement has far exceeded the reservoir of students available. High demand will continue for several years as enrollments at two- and four-year institutions stabilize and the number and size of green-oriented service companies continues to expand.

Landscape management offers the opportunity to work outdoors with plants. Part of the mystique is the opportunity to be creative and to work with people. Job placement after completion of an educational program is excellent. Opportunities are available throughout the country. Students have the latitude of selecting a geographic location they would prefer or like to experience.

Opportunities for women are equal to those of men in the field. Women can be found as crew members, supervisors, pesticide or spray technicians, equipment operators, mid- and upper-management, and company owners. Sexual discrimination still exists, but it is less pronounced in the green industry than in many other phases of the business world. The "Good Ole Boys" will become receptive and accepting once they discover that any person, regardless of gender or ethnic background, can carry their own weight.

Landscape management is hard work. It necessitates developing technical and management skills in preparation for mid- and upper-management positions or for establishment of one's own company. Many things cannot be taught and come only through experience. Promotions for talented, educated, and motivated employees come rapidly. Career earnings potential compares favorably with those in allied fields. From my experience in assisting students with employment opportunities, starting salaries in landscape management and other service phases of the green industry are usually higher than in the production and retail end of the business. Salaries will continue to increase as firms compete for a limited pool of trained students.

Keeping Up

Landscape management, as every business, operates on information. The landscape professional and student must stay at the forefront. This requires procuring and digesting information on the technical and business aspects of horticulture, turf, machinery, and personnel management. Every manager should develop and update a library for his/her or the firm's use. The size and diversity of the library should grow with the number of people utilizing the resources. The publications should be read and used, not just collected.

There are many books that provide excellent resource and background. *Appendix 1* provides a list of several books useful to landscape managers. This is by no means an exhaustive list. New books constantly enter the market. Some will prove invaluable, while others may not. Since books are expensive, determine if the publication is valuable as a reference before purchasing it. If one must err, I would prefer to buy a book that I may use little, rather than not have one that would be useful.

Table 1–2. Positions Available in the Landscape Industry

Positions and career patterns depend on the size of the company, type of work performed, training, and market area. The following are some positions in the landscape industry by desired level of education.

Entry level—High school education—No experience

Crew Person
Landscape Maintenance Trainee
Interior Plant Maintenance Trainee

High school education—Some experience

Crew Chief
Crew Leader
Foreman Trainee
Foreman/Supervisor
Chemical Technician

College Education (Two- or Four-year Program)

Chemical Technician
Foreman/Supervisor
Superintendent
Project Manager
Production Manager
Irrigation Technician
Interior Landscape Technician
Sales Trainee
Sales Representative
Sales Manager
Department, Division, or Branch Manager
Company Management

Positions in accounting, finance, business management, and marketing area are also available in most firms.

Adapted with permission from: *The Landscape Industry—Growing Careers for You!* by the Associated Landscape Contractors of America, Reston, VA.

Magazines, periodicals, and newsletters provide a frequent window to the business and technical aspects of landscape maintenance. *Appendix 2* lists some of those of interest to the landscape professional. Publications specializing in certain aspects of the trade as well as general sources of information are available. Many magazines are available at no cost to professionals and students, while others charge for an annual subscription. The problem today is not one of too little information available, it is finding the time to read all of the sources available.

Video periodicals, monthly video tapes covering a variety of subjects, have been initiated. These offer yet another source of information. Videos may prove popular for quick updates and for those of the television generation.

Reference and training video tapes and interactive computer programs are also available. Videos and computer exercises can be used to train employees on safety, pesticides, equipment operation and care, and many other topics. They are also valuable as library references. Many local associations rent videos to their members.

Professional associations, organizations, and societies provide the best means for the professional to stay attuned to the business and technical information. Join and participate in the professional organizations.

Do not limit participation to only local or only national organizations. Both have value. Local groups allow networking and idea exchange with companies and competitors in the same or similar markets. National and regional groups and meetings allow the manager to meet and learn from people from a wide geographic base.

A large and growing number of trade organizations serve the green industry. Some are very specialized while others provide a more holistic approach. *Appendix 3* lists some of the many organizations directed to the landscape service industries. Again, this is not a complete listing. It omits regional, state, and local groups.

Most associations also provide publications of news, technical developments, new products, business information, and other topics of interest. Organizations organize an annual or more frequent meeting, usually accompanied by a trade show. Trade shows are excellent places to see and compare equipment and material.

Local, regional, and state organizations, as well as university research and extension personnel, also organize educational meetings, trade shows, equipment demonstrations, and field days. Topics are aimed at a narrower geographic or climatic area. Take key employees to beneficial meetings. Meetings serve as a reward for work well done, produce a better trained employee, increase morale and let them know the company cares.

Bibliography

Anonymous. 1985. ALCA publishes survey of maintenance companies. *American Nurseryman,* 161(10):6–7.

Anonymous. 1990. Landscape contracting today and in the year 2000. *Lawn & Landscape Maintenance,* 11(3):20–21.

Anonymous. 1990. Respectable growth predicted this year. *Lawn & Landscape Maintenance,* 11(6):15–16.

Anonymous. 1993. The "green" industry. *American Nurseryman,* 177(4):17.

Code, C. 1988. Going full-service? *ALA,* 9(10):22–26.

Code, C. 1988. Full service lawn care: The shape of things to come. *ALA/Maintenance,* 9(11):24–26, 32–36.

Code, C. 1990. Will strength in numbers prevail? *Lawn & Landscape Maintenance,* 11(11):22–25.

Flemer, W., III. 1988. New kids on the block. *American Nurseryman,* 168(9):45–55.

Fong, H. 1989. The art and science of management. *The Public Garden,* 4(3):20–21.

Hensley, D. 1993. Are you keeping up with trends in the business? *Nursery Manager,* 9(5):70–71.

Jones, D. 1990. Designing programs to guide your firm's work force. *Lawn & Landscape Maintenance,* 11(3):36–40.

Lay, C. F. 1978. The management of grounds of site maintenance operations. In: *Manual of Site Management.* Environmental Design Press. Reston, VA.

Marcellino, M. 1989. Hiring in the 1990's: Will there be enough workers? *ALA/Maintenance,* 10(2):38–44, 75.

Marcellino, M. 1989. Selling, servicing the competitive homeowner market. *Lawn & Landscape Maintenance,* 10(9):22–25.

McGary, R. 1990. Service in the 90's. *Landscape Management,* 29(11):18–22.

McIver, T. 1990. The water's fine. *Landscape Management,* 29(3):54–56.

McIver, T. 1991. Top 50. They can't stand still. *Landscape Management,* 30(4):32–38.

Sobul, J. 1988. Green and growing. *Landscape Management,* 27(2):22–26.

Westrick, D. 1990. Green industry women are taking on leadership roles. *Lawn & Landscape Maintenance,* 11(9):34–38.

Chapter 2
Marketing Landscape Management

Every landscape management firm must market itself to obtain new customers and increase business. Market strategies, advertising, and selling methods vary with: size of the company; scope of services offered; market (residential, commercial, or both); and size of market (city).

Regardless of the variables, every landscape management company claims their number one advertisement is their quality of work. This is the most effective and inexpensive method of retaining present customers and obtaining new ones. Every landscape management contractor with whom I have talked feels he/she is providing quality service for a fair price. Quality, unfortunately, is frequently equated with price. Quality workmanship need not be expensive. A portion of merchandising and selling landscape services is educational. Clients must be shown and taught that price should not be the primary determination for selecting a contractor or management program.

Photo 2–1. Management of residential landscapes is a highly competitive and lucrative market. Clientelle choose management companies on price and quality. Most high-end landscapes are obtained by referral from a satisfied customer. Managing residential landscape requires working closely with the homeowner and understanding their needs. Photograph courtesy of Mark Yahn, Ground Control™ Landscaping, Orlando, FL.

The intensity and scope of promotional activities vary. The greatest amount of advertising occurs in the residential market. Managers can supplement their paid advertising with public relations techniques designed to keep the company's name before present and potential customers. Studies have shown that some of the techniques that bring in the most business also cost the least.

Company Image and Professionalism

One effective method of marketing and advertising is projection of a strong, professional company image. A positive company image inspires confidence in the firm. It tells the client that these people know what they are doing, that they will treat them fairly, that they are trustworthy, and that they are professionals. A negative company image needs no explanation.

The image of the company is exuded in everything it does. Assuming every contractor does or has the potential to do quality work, how is the "image" of a successful company created and portrayed?

Photo 2-2. Many commercial sites are maintained by in-house grounds crews. Commercial landscapes are also maintained on competitive bid. Commercial landscapes may allow use of larger, more profitable equipment. Working hours should be coordinated with the client. The market is very price competitive and quality oriented.

Logos

A *logo* is the visual representation of the company. It is the professional stamp, sign, and signature. The logo is the symbol by which your clients and competitors will, hopefully, recognize vehicles, personnel, correspondence, and the company in general. The logo representing the company should be high quality and professionally drawn; it is your trademark.

Illustration 2-1. Logos are the symbol by which the landscape management firm is recognized by clients and competitors. They should appropriately represent the company and its services and be professional quality. These logos are courtesy of Mark Yahn, Ground Control™ Landscaping, Orlando, FL, Kevin Fateley, Kanscapes®, Manhattan, KS, and Hermes Landscaping, Lenexa, KS.

Many new companies spend an inordinate amount of time selecting just the right image for their company logo. Others, however, do not spend enough. Some go through several logos and symbols before selecting one that they feel justly represents them. Company names and logos can be registered with your state's Secretary of State to prevent others from inadvertently or intentionally adopting them. The company's name and logo should be used on all vehicles, correspondence, invoices, advertisements, and uniforms.

Trucks and equipment

Take a look at the firm's equipment. The trucks should be clean and painted with a uniformly lettered logo and phone number. If the owner and his/her personnel do not take pride in their equipment, then why should the client expect them to take pride in their work or in the care of his/her property? The trucks and other equipment do not have to be new, but they do have to be reasonably clean. Few firms, especially new and small companies, can afford to purchase a fleet of shiny, new trucks and equipment. Serviceable used vehicles can be cleaned and painted. Most successful companies re-paint trucks, trailers, mowers, and other equipment during the off-season.

Photo 2-3. Vehicles should be clean and tastefully display the firm's name and phone number. A company that is paid to bring out the best in a home or commercial site should take pride in its equipment. What better advertising than the vehicle parked in front of a quality landscape being maintained by highly professional employees?

It should be the responsibility of the crew to remove debris and clean the vehicle daily, either before or after starting on their appointed routes. The truck should be washed once a week. Some firms have the crews come in early one day per week for washing vehicles; others have designated personnel that come in off-hours to clean vehicles.

Correspondence

Letterhead, invoices, and other correspondence should contain the company logo, complete address, and phone number. Correspondence must be professional and attractive. Perception is important; using recycled paper for stationery is very appropriate for an environmentally attuned firm. Correspondence should be clear, concise, grammatically correct, and typed without corrections. Nothing dampens client enthusiasm or the company's image more than a letter full of spelling errors and poor grammar. Billings should be correct and timely.

Personnel

The client sees the field employees on at least a weekly basis. They are the company to the client. What do they say about the firm and how do they say it? The employees should be uniformed, clean, and they should be taught how to respond to and deal with client questions and complaints. Every employee should feel that he or she is part of a winning team.

Uniforms are required by most successful landscape management companies. Uniforms distinguish the firm's employees from the others working on-site and enhance a professional image.

Clients prefer contracted service employees to be uniformed. This enhances their own image and makes security easier. Uniforms should be the "company" color and the employee's name and company logo displayed.

Many management companies provide uniforms but employees are responsible for cleaning or laundering charges, usually through a contract uniform company. Some firms are more generous than this, others less. At a minimum, even the smallest employer can provide every employee with Tee shirts and caps in the company color imprinted with the firm's name or logo.

Photo 2-4. Employees represent the company to the client. Employees should be neat, uniformed if possible, and communicate professionalism.

Require employees to keep their hair and person neat. Appropriate footwear should be required, including safety boots where imperative or prudent. Some enterprises provide footwear to employees; the cost must be reimbursed if the employee is dismissed or leaves within a given time.

Instruct employees on dealing with client questions or complaints. Every employee running a mower or string trimmer cannot be expected to provide instant diagnosis of problems. They can, however, be expected to be polite, understanding, and to refer the questioner to the supervisor. The supervisor or employee should pass any questions, complaints, or comments that cannot be immediately answered to someone within the company who can provide action. Encourage employees to report any damage to the site or equipment, regardless of cause. Consider a finder's fee for employees who produce leads that turn into a new contract or additional work on an existing contract.

Develop a professional image when recruiting and hiring employees. Many contractors support and attend career days at colleges and universities and make donations to scholarships and horticulture clubs. Develop a quality recruiting packet for attracting key employees; seek the assistance of a professional designer if necessary. Develop an employee handbook with information on company benefits, insurance programs, policies and procedures, disciplinary rules, and so forth. Have the book available in English and other languages, as necessary.

Organizations

The image and expertise of the company are enhanced by joining and actively participating in local, state, and national professional organizations. Encourage key employees to become certified, if certification is available.

Do not omit associations of affiliated industries, such as landscape architects and designers. Landscape architects and designers are people who may recommend your company. Avail yourself of program and panel discussion opportunities, exhibit at trade shows and help sponsor social gatherings.

Advertising

Numerous merchandising and promotional techniques are available to put the company name in front of potential customers. Each has its successes and disappointments, depending upon the market, budget, locality, and quality of the effort. What works for one company may not work equally for another. Little information, however, is available to the professional on effective marketing of landscape management.

Referrals

Landscape management companies rely heavily upon referrals for increasing commercial and residential accounts, regardless of their market size. Referrals require quality work at a fair price; the customer must feel that he/she has received value for the funds expended. Referrals are especially important with commercial accounts and "high dollar" residential landscapes. There is a definite network between commercial property managers. Most owners of large, expensive residential landscapes will not consider a firm without suitable references.

Keep in touch with companies that contract for office cleaning, general building maintenance, and so forth. Invite principals of such businesses to breakfast or lunch and get to know them. Build a network of contractors with whom information and job leads can be shared.

Few clients are swayed by lunches or other entertainment. The burden is to provide good service and handle complaints fairly. It is important to do whatever it takes, within reason, to maintain a good relationship with the property managers and persons in charge of the landscape.

Traditional advertising

Television, radio, newspaper

Few, if any, companies specializing in or seeking commercial management accounts utilize television, radio, or newspaper advertisements. These traditional media do not target commercial markets and are very expensive. Television, radio, and newspaper advertisements are successfully used to attract residential accounts, however. Lawn service and chemical applicators more typically utilize mass media than full-service management firms. Before using mass media, solicit the advice of a competent consultant to develop effective advertisements. I have seen some local, self-produced television spots for lawn service companies that were quite embarrassing.

Business publications

City, area, or regional specialized magazines, newsletters, or other publications are available for the business community. These provide an opportunity to put the company in front of business owners, managers, property managers, and purchasing agents. Again, think quality; seek the assistance of a professional to develop advertisements.

Write articles for business and property management-oriented magazines. Establish professional competence and a willingness to share expertise. A list of published articles enhances the company's résumé.

Yellow pages

Allowing the customers' fingers to do the walking can be an expensive form of advertisement for the landscape and lawn maintenance companies. Yellow pages advertising charges are based on the dimensions of the ad and the size of the market covered. Several landscape management contractors have told me that they did not feel Yellow Pages' ads were especially effective. They felt that most people used them to look up the company's phone number, not to select a contractor. All contractors believed that it was important to have an advertisement, however. They felt that since everyone else was listed, they also had to have a listing. Several listings under various headings (trees, lawns, spraying, etc) may be required to indicate the extent of services provided.

Direct mail

Many residential and commercial landscape contractors use direct mail advertising. Direct mail can target specific zip codes or segments of the market, depending upon the mailing lists used. Direct mail is a powerful medium. It reaches customers unavailable through other media and allows the firm to present a great deal of information. Direct mail appeals can be accompanied by a post-paid return card or a phone number that the potential client can use to initiate contact with or receive an estimate from the company. Some companies offer direct mail special "deals" or discounts to attract attention.

Consultants can help develop a direct mail campaign, although many contractors formulate their own letter, return cards, and mailing lists. Mailing lists are available from Chambers of Commerce, country clubs, apartment and other management associations, all for a price. Direct mail can be an expensive form of advertising considering the cost of developing, printing, handling, and mailing each piece, even at bulk postal rates.

Direct mail is popular among lawn service companies seeking to expand their residential market. A typical homeowner within a desirable market area will frequently receive several direct mail appeals. Remember this when designing your effort to prevent the campaign from falling into the category of "junk" mail. A piece of direct mail has only a 20 percent chance of capturing the reader's attention for up to 8 seconds. It must attract attention, spark interest, represent quality, and inspire confidence, without having the appeal of a circus barker, "Hurry, Hurry, Hurry,. . . ". Determine what the customer is interested in learning and present this in combination with photographs and art work.

The return on direct mail campaigns is low, usually around 2 percent or lower per mailing. Most direct letters find a direct route to the trash can. *Bona fide* potential customers return their cards or make contact with the company quickly after receiving the mailing. Contractors sometimes use 3 to 4 mailings within a short time span to the same audience. Successive mailings serve as reminders to potential clients who procrastinated in mailing their return card.

Direct mail can also introduce the company to new markets or areas and make clients aware of new offerings. It is typically the first advertising effort a new company makes. Direct mail can be successful in the commercial as well as the residential marketplace.

Newsletters

Newsletters are forms of direct mail advertising bringing the company name before customers and potential customers. Newsletters may well be the marketing tool of the 90s because of the affordability of desktop publishing.

Illustration 2–2. Newsletters can effectively communicate to present and potential clients. They can be adapted to residential or commercial markets, however their style will differ. This commercial market newsletter communicates the firm's accomplishments, tips, company news, tastefully markets a service, highlights the services offered, and promotes their clientele. *The above example shows 2 pages of a 4-page newsletter.*

Newsletters are more frequently perceived as information; the recipient is less likely to discard it as unsolicited advertising. They are effective in residential and commercial markets but the content and approach must differ. The newsletter may be elaborate, typeset, illustrated, printed on high quality paper, or it may be simple, typed, and photocopied. The commercial market will likely respond to the former.

Residential newsletters can discuss almost anything from "how-to hints" on gardening, to recipes. Commercial newsletters generally take a loftier approach, discussing happenings, changes, and promotions within the company. They may discuss the effect of recent weather (drought or unusual temperatures) on landscape plants. Education is an important function and appeal to newsletters.

Avoid overt self-promotion or advertising in the newsletter. According to the experts, if the recipient perceives the newsletter as strictly advertising, they are less likely to read it.

Newsletters require time from the manager to write, edit, and produce. Many companies begin them as a noble effort but soon lose interest. Professionally written newsletters are available. They

16

can be printed with your logo and heading. Some companies will further localize the newsletter by including lead stories from the manager.

Full-time or part-time salespeople

Most landscape management companies eventually grow to the point where the owner or manager is no longer able to keep up with the volume of requests. At this point, dedication of some employees to sales is an option, if not a necessity. Full-time salespeople are more common among companies aimed at commercial accounts.

The role of the salesperson varies. Some are involved strictly with calling on property managers and potential clients to present proposals and bids, and to sell contracts. Others provide follow-ups, property and quality inspections, and handle client complaints. Titles such as Contract Representative, Contract Supervisor, or Sales Representative indicate that the duties are expanded beyond simply eating lunch with, and selling the client.

Successful landscape management salespeople are typically paid by commission and often make good wages. Most managers realize that the more a salesperson is making on commission, the more work they are providing the company, and the more profit for the owner.

Sales support

The most valuable support for a sales force is quality work. Other important support includes lists of potential clients, referrals, and other sources of leads. High quality, professionally designed brochures and sales aids explaining the company's history, philosophy, resources, and services are a necessity. Several firms provide salespeople and clients with brochures to compare the buyer's present contractor with those services and benefits proposed. These client advantages for comparison might include: uniformed employees, number of years in the business, insurance coverage, education and quality of key people, and any other unique, desirable, or vendible attributes of the organization.

Consultants and advertising support

Public relations firms, advertising agencies, and advertising consultants can provide real assistance to landscape contractors in developing marketing strategies, advertisements, and campaigns. The company must be ready to budget significant dollars to advertising. The return for dollars invested may not be the equivalent found for other products. I have spoken with landscape contractors who have made it to the "big time" and hired advertising agency support. Some did not feel the return warranted the investment due to the limited and specialized markets they were approaching. Others felt that outside assistance was critical for specific campaigns.

Advertising education, assistance, and information are available through other trade associations. However, marketing assistance is extremely limited from associations serving the Green Industry. This will improve as markets and budgets tighten in the future. Advertising support and assistance in the residential market is available to companies that are part of a national franchise.

Non-traditional advertising

Many seldom-thought-about, unaccustomed methods of advertising the company and its services are possible. The owner/manager should be amenable to novel ways to place the company's name before potential customers.

Newcomers assistance groups

In most areas there are *newcomers groups,* such as Welcome Wagon®, that meet and greet new families to the community. Newcomer services provide information to people who are new homeowners, who are not familiar with the city, and who may be in the market for landscape services. Several landscape installation and management contractors distribute information, coupons, and other printed material through these groups. This is not a free service. Users can limit exposure to specific zip codes, neighborhoods, or areas.

Lawn and garden shows

Lawn and garden shows are popular in the winter and spring throughout the nation. They provide an opportunity to showcase services and wares to potential residential customers and conduct public education. They permit direct and personal contact with people.

The effort must be first rate since one never gets a second chance to make a first impression. The booth or display must be attractive and eye-catching so that people will stop. Every firm is vying for the time and interest of the same audience. What makes your display and company different and interesting?

Select the best, most out-going employees to host the booth. They must be

Photo 2–5. Lawn and garden shows are common in the spring in nearly every market. Homeowners and gardeners flock to them for their first breath of spring. These shows provide excellent opportunities to meet potential clients for landscape management. Successful advertising efforts for garden shows require investments of time, money, and effort.

able to meet and greet people, inspire confidence and professionalism, and politely sell services. Avoid hard sell; make contact and then follow-up. Also remember that people visiting lawn, garden, or home shows like to pick up something to take home. Have key chains, pens, balloons, letter openers, refrigerator magnets, printed information, or anything pertaining to the company available as souvenirs. Another guise to attract attention is to offer a door prize for a few lucky winners. People will fill out their name and address on the entry forms, thus providing contacts.

Community relations

Good community relations keep the firm's name before potential and present consumers. Serving on a local board or advisory council, such as the parks board, may be as easy as contacting the city or county department and indicating interest and availability. Pick one that is not too controversial.

Some companies donate their services to worthy, non-profit, high visibility sites or organizations, such as Ronald McDonald® Houses. Many organizations will gladly allow signs or mention the donating firm's name when appropriate. Develop news releases of charitable work or donations and send them to local newspapers and publications. If the releases are well-written and of sufficient news value, they will be printed or a reporter will follow-up for additional details.

Local associations

Membership in local or regional associations of commercial clients is an excellent way to make contacts and become known. Most larger market areas have apartment managers, property managers, builders, developers, and other trade groups. Be available for programs on landscape management to these groups, as well as to homeowners' associations. This develops and enhances your reputation as a local expert and gets the company name in front of the market.

Joining and/or attending local service club meetings results in contact with new people. Service clubs are composed of successful and up-and-coming civic-minded members of the business community. People are more likely to patronize the business when they have met someone associated with it. Contact program chairs of local organizations and offer to speak. Develop a few well-illustrated talks on plant selection, lawn care, water conservation, or other horticultural topics that can be used on short notice.

Awards

Awards for quality landscape design, installation, and management for commercial and residential categories are available from national organizations, including ALCA, as well as some state, regional, and local professional associations. Select the best, not necessarily the largest, properties for entry. Take photographs throughout the seasons. Hire a professional photographer, if necessary, to develop a quality presentation.

Winning an award provides a boost to the firm's professional standing, the client, employee morale, your ego, and is an outstanding advertising point.

Provide a copy of the award or plaque to the client. Awards for management of the site hanging in the reception area dampen the enthusiasm of the competitor's salespeople.

Pass the recognition for the award on to the crew performing the work. Some companies provide trips, bonuses, or other tangible forms of gratitude to crews and supervisors who have accomplished award-winning feats.

News releases

Every business makes news regularly. A company may add a new line of merchandise, expand to new service areas, or hire and promote people. These are potentially newsworthy items. Most business owners are shy about promoting themselves through the news media. One secret of getting the business featured in stories throughout the year is to produce and distribute press releases. News departments are not sufficiently staffed to afford the luxury of sending a reporter to dig up local, small-business news. They are, however, interested in including it. Remember those high school and/or college writing classes and practice.

Local radio stations and cable TV channels are always seeking items of interest to their audiences. Contact show managers or hosts and provide information on gardening or landscape management. Furnish information on use of annuals that require minimal water, managing home lawns during water restrictions, or other timely topics. Be prepared to explain your qualifications and ideas in a coherent manner. Hemming and hawing on the telephone reduce the chances of getting on the show. Work yourself into the enviable position of the local expert that newspapers, radio, and television stations contact for comments on plant or landscape-related stories.

In summary, there are many avenues available to present the company's good name to existing and potential clients. Be resourceful and look for opportunities. The bottom line, however, is quality work. If the company provides inferior work, no amount of advertising or high pressure sales will keep a sinking business afloat.

Table 2–1. Service Keeps Customers

Customers and clients demand good service. Service is the only commodity that a landscape management firm or any other service-oriented company has to offer. Customers look for some measurable, universal standards when it comes to service.

Zero Errors in merchandise, orders, or paperwork.

On-time performance. Be on-time 100 percent of the time for appointments, deliveries, or scheduled visits.

Quick resolution of problems. Clients look to the company to correct service or product problems. Satisfaction depends upon time required or needed to "fix" the problem and the amount credited to their account.

Concern. Clients feel they deserve genuine concern and care; after all, they are paying for it. A few positive strokes go a long way. Be truthful. "I don't know, but I'll find out," works better than any line.

The answer to a problem. Clients prefer honest, enthusiastic answers to questions or problems.

Spontaneity and flexibility. Key employees and management should be flexible to handle minor problems and adjustments on the spot.

A positive attitude when curing a mistake. "No problem! It was our fault and we'll take care of it." Bad attitudes beget more bad attitudes.

Bibliography

Bruce, F. and M. Lynch. 1990. Customer service. *Florida Foliage,* 16(9):7–9.

Capozzi, P. 1990. Uniforms: Helping shape professionalism in the green industry. *Lawn & Landscape Maintenance,* 11(10):12.

Carnes, B. 1989. Public relations. *Grounds Maintenance,* 24(4): 90–93, 148.

Code, C. 1988. Going full-service? *ALA,* 9(10):22–24, 26.

Code, C. 1989. Creative marketing targets customer's specialized needs. *ALA/Maintenance,* 10(3):22–26, 75–77.

Evans, J. A. 1993. Keeping in touch. *Lawn & Landscape Maintenance,* 14(5):48–51.

Hensley, D. 1987. Scouting for business. *Nursery Manager,* 3(7):60–62.

Hensley, D. 1991. Taking care of your business. *Nursery Manager,* 7(7):115–116.

Hensley, D. and J. Rathlef. 1991. Choose the right name, logo for your business. *Nursery Manager,* 9(7):97–98.

Marcellino, M. 1989. Selling, servicing the competitive homeowner market. *Lawn & Landscape Maintenance,* 10(9):22–25.

Merrifield, B., Jr. 1993. Perfect Service. *American Nurseryman,* 177(7):67–69.

McNamee, N. A. 1990. When the customer is dead wrong. *Grounds Maintenance,* 25(8):80.

McNiel, R. and D. Hensley. 1981. Improving your advertising. *Southern Florist and Nurseryman,* 94(41):9.

Petree, J. 1988. The write stuff. *American Nurseryman,* 167(8):93.

Petree, J. 1988. Direct mail. *American Nurseryman,* 168(3):91.

Petree, J. 1988. Writing copy right! *American Nurseryman,* 168(9):1, 97.

Ricciardi, C. 1990. Specialized marketing methods attract and keep clients for interiorscape firms. *Landscape Contractor,* 31(5):22–26.

Rose, V. F. 1987. Cracking the commercial market. *ALA,* 8(5):30–33.

Smucker, B. 1984. Image means business for landscape maintenance contractors. *American Nurseryman,* 159(10):63–65.

Stiles, B. 1990. Promotion ideas to boost your sales. *Landscape Contractor,* 31(1):36–38.

Wagner, W. G. 1990. Avoiding the pitfalls of yellow pages advertising. *Lawn & Landscape Maintenance,* 11(9):40–44.

Westrick, D. 1990. Operators turning to franchising more frequently. *ALA,* 11(2):34–40, 77.

Chapter 3
Specifications and Contracts[1]

The relationship between client and contractor must be established on business and professional terms. Although the integrity of the parties is still important, business is seldom conducted with a handshake and a smile. Misunderstandings between clients and landscape management contractors can and do develop. The adoption of well-written specifications and contracts avoid confusion for both parties.

MAINTENANCE SPECIFICATIONS

Mention the word "specifications" to many contractors and they grimace. Specifications are sometimes viewed as inordinate, unnecessary, and the bane of the contractor. Specifications, however, serve to detail the requirements and expectations of the owner and to protect the client and the contractor.

Specifications are simply a method of communication from the client, or his agent (landscape architect, designer, or consultant) to the landscape management contractor establishing the ground rules of what, how, and when maintenance services are to be performed on the site. Specifications may be part of the requests for bid, the contract documents, or the final contract. Specifications vary widely in use, complexity, and adherence. They are not legally binding unless made part of a final, signed contract.

Most frequently, specifications are produced by a landscape architect, designer, or consultant at the request of and to protect the owner. Maintenance specifications or schedules are often part of the client's contractual expectations of the landscape architect. Many landscape architects also insist that maintenance instructions are part of their developmental services. They want to be assured that the landscape they have designed will be cared for properly so that it may achieve its design intent.

Specifications protect the owner by ensuring that all necessary care for the landscape is considered by the contractor and establishing standards for the work. Specifications provide a uniform format for bids and estimates when several contractors are being considered for a property. The owner can evaluate the various prices for conducting the same work; he/she can compare apples with apples.

Likewise, the specified provisions serve to protect the contractor. Specifications describe the limitations of the contractor's responsibilities and can forestall the contractor from doing work not included in the proposal or bid. They may also establish billing and payment dates and requirements.

Specifications, as well as maintenance schedules, may also be produced by the landscape contractor. They are used to detail the program included in a proposal and the obligations of the contractor and the owner.

---

[1]A special thanks to David W. Suddarth, Attorney, for his input and review of this chapter.

Writing Specifications

In this discussion of specifications we will consider the views of the author (landscape architect or designer) and the reader (landscape management contractor). The objective of both the landscape architect and maintenance contractor should be to provide the owner the best landscape care possible for a fair price. The communications set forth within specifications should be between members of the same team; not the weapons of adversaries.

Specifications differ widely; there are no set standards for their preparation, use, complexity, or dimensions. True specifications differ from contracts in that they do not contain the elements of a contract, such as payment schedules, recitation of parties, default clauses, or signature lines. They are not binding agreements in themselves, however, they are routinely made part of a contract by reference. Specifications may or may not contain a schedule of events, may or may not establish standards, and may or may not be understandable.

Good specifications are not easy to write and use a style of their own. Since they usually serve as part of legal documents, the utmost care should be exercised in their crafting. Several "canned" specifications and contracts are available from professional societies, consultants, texts, and other publications. These serve as a format and starting point; however, they should not be adopted verbatim. A good set of specifications and contracts utilize the writer's experience and reflect regional and site variations.

Computers and word processors makes repeated preparation of these documents easier. A "master" outline for specifications or contracts is stored, easily recalled, and modified. This luxury, unfortunately, can result in the specifications becoming stale or not changing with technology or the site. Landscape architects too frequently use specifications prepared for earlier projects or during a college class without rewriting them. Each site has unique problems and requirements and, accordingly, specifications must be adjusted.

If the firm is designing and implementing projects in various regions of the country, then the landscape architect should solicit advice and comments from local extension and university personnel, landscape professionals, consultants, or management contractors. If you don't know what is appropriate in a specific situation, find out.

Specifications from a private firm, for work let to a limited bid list, or for negotiated contracts will be simpler than those issued by public agencies. Public agencies use detailed and stringent specifications to protect themselves from incompetent or unscrupulous contractors. The procedures are detailed and the selection of materials limited. Specifications for federal and other government work may include the wage rates paid laborers and the type of equipment to be used. The qualifications and requirements for the contractor will also be rigid. The firm's records and performance will likely be audited.

As with any writing, specification crafting begins with an outline. List every management area that will be covered and discussed. Consult one of several "canned" sets of specifications, those written by other members of the firm, or those received for other projects for style, guidance, and inspiration. Select a comfortable format and begin writing. A thorough set of instructions requires several drafts; review them for content and clarity.

Specifications, like contracts, are written in sections. Each section is divided into sub-sections, articles, or paragraphs. A workable format for specifications might include: title; location; scope of work; materials; and general instructions.

Title

The *title* is the subject of the specifications, such as:

- *SPECIFICATIONS FOR SITE MANAGEMENT FOR _____.*
- *SPECIFICATIONS FOR THE MAINTENANCE OF _____.*
- *SPECIFICATIONS FOR THE MAINTENANCE OF THE TURF AND LANDSCAPES AT _____.*

The title may also include the specific areas of the proposal, such as turf or annual color beds, if it is limited to these sections.

Location

The *location* describes exactly where the work will be performed. This may be simply an address or include a legal description of the property, such as . . . *bounded by Elm avenue to the North and Magnolia street to the West.* The location is also detailed in contracts.

"LOCATION OF WORK: Corporate Office Center, 2113 Glenda Avenue, Anytown, KS 99999 (a 20 acre commercial site, bounded by Erin Drive on the West, Brooke Avenue on the East and by Jessica Street to the South.)."

Scope of Work

The *Scope of Work* provides an overview of what is to be done.

- "**SCOPE OF WORK:** Furnish all supervision, labor, material, equipment, and transportation required to maintain the landscape in an attractive condition throughout the year, as specified below."
- "**SCOPE OF WORK:** Furnish all necessary, supervision, labor, material, equipment, and transportation to complete the work described herein."
- "**SCOPE OF WORK:** Provide supervision, labor, material, equipment, and transportation, necessary to provide complete and continuous maintenance of all trees, shrubs, groundcovers, lawns, seasonal color beds of annual plants, and all other work connected thereto as specified below."

And so on. Do not get carried away with excessive details in the Scope of Work, that is what the later sections are for. Include exactly what the company is expected to provide: material; labor; and machinery. Some authors also incorporate supervision, transportation, proper licenses and insurance, and other details into the scope. While these items that may be taken for granted, including them in the Scope of Work is worthwhile and recommended.

Materials

This section describes standards for materials. Quality descriptions establish acceptable quality for plants and other material in landscape installation specifications. Material quality standards are not, however, often used in landscape maintenance specifications or in maintenance contracts. Include a separate materials section only if the author needs to guarantee the quality or use of specific plant material (annuals), mulch, or fertilizer.

Landscape installation specifications often request that use or installation of materials or plants be delayed until they are approved by the landscape architect or his/her representative. A delay for approval for using materials in landscape management would be an inordinate and costly inconvenience. I have never seen any maintenance specification or contracts requiring material approval prior to use.

Material quality and limitation in landscape management are most typically dealt with in the later sections involving their use. Fertilizers are briefly discussed in sections involving fertilization, annuals in the color bed section, and water in the irrigation paragraphs. Presume that the contractor will be reasonable and quality-oriented. Allow him/her to make management decisions as to most specific products and material to conduct a first-rate program.

The one material I would address is *water*. Concerns can be easily dispatched with a simple sentence, *"All water will be furnished by the owner."* or similar. Unnecessary as it may seem, I heard of one case where the contractor ended up paying the water bill. Wolves come dressed in all manner of clothing. A separate article or section can be written to address additional concerns, if necessary.

General Instructions

The *general instructions* are the essence of specifications. They communicate the methods, chronology, materials, restrictions, standards, grades, and qualities that are requested and required.

The general section is organized into *subsections* covering each important element within the landscape: Trees, Shrubs, Turf or Lawns, Seasonal Color (annuals and/or bulbs), Groundcovers, Parking Areas, Irrigation System, and others, as necessary. The subsections detail specific care of the particular areas, such as fertilization, weed control, disease and insect control, pruning, and others.

Care requirements in the subsections should be as explicit as necessary. Make the conditions results-oriented where ever possible. The client wants more than the shrub beds weeded, he/she wants "weed-free beds." Consider what the end result should be and put it in writing.

Avoid generalities such as "good" or "workman-like manner" unless these qualities are defined or details are presented to explain what is meant. What is "workman-like" or acceptable to one person may not be to another. Hence, everyone is unhappy and a lawsuit may result. A workman-like manner for weeding shrub beds might include *"avoiding damage to surrounding plants, removing all debris and waste, and redressing the mulch surface."*

Quantify specifications by providing measurable guidelines.

"All newly planted trees will be watered weekly (every 7 days) during the first ten (10) weeks after planting by applying water with a hand-set sprinkler and hose. The sprinkler shall cover an area no less than 10 feet and no more than 30 feet in diameter and will be run for no less than one (1) hour per setting to ensure wetting of the soil below the establishing root zone (2 feet). No sprinkler shall run for more than two (2) hours."

Although these requirements to water newly planted trees may seem excessive and wordy, they leave few questions to interpretation and are verifiable. Other factors that can be quantified or verified include: time, distance, volume, weight, area, unit (per employee or machine), and costs.

In some situations it is impossible to establish quantifiable standards or quality. How does one describe a well-mown lawn? It is difficult, if not impossible, to depict what is expected in measurable terms. In these situations, write the instructions so that if they are followed then only an acceptable job will result. Include drawings, details, maps, plans, or other documents that will make the requirements clearer.

> *"Cool season turf on the site (see attached maps) shall be mown to a height of two inches from the first mowing in the spring until June 15 and at a height of three inches between June 15 and until August 15. The mowing height will be returned to two inches after August 15. Each mowing will be conducted at a frequency so as to not remove more than 1/3 (one-third) of the leaf blade per mowing. A rotary mower with sharp blades will be used so as not to tear the leaf blades. The direction of mowing will be alternated every mowing.*
>
> *All clippings in areas adjacent to the building (marked on attached maps) will be collected by bagging or raking and removed from the site. Clippings in all other areas will be dispersed over the grass so as not to be unsightly. If clippings in these areas remain evident 24 hours after mowing they should be dispersed by blowing, bagging, or raking. All clippings will be removed from walks, curbs, and parking areas."*

If the accepted and recommended standards for, in this example, mowing turf in the given region are detailed, an acceptable quality mowing will result.

Do not use references unless they are included. *"Shrubs shall be pruned with a thinning technique as detailed and set forth in the State Extension Pruning Guide."* Unless a copy of this Extension publication is included with the specifications, the statement is worthless.

Even with results-oriented specifications, it may be necessary to address some *restrictions* or *exceptions*. Specifications give direction, they also provide license. If the trees must be pruned but the climber cannot use climbing spurs, then say so. Write down major restrictions, but be reasonable. No one can anticipate and provide for everything that can possibly go wrong.

Address standards beyond landscape care that are important to the client or users of the site. Some specifications include standards for noise, worker's dress or uniforms, and language. Others address inspections and acceptance of the work, payment schedule and retention, warranties, guarantees, or other items important for the contractor or client to be aware of and understand.

Individual Areas of Concern for Specification Writers

Turfgrass

Recommendations for proper care of turfgrass vary with *type* and *region*. Make sure that the proposed care is appropriate for the species and region.

Pruning

Differentiate between *shearing* and *pruning*. To some people they are the same procedure. To the plant, however, the processes are worlds apart. If the plants are to be pruned correctly with a thinning technique, then state it clearly. Providing proper pruning specifications, illustrations, and incorporating Extension or other pamphlets illustrating proper pruning will help.

Pesticides

Specifying particular chemicals for insect, disease, and weed control is difficult for most design firms. Pesticides constantly enter and leave the market due to research and development, government intervention, and market forces. Several have disappeared and reappeared under different trade names in recent years. Most designers do not have the background or time to keep up-to-date on the latest recommendations. It is generally in the purview of the contractor or landscape supervisor to know what material will provide the most effective control with the least environmental risk and cost. When pest control is indicated, use a generic statement, such as ". . . *shall be controlled with currently recommended and approved (pest)icide.*" This allows the contractor to select the appropriate material for the task and reduces the writer's liability in recommending something inappropriate or illegal. I have read "current" specifications that requested use of pesticides that had been removed from the market by the Environmental Protection Agency or that would have killed the plants involved. Specification, recommendation, and use of pesticides should be left to those who are appropriately trained and knowledgeable.

Fertilizer

Unless a specific ratio or type of fertilizer are required, nitrogen and other nutrient rates should be specified in *pounds* per 1,000 square feet or acre. Again, this allows the contractor to select the most appropriate and economical material. If slow-release nitrogen is desired, then request that the total nitrogen contain a certain percentage of slow-release nitrogen.

Insurance and Licensing

It is prudent to include a section or subsection in specifications addressing *insurance* and *licensing*. Require that the contractor obtain and pay for the following insurance coverage: workmen's compensation, public or general liability, property damage, and any other insurance as required by Federal, State, or Local laws, or the client.

Require contractors to posses valid licenses or certifications required by law. In all states this will include pesticide applicator certification. Several states license landscape contractors, arborists, and landscape maintenance contractors. Any local licenses or certifications necessary to conduct business should also be mandatory.

Contractor Prepared Specifications

Landscape management contractors produce specifications of their own program(s) that are included with proposals, bids, and contracts. The contractor's motive for specifications is the same as for those prepared by the client or his/her agent. That is, to clearly communicate the services to be furnished, establish responsibilities, list the provisions to be agreed upon by the owner, and to avoid confusion during the implementation of the contract.

Specifications prepared by contractors also vary in format and detail. Some will refer to attached schedules listing the exact number of mowings and other tasks. Most contractor specifications are less detailed than those produced by landscape designers. Contractor-produced specifications may also serve an educational function to explain why something is done or not done.

> *"Grass clippings will be left to disintegrate and return valuable nutrients to the soil. If clippings are excessive or clumped due to dampness or delay in mowing because of inclement weather, they will either be spread or removed. Clippings in areas where people might track them into the building will also be removed after each mowing."*

The above tells the client why clippings are not bagged or raked and establishes the conditions under which they will be removed. It shows that the company is interested in maintaining quality in the landscape and demonstrates concern for the client's operation by attempting to minimize the tracking of cut grass into the building. It also teaches the client a little about nutrient recycling.

Limitations to the Work

Regardless of the author, safeguards are mentioned in specifications. These limitations will certainly be part of the signed contract. Limitations to the responsibility of the contractor can be covered by a statement such as,

> *"All items not detailed or listed within these specifications shall be considered extra and will be charged separately according to the nature of the work,"*

or similar.

Other responsibilities sometimes explicitly identified and limited include: working trees greater than a certain height, additions to the landscape after the agreement, care of parking lots and walks, losses due to Acts of God or vandalism, and other issues necessary for the contractor's or client's peace of mind.

To summarize, specifications should be detailed enough to explain and provide standards for the work in question.

1. Tie down loose ends.
2. Clarify unsure areas.
3. List areas where the contractor is not expected to perform.

MAINTENANCE CONTRACTS

Contracts for landscape maintenance are no great mystery and do not require signing in blood. Contracts are simply a communication system to explain exactly what is to be done, by whom, for a given compensation, and over what specified period of time. A contract is an agreement enforceable by law protecting the client and the contractor.

The basics of a good contract are uniform. Local and state regulations, as well as company and client needs will, however, differ. A contract is a *legal document,* it is defense against consumer ignorance, unreasonable demands, Acts of God, and perhaps even trimming the roses.

There are several basic contracts found in the trade. Many of these are "canned" contracts produced by professional associations, consultants, and other groups. Some firms have developed their own "uniform" agreement for their bids or estimates. Have an attorney review any contract before using it or signing it.

Contracts can generally be divided into two sections, the *general scope* and the *specifics.*

The General Scope

The *general scope* establishes the overall business terms of an agreement. The *Scope of Work* for contracts is the same as discussed under specifications. It briefly describes the work to be performed. The *duration* of the contract is included in the general scope of a contract. The duration is from one specific date to another.

The exact *dimensions* and *location* of the site and the number of *site inspections* should be detailed. The general section may refer to attached drawings, schedules, specifications, landscape plans, or other contract documents.

Payment

The *payment schedule* within the general scope is particularly important to the contractor. It specifies the amount the client agrees to pay and the number of installments. Contractors should make sure payment schedules are practical. Maintenance payments are usually made on a monthly basis, which prevents deficit cash flow for the firm, reduces interest accumulation on any borrowed money, and makes an all-around better business agreement.

The contractor may have to invoice the client before he/she can receive payment. There may be time limitations on imposed payments, such as, "*Contractor shall invoice completed work on the 15th day of each month and billings will be payable on or before the 25th day from the date of billing.*" Interest or other penalties attached if payment is not received within the specified period. The maximum amount of legal interest allowed on past due accounts varies with state. There may be requirements for inspections and acceptance of site management procedures detailed before payment can be invoiced or received.

The Specifics Section

The second or *specifics section* of a maintenance contract usually establishes a series of articles, sub-sections, or paragraphs stipulating specific areas of responsibilities. It is within this section that the *specifications* used to established the bid are referenced. The specifications now become part of the contractual agreement.

Some "canned" maintenance contracts, list a cafeteria of maintenance tasks. The contractor and owner "fill in the blanks" to develop a program.

The following is a short example of specific sections of such a document:

Lawn Maintenance
1. ( ) Mow, weather permitting,
   ( ) _____ times per month or
   ( ) as needed.
2. ( ) Equipment: ( ) rotary mowers
                  ( ) reel mowers
3. ( ) Mowing height: Cool season grass _____   Warm season grass _____
                              spring _____
                      summer _____
                         fall _____

4. Clippings   ( ) will   ( ) not be collected
5. Edge ( ), and   ( ) trim   ( ), each mowing or
                                      ( ) _____ times per season.

and so on.

The contractor and client indicate the program to be conducted. Hopefully, the contract will be retyped to show only the agreed upon program, instead of check marks and handwritten numbers.

Regardless of the type of "specifics" section used in the contract, it should provide adequate detail so that the owner will understand what he/she is receiving and the standards that are established. The specifics for a mowing paragraph should address the frequency of mowing, edging, and trimming, the type of machine, cutting height, and the fate of the clippings. As with specifications, clarify the unknown and put it in writing.

I spoke with one contractor who signed a landscape management agreement stating that the area would be mown to the owner's satisfaction. This was a poor choice of wording. No height or other guidelines for the turf were included. The property manager insisted that the turf (Tall fescue) be mown at one inch during the summer. A cool season turf in the Midwest mown at one inch in July is placed under inordinate stress. The quality of the turf declined rapidly and the contractor was blamed. He lost the contract in mid-season.

Granted, he was probably better off without this particular property. However, a well-written specifics-section of the contract detailing mowing operations would have prevented extra work, loss of a contract, hard feelings, and one property manager serving as a less-than-supportive reference.

Safeguards

One of the most important statements of any contract usually appears at the end. This statement establishes the limits of what is expected from the contractor. Such a limitation may read,

- *"All items not detailed or listed within this contract will be considered extra and shall be charged separately according to the nature of the item."*, or
- *"This contract contains the entire agreement of the parties. Any modification, amendments, or changes shall be in writing and signed by all parties to be effective."*

These statements protect contractors against unforeseen circumstances. They also eliminate their obligation to do work they are not prepared to do, nor paid for under the contract.

Other safeguard clauses might also involve:

Adverse conditions: *"The contractor shall not be required to work during adverse conditions, including but not limited to rainstorms, excessive wind, or fires."*

"Work delayed due to rain or adverse conditions will be rescheduled the following day."

Bills are normally prorated to reflect work that cannot be made up due to adverse conditions.

Holidays: *"The contractor recognizes the following holidays* (list of the holidays observed by either the client or the contractor that will preclude on-site work). *A normally scheduled site visit occurring on a recognized holiday will be re-scheduled to an alternate day."*

Additional Work: *"No additional work shall be undertaken by the contractor unless agreed to in writing by the parties."* This avoids failed memories of verbal agreements on tasks and payments. The "in writing" agreement may be as simple as a signed invoice or letter of agreement.

Water and/or Irrigation: "*Owner shall provide all water necessary for irrigation. Contractor will repair any damage to the irrigation system due to mowing or other actions of the contractor, however, any other adjustment or repair to the irrigation system(s) and all accessories will be made on a time plus material basis and charged to the owner.*", or

- "*Hand watering of landscape areas not covered by automatic irrigation systems shall be the sole responsibility of the owner, and the contractor does not assume responsibility for any loss or damage to plant material because of lack or excessive watering by the owner.*"

Exclusions and limitations: "*The contractor shall not be responsible for vandalism, theft, adverse natural conditions, Acts of God, or anything beyond the control of the contractor.*"

Inspections

Inspections are important to the client and the contractor to forestall problems, provide each party the opportunity to comment on the care of the property and performance within the contract, and the opportunity to communicate. Inspections should be looked forward to, not viewed with dread. If the contractor has done quality work, he/she should be proud to show the owner. If not, he/she should be prepared to receive complaints.

The inspection affords the contractor the opportunity to answer the client's questions and point out areas where additional work might be conducted. The sole purpose of an inspection should not be a selling mission, but the opportunity for additional work should never be overlooked.

Determine who will inspect the property and when the inspections will be conducted. The contractor's or owner's representative may wish to provide a check list for the inspection. Always carry a copy of the signed agreement.

Breach

The maintenance contractor should insert provisions regarding what to do if the client breaks the contract. The biggest problem in this area is usually non-payment of fees. As a practical matter, a breach of payment usually results in the contractor's cessation of further work on the project.

However, if substantial work has been performed the contractor may be the financial loser. Losses increase if he/she has to pay additional money for legal fees and collection costs. Therefore, each contract should contain clauses that require the client to pay all costs of collection, including attorney's fees, in the event the client breaks the payment schedule. The following are how such events have been handled by various contractors.

- *Legal Fees and Court Costs:* "*In the event that either party becomes involved in litigation or arbitration arising out of this contract, its interpretation, or the performance thereof, the prevailing party shall be entitled to reasonable attorney's fees and court costs in addition to any other relief that may be awarded.*"
- *Legal Fees and Venue:* "*In the event of litigation to enforce or interpret this agreement, the prevailing party shall be entitled to reasonable attorney's fees. This agreement is deemed made at the contractor's place of business and suit may be brought, at the Contractor's option, in the judicial district serving the Contractor's principal place of business.*"
- *Work Stoppage:* "*The Contractor shall have the right to stop work if any payments are not made to the Contractor as detailed under this agreement. The Contractor may keep the job idle until all payments*

due have been received. Such action by the Contractor shall not be deemed as a breach of this agreement by the Contractor."

Arbitration

No matter how carefully the landscape management contract is drafted, disputes can occur. Therefore, contracts may contain a clause providing for arbitration of disputes arising from the agreement.

If a contract provides an informal mechanism to settle disputes then costly legal action is averted. In addition, arbitration does not require strict courtroom rules of etiquette; both sides can tell their story in plain English. While attorneys may be used to represent one or both sides, they are not mandatory. Arbitration is private and the awards are confidential; they are not accessible to the media or a matter of public record. The arbitrator's decision is legally binding and cannot be overturned by the courts on appeal, except where the referee has gone beyond the issues of the dispute.

Arbitration clauses cover the types of disputes subject to mediation. They allow the contracting parties to choose people to arbitrate the dispute and reach a resolution. The American Arbitration Association, a nonprofit group with offices in 25 cities, is frequently turned to or cited as an arbitrator in many commercial situations.

The following example of an arbitration clause established the actions that may lead to arbitration and the arbitration procedures.

> ***Arbitration:*** *"If, at any time, a controversy develops between the contractor and owner with respect to any matters in question arising out of, or relating to this agreement, or the breach of this agreement in which the parties do not promptly adjust and determine, the controversy shall be decided by arbitration administrated by and in accordance with the rules of the* (American Arbitration Association or other organization), *unless the parties mutually agree otherwise. This agreement to arbitrate shall be specifically enforceable under the prevailing arbitration rules or law. The award rendered by the arbitrators shall be final, and judgment may be entered upon it in any court having jurisdiction thereof."*

The last two sentences of the above clause may be void in some states.

Cancellation

Most contracts have a clause allowing cancellation of the contract by either party upon written notification. This usually requires an extended notice, such as 30 days. Written notice is usually taken to mean registered mail. Other contracts specifically prohibit cancellation of the contract without a penalty or payment of a portion of the unfulfilled contract as *liquidated damages.*

> ***Cancellation of contract:*** *"The contract may be canceled by either party after 30 day written notice. The final billing must compensate the contractor for the full value of work done up to that time."*
>
> ***Liquidated Damages:*** *"It is agreed that the actual damages that might be sustained by the Contractor from breach of this contract by the Owner by terminating the contract prior to its term are uncertain and would be difficult to ascertain. It is further agreed that the sum of _____ percent of the remaining unpaid contract price would be reasonable and just compensation for such breach. The Owner hereby promises to pay and the Contractor agrees to accept such sum as liquidated damages, not as a penalty, in the event of such breach."*

Signature line

A final small, but powerful, caution occurs at the signature line. If you are signing a contract representing the corporation, then include your title when signing the papers. Failure to do so could put the signer at risk of becoming personally liable should everything go sour.

If a contract does not have your office title typed below the signature line, write it in manually after signing your name. Make sure the name of the organization is stated somewhere in the contract. As an example, the signature line on a contract should read *"by John Doe, president"* or *"John Doe, President of X Corporation."*

Negotiations

Contracts must be mutually agreed upon. Signatures of both parties indicate that the provisions are agreeable. Contracts written by one party in the accord or their agent will, naturally, be one-sided. It is only natural to construct a fair agreement but one where the author retains advantages in certain situations. Before signing a contract that places the firm at a severe disadvantage or that contains unacceptable provisions, ask that they be changed or modified. Few agreements in the business world are not subject to negotiation.

Indicate the objections and substantiate them to the other party. Provide alternatives that would be fair to both principals. Any changes to a contract must be made in writing. Minor changes can be made on the original document and initialed or signed by both parties. Major changes may require rewriting the contract or attaching amendments. Do not accept verbal agreements to change a contract after signing without something in writing at the time of signing.

If changes in the presented document cannot be made to the mutual satisfaction of both signers, then the alternative is to not accept or sign the instrument. A contractor is better off without the work if the conditions are not fair or agreeable. Likewise, the owner will be able to find another contractor to do the work according to his/her requirements and wishes. The price, however, may be greater.

Bibliography

Bourne, J. A. 1984. *Grounds Maintenance Management Guidelines.* 1st ed. Professional Grounds Management Society, Pikeville, MD.

Carpenter, P. L., T. D. Walker, and F. O. Lanphear. 1975. *Plants In the Landscape.* W. H. Freeman and Co., San Francisco, CA.

Day, S. 1989. Site planning, maintenance specifications pay off. *ALA/Maintenance,* 10(6):36–38.

Griffen, J. M. 1970. *Landscape Management.* California Landscape Contractors Association, Los Angeles, CA.

Hall, J. R. 1978. Guidelines for writing lawn maintenance specifications. In: *Manual of Site Management.* Environmental Design Press, Reston, VA.

Hensley, D., W. McCoskey, and D. Suddarth. 1990. So, what if he doesn't pay. *Nursery Manager,* 6(3):108–112.

Lofgren, D. E. 1978. General landscape specifications-how to write maintenance specifications. In: *Manual of Site Management.* Environmental Design Press, Reston, VA.

Lofgren, D. E. 1986. How to write good specs. *Grounds Maintenance,* 21(1):112, 114.

Marsh, D. 1985. Specifications for site maintenance and contracts. In: *A Guide to Developing a Landscape Maintenance Business.* Associated Landscape Contractors of America, McLean, VA.

Marsh, J. 1978. Practical specifications for contract landscape maintenance. In: *Manual of Site Management.* Environmental Design Press, Reston, VA.

Milburn, S. A. 1988. A bad sign. *American Nurseryman,* 167(8):67–68.

Stessin, L. 1990. Arbitration: A quick solution to quarrels. *Landscape Contractor,* 31(5):36–37.

Suddarth, D. W. and D. L. Hensley. 1984. Specific contracts guard maintenance companies against misunderstandings. *American Nurseryman,* 159(6):163.

Suddarth, D. and D. L. Hensley. 1988. Know your lien laws. *American Nurseryman,* 168(6):91–95.

Suddarth, D. 1990. Muller and Suddarth, Attorneys. Troy, MO Personal communication.

Table 3-1. Sample Contracts

The following are samples of landscape management contracts. They should serve *only* as examples and not as the exact construction required for a valid contract. Many different types of contracts are used by the landscape management industry and the contract laws of each state differ.

The first example is a *simple* document that resembles little more that a "Gentlemen's Agreement." It states simply that the contractor agrees to perform the work indicated for the amounts listed. The agreement constitutes a legal and binding contract when signed, but it is extremely limited in its scope or protection. Quality standards, limitation of responsibilities, and remedies for breach or other problems are omitted. The contractor's only recourse to nonpayment by the client is to charge interest. The contractor must perform work for an additional 30 days beyond written notification, even if no payment has been forthcoming. The agreement also negates starting dates, name of the owner or representative, and other important aspects found in more complete and tighter instruments.

Many contractors prefer to operate with simple, loose agreements. They feel that their word is enough. Some contractors feel that the client may be turned-off or on-guard if the agreement contains too many contingencies and too much "legalese." I am aware of at least one case where a contractor lost a job that he had maintained for several years because he presented an unnecessarily detailed and protective contract to a client.

Other contractors, however, feel they would rather have the client be wary as opposed to performing work for which they are not paid. Disputes develop because no one really understands the details or limits of the agreement.

The second example contract refers to detailed specifications that are not shown for the specifics of what is to be done, the frequency of the tasks, and quality standards. The contract presents remedies for various contingencies. It explains a number of the duties of the owner and the contractor. Since it is written by a contractor for signature by the property owner, it reflects various protection mechanisms in favor of the contractor. These include liquidated damages, penalties for owner's breach, holiday exclusions, and others. The instrument also provides methods to solve future disagreements via arbitration. A contract constructed by the property owner's representative would likely provide stringent protective clauses in favor of the owner.

Most contractors use contracts somewhere between these examples in wording and protection. Remember, the more that can be written down and agreed upon, the fewer disputes will erupt in the future.

Table 3–1. (con't)

SAMPLE CONTRACT 1

DAVE'S LANDSCAPES-AR-US
P.O. Box 123, Anytown, KS

AUTHORIZATION

I hereby authorize DAVE'S LANDSCAPES-AR-US to perform the landscape maintenance at _____ _____ as listed on the reverse side of this page. (Applicable taxes will be added) DAVE'S LANDSCAPES-AR-US will invoice for each service, as performed. Terms are net 30 days. A service charge of 18% per year (or 1.5% per month) will be assessed on any delinquent balance.

   This contract may be terminated by either party by giving 30 (thirty) days notice with agreement between both parties on charges due.

_____
DAVE'S LANDSCAPES-AR-US

_____
AGENT

_____
DATE

MAINTENANCE SCHEDULE

STANDARD OPERATIONS	COST PER	# TIMES	TOTAL
Mow, Trim, Sweep, and Bag as needed	$280	22	$6,160
Edge Walks and Curbs	120	8	960
Turf Fertilizer, Weed and Insect Control	375	4	1,500
Grub Control	425	1	425
Pruning	50	2	100
Shrub and Tree Insect Control	90	2	180
Irrigation Service - Timer Adjustments Only			no charge
		TOTAL	$9,325

OPTIONAL OPERATIONS	COST PER	# TIMES	TOTAL
Aeration	$600	1	$600
Mulching beds	0.50/sq. ft.		
Turf Fungicide	$15.00/1,000 sq. ft.		
Grassy Weed Spot Spray	$12.00/1,000 sq. ft.		
OPTIONAL OPERATIONS TOTAL			$600

Table 3-1. (con't)

SAMPLE CONTRACT 2

LANDSCAPE MANAGEMENT CONTRACT

Agreement made on _____, 19___ by and between DAVE'S LANDSCAPES-AR-US, 123 Oak, Anytown, Kansas, hereafter referred to as "DAVE'S" and NOAH'S PROPERTY MANAGEMENT, hereafter called "OWNER", 1220 W. Palm, Suite 12, Anytown, KS 65555 (913-555-1234).

Purpose of Agreement

The purpose of this agreement is to state the terms and condition under which DAVE'S will provide landscape management for the property of the Owner. This property is located at 1220 W. Palm, Anytown KS, a 5 acre commercial office site, bounded by Elm Blvd. to the North, W. Palm to the East, Cercis Ave. to the South and by Broadway to the West, and is hereafter referred to as "property." The name of the "property" (if any): Joshua Place Corporate Park.

Upon acceptance by duly authorized representatives of DAVE'S and the Owner, this agreement becomes a legally enforceable, binding contract. If the Owner has any questions concerning this contract, legal advice should be obtained.

In consideration of the mutual promises herein, the parties agree as follows:

1. Scope of Work: DAVE'S agrees to furnish all materials, equipment, labor, supervision, and transportation, insurance, and licenses necessary to perform the management services set forth in the attached specifications on the property.

2. Payment: Owner agrees to pay DAVE'S the "Contract Price" for performance of the services set forth in the attached specifications. The "contract price" is to be paid in 12 equal monthly installments of $1367.00, the first installment being due and payable upon execution of this agreement. Each additional installment is due and payable on the 15th day of each succeeding month thereafter until the "contract price" is fully paid. All accounts not paid within ten (10) days of the date due shall accrue interest on the unpaid balance at 18% per year (1.5% per month).

    b. Breach: Failure of the Owner to pay any or all of any accrued portion of the contract price as provided above within fifteen (15) days from the date due shall constitute a breach of this contract and shall entitle DAVE'S to recover damages for this breach as provided herein at the sole election of DAVE'S.

    c. Work Stoppage: DAVE'S has the right to stop work if any payments are not be made to the contractor as detailed under this agreement. The contractor may keep the job idle until all payments due have been received. Such action by the contractor shall not be deemed as a breach of this agreement by DAVE'S.

3. Term of the Contract: The term of this agreement is for 12 months, beginning August 1, 199___ and ending July 31, 199___. This agreement may not be terminated during this period without the prior written consent of the other party.

4. Owner's Duty to Inspect the Work. The Owner has the duty to inspect the property within three (3) days after any service described in the attached specifications have been completed by DAVE'S. If the Owner is dissatisfied with any of the work performed, notice of such dissatisfaction must be given to DAVE'S within five (5) days from the completion of the services. DAVE'S shall then have ten (10) to repair or correct such work at no additional cost to Owner. Owner's failure to properly notify DAVE'S of dissatisfaction in any services called for under the terms of this agreement constitutes a waiver of any claim or offset the Owner may be due in regard to work rendered under this contract.

5. Insurance and licenses: DAVE'S will carry complete workmen's compensation, public liability, and property damage insurance, as well, as all Federal, State, and Local licenses appropriate and necessary to conduct the work described in the attached specifications.

6. Water and/or Irrigation: Owner shall provide all water necessary for irrigation as described in the attached specification. DAVE'S will repair any damage to the irrigation system due to mowing or other actions of the contractor, however, any other adjustment or repair to the irrigation system(s) and all accessories will be made on a time plus material basis and charged to the Owner.

7. Adverse conditions and holidays: DAVE'S will not be required to work during adverse conditions, including but not limited to rainstorms, excessive wind, public insurrection, or fires. DAVE'S recognizes the following holidays: Labor Day, Memorial Day, and Dave's Birthday (October 27). If a regularly scheduled work day coincides with one of these, or if it rains on three or more consecutive visit days, DAVE'S will work an alternate day or prorate the monthly bill by 15 percent.

8. Exclusions: DAVE'S shall not be responsible for damage or interruption of services due to vandalism, theft, adverse natural conditions, Acts of God, or anything beyond the control of the Contractor.

Table 3–1. (con't)

9. Liquidated Damages: It is agreed that the actual damages that might be sustained by DAVE'S from breach of this agreement by Owner terminating the contract prior to its term are uncertain. These damages would be difficult to ascertain. It is further agreed that the sum of 30 percent of the remaining unpaid contract price would be reasonable and equitable compensation for such breach. The Owner hereby promises to pay, and DAVE'S agrees to accept, this sum as liquidated damages, not as a penalty, in the event of breach by the Owner.

10. Legal Fees and Court Costs: In the event that either party becomes involved in litigation or arbitration arising out of this contract or the interpretation or performance thereof, the prevailing party shall be entitled to reasonable attorney's fees and court costs in addition to any other relief that might be awarded.

11. Arbitration: If, at any time, a controversy develops between DAVE'S and Owner with respect to any matters in question arising out of, or relating to this agreement, or the breach of this contract in which the parties do not promptly adjust and determine, the controversy will be decided by arbitration, unless both parties agree otherwise. This agreement to arbitrate shall be specifically enforceable under the prevailing arbitration rules or law. The award rendered by the arbitrators shall be final, and judgment may be entered upon it in any court having jurisdiction thereof.

12. Entire agreement: This contract contains the entire agreement of the parties. Any modification, amendments, or changes must be in writing and signed by all parties to be effective. Any work in addition to that contained within the attached schedule will be charged separately and additionally according to the nature of the work.

Upon acceptance by DAVE'S and the Owner, the parties shall be contractually bound and shall be entitled to and responsible for any and all rights and obligations created herein.

Accepted

OWNER

By: _____

      Name   Title   Date

Address: _____

DAVE'S LANDSCAPES-AR-US

By: _____

      Name   Title   Date

Chapter 4
Estimating Landscape Management Services

Landscape managers in the contractual arena must determine the amount of material, labor, and equipment necessary to perform a task or maintain a given property at a profit. Supervisors of in-house landscape management must develop and adhere to meaningful budgets. Accuracy in estimating costs determines whether or not the operation will obtain a contract, make a profit, or stay within a budget. Accurate estimating determines if the operation or manager will succeed or fail.

Project Evaluation

Contract landscape management companies are in business to make a profit and expand. However, the firm does not want *every* job that may be available or offered. The company must maintain quality workmanship, respect, and a good reputation. New work should fit into established goals. Consider the following when projects to bid are offered to the company:

1. Size. Can the firm handle the job? If the job is too small, the firm may not be able to do the work efficiently. Many landscape management contractors, especially those targeting commercial properties, establish a minimum size for maintained sites. Residential oriented companies also operate on a minimum site size, or more likely, a minimum charge sufficient to pay for the "inconvenience" of a small site.

If the job is too large, the company may not have the capability or equipment to handle it. If the firm obtains the contract, can it mobilize the personnel and equipment to do the work efficiently and for a profit?

2. Work schedule and current commitments. Will the job fit into the existing work schedule? Will it require a different route or new crew(s)? If new crews are added, can additional work be found to fill their schedule? Does the company have the equipment, personnel, and supervisory staff to add the work efficiently?

3. Procedures. Are special equipment, techniques, or crews required? Does the company have or can it obtain the expertise, equipment, or personnel to do the work? Are subcontractors available for specialized work beyond the firm's capabilities?

4. Examine the specifications and contract carefully, especially if it is a public property. Do the owners require techniques or requirements different from those usually conducted? If so, are these requirements reasonable? If the specifications will be time consuming, then adjust the bid. Will the management firm be held responsible for the actions of others, such as vandalism? In some instances, the landscape manager may be asked to anticipate and estimate the cost of replacement and repair of the landscape due to damage of tenants or others in the bid. A difficult task, at best.

5. Does the project fit the image of the company? Is it the type of work that the firm is known for or would like to be known for?

6. Geographic area of the work. Can the additional travel cost be turned into a profit? If the work is out of town, are there reasonable places for the crew to stay overnight? Can local crews and supervisors be obtained?

7. Who is responsible for inspection of the work and determination of payment? Inspection and arrangement for payment may be conducted by the property manager, the designer, or a consultant. The consultant may be a landscape architect or designer or an independent consulting company. Know who will judge the work against the specifications set forth.

Is the evaluator competent and fair? The manager may wish to increase the bid if there are indications that a percentage of the work will regularly have to be redone, if there are likely to be requests for *gratis* work in addition to the contract, or if there has been a history of withholding partial payment. Some landscape management contractors have an unlabeled "Mickey Mouse factor" that is included when they are dealing with notorious property managers or contract representatives.

8. Payment: when and how? Does the payment schedule fit cash flow needs? Is payment dependent upon "passing" inspections? Potential problems in this area have been discussed.

How much time will be required for payment for extra work beyond the contract? Some companies must go through many layers of approvals and paperwork to obtain payment for additional work. Some owners delay payment as long as absolutely possible. Remember, your company is not a bank. Do not allow the client to use the firm's money without interest added or an adjustment to the bill up front.

9. Are there potential problems that might prevent the efficient completion of the contract? Labor problems on the site, contract disputes between the owner and installation contractor, or water rationing affect performance of site maintenance. Be aware of any business difficulty that may result in failure of the client.

If the bid is for management of a new landscape, will it be completed on time? Also, remember that the site will change drastically during the construction phase. If possible, wait until installation is complete before submitting a final price.

10. Will design and installation factors affect maintenance efficiency or price? Items to consider, especially with newer landscapes, are plant selection and location. Have microclimates been compensated for? Has the designer selected plants tolerant to the site and conditions? Will the management firm be required to do the impossible? How much winter (or summer) damage can be anticipated? Was the landscape properly installed; how much loss is anticipated and who is responsible?

11. Was the irrigation system installed properly and is it functional? Irrigation, more than any other factor, determines the summer quality of the turfgrass and landscape. Who controls the operation, scheduling, and repair of the system? Does someone else determine the quality of the maintenance program without the firm's input or control?

Site Evaluation

A fundamental rule of landscape management contracting is to visit the site before submitting a bid or estimate. Elementary as this may seem, too many contractors rely on windshield or drive-by estimates. I spoke with one young "would-be" contractor who successfully bid and signed a contract for maintaining a motel "landscape." He did not realize that there was a large courtyard with extensive plantings when he submitted the price. He couldn't see it from his pick-up, so all that was bid was the mowing and snow removal from the parking lot. This was an expensive lesson.

Walk and evaluate the site. Measure the turf areas and shrub beds, count the trees, and determine any problems that must be corrected or that will affect performance and price.

Estimating is a management or sales responsibility. Make sure the evaluator is responsible and trained. Some companies have site evaluations or estimates checked by someone in production to make sure it is reasonable and accurate. The manager is responsible for checking all estimates for large or prestigious properties.

Checklist

Most firms use a *checklist* or form that is filled out during on-site inspection. Such written reminders assure that valuable information necessary for pricing and program development are not neglected. Checklists also record site conditions that can be used in later evaluations of bid and pricing performance. The following are some items to consider during on-site evaluations:

1. If history or company procedures warrant, obtain a soil sample for analysis to determine nutrient status, soil *p*H, bulk density, and possibly cation exchange capacity.
2. Note the surface and subsurface drainage. Look for drainage problems and wet areas.
3. Examine entrances and determine if there is access for equipment. Roof gardens and courtyards often present problems.
4. If the site does not contain an automated, underground irrigation system, is there access to water? Are there sufficient numbers and size of outlets? Will water have to be hauled to the site?
5. Who determines and controls the schedule for the irrigation system?

Records

Records are a critical part of determining business costs and developing budgets, estimates, and bids. Good records allow determination of actual costs and provide accurate information for production times and rates. Historical records are used to determine what impact changes in equipment and supplies will have on costs and profits. Records also identify profitable and unprofitable service areas. The lack of accurate performance records and comparisons of actual and estimated costs are the greatest hindrance to effective bidding and pricing for new firms.

Many different record forms have developed and are used in the landscape management industry. The specific forms needed and used vary with each operation; there are no industry standards. Records forms must generate the information necessary for the particular operation.

Several different forms will be illustrated in the following discussions; these are by no means "the best," most efficient, or only records that will be needed or adopted. Business record forms must be sufficiently complete and accurate to generate the necessary information, yet simple enough that they can be filled out correctly by the employees. Business computer systems have made record keeping and tabulation immensely easier than it was in the pre-computer dark ages. Today, the manager has more and better information at his/her fingertips than anytime in the past. The accumulation of business data, however, does not ensure success. *People* still must interpret and respond to this information.

Developing an Estimate

When evaluating a property to develop a bid or budget, the manager or estimator must determine: 1) the work to be accomplished; 2) the area involved; and 3) the time required and the costs involved. Less simplistically, an estimate or budget will consider:

1. The individual jobs or tasks included in the total project.
2. The size of the area for each activity.
3. The supplies and material required.
4. The personnel and equipment needs for those jobs.
5. The frequency at which each task will be performed.
6. The quality level required for each task.

Table 4-1 illustrates the basic inputs that must be brought together to formulate estimates and budgets.

Landscape Programs and Schedules

Hopefully, a great number of the "what, when, and how" questions will be answered by clearly written specifications or schedules supplied by the prospective client. In most instances, however, the contractor or estimator bears the responsibility of determining the needs of the site and desires of the client. The maintenance program should be clear and detail the tasks involved, their frequency, and the quality level.

The *frequency* of each task is determined by the maintenance schedule or program, the quality expectations and budget of the client, the maintenance level of the site, and the region of the country.

Maintenance "Take offs"

Landscape management contractors have adopted a *take off* forms for listing items from maintenance specifications, schedules, or programs. Take off forms make sure that nothing is omitted. Table 4-2 is a rudimentary example of a take off. Construct the form to include space for frequency, areas, type and amounts of material and equipment necessary, and other pertinent information.

Determining the Area

The size of beds, lawns, and parking areas, exact number of trees and shrubs may be easily obtained from an as-built landscape plan from the client or designer. Specific acreage can be measured by hand or with the aid of a planimeter. A *planimeter* is an instrument used to measure the square inches or area of regular or irregular segments. As built plans, unfortunately, are not always available.

Aerial photographs, in scales as large as 1 inch = 50 feet, are available from some county appraiser offices or other local government offices. Again, unit areas can be determined with the aid of a planimeter or geometry. Several contractors have mentioned the value of aerial photographs when bidding mowing, snow removal, and turfgrass care for apartments, commercial sites, or other large properties.

Table 4–1. The components that must be brought together when developing a landscape maintenance estimate or budget.

1	2	3	4	5	6	7	8	9
Maintenance activity or task	**Frequency**	**Area or unit**	**Production rate**	**Production hours**	**Labor rate**	**Material**	**Equipment rate**	**Equipment costs**
From take off or list from specifications or maintenance program	*(times per year)*	*(sq. ft. or unit)*	*(time per unit)*	*columns (4×3×2)*	*($ per hr)*	*(material cost × column 2)*	*(cost per hr or unit)*	*columns (2×3×8)*

Table 4–2. Maintenance Take Off

Job Title	
Location	
Specification or Bid	
Dates in Effect	
From: To:	

Maintenance Activity	Frequency					Unit or area	Material Needed
	Daily	Weekly	Monthly	Yearly	As Required		
Lawn Areas							
Irrigation							
Mowing							
Edging							
Weed control							
Pest control							
Fertilization							
Trash and debris removal							
Raking							
Aerating							
Other							
Planted Groundcover Areas							
Irrigation							
Edging/trimming							
Weed control							
Pest control							
Fertilization							
Trash and debris removal							
Other							
Shrubs							
Irrigation							
Pruning							
Weed control							
Pest control							
Fertilization							
Trash and debris removal							
Mulch/re-mulch							

Table 4–2. (con't)

Maintenance Activity	Frequency					Unit or area	Material Needed
	Daily	Weekly	Monthly	Yearly	As Required		
Trees							
Irrigation							
Pruning							
Weed control							
Pest control							
Fertilization							
Other							
Public or Patio Area							
Trash and debris removal							
Sweeping							
Washing							
Snow Removal/deicing							
Other							
Parking Areas and Drives							
Trash and debris removal							
Sweeping							
Washing							
Snow Removal/deicing							
Re-stripe and mark							
Surface seal							
Other							
Walks							
Trash and debris removal							
Sweeping							
Washing							
Snow Removal/deicing							
Weeding cracks							
Other							
Walls and Fences							
And so on for the services rendered							

The last method is to *physically measure* turf, parking, plantings, and other areas with a measuring wheel or tape, and to count the trees and shrubs. Even if an as-built plan or aerial photo exists, a site visit is still absolutely necessary to determine topography and anything else that impedes management operations.

The degree to which the individual components of the site are broken down for bidding depends on the size and complexity of the job, the competitiveness of the marketplace, and the contractor's personal preference and methodology. At the very minimum, the square feet of turf, seasonal color beds, shrub beds, and the number of trees must be cataloged. Measure parking lot areas and walks if snow removal or cleaning is included in the bid. Do not rely on windshield surveys or comparing a new property with an existing contract for size and complexity. This may result in a surprise.

Estimating Time

The *time* required for various jobs in landscape management is, literally, the $64,000 question. Ask any contractor what it costs to mow a given area and answers range from, "I wish I knew," or "Probably more than I think," to pretty exact figures. Every contractor seeks a better handle on his/her costs, estimates, and hopefully profits. The exploding use of computers makes this task easier but can also complicate it further. Many contractors currently use computer-based bidding; many others want to and will in the near future.

Estimating production time is a dilemma for every new contractor since new firms do not have historical records or experience to rely upon. They may also have a mixture of equipment, varying in serviceability and size.

Production Rates

Numerous management firms use *production rates* or standards for estimating purposes. Production rates are the time required to mow, prune, spray or perform other specific work on an individual or unit basis (per square feet, acre, or linear foot, or mile).

Figures for average production rates for landscape management tasks can be found in publications from Associated Landscape Contractors of America (ALCA), Professional Grounds Management Society (PGMS), and in several texts. Table 4–3 lists production numbers for various landscape maintenance functions gathered from various sources. Such figures are "average" estimates for the average employees using average equipment on an average site. They serve only as guides, but at least provide a starting place for the young contractor. Some contractors have told me they would fire their employees if they couldn't produce more than that indicated in these publications. Others would love to replace their entire work force with these "average" workers.

Developing Production Rates

Specific production rates for each job and company depend on the equipment used, the skill and enthusiasm of the worker, and the condition and terrain of the area. The influence of size and speed on mowing is found in Table 4–4. Managers try to develop generalized figures that work in most situations. There are no average workers, as there are no average jobs. Adjustments to production figures will be discussed later.

Production rates can be developed from records of actual time-on-the-job from past contracts. Production figures can also be developed by measuring the work of employees with various equipment over known areas. Fine-tune and check production rates by comparing estimated time with actual times for specific tasks over the firm's many contracts.

Table 4-3. Maintenance Task Estimating

AREA AND OPERATION	Average Frequency per Year	Average Minutes per 1,000 sq. ft.	AREA AND OPERATION	Average Frequency per Year	Average Minutes per 1,000 sq. ft.
TURF MANAGEMENT			Fertilization (broadcast)	2	5
Mowing 16" hand mower	30	10	Mulch	1	30
19" power	30	9	Spray for pest control	2	30
21" self-propelled	30	6	**TREES**		Min./small tree
36" self-propelled	30	4	Pruning	2	20
48" rider	30	45 Min./acre	Fertilization		
72" rider	30	36 Min./acre	broadcast	2	5
Fertilization	2	3	deep root feed	1	30
broadcast (PTO powered)	2	.25	Pest control—spray	3	15
36" spreader			Injection	1	10
Preemergent herbicide application	1	15	**SEASONAL COLOR BEDS**		Min./1,000 sq. ft.
Postemergent herbicide application back-pack sprayer	2	15	Bed preparation	1	200
15" boom, power	2	4	Planting (flats)	1	600
30" boom, power	2	8	Weeding (no mulch)	15	60
Rake			Cultivation (no mulch)	15	30
hand	1	60	Mulch	1	30
power	1	10	weeding (in mulch)	7	20
Vacuum—30" machine	3	10	Pest control (spray)	3	10
Overseeding (machine)	1	30	Preemergent herbicide (broadcast)	1	5
Aeration (core aerator)	1	30	Fertilization (broadcast)	2	5
Edging shrub bed—hand	10	Min./1,000 linear feet - 60	Policing—debris removal—hand	25	15
power—walks	30	5	machine—vacuum	5	10
power—shrub beds	10	10	Plant removal and clean-up	1	400
Trim around objects			**PAVED AREAS**		Min./1,000 sq. ft.
string trimmer	25	10	Walks		
chemical	2	10	Sweeping—hand	15	25
SHRUB AREAS		Min./1,000 sq. ft.	Vacuum	15	4
Weeding			Blower	25	2
hand	15	60	Snow removal	?	
postemergent spot spray	3	15	hand	?	60
Preemergent herbicide application	2	5	power	?	12
Policing-debris removal hand	30	15	Drives and Parking	?	
machine—vacuum	30	7	Cleaning—vacuum	10	3
Pruning	2	60	Snow removal	?	10

Table 4-4. Average square feet mowed per hour using mowers of various deck widths at various mowing speeds.

Mower Deck Size (inches)	Square feet per hour			
	Average Mowing Speed (miles/hour)			
	2.5	3.0	3.5	4.0
21	18,500	22,000	26,000	–
26	23,000	26,000	32,000	36,500
28	24,500	29,500	34,500	39,500
30	26,500	31,500	37,000	42,000
32	28,000	33,500	39,500	45,000
38	33,500	40,000	47,000	53,500
42	37,000	44,500	52,000	59,000
48	42,000	50,500	59,000	67,500
60	53,000	63,500	74,000	84,500

Landscape contractors break down production rates into *unit areas,* such as square feet of turfgrass, linear feet of edging, square feet of bed, and number of trees and shrubs. Distinguish between the various size machines, such as mowers, in the company; the production time for each differs significantly.

Production factors will be needed for all operations that are routinely performed, as well as those that are undertaken occasionally. The list in Table 4–5 is a compilation of production factors included by many contractors.

Adjustments to production rates

Production and efficiency vary with site. Adjustments to production rates reflect differences in conditions, difficulty, and other parameters. Adjustments to mowing production rates include increases for: collecting clippings; corner lots; hills and berms; cut-up areas (sidewalks and scattered ornamentals); jobs specifying end-of-the-week mowing; increased edging and trimming. Pruning time depends upon plant size and their degree of neglect. Weeding times depends on the present and past herbicide programs.

Adjustments to production rates are applied by adding a *percentage* to the final total of estimated hours or prices or by multiplying by an "efficiency" factor or "*burden.*"

Travel Time

The time required for travel, unloading, and loading the equipment must be accounted for as part of the final price. Some contractors increase estimated hours by a standard percentage to account for these non-productive functions. Others calculate and list travel as a trip charge or "mobilization" charge. At least one company has a "debris removal" charge for each crew trip to the property that

Table 4–5.		
Some of the many landscape operation for which a firm may want to develop production rates. Determining the time or *rate* required to perform the various tasks allows more rapid and accurate estimating. Develop production rates for each machine used and adjust the rate to reflect site and weather variations.		
A.	**TURFGRASS**	
	1.	mowing (for each size machine in inventory, with and without collecting clippings).
	2.	edging and trimming (string trimmers and edgers)
	3.	fertilization (dry and liquid materials)
	4.	pesticide application (dry and liquid material)
	5.	leaf removal (open and small areas)
B.	**SHRUBS AND GROUNDCOVERS**	
	1.	pruning (easy and difficult)
	2.	shearing
	3.	fertilization (dry and liquid materials)
	4.	pest control (insect and disease)
	5.	herbicide application
	6.	weeding
	7.	leaf removal
	8.	mulching
C.	**TREES AND LARGE EVERGREENS**	
	1.	pruning (large and small)
	2.	fertilization (dry, liquid, injection)
	3.	pest control
D.	**SEASONAL COLOR**	
	1.	planting
	2.	fertilization
	3.	watering
	4.	pinching
	5.	removal
E.	**MISCELLANEOUS**	
	1.	irrigation checks and adjustments
	2.	travel, loading, unloading, and clean-up

serves as the travel charge. How travel and other adjustments are handled will depend on the client, local market characteristics, and company philosophy.

Production Budgets

Time budgets for maintenance of a site can be developed from production rates. *Production budgets* supply crew supervisors and scheduling personnel with a planning tool. Production can be estimated so that work loads and routes can be planned accordingly. Production estimates provide field personnel with figures for exactly what is expected and how long each function should take. Budgeting also provides an efficient and accurate method to track actual versus estimated time by task. The contractor will know where any problems lie, not simply that they exist.

Putting Estimates Together

Bid summaries bring production figures, supplies, equipment and other costs, and the maintenance program together. Each company must develop estimate sheets to meet their specific needs.

Computer programs are available to take job task requirements, area measurements, production rates, and other information and produce direct costs or estimates.

Determining Cost Estimates

Many different costs must be determined or estimated to produce a bid or budget. Table 4-6 shows how these components blend to form the final price or budget. Each segment of the process must be carefully derived and considered or the final product will be in error. No estimating process is perfect. Hopefully, the intrinsic errors inherent in any estimating process can be balanced making the end result acceptable to the client and the estimator.

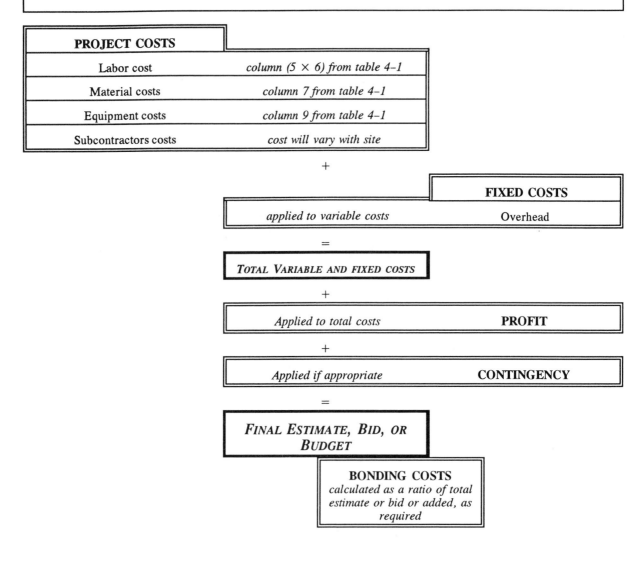

Table 4-6.
A summary of inputs for preparing an accurate estimate, bid, or budget. The final figure accounts for the **project costs** (labor, materials, and equipment) and subcontracting expenses, a part of the total **overhead** of the firm, a **profit** for entrepreneurial companies, and possible **contingency** factor. If the project requires bonding, the cost of the **bond** may be: 1) calculated as a *ratio* of the total price, if the cost of the bond is calculated as a percent of the total price; or 2) added into the final price if the cost of the bond is a flat fee.

PROJECT COSTS	
Labor cost	*column (5 × 6) from table 4-1*
Material costs	*column 7 from table 4-1*
Equipment costs	*column 9 from table 4-1*
Subcontractors costs	*cost will vary with site*

+

	FIXED COSTS
applied to variable costs	Overhead

=

TOTAL VARIABLE AND FIXED COSTS

+

Applied to total costs	**PROFIT**

+

Applied if appropriate	**CONTINGENCY**

=

FINAL ESTIMATE, BID, OR BUDGET

BONDING COSTS
calculated as a ratio of total estimate or bid or added, as required

Project Costs

Project or *variable* costs include material, labor, equipment, subcontracting, and other expenses incurred by the firm that are directly attributed to the fulfillment of the contract or management of a site. The magnitude of individual costs vary with each property and are directly correlated to the amount of work and expectations for the site.

Materials

Material costs are probably the easiest expenses to calculate. The manager or estimator has a known amount of turfgrass area, landscape beds, and seasonal color for any property and a known amount of fertilizer, herbicide, insecticides, mulch, flowers, and other expendable materials that are applied or planted per unit area.

Each firm must determine its philosophy as to whether materials will be estimated in *whole* or *partial units*. For instance, if a property requires 92 pounds of fertilizer for the turf, and fertilizer is purchased in 50 pound bags, is the material priced at 92 pounds or at 2 bags? This is an insignificant question when dealing with low cost items such as fertilizer or mulch; rounding to whole units will probably not make any difference in obtaining a competitive contract. However, with more expensive chemicals, such as pesticides, pricing per whole bag or unit may increase materials' cost estimates dramatically. One should price these on the basis of the amount actually used; partial bags will undoubtedly be utilized on subsequent jobs.

Material costs include more than simply the invoice price of materials divided by number of bags or pounds. Include freight and sales tax. Apply a handling and storage cost to all materials, especially bulky items requiring handling time, or those requiring covered, secure, or special storage. Do not forget to add a factor for broken, damaged, and "lost" material. Also, add any interest incurred on the purchase from either a supplier or lending institution.

Labor costs

An *employee* costs the firm considerably more than his/her hourly wage. The actual cost to the company includes the base pay rate plus all mandatory and voluntary employer contributions to the employee. Legislated contributions, often referred to as *labor burden,* include: employer's share of FICA (social security), federal and state unemployment insurance, workman's compensation, and other statutory contributions. *Fringe benefits* or "perks" vary with company, but include: insurance benefits; retirement plans; paid holidays, vacations, and sick leave; uniform allowance; educational, license and meeting expenses; memberships; profit sharing or bonuses; and many others.

Some firms do not calculate employer-furnished insurance or pension plans as part of direct hourly labor rates. Since these costs are fixed on a monthly or annual basis, these employers prefer to establish them as part of overhead.

Several employers also incorporate a factor for unproductive time, such as rain days and breaks, when determining labor rates. Table 4–7 is useful in determining and understanding the total cost per hour of an employee.

Many managers also incorporate probable overtime in calculation of *effective* hourly rates. Contractors in some regions can schedule a uniform work program without overtime. In most areas, however, seasonal peaks, weather, and other happenstances must be addressed through overtime.

Table 4-7. Labor Cost Estimating Worksheet		
COST ITEM	Employer Cost	Employee Income
Direct Wage Costs		
1. Total regular wages	$	$
2. Overtime wages		
3. Cash bonuses		
A. Total Wages (1+2+3)	$	$
Mandatory Wage Costs		
4. Employer's share FICA (Social Security)	$	$
5. Federal Unemployment Insurance		
6. State Unemployment Insurance		
7. Workman's Compensation Insurance		
8. Other		
B. Total Mandatory Wage Costs (4+5+6+7+8)	$	$
Fringe Benefits		
9. Insurance	$	$
Life		
Health		
Dental		
Other		
10. Retirement (employers contribution)		
11. Uniforms		
12. Training/education		
13. Transportation allowance		
14. Other		
C. Total Fringe Benefits (9+10+11+12+13+14)	$	$
Other Benefits		
15. Holiday pay	$	$
16. Paid vacation leave		
17. Paid sick leave		
D. Total Other Benefits (15+16+17)	$	$

E. Total Employee Costs		
(A+B+C+D)	$	$

F. Productive hours worked per year[1]	

G. Average Cost Per Hour—E divided by F	

[1]Productive hours should not include breaks, weather related down time, training, or any other non-productive time.

Midwest seasons run approximately 30 weeks from mid-April to mid-November. Some contractors plan for 11 weeks at six days per week and 19 weeks at five days per week. A labor budget may call for 11 weeks of 51 hours-per-week and 19 weeks of 42 hours. The increased wages for overtime can, therefore, be factored over a year and estimated as part of the hourly labor rates.

Equipment Costs

Equipment costs are a significant expenditure of any management firm. Equipment expenses can be considered direct project costs or as part of overhead. There is no "correct" answer.

Developing equipment expenses as a project or variable cost allows realistic recognition of the cost of equipment on a per-job basis. This aids the manager in evaluating and differentiating between equipment- and labor-intensive procedures and make his/her pricing of each more realistic and competitive. Hourly equipment and labor costs allow the manager to make efficient and economic decisions on equipment purchases, efficiency, and how changes in equipment will affect productivity, costs, and the bottom line.

Assigning equipment cost as part of overhead, however, is simpler. It is also more appropriate to assign costs of relatively inexpensive, long-lived, or seldom used machinery as overhead.

When determining the cost per hour or unit area (1,000 square feet,

Table 4–8. Worksheet for calculating equipment operation costs.

The cost per hour for any machine or vehicle can be determined by adding the fixed and variable costs and dividing by the estimated use over its life.

FIXED OR OWNERSHIP COSTS

1. Purchase price	=	$
2. Salvage (10%) or trade-in	-	
3. Non recoverable Price (1-2)	=	$
4. Finance or opportunity cost	=	$
5. Insurance/taxes/licenses	=	$

A. Total Fixed Costs (3+4+5)	=	$

OPERATING OR VARIABLE COSTS

6. Fuel	=	$
7. Oil/lubricants/antifreeze	=	$
8. Estimate repairs	=	$
9. Tires	=	$

B. Total Variable (6+7+8+9)	=	$

USE

11. Estimate use per year (area or hours)	=	
12. Estimate life (years)	=	

C. Total Use (hour or area) of machine (11 × 12)		

COST PER HOUR OR UNIT OF USE

Fixed plus variable costs divided by total use (A+B÷C)	=	$

acre, or mile) of ownership and operation, manufacturer and suppliers' claims must be considered with a grain of salt, or two. Evaluate and develop the hourly costs of ownership on realistic estimated annual hours of use and the useful life span of the machine. For instance, a mower used 30 weeks per year, five days per week, six hours per day is operated for 900 hours per year. A machine kept for 5 seasons would be operated for 4,500 hours.

The worksheet in Table 4–8 will be useful for determining the individual expenses that comprise the cost of operating landscape maintenance equipment.

Ownership Costs

The *cost to purchase* a machine is the actual costs plus finance charges. Some managers prefer to calculate actual cost for hourly computations based on the replacement cost for the machine, rather than purchase price. Either calculation should include a realistic scrap or trade-in value (often around 10 percent) to be deducted from the overall costs. Calculating equipment cost on replacement rather than purchase price may be more prudent during inflationary periods.

The *cost of the money* used to purchase this equipment must also be included. If a contractor finances $4,000 of the cost of a $7,000 machine, then the interest paid can easily be seen and understood as part of the overall ownership expense.

Is there a "cost" for the $3,000 cash portion of the price? What if the owner paid cash for the entire purchase? Business advisors urge judicious managers to consider the cost of money as the best return available on the entire $7,000 purchase price or $3,000 down payment, rather than just finance charges. This return on cash, or *opportunity cost,* is the gain that can be realized if the purchase price was invested in a safe income source, such as a certificate of deposit, money market certificate, or within the owner's own business. The cost of money would be determined by the duration of the investment, just as finance charges. Opportunity costs should be considered for cash portions of equipment purchases, in addition to any finance costs.

Equipment operating costs

Include fuel and oil in *hourly operating costs*. Determine fuel consumption per hour under normal use. What will happen to fuel prices next year, or even next month, is a guess. Increases in fuel price affects the cost of operation but the overall impact is actually quite small. The oil changes and other routine service are estimated over the machine's life.

Repairs and maintenance are estimated by including the cost of expected overhauls or major repairs, periodic tune-ups, and replaceable items (belts and blades) in the total operating expenses. Experience with similar machines, manufacturers and suppliers, and mechanics can provide information on repair costs.

The manager must include the cost of insurance for a true cost of equipment operation. Once more, some firms prefer to consider insurance as overhead since it is an annual fee. Most policies do not itemize charges for specific pieces of equipment, except for large equipment, such as trucks.

Hourly costs for equipment can be carried to the extreme. The majority of contractors using the hourly charges develop costs for major equipment (vehicles, tractors, mowers). Some will compute the time cost for smaller equipment, such as blowers, edgers, and string trimmers. Other managers consider small machine costs as part of their overhead. Hourly figures are sometimes used to account for rakes, hoes, and other small tools. Basic small tool inventories, however, are best considered overhead. The estimator will go crazy trying to anticipate every minute a broom or pruner is used.

Subcontractors' Costs

Subcontracting is a necessary and profitable part of landscape management. Only very large, diverse companies have all of the equipment and expertise to perform every required management task. Select subcontractors carefully; they represent your firm. Always request and check job references before hiring a

Table 4–9.
Criteria for selecting subcontractors:
• Performance quality • Volume of work the contractor can perform • Financial backing • Reliability • Professionalism

subcontractor. Be sure the subcontractor carries proper insurance and licensing to protect the hiring firm and the client.

Subcontractors' costs are relatively easy to apply as direct costs. An estimate or bid from a subcontractor for their services is received. Many firms "markup" or add a percentage to the subcontractor's bid. The markup compensates for the hiring firm's time and

Table 4-10.
Subcontracting:
• Allows the firm to offer the client complete service management. • Extends the scope of work the firm is able to accomplish or participate in. • Provides additional personnel, equipment, and expertise without extending the firm's resources.

expenses for monitoring the work. There is no accepted formula for markups. Markups range from 10 to 50 percent of the subcontractor's price, depending on the complexity of the job, the budget, and the market. Ten percent is the most common figure. The larger the job, however, the smaller the markup typically is.

Working as a subcontractor

Prompt payment and extended liability are the primary issues to consider when working as a subcontractor. General contractors may delay payment to the subcontractors until the job is finished and accepted. A subcontractor must be held responsible for his/her actions on site. However, make sure that the subcontracting firm will not share in liability for actions they were not concerned with. Some generals contractors like to spread the potential liability and "blame" among all of the participating subcontractors. Read the contract very carefully.

Overhead

Overhead is the cost of doing business. Overhead expenses can not be directly attributed to a single job. Overhead is incurred whether the company has work or not. These include salaries and benefits for administrative, management, secretarial, and accounting staff, payments or rent for land and buildings, and utilities (Table 4-11).

Table 4–11.

Overhead reflects those business expenses incurred whether or not the firm receives any work or income. Overhead is comprised of many, sometimes forgotten, but very important costs. The following illustrates some typical overhead expenses associated with landscape management.

Costs for Facilities

Land—Payment or Rental
Structure—Improvement and Upkeep
Furniture and Furnishings
Utilities:
    Heat
    Electricity
    Water
    Sewer
    Waste Disposal
    Telephones
Taxes
Insurance
Janitorial Service
Grounds Care by Employees
Security

Administrative/Management Expenses

Administrative Wages and Benefits
Management Wages and Benefits
Support Wages and Benefits
Secretarial and Accounting
Finance Costs
Advertising and Marketing

Account Collections
Licenses/Fees/Permits
Office Supplies
Insurance
Postage
Office Equipment
Travel/Meetings/Training
Publications and Memberships

Contracted Services

Labor and Materials Acquired by Contract
Legal Fees, Audits
Consultants

Tools, Equipment and Vehicle Costs

Purchase or Lease
Service and Repair
Replacement
Fuel and Fluids
Parts
Vehicle Insurance/Taxes/Licenses
Storage
Rental
Small Tool Inventories

The salaries or wages of "non-working" supervisors or managers who coordinate a number of people or crews can be included as management overhead. Some contractors do, however, consider these people as direct costs to the sites their crews are responsible for and apply their salary as an hourly expense. It is more efficient and reasonable to consider such employees as management overhead.

Applying overhead

There are as many ways to apply or factor overhead into a bid or estimate as there are companies. Some companies simply determine labor and material costs and multiply by a *magic number* to cover overhead and profit. The numbers two and three seem to be the most bewitching. This may be acceptable to some, so long as they are in the black at the end of the year. Most business owners and managers feel, especially in a competitive market, that the company must know and be able to control its costs.

Each property or contract must pay its share of the overhead costs. An accountant, business manager, or a consultant can assist in developing specific overhead figures and application formulae. The accounting is not difficult and annual expenditures by category must be determined for tax purposes anyway. Most overhead recovery systems develop a relationship (or ratio) between overhead and direct costs. Some procedures are based upon a relationship or ratio between indirect costs and labor, since labor is the greatest direct cost.

Other Costs

Supplements to total job costs may be added to the bid in some cases. For a new company, a new or difficult landscape, or unusual contract, a *contingency* factor is sometimes added. A contingency is an amount or percentage added to the calculated costs to protect from omission, gross error, or site factors that were unnoticed or unable to be factored in. Contingencies are sometimes referred to as a "fudge factor." They will serve as insurance if something was omitted or misfigured or a substantial boost in profits if everything was calculated correctly. They may, however, result in loosing the contract in competitive situations, since they will boost the bid.

The cost of *bid bonds* or *performance bonds,* if required, must be added after the entire bid, including profit, is calculated. The price for the guarantee of a surety may be charged as a *percent* of the total contract or as a *flat fee.* If the bonding fee is a percent of the entire contract, include the fee in the final price using a ratio equation. Flat fee bond charges can be added to the total costs plus profit to determine the final price.

Profit

Profit is not the only reason people go into business. It is, however, the principal inducement for remaining in business. As someone once said, "Work without profit is exercise." The amount of profit, or return on investment, desired or required, must be determined by the owners of the firm.

How much profit is enough? How much is too little? The profit margin of a firm is usually a variable floating around an ideal. It depends upon several facets and is ultimately determined by how accurately costs were estimated. Hopefully, either estimates will be reasonably accurate or the shortfalls will be balanced by the windfalls to equal an acceptable overall rate of return. One benchmark for lowest level is current rate of returns on safe investments, such as certificates of deposit (CD). How much could the owner make if he/she sold everything today and invested in a 10-year CD? Why would the manager be willing to accept a lesser return with all of the work and headaches that go into operating a business?

The profit applied to individual properties is a figure within range influenced by need, size, risk, and the marketplace. What is the lowest and highest (without feeling guilty) profit acceptable on a job? If the firm needs the job to fill its schedule, as an advertising point, to simply keep afloat, or as a point of honor, then it should be more willing to do it for a lower profit margin. The greater the need, the lower the profit the owner is willing to consider.

With risk comes increased expectations of profit. If the job is risky from any of a number of views (labor, difficulty, or age of the landscape) then seek a greater profit. If the job is one that everyone can do, then be assured that everyone will bid on it. Larger jobs are sometimes bid at lower profits than are smaller properties. The lower profit rate is compensated for by increased volume and efficiency. Smaller jobs often have increased costs due to their scale, and higher profit margins are applied.

The number of competitors in the marketplace causes a landscape management company to adjust its profit to become more competitive on specific jobs. Good work at a reasonable, or at least acceptable price, is always more honorable than a reputation as a low bidder at any price.

Profit is applied to the final price of any job according to the business statement and requirements of the owner. If profit is a percentage of total costs or investment, then the total cost of a job (direct + indirect) is multiplied by this figure. If the profit is a percent of the final price, billing, or volume, then it must be calculated by using a ratio equation. Again, seek the assistance of an accountant or a business consultant in setting up the firm's books and goals.

Table 4-12. Bid Comparison Form

Comparison of actual versus estimated costs is critical to improve estimating accuracy and identify true costs. The following is a simple example of a form that might be used to compare estimated or bid figures with actual costs or times. The actual costs would be derived from job and time sheets.

Job: _____

Activity	Estimated	Actual cost	Difference	Reason
Material				
Pesticide				
Fertilizer				
Labor				
Mowing				
Tree care				
Shrub care				
Detailed Listing of other Operations				
Gross				

Hourly Charges

A large number of companies have developed a pricing system in which direct costs, overhead, and profit is applied directly to hourly production rates. Total direct hours for labor during the past fiscal year are divided into the total income for the year. This yields a bid price per man-hour that includes direct, indirect, and profit. The *hourly rate* is adjusted to reflect the desired profit level. This pricing method depends on last year's business figures so changes in costs, wages and inflation must be anticipated.

Companies using this system develop different hourly labor rates to reflect the amount or expense of equipment and materials involved. For instance, mowing is more expensive than general labor. Spraying and irrigation repair are more expensive than mowing.

A company that I am familiar with used the following labor rates (in 1989 dollars):

$20.00 per man-hour for mowing, edging, trimming, and other general maintenance activities;

$70.00 per man-hour for herbicide application to shrub beds;

$75.00 per man-hour for herbicide application to turf;

$80.00 for seasonal insect applications; and

$40.00 per hour for irrigation checks, adjustment, and repair.

Hourly price differences reflect the equipment, material, and increased salary for technical and professional personnel for the individual operations.

Other companies have extrapolated the income per man-hour to develop charges per unit area (1,000 square feet or acre) for mowing or chemical applications. Pruning is sometimes calculated on a per-plant basis; seasonal color is frequently estimated on per-flat or per-plant or per-bulb charge.

Per-hour or per-unit estimating systems provide simple and rapid methods of determining charges. Per-hour charges are based on company history. Good managers will monitor interim financial statements and cumulative costs for individual jobs. New companies adopting this practice tend to utilize per man-hour figures pulled from the air, usually very close to, but slightly below the larger firms in the area. The result is a large profit per hour during the first few seasons, however, total profit and profit per hour will decline as overhead increases.

Bibliography

Anonymous. 1981. *Guide to Grounds Maintenance Estimating.* 2nd ed. Professional Grounds Management Society, Pikesville, MD.

Anonymous. 1985. Estimating techniques that will make you successful. *Landscape Contractor,* 26(12):10.

Anonymous. 1987. Costing mowing jobs. *American Lawn Applicator,* 9(3):44–46.

Anonymous. 1990. Equipment operating cost survey. *Pro,* 2(7):30.

Anonymous. 1990. *Grounds Maintenance Estimating Guidelines.* 6th ed. Professional Grounds Management Society, Cockeysville, MD.

Anonymous. 1992. Calculating mowing costs. *Landscape Management,* 31(1):22–24.

Anonymous. 1992. Subcontracting for pleasure and profit. *Landscape Contractor,* 33(5):26–28.

Anonymous. 1993. Computing mower costs. *Lawn & Landscape Maintenance,* 14(4):49–52.

Christian, P. D., III. 1990. When the rubber meets the road. *Grounds Maintenance,* 25(6):36, 38–39.

Copley, K. 1983. How to estimate the job. *Grounds Maintenance,* 18(1):10–11, 14, 18.

Copley, K. and D. Lofgren. 1983. Estimating. *Grounds Maintenance,* 18(2):18–24, 28–30.

Garber, T. 1990. Accurate estimating, pricing stems from a solid budget. *Lawn & Landscape Maintenance,* 11(11):26–29.

Garber, T. 1990. Accurate estimating, pricing stems from a solid budget. *Lawn & Landscape Maintenance,* 11(11):26–29.

Garber, T. 1990. Competition increases need for insightful bidding. *Lawn & Landscape Maintenance,* 11(12):102–111.

Haupt, S. B. 1993. What does $10 cost? *Tree Care Industry,* 4(9):22–26.

King, J. C. 1987. Three ILCA members help take the mystery out of estimating. *Landscape Contractor,* 28(11):14–15.

Landis, D. 1989. Landscape bidding and job costing—a CPA's perspective. *Landscape Contractor,* 30(5):10–13.

Legg, D. 1990. The cost of mowing. *Grounds Maintenance,* 25(3):110–116.

Lofgren, D. E. 1978. Budgeting, estimating and management. In: *Manual of Site Management.* Environmental Design Press, Reston, VA.

Lofgren, D. E. 1991. Projecting labor costs. *Grounds Maintenance,* 26(11):38, 51–52.

Martin, S. 1991. Multi-year contracts. *Grounds Maintenance,* 26(10):16–22.

Marx, W. 1991. Job costing. *Pro,* 3(5):5.

Moore, M. 1985. Bidding, installation and maintenance—how we do it. *Foliage News,* 10(5):1–6.

Phillips, T. 1991. Pricing for profit: an introduction. *Landscape Management,* 30(2):32–34.

Phillips, T. 1991. Pricing for profit II. *Landscape Management,* 30(3):56–61.

Post, C. A. 1981. How to bid for profit. *American Nurseryman,* 153(9):80–83.

Purdy, W. F. 1984. Landscape estimating. *Southern Landscape and Turf,* 29(1):24, 29.

Trusty, M. and S. Trusty. 1992. Making a profit at mowing. *Lawn & Landscape Maintenance,* 13(12):27–31.

Vander Kooi, C. 1985. *Estimating and Management Principles for Landscape Contracting.* C. Vander Kooi, Littleton, CO.

Vander Kooi, C. 1989. Developing a bidding strategy. *Pro,* 1(6):5.

Ward, M. 1991. Pondering mowing costs. *Lawn & Landscape Maintenance,* 12(2):34–36.

Wilbraham, S. 1989. How to bid large properties. *Pro,* 1(6):4.

Chapter 5
Personnel Management[1]

Landscape management is a labor intensive service industry. The largest single budget item is labor. The greatest challenge to graduating students and new managers is not problem diagnosis or product knowledge. It is the lack of experience in supervising people. The quality of the work force determines the success or failure of the company. Most of the "problems" expressed by managers concern finding and keeping qualified labor. This will continue to be a dilemma in the future.

Photo 5-1. People are the strength, reputation, and future of every landscape management company. Photograph courtesy of Mark Yahn, Ground Control™ Landscaping, Inc., Orlando, FL.

Interviewing and Hiring

There is more to hiring field employees and supervisors than running an ad and selecting the "best" person for the job. Managers and potential managers must be cognizant of employee's rights. Employee rights are among the forefront of changes encountered in the green industry. Wrongful discharge is one of the most rapidly expanding features in the legal landscape. Anyone who applies for a position within a company deserves consideration and has certain rights guaranteed by law.

Hiring requires several critical steps to find the "right" person for a position. The manager must knew what he/she wants in an employee before beginning the search process. To do this, write a *job description*. A job description lists the responsibilities and duties attached to the position. Obtain input from several appropriate people in the company. If the position is supervisory, exclude input from the departing employee. The employee may exaggerate the complexity of the job or make invalid suggestions.

Realize that an opening provides the opportunity to restructure. Is a new employee needed or can the responsibilities be divided among existing staff? Should someone presently within the company be promoted to fill the vacancy?

Determine the skill level and experience required to handle the job effectively. What was it about the previous employee that made him/her effective in the position? What skills would have made them more effective? Criteria often considered include: education; experience; appearance; and

[1]Special thanks to Glenda Hensley for assisting with this chapter. Her personnel experience and training as an Administrative Assistant with the College of Veterinary Medicine, Kansas State University and with the Joint Institute of Marine and Atmospheric Research, University of Hawaii were invaluable.

personality. Avoid the temptation of setting the qualifications too high. Are you willing or able to offer a pay and benefits package that a "super star" candidate will require?

Job Applications

Construct application forms so that they do not violate state or federal antidiscrimination laws. Many companies use commercially prepared forms specifically designed to avoid discrimination. Some application forms, however, have shortcomings.

Many historical questions on application forms have been ruled as dangerous. A company or manager can transgress by asking applicants, on application forms or during an interview: their age; dates of public school attendance; birthplace; religion; citizenship; race; height and weight; color of hair, eyes, or skin; marital or family status; non job-related handicaps; whether the applicant owns or rents a home; transportation arrangement for getting to work; type of military discharge; or name or address of any relative. Employers may not inquire about an arrest record (you can ask about convictions in some states), whether the applicant has been sued, refused a surety bond or government security; hobbies, activities or memberships not related to job qualifications; or past workers' compensation claims.

Table 5-1.
Job description[1] The following is a sample of a job description for a supervisor, foreman, or crew leader of an institutional or public grounds.

I. *Scope of Work*
    All exterior grounds, walks, roadways and facilities.

II. *General duties and responsibilities:*
    1. Assign all tasks and jobs to grounds employees on a timely basis.
    2. Fill out time reports daily.
    3. Plan and organize all work including scheduling and follow-up inspections on a routine basis.
    4. Assist supervisors in the budgeting process, data collection, report preparation, and designing and analyzing training.
    5. Cooperate with other departmental personnel in completing assigned tasks, either as a leader or as a member of a team.
    6. Make routine purchases of material, services, rentals, repairs, and equipment as required and authorized.
    7. Cooperate with other personnel and supervisors.
    8. Fill-in, as needed, for grounds department personnel when others are absent or unavailable.
    9. Participate in fire and disaster programs as directed.

III. *Qualifications:*
    1. Good health with adequate physical strength and endurance to perform the work described.
    2. Knowledge of how to work effectively and safely.
    3. Willingness to be trained in any categories of grounds or personnel management that may be needed.
    4. Knowledge of the safe use of hand and power equipment involved with grounds management.
    5. Five (5) or more years working directly in horticulture, gardening, and/or landscaping.
    6. Two (2) or more years supervisory experience of 2 or more employees.
    7. A valid drivers license.

IV. *Education:*
    High school graduation or equivalent. Some post-secondary horticultural courses are desirable.

---

[1]Adapted from Professional Grounds Management Society. 1989. *Ground Management Forms and Job Descriptions Guide*. 3rd ed., Cockeysville, MD

Table 5-2.

The questions asked of perspective employees must be phrased carefully as not to infringe upon their rights and so the employer does not appear guilty of discrimination. Here are some "problem" questions and acceptable substitutes.

TOPIC	ACCEPTABLE	UNACCEPTABLE
NAME	<ul><li>Name</li><li>Have you ever used another name?</li><li>Is any additional information relative to change of name, use of an assumed name, or nickname necessary to check on work and education record?</li></ul>	<ul><li>Maiden name</li></ul>
RESIDENCE	<ul><li>Place of residence?</li></ul>	<ul><li>Do you own or rent your own home?</li></ul>
AGE	<ul><li>Statements indicating that hiring is subject to verification that the applicant meets legal age requirements.</li><li>If hired can you show proof of age?</li><li>Are you over eighteen years of age?</li></ul>	<ul><li>Age</li><li>Birthdate</li><li>Dates of attendance or completion of elementary or high school.</li></ul>
BIRTHPLACE CITIZENSHIP	<ul><li>Can you, after employment, submit verification of your legal right to work in the US?</li><li>Are you a US citizen?</li></ul>	<ul><li>Birthplace of applicant's parents, spouse or other relatives.</li></ul>
NATIONAL ORIGIN	<ul><li>Languages the applicant reads, speaks or writes.</li></ul>	<ul><li>Questions about applicant's nationality, ancestry, national origin, or parentage.</li><li>What is your mother's tongue?</li><li>Specific language commonly used by applicant.</li></ul>
SEX, MARTIAL STATUS, FAMILY	<ul><li>Name and address of parent or guardian if applicant is a minor.</li><li>Statement of company policy regarding work assignment of employees who are related.</li></ul>	<ul><li>Questions that indicate applicant's sex.</li><li>Questions that indicate applicant's marital status.</li><li>Number and/or ages of children or dependents.</li><li>Provisions for child care.</li><li>Questions regarding pregnancy, child bearing or birth control</li><li>Name or address of relative, spouse or children of adult applicant.</li></ul>
RACE, COLOR		<ul><li>Questions about the applicant's race or color.</li><li>Questions regarding applicant's complexion or color of skin, eyes, or hair.</li></ul>

Table 5–2. (con't)

TOPIC	ACCEPTABLE	UNACCEPTABLE
RELIGION	• Statements by employer of regular days, hours, or shifts to be worked.	• Religious days observed. • Does your religion prevent you from working weekends or holidays? • Questions about the applicant's religion.
PHYSICAL DESCRIPTION OR PHOTOGRAPH	• Statement that photograph may be required after employment.	• Questions as to applicant's height and weight. • Require applicant to submit a photograph with application.
PHYSICAL CONDITION, OR HANDICAP	• Statements that employment may be made contingent to the applicant passing a job-related physical examination. • Do you have any physical condition or handicap that may limit your ability to perform the job applied for? If so, what can be done to accommodate your limitation?	• Questions about applicant's general medical condition or, state of health. • Questions regarding receipt of Workers' Compensation Insurance. • Do you have any physical disabilities or handicaps?
CRIMINAL RECORD	• Have you ever been convicted of a felony, or a misdemeanor that resulted in imprisonment? (Such a question must be accompanied by a statement that a conviction will not disqualify any applicant from the job.) (Legality of this question varies with states.)	• Arrest record. • Have you ever been arrested?
BONDING	• State that bonding is a condition of employment.	• Questions regarding refusal or cancellation of bonding.
MILITARY SERVICE	• Questions about relevant skills acquired during applicant's US military service.	• General questions about military services, such as dates, or type of discharge.
ECONOMIC STATUS		• Questions about applicant's current or past assets, liabilities, or credit rating, including bankruptcy or wage garnishment.
ORGANIZATIONS, ACTIVITIES	• Please list job-related clubs, professional organizations, societies, or other associations to which you belong. Omit any that may indicate your race, religious creed, color, national origin, ancestry, sex, or age.	• List all organizations, clubs, societies, and lodges to which you belong.

Table 5–2. (con't)

TOPIC	ACCEPTABLE	UNACCEPTABLE
REFERENCES	• By whom were you referred? • Names of persons willing to provide professional and/or character references for applicant.	• Questions about applicant's former employers. • Questions that obtain information about the applicant's race, color, names, creed, national origin, ancestry, physical handicap, medical condition, marital status, age, or sex.
NOTIFICATION IN CASE OF EMERGENCY	• Name and address of *person* to be notified in case of accident or emergency.	• Name and address of *relative* to be notified in case of accident or emergency.

Employers cannot ask questions that permit them to deduce an applicant's age, sex, or minority status. Requesting information on the applicant's height and weight, for example, might suggest that the applicant is a woman or a member of a certain racial or national group. These questions cannot be asked even if the information will become readily apparent during an interview. Photographs may not be requested as part of the application.

Where to Look

Field positions can be filled by advertising in the "Help Wanted" section of one or more local newspapers. Public employment assistance offices and programs may also provide applicants. Lawn and landscape companies face competition from the construction industry, factories, and other service industries such as fast-food, retail, and delivery industries. Trade publications can provide a source of more experienced and supervisory candidates. Technical schools have names of qualified applicants for positions requiring specific training and/or advanced education.

Consider *non-traditional employees,* such as older people. Typically entry-level workers are in their early 20's. Many firms successfully recruit employees in their 30's and 40's. They find that although these workers may require a higher wage, they provide additional skills, experience, and reduced turnover. The green industry is still dominated by men, but employers should recruit and consider the entire labor market: women; minorities; immigrants; and displaced workers.

Establish contacts with local and regional two- and four-year colleges. Build rapport with the various departments by meeting instructors, offering to present guest lectures to classes and student clubs, and for field trips. Do not restrict the search for key or supervisory employees to horticulture, landscape architecture, and allied departments. Companies recruiting at universities seek people from agricultural economics, business, crop protection, agronomy, and a host of other departments.

Internships are mutually beneficial opportunities for students and management. Employers have a chance to assess prospective employees and the opportunity allows students to gain valuable experience and training. The internship should not necessarily be looked upon as a profitable position. Ideally, the student will gain experience in all phases of the company. An intern should be more than a summer employee. Managers should explain the how's and why's, as well as the what's.

A surprising number of students who have completed good internships return to that company for their first full-time job.

Seasonal employees are an important resource during busy periods. Landscape management work is seasonal. A lot of work must be done in a short time. Begin hiring seasonal employees early in the year, don't wait until the day before they are needed. Hold mass hiring seminars at local schools. Stress the importance of the part-

Table 5–3.
Where to advertise for part-time or seasonal employees.   • Daily newspapers   • School bulletin boards   • Word of mouth   • Weekly newspapers   • State employment agencies

time people to supervisors and existing crews. Ask for their tolerance and help in training the part-timer's. Offer good part-time or seasonal employees as much work as possible throughout the year to keep them interested in the company.

As the company grows, consider appointing or hiring a *personnel officer*. This person can keep applicant files, learn and understand the necessary paperwork, and make the manager's life easier.

The general operation and management of the company play an important part in hiring, as well as employee retention. Develop programs that adequately train and reward employees. Create an environment that encourages people to seek career opportunities with the company.

Promotion From Within

A prime place to seek supervisory or management candidates is within the company. You are dealing with a known quantity and do not have to research their background. The current employee is familiar with the organization, its goals, the management, equipment, and employees.

When comparing internal and external candidates, do not confuse credentials with accomplishment. Every manager or supervisor need not have a college degree. Possession of a degree does not assure expertise or ability to supervise people. Experience, motivation, and enthusiasm go a long way.

Promotion from within creates higher morale. The opportunity for upward movement shows employees that the company believes in their accomplishments, and abilities. Promotion also indicates to the employee that he/she has a career rather than just a job.

There are also negative aspects for promoting from within. The applicant pool is limited. None of the employees may be suitable for the available position. A current employee that is interviewed but then not promoted may become disgruntled and a liability. The manager must assure the employee of his/her value to the organization or risk losing the disappointed person. Promotion from within still leaves a vacancy that must be filled. Other employees sometimes resent a former co-worker becoming their "boss." Additionally, new talent or expertise has not been added to the company.

One difficult task for some firms is to expand the number of field crews for increased work loads. Good crew supervisors are difficult to find on short notice. One company anticipates crew expansion with a position of "assistant crew supervisor" on every field crew. The assistant supervisor has the opportunity to work directly under a supervisor and has leadership responsibilities in his/her absence. The assistant is paid slightly more than other field employees on the crew. The assistant is familiar with the work routine and can assume a supervisor's position with minimal preparation when required.

Recruiters

Several employment firms have emerged to serve the green industry in recent years. Recruiters or "head hunters" aid managers in filling certain positions. Recruiters can sometimes find more qualified candidates in a shorter time. They can perform initial screening and provide potential people who meet pre-established qualifications.

Evaluating Résumés

The quality of the résumé and that of the candidate are not necessarily related. Many applicants seek the assistance of a professional résumé service. Hopefully, all of the information is true and accurate. When reading résumés look for specific accomplishments such as sales increases, measurable productivity improvements, and examples of leadership.

Grades are not the most important indicator of knowledge or success. Grades, however, do indicate something about self-discipline, goal orientation, and intelligence.

Take note of noticeable gaps in work chronology. Do not eliminate a candidate for having had several jobs, but do inquire about it during the interview.

The résumé can indicate how hard the candidate will work. Look for instances where the person went above and beyond the call of duty. This may be evidenced by volunteer work and college club activities, especially committee chair and officer positions. Extra-curricular activities indicate high energy levels, a willingness to take responsibility, and ambition.

Seriously question résumés that: over-emphasize education or training; have distinct gaps in their background; contain trivia; those that sound egotistical or bitter; and those that appear too slick or too cute.

Read the cover letters carefully. In a cover letter, expect to learn what makes this applicant or student different from any of the others. The letter should be well-written, grammatically correct, and typed without error. Again, there is plenty of assistance available in writing cover letters.

Interviewing

The interview is the period when the employer and employee meet and evaluate each other. Conduct the interview in as relaxed a setting as possible. Allow adequate time to answer the applicant's questions as well as have yours answered. Prepare for the interview by reading the credentials provided. Review the applicant's background and application with him/her to see if the information is correct and if there are any pertinent additions.

By all means, check references. During the years I have assisted students to find jobs throughout the green industry, I am appalled by how few employers bother to check references. Many feel that a person would not be listed as a reference unless he/she had positive comments about the applicant. In general, this is probably true. On the other hand, technical school and college instructors or advisors will likely provide an honest opinion of the person. They fully realize the student's limitations and are concerned about the success of the employer/employee relationship from both sides. Most instructors will not recommend students for positions they will not be able to handle.

When interviewing an applicant for any position, know what information is sought. Have some questions planned. Know what points on the résumé or application require discussion. Assume a conversational tone rather than a direct question 1, 2, 3 format. Encourage the candidate to do most of the talking and be a good listener using silence, nodding, and eye contact. Ask open-ended questions rather than those that can be answered yes or no.

Know what questions are appropriate and what behavior may be interpreted as discrimination. Ask only job-related questions. Ask women the same questions asked of men. If physical standards are set, i.e., height, weight, or strength, then be prepared to show how they relate to the position.

Table 5–4.
Supervisors must be able to work with people. Outstanding performance, attendance, and company loyalty may not be enough to indicate success as a people manager. The business is entrusted to supervisors. Evaluate a person for a supervisory or leadership role in relation to the following questions:
• Does the person have adequate supervisory ability? • Can the applicant assume the added responsibility? • Can the person communicate readily and clearly with employees, other managers, and clientele? • Does the prospect have sufficient stamina? • How does the person work with others? • Can the prospect make decisions? • How successfully can the individual delegate responsibility or assignments? • Will the person overreact to the promotion or new authority? • How will the person accept advice or criticisms from superiors? • What is the emotional stability of the individual?

Do not force issues that the applicant clearly wishes to avoid. Ask about duties and responsibilities of their current position. Ask what the applicant's most important professional accomplishment was and their greatest frustration. Ask about the strengths the applicant perceives they possess to make them a success in this position. Avoid trap questions, "Are you any good at firing people?"

Give extra credit to applicants who have done their homework and know something about your company. Find out why they are interested in this position and willing to leave their current position. Inquire about the applicant's goals over the next two to five years. Can they grow within the company?

Do not oversell the position. Explain the negatives about the job. What may be a negative to one person may be a positive to another. The applicant should have a true picture of their responsibilities to make an informed decision and reduce turnover.

Explain briefly the opportunities the company offers including: salary range; merit raises; benefits, insurance; any and all leave provided; and the payroll schedule.

Close the interview by asking for further questions from the applicant. Be sure to give the applicant a date to expect notification of selection for the position.

Write down your opinions immediately after concluding the interview. What did you like and not like? If several people were interviewed for a position, they will blur and blend after a while. Interview the entire applicant pool before extending an offer. If a person appears perfect for the job, he/she will still be perfect after talking to the remaining applicants.

Make the offer to the selected candidate as quickly as possible by phone and by mail. Do not include anything that indicates the duration of the job, such as referring to a secure position. Do not promise anything that cannot be delivered. This can lead to trouble if the person does not work out. Ask the candidate for acknowledgment of acceptance and indicate that you are looking forward to working with him/her.

Salary

Determine the salary for the position based upon responsibilities and expectations. Know the current market value of the position being offered. Do not automatically base the new employee's wages on those of the previous. Exiting employees may have been paid more or less than they or the position is worth.

Salaries vary with market area, the size of the applicant pool, company policy, and budget. As the market for employees becomes more competitive, salaries are forced to increase. Employers should not only consider the starting salary but develop equitable pay practices. Fringe benefits are very important to an employee trying to raise a family.

Salaries in the landscape management industry are more competitive than most other segments of the green industry. There is also greater concern about fringe benefits. This is based loosely on fact and a great deal on observation of offers and success of past students in various areas of ornamental horticulture. I have heard fewer concerns from prospective employees about salary levels in the landscape management industry than in the nursery and garden center industries.

Reserve salary discussions until a job offer is made. I do, however, encourage students to come away from an interview with at least some idea of a salary range. Schedules for evaluations and raises are probably as important as initial salary. An employee may be more willing to accept a lower starting salary during an evaluation or training period if there is promise and hope for fair, periodic increases based on production and the health of the company.

Some companies require new employees to sign *non-competitive contracts*. In essence, non-competitive contracts state that an employee will not compete with the company after leaving the company, for any reason. The contracts are meant to prevent employees from starting his/her own business using the expertise and client base gained from the employer.

Some contracts are reasonable in their language and intent, others are not. I am aware of one former student asked to sign a contract a few days after arriving on a new job. He had not been informed of this requirement before accepting the position and moving his family. The contract prevented him from starting or working for any firm providing any landscape commercial or retail product or service within a 60 mile radius for 3 years after leaving the company. He thought the contract was inordinate, refused to sign it, and was dismissed a few days after beginning employment. He now has a very competitive and profitable firm in the same town. The employer deprived himself of an excellent employee and undoubtedly exposed the company to a nasty and expensive lawsuit had the employee elected to pursue it.

Courts have upheld some non-competitive contracts that protect the firm's customer lists, client base, and trade secrets. More often, however, courts throughout the country have found non-competitive contracts an unreasonable restriction on the employee and free trade.

Orientation

The new employee should be made to feel welcome. He/she should be introduced to everyone appropriate within the firm. Care should be taken that the employee understands the benefits available and correctly fills out all paperwork. A volume of paperwork has become necessary to assure compliance with the changes in the Immigration Reform and Control Act and other governmental mandates. Company policies and organization must be explained clearly. The employee must be made to feel that he/she is part of a team and has something valuable to contribute to the effort.

Every employee should be provided with an employee handbook. An alternative is a brief history of the company and the organizational format. Include a written welcome from the owner, if he/she should not be affiliated with the firm's daily operations.

Employee Handbook

In most organizations *employee handbooks* are used to summarize the relationship between the employer and the employee. Handbooks describe the employer's philosophy and set the tone for employee relations. Handbooks present rules and policies, standard procedures, and expected standards of conduct. They also explain what the employer provides the employee: benefits; services; and so on. Handbooks present the information necessary to make employees feel good about the company, build loyalty, and feel as if they are part of a team.

Another function of an employee handbook is to show the value of the benefits. It may be the only place where all the benefits are listed. A handbook can be a good recruiter, motivator, and assist employee retention. Few employees realize the true dollar value of their benefits.

A well-prepared handbook saves time by answering routine questions like, "How soon can I take a vacation?"

Potential implications of employee handbooks

There are also some legal implications to consider. In some instances, an employee handbook is viewed as part of an explicit contract between the employee and employer. Handbooks also provide written proof that the employees have been told the rules and policies. Some employers require the employee to sign a card indicating that he/she has read and understood the rules and policies in the handbook. If this is done, then be sure that the handbook is written so it is understandable, and that it is available in as many different languages as necessary. Also, make sure that it has actually been read.

Regardless, avoid dangerous phrases, such as "you are now part of the company family," or "you can expect to be employed as long as you do a good job." Refer to "permanent" employment as "regular" employment. These statements can be construed as promise of long-term employment.

Other specific areas of concern within employee handbooks include: grounds for dismissal; performance reviews; pay raises; and probationary periods. State specific offenses that will be grounds for dismissal or discipline, but do not limit the firm to these.

Establish performance review procedures and conduct them fairly. Referring to annual reviews suggests that the employee has a year-long contract. Again, "annual" pay increases may be interpreted as a year-long employment contract. Salaries and subsequent adjustments can be described in terms of actual pay periods, with reference to *annual* rates only as an example.

Refer to the probationary period as an orientation or introductory period. It may be interpreted that an employee can only be dismissed for cause after the probation.

The advantages of an employee handbook certainly outweigh any problems associated with it. These short-comings can be neutralized with careful writing. The handbook must be fair, consistent, and updated to remain current. As with any potential legal document, write it with an eye toward interpretation and have an attorney review it.

Developing an employee handbook

Most handbooks provide general information about the company, including a letter from the chief executive, a brief history of the company, an organizational chart, and a statement of the company philosophy. Other areas included are employer services, work and discipline rules, and pay issues.

Cover the topics that pertain to the majority of employees. Be careful of items that differ among classes of employees. Discussing the perks for top management creates ill will among the troops.

Keep the book positive. Do not dwell on discipline. One of the aims should be to boost employee morale.

Do not try to discuss complicated topics. Refer employees to a designated person within the company for questions on health insurance and other complicated benefits. Do not try to reprint the entire insurance policy. This can be handled by the personnel officer.

Determine how often the information in the handbook will change. Every time specific salaries, vacation, sick or holiday leaves are mentioned, you risk revision of the figures. On the other hand, if the handbook does not deal with specifics, then how useful is it?

Fringe Benefits

Employers are required by governmental mandate to provide some fringe benefits to employees. These include Social Security, workers' compensation, and unemployment

---

Table 5–5. Common Employee Handbook Topics

Personnel manuals vary in length and complexity. To be useful, the handbook should cover the following company policies:

Working Hours
- starting times
- time and extent of breaks
- lunch policies and limitations
- overtime
  - authorization
  - meal reimbursement
- absence/tardiness
- time clocks/cards

Leave
- vacation
  - when allowed
  - scheduling
- holidays
- sick leave
- family illness
- funeral leave
- jury duty
- military duty

Discipline/Work Rules
- termination/probation
  - reasons
  - procedure

Pay Policy

Grievance Policy

Employee Benefits
- insurance programs
- profit sharing or bonuses
- retirement
- promotions
- educational opportunities
- employee purchase discounts
- parking
- dress code
- uniforms
- conduct
- honesty
- tools

Travel
- reimbursement
- travel time

Safety
- reporting accidents
- safety equipment

And other topics as pertinent

71

insurance. Other benefits are provided by agreement between the employer and employee. These include pension, profit sharing, bonuses, continuing education assistance, notary public service, paid vacation, holidays, sick leave, health insurance, life insurance, and many others.

Fringe benefits are important in recruiting and retaining employees. It is, therefore, important to make employees aware of what the company provides for benefits and their costs. Fringe benefits boost the employee's real income because they are tax exempt. Fringe benefits can be beneficial to the employer. Fringe benefits cost the employer less than the comparable salary increase necessary for the employee to provide the same services his/herself.

Consider several items when evaluating fringe benefits for employee packages. First, determine which benefits are most advantageous for the employees. Medical plans are usually the most often requested. To ensure the maximum effectiveness at minimal after-tax cost, an employee benefit should meet two tests. 1) The cost of providing the benefits should be tax deductible. A small company cannot economically embark on a program that does not permit the expenditure to be deducted. 2) The cost of the fringes should be tax-free to the employee.

The Tax Reform Act of 1986 imposed strict guidelines governing non-discrimination of fringe benefits. Each benefit has a set of eligibility tests to ensure that the plan does not discriminate against lower-paid employees. Check with an accountant to make sure the benefits meet the mandated requirements.

Employee Evaluation

Evaluation of employees is one of the most challenging functions for a manager. Good evaluations are a pleasure. However, no one enjoys telling someone that his/her work is not up to par. Employee performance should be tied to pay increases, advancement, and job retention.

Evaluations are easier when they are joined to job descriptions and goals. Some firms have a set of performance standards or goals for each job that are agreed upon by the supervisor and employee at the beginning of the evaluation period. Define performance standards so that everyone understands. These same standards are used at the time of evaluation. Standards makes it easier for the manager to evaluate the worker and for the employee to understand the evaluation. Goals encourage superior performance and should be re-negotiated every evaluation period.

Make the evaluation as positive as possible. Emphasize strong points and indicate areas where the employee could improve. One aim of the evaluation should be to help and educate the person as to how he/she can improve their effectiveness and efficiency. Using evaluations as gripe sessions and to berate the employee is not effective management. Do not wait until annual evaluations to discuss areas where the employee is not performing as expected or doing an excellent job. Allow the employee to input his/her opinion of performance. Do not allow friendship to cloud your perception of the person.

Motivating Employees

"Keeping their jobs is the only motivation my employees need," according to some managers. Motivation by punishment and fear is the least effective management style. Unfortunately, it is too frequently used. Many supervisors think little of dressing-down, suspending, or firing employees.

Punishment and fear may achieve short-term results, but not long-term encouragement or efficiency. Adults are not inclined to remain in a position where they are threatened or intimidated. Yelling and intimidation create animosity toward a superior and the company. Employees may respond with hostility and subversion. Equipment will break more often and employee attitudes toward the client will reflect the supervisor's attitude toward them.

The manager must realize and communicate to his/her supervisors that the employee is the backbone of the business, the foundation of his/her reputation, and future. If the supervisor is interested in performance levels, job satisfaction, and internal motivation of the workers, effective and demanding managerial strategies must be used.

Peer pressure can induce higher levels of quality and performance. Encourage *team work.* Individuals are more concerned with living up to the expectations of fellow employees than those of their bosses. There is evidence that employees are more motivated when they perform a variety of tasks, as part of crew, rather than a single, repetitive function, such as only mowing.

Employees who are allowed to set their own performance levels will usually try to meet or exceed their own expectations. It is important to have the employee make a *verbal commitment* regarding written objectives. Individuals and groups are more likely to attain their goals when they make a public commitment to do so. They view verbal commitments with witnesses as promises and most people view themselves as the type who keeps their word.

Words of praise to an employee or crew that truly deserves it will lift their spirits. Improved self-image can lead to greater interest in daily work and a desire for improvement. Proper use of praise and rewards cannot be over-emphasized. Praise, after all, is free.

One company has a *gold card system;* any compliments to a crew or individual from clients are written up on a gold index card and posted on the bulletin board. This form of public recognition is well received.

Use of *rewards* is management based upon behavior modification. Workers will increase or repeat the desired work performance if they are given rewards or positive motivation. Poor performance is eliminated when the employee comprehends the relationship between commendable performance and rewards, in theory at least.

This approach is successful, but there are complications. What may be an inducement to one individual is not to another. However, money talks! Bonuses funded from savings on contracts or performing under budget on a contract can be rewarded with a percent of the windfall. Consider small bonus programs rather than salary increases. Salary increases are permanent.

Photo 5–2. Pass compliments from clients to the crews. This company uses "gold cards" to show everyone in the shop compliments received for crews or individuals.

There are many *bonus systems* in the industry. Some provide additional time off in exchange for performance. Others tie bonuses to successful completion of classes, achieving certification, or licensing associated with the job. Some employers provide recognition dinners for employees and their families, and other inducements. Find out what would grab the attention of your employees.

There may be one or two employees who degrade these efforts. These are the type of people, however, that are not needed in the organization.

Take care to develop a bonus program solidly based on performance. Make sure everyone understands the rules and that they are applied fairly. Also remember the office staff when initiating any bonus program.

Some firms have developed a *competition* among crews and supervisors. The prizes may be cash, vacations, appliances, dinners, or plaques. The contest must be fair to all. If the same individual or group wins time after time, the motivation of the other workers declines.

Motivation is good management. When employees have a higher sense of worth, they are a more valuable asset. Motivated employees save money, jobs go smoother, and equipment lasts longer. Employee turnover is also reduced and profits increase. Motivation requires planning and work on the part of the manager. After all, that is the manager's job: to manager and inspire.

Table 5–6. What causes employee turnover?
Employee turnover is costly for any industry. The cost of recruiting and training are lost when an employee leaves. New employees require an acclimation period before they can work efficiently, effectively, and profitably. There are many reasons why employees move to different jobs. The following are some of the causes of turnover in the landscape industry. They are in no particular order of importance.
• Hiring under- or over-qualified people. • Feelings of isolation from the social groups at work. • Employee is unable to adjust to the physical surroundings. • Difficult or strenuous work. • Poor supervision and management. • Employer or supervisor attitude toward employees. • Unclean or poor facilities. • Little possibility of advancement—a dead end position. • Money. • Benefits. • Stress or burnout. • Personality problems with fellow employees or supervisors.

Absenteeism

Absenteeism is an expensive problem in every industry. Besides illness, there are many reasons that employees do not come to work. Poor working conditions, boredom, uneven work distribution, undependable transportation, and substance abuse are but a few. An employee may also stay away because of work-related personality problems. Personality clashes between employees and jealousies are contributing factors. Minor conflicts among workers, if not settled by the supervisor, can develop into costly running feuds.

Poor relations with supervisors are a common problem. A surly and uncommunicative overseer can make for a miserable day. Lack of responsibility and recognition may also lead to job dissatisfaction and irregular attendance.

Solving absenteeism universally is impossible, however, improved management and motivation minimizes the impact. Establish and adhere to a company policy on absenteeism. A continuing survey of the causes of absenteeism within each department can discover chronic abusers and identify problems. Verbal recognition for a job well done and other reward-related management improves employees' esteem and attendance. Try to make the workplace a pleasant place. Keep lunchrooms and bathrooms clean. This reflects the employer's attitude toward the employees.

The manager should know his/her subordinates. Show interest, without prying, in their personal lives. Encourage employees to discuss problems, as appropriate.

The manager should determine the needs and attitudes of the subordinates. Compare department and crew attendance between areas within the company. Absenteeism, like many employee problems, is a symptom, not a disease. A knowledgeable and progressive manager works with employees and supervisors to discover and rectify work-related causes.

Employee Theft

Many employees have dual standards. Those that would never think of taking a candy bar without paying for it, may remove paper, pens, fertilizer, and chemicals from work, or make long-distance calls on the company phone without compunction. Casual *theft,* and that is what it is, theft, costs employers billions of dollars annually. Add to this *time theft.* Workers leaving early, arriving late, or taking extra-long breaks, accounts for even more dollars lost to employers. Two hundred billion dollars of employee time is "stolen" annually.

Employee theft is any abuse of an organization's time, benefits, or resources. Theft can be devastating for any small business but hits service industries especially hard because of the competitive nature and financial constraints of the market.

Make honesty and ethics job standards. List theft and dishonesty as reasons for dismissal or disciplining employees. Let every employee know from the outset that honesty is expected.

Lead by example

A statement in the personnel handbook is not the only answer. Employee theft is a "people problem" and managers must lead by example. Management should create a climate that supports and reinforces honesty and integrity. Make honesty a policy beginning with the owners and managers. A dishonest or lax supervisor is a poor example for employees. Owners and managers cannot take home unauthorized supplies or leave early without recording the absence. They cannot send employees to care for their personal grounds during business hours. Ownership and management do have privileges, but these should not be abused.

Internal controls

Adopt security measures such as phone logs, or supply and equipment sign-outs, but do not let anti-theft measures become a crusade. Protective measures work best when instituted matter-of-factly and without personal or individual suspicion. They should be initiated before a problem occurs, not after.

Equipment can be checked-out to individual employees or to crew supervisors. Many companies hold crews and employees personally responsible for the equipment they are issued. A few require employees to purchase their own small equipment such as, pruners, pliers, and shovels. Imprint equipment with identification numbers; hand tools can be marked with a bright paint.

Controls can also be implemented in the office and bookkeeping departments. Employees that handle money can be bonded. Limit access to the cash drawer. Periodically change file cabinet locks and computer passwords. Keep postage meters and stamps secured. Record the number of letters posted daily. Mail should not be opened by persons not having access to cash receipt records. Supporting documents should accompany all checks submitted for signature.

Dealing with theft

Control measures do not prevent theft, they only make it more difficult. Managers must pay attention. Investigate problems as they arise; do not wait for a crisis. If things start disappearing, phone bills become inordinately high, or if too much time is wasted, then ask the employees what is going on. Many times simply focusing the manager's attention will nip potential problems in the bud. If theft is serious, seek assistance from the insurance company or police. A police investigation will certainly grab the employee's attention and send a message.

It is the supervisors' responsibility to initiate the appropriate level of control to deter theft. If control measures are too strict, productivity, and creativity suffer. Theft prevention and control are merely a state-of-awareness and caring by owners and supervisors.

Terminating Employees

Dismissing employees should be the last resort. No one likes to be the "bad guy" and fire people. Dismissing incompetent, dishonest, or irreconcilable employees is sometimes the most expedient alternative. Termination should be carefully considered and done with care.

Dismissed employees have taken employers to court and won large settlements for wrongful dismissal. California seems to be the leader in this area.

When dismissing an employee, an employer should clearly state the reason for termination. In most instances, the manager must show that dismissal is the direct result of substandard performance, job-related negligence, or serious violation of policies. An example might be an employee who is a substance abuser. An alcoholic should not or can not be dismissed because they have the disease. They may, however, be terminated for negligence if he/she comes to work drunk or drinks on the job.

Discuss procedures for dismissal in the employee manual. By all means, they must be adhered to. As a critical measure of protection,

Table 5–7.
What are the most common errors committed by employers when terminating employee? Be aware of mistakes that can land the company in legal difficulties. Establish proper hiring and termination practices. Train supervisors to respect employee rights.
• Failure to put honest evaluations in writing. Try to accumulate several written evaluations documenting inadequate performance before dismissal.   • Including dangerous wording in employee handbooks. Detail termination and grievance procedures and avoid "wiggle" words that can be interpreted several ways.   • Making informal verbal contracts.   • Firing for bogus reasons.   • Terminating an employee for refusing a polygraph test. Employees can be required to submit to "lie detector" test only if there is sufficient and clear justification.   • Forcing an employee to resign by making working conditions intolerable.   • Terminating an employee for refusing to commit an unlawful act, violate public policy, or take other improper actions.

a manager must document substandard performance. Make sure solid documentation exists before initiating disciplinary action. Also document attempts to address and remedy the employee's problems. The importance of the proverbial "paper trail" cannot be overlooked.

Always conduct a pre-dismissal "hearing" before terminating anyone. Explain the reasons for dismissal and present the evidence resulting in the conclusion. Give the employee the opportunity to respond. Never dismiss an employee without a fair, thorough hearing. Again, document this. If a grievance procedure exists, then apprise the employee of his/her options.

Never use demeaning words or phrases when writing dismissal letters or during disciplinary conferences. Define "disloyalty" and "gross insubordination." Focus on the facts; absence of facts provides legal grounds for challenging the termination.

Employee dismissal is not punishment. Termination is the last resort after trying to rectify employee problems. Dismissal as a vendetta or punishment encourages mistakes, results in eventual problems, and is an abuse of power.

No one likes to "fire" people, however, it is part of the burden of management. Incidents of termination are reduced with careful hiring and orientation practices, regular review of policies and procedures, effective communication, and leadership.

Employee Education

Employee training and education are ongoing processes that improve attitudes and profits. Many companies spend significant time, money, and effort on employee training. This does not, however, mean every training effort is effective or cost efficient. Poor training is costly. It contributes to employee turnover, customer callbacks, equipment abuse, violations, lost opportunities, and reduced profit.

Managers have greater opportunities for high quality employee training than at any other time in history. In the past, employee training was conducted by the owner or supervisors. Instructors from local colleges and universities, sales representative and technicians, consultants provided periodic programs and workshops. These opportunities still exist and are certainly viable.

Today, however, there is an increasing host of slide-tape programs, video tapes, computer programs, audio tapes, books and pamphlets, and other educational supplements available. These may be rented or purchased from local and regional professional associations, Extension services, colleges and universities, or other landscape management firms. Equipment manufacturers supply material on proper maintenance of their products. Some maintenance companies have produced very high-quality learning and training aids and videos internally. Topics range from safety, proper equipment use and care, pesticide safety and use, to horticultural techniques.

Photo 5-3. Field days provide a view of university research, product comparisons, and equipment demonstrations. They also provide invaluable opportunities to meet and learn from Extension Specialists, researchers, and other professionals. Field days are important educational opportunities for key and field employees. They provide a welcome change in routine and a little reward for jobs well done.

The number of voluntary and mandated certification programs is growing. Assisting employees to become certified increases their self-esteem and the firm's profitability. Support the employee's quest toward certification. Purchase the badges or caps recognizing certification by professional organizations for those who pass the examinations. Consider rewards for completing training or certification programs.

Training should not be relegated to rainy days or the dead of winter. It should be an on-going, organized process; repetition is a key to learning. Training should not be an "event," viewed as punishment, or a chance to nap. Some companies have established training sessions during the orientation phase of an employee's tenure. Others continue with supervisor training and updates or whole-staff sessions on a regular basis.

To attain maximum effectiveness, training must occur throughout the year, should involve many staff members, and should be frequently reviewed. It has been suggested that 50 percent of the information gleaned during a training session is lost almost immediately. Approximately seventy percent of the new information is lost by the next day and seventy-five percent is lost during the first week. Eighty-five percent of the information is lost by the end of a month without review or reinforcement.

A review of the training after 24 hours increase information retention by 55 percent. Retention rates after one week and one month are improved to 85 percent with periodic reinforcement or review.

Management should also rein-

Table 5–8. Who teaches the classes?	

According to the SBA and US Census Bureau, colleges and universities are the most common source of employer-sponsored training. A large portion of this training for the landscape industry is through the Cooperative Extension Service. There is a Cooperative Extension Service in every state. Addresses are listed in Appendix 4. County Agents and Area and State Subject Matter Specialists serve as resource people and provide training and programs for various aspects of agriculture, management, human resources, and sometimes business. To find out more, contact your Extension Service.

Source of Training	Percentage
Colleges and universities	31
Professional training industry	16
Community colleges and technical schools	15
Professional, trade and labor organizations	14
Vocational schools	7
Other school and community organizations	6
Government	6
Other	5

force training. Reinforcement may be simply showing some type of appreciation. Reinforcement and appreciation can be verbal or written. New techniques and practices learned should be adapted by the company.

Finally, make sure those that need and would benefit from the training attend meetings and educational opportunities. Key employees without the benefit of college training should be given first priority. It seems that the company representative at most association meetings, field days, or educational meetings is the owner or manager. Wouldn't it be more effective to send the people who were actually in the trenches?

Bibliography

Abrahamson, S. 1990. Retaining seasonal employees. *Grounds Maintenance,* 28(8):93–96.
Anonymous. 1991. Uniforms. *Grounds Maintenance,* 26(1):102.
Anonymous. 1991. The hiring game: who will succeed? *Lawn & Landscape Maintenance,* 12(5): 18–19.

Arkin Magazine Syndicate. 1989. Motivating your employees. *ALA/Maintenance*, 10(1):66.

Baetz, R. L. 1989. Motivate your muscle. *American Nurseryman*, 169(12):67–69.

Block, L. 1989. Mandated management. *American Nurseryman*, 170(10):33–49.

Bruce, S. D. 1989. Employee handbooks. Time-saver and morale booster—or potential time bomb? *American Nurseryman*, 170(10):24–30.

Covington, S. 1989. Twelve questions to ask before selecting a supervisor. *Landscape Contractor*, 30(9):40–41.

Curry-Swann, L. 1989. White-collar theft. *American Nurseryman*, 170(10):123.

Davis, S. L. 1978. Management by objectives in grounds management operation. In: *Manual of Site Management*. Environmental Design Press, Reston, VA.

Deyoung, J. 1989. People still call me "boy." *Pro*, 1(2):14.

Dittmer, N. K. 1989. The cafeteria plan—an attractive employee benefit. *Landscape Contractor*, 30(12):18–19.

Drexler, M. 1989. Maintenance professional on a proactive course to training. *ALA/Maintenance*, 10(3):28–30.

Faizst, J. 1978. Labor relations and personnel management in site maintenance. In: *Manual of Site Management*. Environmental Design Press, Reston, VA.

Grahl, C. 1990. Bonuses, rewards popular in the race for employees. *Lawn & Landscape Maintenance*, 11(10):40–44.

Gregg, R. E. 1989. Harassment. *American Nurseryman*, 170(10):53–63.

Hensley, D. 1992. Off months are perfect time to replenish your workforce. *Nursery Manager*, 8(1):73–78.

Hensley, D. 1993. Ask the right questions when hiring. *Western Turf Manager*, 4(1):24–25.

Hensley, G. 1990. Administrative assistant, College of Veterinary Medicine, Kansas State University. Personal communication.

Human Resource Associates. 1990. Turnover: Your most expensive problem. *ALCA Personnel Notebook*, ALCA, Reston, VA.

Jones, D. 1990. Designing programs to guide your firm's work force. *Lawn & Landscape Maintenance*, 11(3):36–40.

Jones, D. 1990. An effective outline promotes favorable training. *Lawn & Landscape Maintenance*, 11(4):40–42.

Jones, D. 1990. Follow up training increases task retention. *Lawn & Landscape Maintenance*, 11(5):30–33.

King, J. C. 1987. Avoid hiring mistakes. *Landscape Contractor*, 28(8):17–18.

Lehmann, D. and D. Hensley. 1991. Employee theft. An avoidable problem. *Northern Turf Manager*, 2(8):37–40.

Perry, P. M. 1993. Terminating Employees. *American Nurseryman*, 177(2):85.

Perry, P. M. 1993. Let the employer beware. *American Nurseryman*, 177(5):93.

Professional Grounds Management Society. 1989. *Grounds Management Forms and Job Descriptions Guide*. 3rd ed. Cockeysville, MD.

Roche, J. 1989. Whither comest the people? *Landscape Management*, 28(10):20–26.

Roche, J. 1991. Employee education. *Landscape Management*, 30(5):24–28.

Rosenberg, H. R. 1986. Learn how to use job descriptions. *American Nurseryman*, 163(5):73–74.

Scholtz, C. G. and J. Arkin. 1989. Fringe benefits: finding the right mix for employer and employee. *Landscape Contractor,* 30(11):18–20.

Seidel, A. W. 1978. Employee education. *American Nurseryman,* 147(2):6.

Seidel, A. W. 1978. Employee absenteeism. *American Nurseryman,* 147(8):6–7.

Shumack, R. L. 1977. Alabamians review pension and profit-sharing plans. *American Nurseryman,* 145(7):14,127–128.

Smith, S. 1990. A top-notch performance evaluation. *American Nurseryman,* 172(2):59–65.

Smith, S. 1990. Four steps to a happier staff. *American Nurseryman,* 171(8):48–53.

Smucker, B. 1980. Fringe benefits—the hidden asset. *American Nurseryman,* 151(8):102–103.

Steingold, F. S. 1990. The hazards of employers dealing with employees' rights. *Grounds Maintenance,* 25(3):132–135.

Taylor, B. 1990. Finding the perfect employee. *Landscape Contractor,* 31(3):34–35.

Turner, T. 1990. The hire road to success. *American Nurseryman,* 171(8):38–41.

Urbano, C. 1989. Labor. *American Nurseryman,* 170(10):69–75.

Wandtke, E. T. 1990. Working overtime on morale. *Landscape Management,* 29(6):52.

Chapter 6
Equipment Selection and Acquisition

Equipment is a major portion of the expenditures of every landscape management operation. Equipment needs grow and change as a company increases its customer base and services. Equipment decisions must be carefully made before the manager commits precious capital. Knowledge of equipment is but one more challenge to the landscape manager.

Equipment Selection

The criteria for determining if a piece of equipment is needed or economical vary with each operation. The first question is whether or not the company needs or can

Photo 6–1. Large and small equipment represent a major portion of the investment required by in-house and contract maintenance organizations. Equipment selection requires thought to maximize the investment.

afford the equipment. If a piece of equipment can do the work more efficiently, inexpensively, or more quickly than hand labor, the company can afford to operate it. Equipment is also important when it is necessary to do the work rapidly, such as plowing snow, even though adequate labor may be available to do the work manually. Equipment that has a range of performance, or can perform several tasks instead just one, is easier to justify. Also consider how the equipment can grow into or adapt with the company's future goals and plans. The bottom line is whether or not the equipment will make money for the company.

Table 6–1. Common Equipment Selection Mistakes
In no particular order:
1. Not purchasing commercial-quality equipment.
2. Making the purchase decision on price alone.
3. Purchasing over- or under-powered machines.
4. Failing to consider service, the availability and cost of factory-authorized technicians, and parts.
5. Selecting machinery from too many different manufacturers. Parts are not interchangeable. The parts inventory becomes unmanageable and an economic burden.
6. Failing to obtain a pre-purchase demonstration on your site and with your personnel.
7. Not considering fuel source or 2- or 4-cycle engines and purchasing the wrong one.
8. Failing to consider the size and weight for maneuverability, transportability, and employee fatigue.
9. Not checking with other managers to confirm the sales pitch.
10. Relying solely upon brand name.

Once the decision to buy a machine has been made, the manager's job has just begun. The manager must determine what brand, size, and capacity of machine. The objective is to purchase the least costly piece of equipment that will do the job efficiently and correctly. Should the equipment be purchased, leased, or rented? Will the current employees be able to operate the machine safely, efficiently, and productively, or will operators have to be trained or hired? What problems can result from using the equipment?

New or Used?

The cost difference between new and used equipment is substantial. However, look at more than just price. Saving a few thousand dollars is not prudent if more money is spent keeping an older machine running. If the equipment must withstand rugged, stressful work, or is used frequently, then *new equipment* is a better buy. If the anticipated use will be light, undemanding work, then *used equipment* must be considered. Equipment that will be used infrequently is best purchased used or rented.

Table 6–2. Buying Used Equipment
COMPARE. Don't buy the first unit evaluated. Compare models, brands, service, warranty, and machine quality. Do not compromise needs, standards, or requirements.
TRY IT. Ask the seller if the unit can be operated by the firm's operators for a few days.
LOOK. Develop a checklist. Inspect the general appearance, engine, oil, air cleaner, fuel tank, electrical system, drive system, gear box, safety equipment, and other crucial areas. Has the machine received proper care and service or is it dirty where it shouldn't be? New paint can cover a multitude of sins.
ASK. Request a complete service and repair record. If purchasing the unit from a dealer, obtain the name of the previous owner and contact him/her. If the dealer refuses to provide this information, keep looking.
HELP. Have the machine inspected by a trustworthy mechanic if purchasing from an individual. Obtain a reasonable warranty or service agreement from a dealer.

Reconditioned equipment purchased from dealers often carries a short-term limited warranty. It is priced from 15 to 35 percent below the cost of new equipment. Used equipment warranties must usually be serviced by the selling dealer. Know your dealer!

Table 6–3. Selling Used Equipment
DETERMINE THE VALUE. Consult the "blue" book and determine what the local market is for the unit.
TIMING. Used equipment brings higher prices just before or during the normal season, especially if it is ready to go.
QUALITY. Make all necessary minor repairs, tighten loose bolts, and change fluids. Have the service history available. Spiff up the unit, some buyers associate cleanliness with quality. A coat of paint does hide a multitude of sins, but buyers are also well aware of this fact.

Equipment acquired from individuals or purchased "*as is*" from dealers carries no warranty or guarantee. Such items are usually priced from 50 to 65 percent below the cost of a new machine. Check this equipment very carefully; what you see is what you get. List all items that require repair and add these estimated costs to the initial price for a true comparison with other used or new machines.

Size

Select the largest piece of equipment available for the job, within reason. Larger equipment will do the task more rapidly and more efficiently and will pay for itself. Consider the maneuverability of the equipment in tight areas and the potential damage that an oversized unit could impose on the site or adjacent properties. A 48-inch walk-behind mower has a minimal effect on improving productivity if it must be taken through 28-inch gates.

Energy Source

Managers may choose between gasoline and diesel powered equipment. There have been many articles written on the advantages of each and personal preference certainly plays a part. Diesel fuel offers

Photo 6–2. Equipment must meet the needs of the site and operators. In general, larger equipment is more efficient and will usually pay for itself with increased production. The equipment must be versatile and appropriate for the type of sites most frequently encountered. Oversized equipment is a liability if it cannot maneuver on the site or damages plants or structures. Photograph courtesy of Excel Corporation, Hesston, KS.

advantages, but its use requires installation of an extra fuel reservoir. Fifty-five gallon drums are impractical because of the storage requirements and inconvenience. A mixed fleet using diesel and gasoline results in one fuel being used in a machine in which it shouldn't. Count on it!

Many of the same comments can be made about two- and four-cycle engines. Select two-cycle engines with as near the same mixture as possible or select an oil-gas mixture that will operate efficiently in all. This allows the mechanic, foreman, or someone with responsibility to mix a drum of fuel for everyone to fill their individual cans. Label two-cycle engines clearly.

Service

Availability of parts and qualified service from a local dealer is one of the most important aspects of equipment selection in the commercial arena. Service may be as important as price in determining specific brands for the smaller operator. A piece of equipment does no good if it doesn't run or requires an inordinate time for repair. Dealers commonly loan equipment if repairs cannot be completed within one or two days.

Warranties vary. Understand what is guaranteed, by whom, and for how long. Some equipment manufacturers purchase and modify engines, transmissions, and other major components. Determine who has responsibility for the warranty of these items.

Information

Before purchasing equipment get as much information as possible. Be an informed consumer. Plan. The worst time to buy a piece of equipment is when it is needed. Take advantage of off-season or trade show discounts that may be available.

Trade magazine and manufacture's literature provide specifications and operating information. Trade shows and equipment demonstrations allow the manager to see, stand behind, and compare different brands. Visit with other management companies that own the brand of machine being considered.

An ideal way to find out how the equipment will work is to observe it under field conditions. Most dealers will be happy to demonstrate their equipment on site.

Photo 6-3. Field days are good places to see and "try on" equipment. Look at several brands and request a demonstration on your site.

Operators

Can current employees operate the machine profitably? Are qualified operators available? Allow the firm's most experienced people to break-in new equipment. If the sales representative provides an on-site preparation review or demonstration, include all crew members. The review should stress proper adjustment, maintenance checks, and safety.

Operators must have time to acclimate to the machine before their production rates reach an acceptable level. Some operators may decide the machine is "no good" before getting used to it. The manager must be patient but persistent. Leaving new equipment in the garage wastes capital and time, while creating doubts about the manager's ability to make decisions.

Preparing Specifications

Public agencies live and die by specifications. The grounds manager must become familiar with the various brands of equipment available and take the time to list the capabilities, attachments, and other requirements for the planned purchase. He/she must also master the specification requirements imposed by the purchasing department for the agency or company.

Often the manager lists the brand and model requested, followed by the words "*or equal*". This may be appropriate and save money if alternatives are acceptable. If several brands of "equal" equipment present bids, the lowest cost machine will be selected. Problems occur if the manager does not have a voice in determining what is equal and what is not. One way to increase the chance of obtain the specific brand desired is to specify something unique for the make or model that is not found on similar brands.

Replacing Existing Equipment

Replacing machinery produces serious questions that the manager must answer. Will the new equipment improve the profitability? Will new equipment cost less to own and operate? Will the new machine reduce direct labor costs or allow the crew to accomplish more with the same effort? Is the old machine obsolete? Will the new machine do a higher quality job?

Comparing costs

Determining true operation cost difference between old and new equipment requires careful analysis of ownership costs, interest, repairs, and impact on cash flow. A machine that is paid for and fully depreciated for tax purposes can look a lot better when compared to the cash outlay for a new machine. The latest model brings with it the tax benefits of depreciation and interest, but also a drain of cash. These must be weighed against production costs, repairs, and downtime costs of keeping an old machine running. Accurate records allow informed decisions.

Interest costs can be significant. Examine current and projected interest rates. Delay an equipment purchase or replacement if it will have a significant adverse impact on the company's cash position. When considering repair costs, a new machine should be relatively free of repairs during the first year. A comparison of buying new versus maintaining the old will generally lean in favor of the new purchase.

Productivity

New equipment should, by definition, improve productivity and will justify itself on paper. Keep in mind that the advertised improvements in production rates may never be achieved. Test the equipment on your sites with your operators. Manufacturer's claims assume the best of conditions and terrain. New or larger equipment can reduce costs and increase profitability by allowing a crew to do more work in a day. There is also a certain psychological impact with new equipment. Employees often feel that their work will be made easier or less physically demanding.

Obsolescence

Technological improvements evolve rapidly. Equipment becomes obsolete because of technology or because the manufacturer stops making it. Obsolescence alone is not a reason to purchase new equipment. The machine had distinct advantages and a positive effect on productivity when it was purchased. These reasons still hold true if ownership and repair costs have not escalated. If repairs or parts become hard to find or down time increases, newer equipment will be an economic alternative. There are situations, however, when older models of machines are superior to their new replacements. Don't let the "got to's" for a new, shiny machine obscure good judgment or the facts.

To Buy or Not to Buy

Once the type, capacity, and brand of equipment have been selected, the next dilemma facing the manager is whether to *buy* or *lease* the machine. Buying equipment, or *ownership,* has been the traditional means of acquiring control of machinery. In recent years, however, increasing numbers of firms have leased landscape management equipment. Manufacturers, distributors and dealers, financial institutions, and other opportunity-minded companies are entering the equipment leasing field.

Ownership, leasing, and other alternatives offer certain advantages for the established or new companies. Investigate all options thoroughly, however, before committing capital.

Table 6–4. Total Life Cost and Cost Per Acre For Three Mowers

The following compares the costs associated with three different mowers. The figures are *relative* costs and are not intended to establish standards or reflect actual costs and prices. They are used for comparison purposes only. Assumptions made on fuel consumption, repair costs and other aspects are also for comparison only.

The table indicates the various aspects of machinery operation that should be considered when comparing actual cost, not just purchase price. There can be a magnitude of savings associated with more expensive but higher-capacity mowing equipment.

	36 inch Walk Behind Mower	52 inch Riding Mower	72 inch Riding Mower
1. Years of operation	6 years	6	6
2. (×) Acres to mow	100 acres	100	100
3. (×) Times mowed/year	20 mowings	20	20
4. (=) Total acres mowed	12,000 acres	12,000	12,000
5. Purchase price	$2,400	$7,000	$11,000
6. (−) Trade-in value (10%)	$240	$700	$1,100
7. (=) Depreciation	$2,160	$6,300	$9,900
8. Total acres mowed	12,000 acres	12,000	12,000
9. (÷) Acres mowed/hour	0.9 acres/hour	2.00	2.8
10. (=) Hours Mowed	13,333	6,000	4,286
11. (×) Maintenance/hour	$0.90	$1.15	$1.15
12. (=) Routine maint. costs	$12,000	$6,900	$4,929
13. (+) Extraordinary maintenance costs	$5,500	$3,500	$3,000
14. (=) Total maintenance costs	$17,500	$10,400	$7,929
15. Purchase price	$2,400	$7,000	$11,000
16. (×) Interest rate	6% per year	6%	6%
17. (×) Number of years	6 years	6	6
18. (=) Opportunity/Investment cost	$864	$2,520	$3,960
19. Fuel consumption, gallons per hour 20. (×) Hours mowed	.75 gph 10,000 gallons	1.10 6,600	1.20 5,143
21. (×) Fuel cost/gallon	$1.30 per gallon	$1.30	$1.30
22. (=) Fuel cost (total)	$13,000	$8,580	$6,686
23. Hours mowed	13,333	6,000	4,286
24. (×) Labor rate	$7/hr	$7/hr	$7/hr
25. (=) Labor cost	$93,331	$42,000	$30,002
26. TOTAL LIFE COSTS (7+14+18+22+25) = 27. (÷) Acres Mowed	$126,855 12,000 acres	$69,800 12,000	$58,477 12,000
28. (=) Total Cost per Acre	$10.57	$5.82	$4.87

Ownership

Purchasing the machine outright provides complete control. The owner makes all decisions. However, there are several potential disadvantages. Purchase requires a large capital commitment. The cost to the user is high if the machine is not used to capacity. There is also the risk of obsolescence. The owner also assumes all operation and maintenance responsibilities and costs.

The owner, however, has full freedom in use of the machine. Depreciation and investment tax options belong to the owner. Some lending institutions and implement companies have creative financing available to match the cash flow of the maintenance industry.

Photo 6–4. Older equipment is often refurbished and saved for backups for front line machines. Backup pieces reduce down time and are critical if the firm relies on in-house service. Keep backup machines in good running order and ready to hit the road. Repairing a secondary machine before it can be used is frustrating and inefficient.

There is also the intangible, pride of ownership factor. I have yet to visit a landscape management firm without eventually wandering to the shop to look at the equipment. Most managers take pride in discussing their purchases.

Leasing

A *lease* transfers control of equipment from the owner (leasor) to the user (leasee) for a specific period for an agreed price. Ownership responsibilities, including taxes, insurance, maintenance, and repairs are assumed by the leasee. A *full-service lease* provides all of these expenses as part of the lease agreement, but these are unusual in the landscape industry. The leasee may have the opportunity to purchase the equipment at the end of the lease. Terms and purchase agreements are often favorable.

According to the American Association of Equipment Lessors, more than 80 percent of the nation's businesses acquire at least a portion of their equipment through leasing. The percent is probably less in the landscape management industry, but a large number of companies lease at least part of their field or office equipment.

Advantages

Leasing offers flexibility and some attractive advantages. The popularity of leasing in landscape management is growing and new options continue to evolve to meet the green industry market.

Leasing does not require expansion of a company's credit line. Expensive credit can be used elsewhere in the company. The long-term expenditure for equipment is greater over the period of the lease than if the item was purchased. A lease must recover the purchase price of the machine, interest, risk, overhead, and a profit for the leasor. Most leases do not require a "down payment," allowing the manager to again use the capital elsewhere. Leasing is a viable option for a firm with considerable debt. Lease payments are fully deductible as a business operating expense. Leasing offers some before tax advantages in that the payments for a machine are usually lower.

Leasing results in higher annual operation cost than ownership, partially because of the seasonal nature of the industry. However, the initial capital commitment is not as great. Manufacturers, dealers, and leasing firms offer varied payment schedules (to compensate for seasonality), low minimum leases, and alternatives for end-of-lease purchases.

Leasing may be especially attractive to the new operator. Most leasing companies are interested in selling and servicing new accounts. However, this does not mean than anyone can walk into a dealership and walk out with several thousand dollars of leased equipment by signing their name. Leasors require potential leasees have a very good credit rating. Leasees must meet established requirements for net worth and collateral and nearly all leasing companies require a credit analysis.

Disadvantages

There are disadvantages to leasing. Leases vary widely in their language, requirements, and eventual cost. Selection is limited to brands available from that particular dealer. There is still a risk of obsolescence before the end of the lease. The firm may be forced to operate an under-sized machine that would have been replaced as the operation grew.

The value of the equipment is lost at the end of the lease term, since the machinery is not owned. If a lease is canceled, even if the company goes "belly-up," the firm may be required to pay a very large penalty or the entire amount owed.

Push a pencil before inking the line. All leases are not created equal; compare the actual costs of all acquisition options. Beware of hidden costs. Most leases have interest built in, some at very high rates. Others require one to three months "payments" up-front. Some leases require a processing fee.

Rentals

Equipment may be *rented* from dealers and rental companies by the hour, day, week, or longer. Infrequently used equipment can be rented as needed. Renting is also a source of short-term backup or extra machines.

Understand the rental contract before signing. In most instances, rental equipment is the renter's responsibility while in his/her possession. The renter is usually responsible for all maintenance and upkeep. It may be stipulated that the equipment be returned in the same condition as when rented, subject to ordinary wear and tear. It is the intent that the property be returned undamaged.

Photo 6–5. Infrequently used equipment such as this trencher used to prune tree roots or service irrigation may be rented. Photograph by James Robbins.

The firm's insurance may or may not cover rented equipment. Check with the insurance carrier to determine if the company's policy covers rented items. Insurance is available from the rental company, but is always expensive. Rental insurance is not necessary if the equipment is protected by other policies.

Custom Hire

Custom hire is renting the *equipment and operator*. Custom hiring or subcontracting the work requiring specialized equipment or licensed and trained operators, such as heavy equipment, or aerial trucks may be the only viable option.

Shops and Service

Most management companies eventually initiate some sort of in-house equipment repair or service operation. In-house repair is more convenient and *may* cost less than outside repair. Some management consultants suggest that a firm should initiate in-

Photo 6–6. Custom hiring equipment requiring special operators saves time and dollars.

house service by the time it reaches $1,000,000 in volume. There are many companies, however, who operate successful in-house service at far less than this benchmark. There is no magic number. The manager who operates a shop thinking it will save money on repairs and service may be disappointed. The major justifications come from savings in lost time, reduced equipment down time, and higher quality work. In-house service requires that the manager pay for the mistakes of the mechanic, while dealers generally guarantee their work.

Operate the in-house facility with profit in mind. Develop a system for allocating shop costs to equipment. Cost allocation is frequently accomplished by setting up separate accounts for the shop within the company operating budget. Income (paper charges for parts and labor) and expenses (parts, labor, and overhead) can be recorded and analyzed. The charges for labor and parts should be competitive with those for local dealers for comparable service. If an in-house service operation costs more than a dealer, give careful thought to the necessity for the operation or find the reasons for the disparity.

A parts inventory and shop create their

Photo 6–7. In-house service shops can save time and dollars. In-house service is not always less expensive than dealer service; carefully consider all costs. Establishing a shop brings its own management challenges.

own challenges. The manager must deal with theft of parts and labor (mechanics working on their own vehicles or those of others during working hours).

Establishing a parts inventory

A parts inventory reduces equipment downtime and expenses. Having spare parts on-hand saves labor and capital. However, landscape management equipment is specialized. Finding parts, especially for older machines can be expensive and time consuming. It is impossible to stock quantities of every conceivable part for every possible machine.

Standardize equipment as much as possible. Regardless of the "color" of the equipment, choose a favorite and make it the standard. At the least, keep the number of brands to a minimum within each machine category. New or smaller companies tend to have a mixture of brands, purchasing on price initiative and searching for the right brand. Larger and successful firms rely on one or a few, usually major brands.

The mechanic will become more skilled by concentrating on and learning the peculiarities of few models. The parts inventory is simpler to determine. A single part will provide backup for several machines.

What parts and how many should be purchased and stocked? Parts are expensive. It will not take long to parlay the shop and parts inventory into a several thousand dollar investment. Service records, experience of the manager and mechanic, the dealer, and the parts supplier will provide insight as to what and how many will be enough or too many.

Photo 6-8. Spare parts are essential to maintenance operations of every size. Standardizing the brand of equipment simplifies parts stocking. Photograph courtesy of James Robbins.

Stock *common wear* items, those with predictably short lives, such as bearings, bushings, and seals. Purchase enough to take care of needs for a reasonable period. Take advantage of the quantity discounts. Landscape management firms, with or without a shop, stock routine and service items, such as oil, filters, belts, and blades.

Stock *routine breakage* items, such as hoses, starters, water pumps, and pulleys. The number on-hand depends on the likelihood of breakage. If the fleet loses one water pump every four months, then one in supply is adequate. Remember that service increases with the age of the equipment.

Plan for emergencies by stocking some *critical breakage* items. These items rarely break so they are seldom stocked by parts departments. Infrequent breakage parts must be ordered from central supply, wherever that is. Having these on hand saves time and money by minimizing downtime but require capital commitment. Keeping critical parts on-hand is less critical if backup machines are available.

Spread the investment for a parts inventory over several years. Enlist the assistance of the company accountant to set up inventory procedures and cost recovery procedures for the parts inventory, as well as the shop in general.

Records

Careful records promote good service, track costs, and assist in equipment purchase and replacement decisions. A *service chart* is a composite of the service schedule for a piece of equipment. Adjust service and oil changes to fit the operation. The service chart for every machine listing date and type of service or repair should be kept where the operator, mechanic, or shop supervisor can easily consult it.

Adapt a simple, internal work order system for equipment repairs. *Work orders* should include a description of the problem, the repairs made, parts used and their cost, and the labor required.

Service

Teach operators and crews to conduct *daily maintenance checks*. Equipment should be part of the company training and orientation program to instruct operators on how to check over, service, and operate their machines safely. A piece of equipment should never be started before the oil level is checked. This is *everyone's* responsibility.

Periodic or *seasonal service* and adjustments may be the responsibility of the crew or the mechanic. A shop can make a more thorough check and service of the machine. The crew or operator can use a backup while the mechanics give the front-line equipment the once over. Some companies have mechanics service equipment at night or during off days.

Equipment for the Crew

The tools and spare parts included with the crew depends on the equipment used, the skill of the operators or supervisor to diagnose and repair problems in the field, and the distance to the shop. At a minimum, pre-gapped spark plugs for each piece of field equipment and spark plug wrench should be available. Also include standard and Phillips screwdrivers, an adjustable wrench, a pliers, and a reasonable selection of box and/or open-end wrenches. Metric wrenches are necessary to work on imported machines. Include a selection of bolts, nuts, washers, and cotter keys.

Photo 6-9. Organize equipment storage for efficiency and security. This firm paints the area for each crew a different color. Equipment can also be color coded. Part of each crew's responsibility must include cleaning and servicing equipment at the end of each shift. Photograph courtesy of James Robbins.

Include pre-wound reels of line for string trimmers and goggles for operator safety. Supply replacement nozzles, strainers and hose fittings to crews working with sprayers. Require all spray operators to use safety equipment.

Keep the tools in a quality tool chest that can be secured to the truck. The tool box should be able to be removed quickly when tools are needed on the work site or transferred between vehicles.

Mark all tools and equipment or paint them a bright color. Establish responsibility for replacing tools that are stolen or abused.

Keep a first-aid kit with bandages, gauze pads, disinfectants, first-aid spray, and other simple first-aid appliances in each truck or tool box. Replenish the first-aid kit frequently. Include a container of fresh water to flush skin, eyes, or clothing in case of an accidental chemical spill or exposure. Enclose phone numbers for a doctor, ambulance service, poison control center, and fire and police departments. Encase phone number and emergency instructions in plastic so they will remain readable. Instruct crew supervisors in simple first-aid and emergency procedures.

Photo 6-10. Each crew must carry an adequate selection of tools and spare parts for simple field service of equipment.

Photo 6-11. This firm uses a dove-tail trailer to transport equipment. Machines are rolled or driven down the ramp. The pickup provides quick access to tools and machines by the crew and passersby. The heavy-duty truck does double duty by pushing snow in the winter.

Photo 6-12. Enclosed vans, trucks, or trailers increase the security for the machines and other equipment.

Photo 6-13. This enclosed trailer contains a small shop for in-field service, safe storage for fuel, and secure storage for equipment and chemicals.

Bibliography

Anonymous. 1982. Purchasing equipment. *Landscape Contractor*, 23(12):8–12.

Anonymous. 1985. Leasing—an alternative to major purchases. *Lawn Servicing,* November/December:38.

Anonymous. 1986. Rent, lease or buy? *Landscape Contractor*, 27(9):9–10.

Anonymous. 1990. Maintenance checklist for commercial mower safety. *Lawn & Landscape Maintenance,* 11(6):48–50.

Anonymous. 1993. Computing mower costs. *Lawn & Landscape Maintenance,* 14(4):49–53.

Berkman, S. 1990. To buy of not to buy? *American Nurseryman*, 172(1):70–75.

Bradley, A., Jr. 1982. Lease or buy? *Landscape Contractor,* 23(12):14.

Buckingham, F. 1986. Should you rent, lease or buy equipment? *Grounds Maintenance,* 21(7):60, 64–68.

Buckingham, F. 1986. Tools to send to the job site. *Grounds Maintenance,* 21(3):40–42.

Buckingham, F. 1987. Buying and selling used equipment. *Grounds Maintenance,* 22(7):12–14, 80.

Clark, B. 1989. Look before you lease. *Pro,* 2(10):10.

Copley, K. 1986. Avoiding common equipment selection mistakes. *Grounds Maintenance,* 21(2):58, 112–114.

Fuller, J. D. 1990. Selecting a walk-behind. *Grounds Maintenance,* 25(5):33–34, 42, 46–52.

Hammond, C. 1987. Save money and lives by using equipment properly. *American Nurseryman,* 165(3):126.

Howard, H. F. 1989. Establishing a parts inventory. *Grounds Maintenance,* 24(9):26–28.

Howard, H. F. 1990. Looking for Mr. Good Mechanic. *Grounds Maintenance,* 25(1):74–77.

Kemmerer, H. 1982. Equipment: Use it wisely. *Grounds Maintenance,* 17(4):88, 92–94.

Pinkus, R. 1985. Equipment costing systems. In: *A Guide to Developing a Landscape Maintenance Business.* Associated Landscape Contractors of America.

Skinner, D. 1988. Deciding to buy used equipment. *Grounds Maintenance,* 23(11):32, 74–75.

Seaman, M. 1989. Love it? Lease it! *Pro,* 1(10):11.

Siegfried, C. A., Jr. 1983. Why rent equipment? *Landscape Contractor,* 24(9):12–14.

Smith, C. 1989. Alternatives to spending a fortune on your equipment. *ALA/Maintenance,* 10(4):48–49.

Steele, B. 1990. Productivity is key to equipment purchasing decisions. *The Landscape Contractor,* 31(11):12–13.

Steele, B. 1990. Rent, lease or buy: what's best for your business? *The Landscape Contractor,* 31(11):14–15.

Chapter 7
Designing to Reduce Landscape Maintenance

Responsible design, as defined by one landscape architect, is sensitive to the environment, the client or user over an extended period of time, and to the requirements of maintenance personnel. The decisions by a landscape architect or designer tremendously impact site management for many years. Likewise, potential maintenance of the site affects design decisions in infinite ways. Every landscape requires management; there are no "maintenance-free" designs.

A landscape is enhanced or destroyed by on-going management during its growth and maturation. Design has maintenance implications, and maintenance has design implications. With the designer's conception and the efforts of the maintenance personnel so inter-twined, why is there so little communication between these two camps? They, after all, serve the aspirations of the same client.

Responsibilities of the Designer

It is the obligation and responsibility of the *landscape architect* or *designer* to produce a landscape proposal attentive to the site. He/she must also create a project capable of being efficiently maintained. The design intent must be communicated in some way to the eventual site manager.

It is also the designer's obligation to develop the project within the management resources that will be available or budgeted in the future. These resources may be in terms of money or labor for the commercial client, or time and willingness for a homeowner. The designer must assess the owner's commitment to provide for long-term maintenance.

The designer can assist the owner in establishing yearly budgets. These budgets, however, must be realistic, not figures pulled from the air to sell the project. When in doubt, the designer should seek the expertise of a management contractor or consultant to obtain a credible "ball park" figure for maintaining the property.

The designer may be called upon for a maintenance schedule or specifications as part of the contract documents. The designer, however, must first understand maintenance processes before he/she can suggest what the management requirements will be.

The Landscape Manager

The *site manager,* whether part of an internally budgeted or entrepreneurial organization, must maintain the landscape at the highest quality and efficiency feasible within budgetary constraints. The professional manager will not sacrifice quality for price.

The site manager must be able to *communicate* management requirements, operations, and goals in a form the owner and designer can realize and understand. Few site managers or contractors for established properties request or study the original plan to determine how the existing compares with the proposed. Communication is most effective if there is an arrangement for the designer to periodically evaluate the work as it grows and develops. Adjustments can be made. This may be somewhat idealistic but it can be achieved. It will be easier in the public realm than in the private.

Landscape management is more than mowing the grass and pruning the shrubs. Management has developed into a highly specialized field involving administrative, scientific, economic, social, and political functions. Site managers must be competent stewards of time, machinery, and capital, and adopt technology as it becomes available. Quality training and supervision for maintenance personnel are essential. The gardener of old, who accomplished everything by hand, has been in large part replaced by specialists and technology.

The Landscape

A *landscape* is not analogous to a building. A building is at its optimum condition on opening day. A building requires continual maintenance to delay its deterioration and obsolescence. A landscape, however, requires many years of management to develop as the designer and client envisioned. The fertilizing, spraying, pruning, and mowing continue for as long as the landscape exists. Many European gardens have been continually maintained for hundreds of years, adhering to the original design tenets, but shaping the landscape to present a civility that would soon disappear without thoughtful care.

Relative Costs Within the Landscape

Some authors estimate that maintenance may account for 75 percent of the total life-time costs of any specific project.

Trees, the most expensive part of a landscape installation, require the least maintenance. Shrubs and groundcovers require more management, but usually have a lower initial cost. All of these require much less management input than turf. With the stroke of a pen and a four letter word, *"turf,"* the designer inserts the least costly of all landscape plants, and the single largest element in typical management budgets. Differences in initial versus long-term maintenance costs must be brought to the owner's attention.

Photo 7–1. Turf provides many desirable aspects to active and passive landscapes. However, the lawn is the most expensive portion of the landscape to maintain over time. Careful selection of turf eases maintenance costs. Areas with regular or heavy traffic, such as this outdoor banquet area, require additional care to alleviate compaction.

Budgets

Landscape work comes toward the end of construction when funds run short. There is the obvious tendency on the part of some owners to skimp, that is, to reduce the landscape construction budget. Everyone involved (especially the owner) must realize that while plants will grow and eventually achieve the desired results, a reduced installation budget forces significant changes.

Groundcovers may be planted further apart and smaller trees and shrubs may be installed. This increases maintenance costs, especially in the early years of the project. Skimping on quality installation results in potential dissatisfaction by the owner, designer, installer, and management contractor. A thing of beauty has in actuality become a headache for everyone because of poor budgeting.

Table 7–1. Maintenance requirement of landscape plants ranked from high to low.

Turf
Plants requiring special care, such as espalier and topiary
Annual and perennial flowers
Groundcovers
Deciduous and evergreen shrubs
Evergreen trees
Deciduous trees

Landscape maintenance budgets may be reduced because of economic or business forces. Re-designing and changing problem maintenance areas will reduce costs. Spending a little money now can produce long-term savings. When changing or re-designing any landscape, maintenance must be a primary consideration. The designer can actively seek the input and expertise of those familiar with the site and its peculiarities.

Designing To Reduce Maintenance

Every landscape site, client, designer, and proposal are different. The design must be sensitive to the needs and requirements of the client, the site, aesthetics, and function. There are, however, common considerations that can and do affect site maintenance requirements. The following discussions may not have a place in every landscape. They are, however, concepts that the designer, the maintenance supervisor, and the owner may wish to consider.

Table 7–2. Guidelines for designing a landscape for reduced maintenance

- Avoid plants that require constant pruning or that overgrow the intended space.
- Avoid plants with leaves, fruits, or seed pods that become litter.
- Choose plants resistant to pests and environmental problems.
- Mulch all beds and use a durable edging.
- Use grass where appropriate but provide alternative surfaces where necessary.
- Lay out planting beds so that machines can be used efficiently.
- Keep ornamentals in beds; keep scattered landscape elements to a minimum.
- Understand the needs of the client and his/her maintenance abilities.

Installation

Establish the *best possible soil conditions* before planting. A good root environment reduces plant maintenance. Particular attention should be paid to soil structure and porosity, since these cannot be changed once the landscape and lawn are installed.

Topography

Changing topography, the rise and fall of the land, results in more appealing designs but also influences management expenditures. The optimum slope for a maintained landscape is around 2 percent; a slope of 5 percent is common around structures to assure dry foundations. Absolutely flat

Photo 7-2. Quality landscape installation and selection of plant materials affect long-term maintenance. The junipers in this nursery are covered with fruiting structures of cedar apple rust. Every one of these plants were eventually planted into landscapes. The maintenance contractor or supervisor will now have to deal with the problems and complaints resulting from installation of poor quality nursery stock.

sites (0 percent slope) should be avoided. Inadequate drainage and standing water increase disease, reduce oxygen within the root zone, and make mowing difficult in wet weather. Standing water also increases the likelihood of personal injury from slipping and falling.

Slopes of 15-20 percent are pleasing and within the range usually maintainable with standard equipment. Berms increase mowing time but are frequently justified from an aesthetic standpoint. Slopes over about 30 percent make mowing and other operations more dangerous and expensive. Steep slopes should be planted in groundcover or terraced to avoid mowing.

Photo 7-3. A very difficult area to mow. Consider alternatives to turf for steep areas. Photograph courtesy of James Robbins.

Structures

Man-made landscape features (patios, decks, walks, walls, fences, benches, and light fixtures) must be maintained against normal wear, the elements, insects and decay, and plant invasion. Using the highest quality, strongest, most durable material or equipment available reduces long-term upkeep.

Material selection should reflect the intended function or anticipated use. When considering landscape and construction materials, compare the initial cost to long-term maintenance and durability. A wooden deck is expensive to maintain in a heavily used or trafficked area. Concrete may be less aesthetic, but it is a more maintenance-free choice.

Use decay resistant or preserved woods and avoid painting wood when possible. If the surface is painted, carefully consider the use of vines or other types of vegetation allowed to grow on the

98

structure. Removing tangled vines or over grown vegetation for painting every few years is a major expense and problem.

Paved Surfaces

Apart from the intrinsic beauty of a lawn, its most notable characteristic is that of being a planted surface that can be walked and played upon. However, this generalization has distinct limitations. Location and use must be considered. Paved surfaces cost less to maintain than turf in areas where significant or frequent traffic occurs.

Design walks to accommodate the anticipated amount of pedestrian traffic. The walk surface and texture should correspond to potential environmental conditions. Heavily textured talks make snow removal difficult. A major walk in commercial circumstances should be a minimum of six to eight feet wide; minor walks need to be four to five feet wide. Residential walks should allow two people to walk comfortably side-by-side.

Photo 7–4. Headstones set level with the surface speed mowing and eliminate trimming at this national cemetery.

Table 7–3.

The following floor surfaces are listed from high to low maintenance.
 	
  Turf
  Earth
  Gravel
  Brick with sand joints
  Asphalt
  Brick with mortared joints
  Concrete

Design walks be to direct pedestrians to their destination in the straightest possible or reasonable manner and define entrances. People in a hurry tend to make their own path; the shortest distance between two points is a straight line. This can be witnessed on any college campus.

Avoid 90 degree angles with paved surfaces where possible. Rounded corners reduce stop and go mowing and deterioration of the turf or landscape planting by people cutting corners.

Consider access of maintenance equipment throughout the landscape. Gates and entrances should be wide enough to anticipate maintenance equipment. Large backyards should allow for entrance of more than a 20-inch mower.

In the snow belt, design walks to accommodate and facilitate snow removal. Clearing steps and stairs requires hand shoveling and sweeping. Gentle slopes provide better access to physically challenged patrons and can be cleared with equipment. Plan for areas for dumping and storing snow on site. Natural snow fences can be created by proper placement of plants and raised planters. Poor plant placement, however, accumulates snow on walks and drives.

Parking

Design *adequate parking* space to avoid parking on grassed areas. Place a gravel or bark mulch strip along the edge areas where cars nose in to park. The mulched strip prevents cars from hanging out over the mowing area. Mowing and trimming time is decreased. Damage to the grass from engine heat and leaking fluids is eliminated. Potential scratching of the cars is reduced.

Water

Water features are notorious for requiring inordinate care and upkeep. Avoid water features in reduced maintenance landscapes. Locate any water feature where it can easily be serviced.

Photo 7-5. Poorly designed parking area divider. The planting bed is too narrow; the trees will be wounded by automobiles.

Photo 7-6. Water features are notoriously high maintenance.

Photo 7-7. Maintenance around this pond is reduced by use of a stone edge or coping. The edge eliminates trimming along the water's edge and provides footing for mowers.

Locate swimming pools away from deciduous trees to reduce leaf removal. Direct water overflow from pools and fountains away from plantings and building entrances.

Gutters and down spouts reduce excessive water run-off, erosion, and washing of mulch. Where gutters are impractical or displeasing, consider installing a modified French drain or gravel strips beneath the drip line to carry away water and reduce splashing.

Plant Selection

Select only *culturally adapted, pest-free plants* that stay within the size limits afforded by the area or design criteria. Plants requiring different degrees of sun, shade, or irrigation will not grow well together.

Designers, nurserymen, and clients tend to push the hardiness zones of plants, regardless of the region. People in central Texas try to grow plants that prefer southern Texas. People in Missouri like to try plants that prefer central Texas or Tennessee. Every few years, however, Mother Nature sets everything back to normal with an exceptional winter. The cycle then begins again.

There are many newer cultivars of common and favorite plants that are less susceptible to age-old maladies. Crabapples serve as good examples. Some cultivars are resistant to apple scab, rust, and fireblight (and fruitless to boot). Other crabapples are susceptible to all three diseases with fruit the size of 'Jonathon' apples. Which requires less maintenance? Why the nursery industry still plants and sells cultivars that are defoliated by June is a mystery.

Some plants are notorious for their susceptibility to chronic problems. Avoiding these is a professional responsibility to the client and management of the site. Although plant problems vary with location, the following are a few that require constant attention:

Photo 7–8. Common lilac is prone to powdery mildew in many areas. Excessive shade and moisture aggravate the situation. Consider more easily maintainable plants in problem areas and avoid problem plants all together.

Euonymus spp. inevitably contract scales, mildew, and crown gall. An exception is burning bush or winged euonymus *(E. alatus)*. Many euonymous have cold hardiness problems.

Pin Oak *(Quercus palustris)* succumbs to iron chlorosis if soil pH is greater than 6.5. The cure, don't plant them.

Roses are noted for blackspot, mildew, winter injury, and an enormous amount of labor.

Gardenia spp. too frequently attracts white flies and also has pH problems.

Select compact cultivars rather that fighting to make a 12-foot tall plant stay beneath a 4-foot window. Plants that overgrow the allotted space require continual pruning. Place and space plants so that they will have room to mature without being crowded. Plants with invasive root systems can cause trouble with other plantings, pavement, curbs, walks, and underground utilities.

Select trees that are strong-wooded. Avoid species that surface root or sucker badly. Avoid trees with fruit or pods or excessive leaf drop that can litter walks or lawns. If messy trees are used, keep them away from walks, patios, or areas that require extra cleanup. Also avoid areas where pedestrians might slip and fall.

Some plantsmen feel that trees with small leaves require less maintenance than those with large foliage. The theory is that small leaves do not distract from the landscape as much as large leaves that have fallen. There is some merit to the fact that raking and removal of small leaves requires less effort than large leaves. Contrast the effort required for thornless honeylocust (*Gleditsia tricanthos* var. *inermis*) and sycamore (*Platanus occidentalis*). Honeylocust foliage is simply macerated and spread by mowing; no raking is usually involved. Sycamore leaves, however, hit the ground with a resounding thud and apparently multiply once they have fallen.

Photo 7-9. Leaf cleanup for some trees is no problem at all, as with this thornless honey locust. If leaf cleanup will be a major undertaking, carefully select tree species, locate them near roadways or other access, keep trees away from water features, and invest in adequate power leaf removal equipment (Chapter 14). Photograph courtesy of James Robbins.

Turfgrass Selection

The type of *grass* selected for lawn areas seriously affects maintenance. Select species on the basis of use and traffic, the level of management available, and those adapted to the region. Trying to grow cool or warm season grasses out of their element results in added management and replacement costs. The turf management chapter of this text provides detailed information on efficient maintenance of turfgrass.

Great differences between species and cultivars in water and fertilization requirements, as well as disease, insect, and stress susceptibility are documented. For instance, management requirements for tall fescue in the "transition zone" are much less exacting than bluegrass to maintain acceptable quality. Many new, improved selections of bluegrasses and fescues require higher levels of water and nitrogen than the common species.

Some turfgrass species are more invasive of planted landscape beds. Bunch-type grasses require less frequent edging to keep them out of plant beds than do bermuda-

Photo 7-10. Avoid trees with messy fruit around walks, roadways, or where people gather. Photograph courtesy of James Robbins.

grass, bluegrass, or other creeping species. Finally, since grass is the most expensive plant to maintain in the landscape, eliminating grass in small areas by using groundcovers or mulched beds significantly affect long-term budgets.

Groundcovers

Groundcovers are one of the most useful plants in landscape design. In addition to providing a "finished" look, groundcovers suppress weed development in landscape beds. Groundcovers substitute for turfgrasses in heavily shaded areas that would not support a quality lawn. Plant steep slopes to a groundcover instead of mowing. Groundcover small, odd-shaped landscape areas where maintenance with power tools would be unreasonable. Since some groundcovers have lower water use requirements than turf, they can be used in water conservation or xeriscape landscapes.

Photo 7–11. Groundcovers can reduce landscape management. The groundcover in the parking island is less maintenance intensive than turf and produces a quality appearance. Additionally, people are less apt to walk across a groundcover planting than turf, reducing compaction.

Groundcovers are expensive to install and require vigilance in watering, fertilization, and weed control during establishment. The long-term inputs required to grow many groundcovers, however, are significantly less than that of lawn grasses, especially in less than favorable turf environments.

Some groundcovers grow rampantly and require frequent trimming to keep them in bounds, are prone to insect and diseases, and have other problems. Select groundcovers carefully, do not trade one maintenance problem for another.

Annual Flowers

Seasonal color beds of annuals require large inputs of resources and labor to maintain quality. Chapter 11 (Color in the Landscape) in this text details growing annual flowers in the landscape. In low maintenance situations, however, keep beds of annuals to a minimum. Consolidate landscape color in high impact areas. Keeping the color beds together rather than scattered throughout the landscape reduces the maintenance time. Select species and cultivars adapted to the particular environment in which they will be used, i.e., sun, shade, moist, or dry.

In addition to environmental tolerances, select annuals for herbicide tolerance. There have been dramatic strides in labeling of weed control products for use in annual flowers. However, there remain differences in tolerance among cultivars and species to pre- and post-emergent materials. Limit selection to those that can withstand herbicides and hand weeding may be essentially eliminated.

Native Species

Native plants may require less attention than some exotic species. The plants are successful in their native environs because they can withstand the rigors of the environment and pest pressures. Large sections of the Kansas City International Airport, Kansas City, MO have been re-established to native prairie species. These require significantly less frequent mowing than the previous bluegrass, and receive little fertilization or irrigation.

Native plants are not a panacea, however. The compacted, urbanized site the native plant is exposed to is far different from the pristine environment that it developed in. Just because a plant is "native" does not necessarily mean that it is more drought tolerant or appropriate for the site than "exotic species." A "native" plant placed in an unfriendly "foreign" environment will fail.

Photo 7-12. Native wildflower mixes are becoming popular for low maintenance or stressful sites. They are often able to tolerate the local conditions with less input than turf and some other plants. Native plants add a local flavor and identity to the landscape.

Mulches

Using *mulch* in planting beds minimizes watering, weed competition, and soil compaction. Mulches help keep plants healthy and attractive. Organic mulches improve the soil. Organic mulch must be replaced periodically. While inorganic mulches do not decompose, they do require occasional raking and refreshing.

Do not use impermeable bed coverings, such as black plastic, beneath mulch. Impermeable coverings reduce soil gas exchange and water infiltration. Open weave mulch liners allow normal water and air movement into the soil. Mulch blankets, however, do not guarantee a weed-free landscape. They will not control some ambitious perennial weeds, weeds germinating from wind-blown seeds landing on the mulch, or weeds growing through openings made to plant the ornamentals.

Photo 7-13. Mulch gives a finished look to the landscape, modifies the environment, and reduces maintenance.

Photo 7–14. Mulches are typically associated with more refined landscapes. Mulches are even more valuable investments for large scale, low maintenance landscapes. Applying mulch around these highway plantings controls weeds and conserves water. Photograph by James Robbins.

Photo 7–15. Too mulch of a good thing? Applying mulch deeper than 3 or so inches can damage plants. Anaerobic respiration occurs producing plant damaging byproducts. Excessive mulch is also unsightly.

Table 7–4.

A comparison of longevity, availability and relative cost for several mulches in a midwest market. Costs are relative and vary with market, supply, and transportation costs.

	Replacement (in years)	Availability- (in Manhattan, KS)	Cost*	Texture
			Mulch matrix	
Organic:				
Straw	1	H	0.30 CF	Coarse
Leaves	1	H	--	Coarse
Leaf mold	1	H	1.45 CF	Medium
Manure	1	H	--	Fine
Pine needles	1	M	0.50 CF	Fine
Peat moss	1	H	1.00 CF	Medium
Lawn clippings	1	H	--	Fine
Cocoa-bean hulls	1–2	L	3.20 CF	Medium
Shredded bark	1–2	H	1.80 CF	Medium
Wood chips	2–3	H	0.50 CF	Coarse
Sawdust	1	M	--	Fine
Crushed corncobs	1–2	M	0.75 CF	Coarse
Compost	1	H	--	Medium
Pecan hulls	1–2	L	2.82 CF	Medium
Inorganic:				
Marble chips	–	M	7.15 CF	Varies
Limestone	–	H	1.20 CF	Varies
Granite chips	–	L	3.85 CF	Varies
Volcanic rock	–	M	1.70 CF	Varies
River gravel	–	M	1.80 CF	Varies
Crushed brick	–	L	--	Varies
Fiberglass mat	–	H	1.07 SY	--
Black plastic films	–	H	0.29 SY	--

Legend: H = high, M = medium, L = low, CF = cubic feet, SY = square yard

*Prices are averages for comparison only (1986 dollars). Actual prices fluctuate with locality, season and supply.

Source: T. H. Spaid and D. Hensley, 1986. Mulch Selection Guide. *Nursery Manager,* 2(3):113–114.

Photo 7–16. Mowing strips maintained by herbicides eliminate trimming.

Mowing Strips and Edging

Mowing strips and edging along planting beds assist in keeping grass from encroaching into planted areas. Edging also prevents mulch from moving into turf areas.

Use steel edging instead of plastic. Plastic edging sticks up higher than steel exposing it to more damage. Steel is also more durable than plastic edging.

Bed Design

Keep the landscape area as free of scattered ornamentals as possible, without hindering the design. Scattered beds are more costly to maintain. Mowing is more difficult when plants are scattered in open turf areas.

Photo 7–17. Mowing strips carried a bit too far. In this case mowing is impeded by the design and size of the mulched areas. Photograph courtesy of James Robbins.

Design planting beds with a continuous sweep allowing easier mowing. Right angles and small bed interrupted by turf require more time to mow and trim. Sweeping beds reduce mowing time. The curves can add emphasis and line to the composition.

107

Massing Plants

Designers find that simple arrangements or broad masses require less diverse and exacting maintenance. Massing produces a cleaner design and increased impact.

Plants in mass require less pruning, weed control, and general care than individuals. Placing several species in compositions or groupings reduces maintenance only if they have similar cultural requirements. Ideally plants should have similar requirements for water, light, soil pH, and fertilization.

Irrigation

A *well-designed*, automated *irrigation system* is one of the most important aspects

Photo 7-18. Massing plants reduces maintenance and is an effective design tool.

and cost effective methods of establishing a manageable, superior landscape in most regions of the country. Irrigation systems are cost effective methods to provide a lower level of long-term landscape management. A poorly designed or installed system, however, results in increased maintenance costs and innumerable woes. Make sure the designer and installer know their business.

Photo 7-19. Edging slows spread of grass into planting beds, speeds mowing and gives a clean edge. Many suitable materials are available. The concrete edging in this photo provides an effective edge, but is too expensive for most landscapes.

Photo 7–20. Poor design resulting in impossible maintenance. How will the grounds crew efficiently maintain this turf? The planting area and mulch should have been expended to incorporate this tiny problem area.

Photo 7–21. The mulch line could be extended to eliminate mowing of this long, narrow grassed area. Photograph by James Robbins.

Photo 7-22. Why? Grass growing among plantings is costly to maintain and looks horrible. Mulch in plantings and keep maintenance in mind when designing.

Separate the control zones for woody beds from the turfgrass irrigation zones. The water requirements for the two are vastly different. Make sure the system can be winterized and there is room for expansion as it becomes necessary.

Mission Impossible Areas

There are places in some landscapes where it is simply impossible to grow plants. These may be small or narrow areas between buildings and walks, narrow, non-irrigated spots on the south side of a wall or structure, or portions of a bed beneath an extended overhang. Regardless of planning, there may be spots where the microclimate makes plant growth unachievable or incredibly expensive. Use a permanent mulch for impossible areas. Do not sacrifice plantings that are doomed to failure.

Understand the Client

Understanding the landscape requirements, desires, capabilities, as well as the daily operation of the client's business produces a more maintainable landscape. For instance, simply including trash receptacles where necessary enhances the appearance and reduces maintenance costs dramatically.

The designer must understand and plan for the mainte-nance capabilities and interest of the client. If he/she is only

Photo 7-23. An impossible area to grow plants because of cars, engine heat and fluids, confined space, and lack of irriga-tion. Stone or mulch is the best choice for this and many areas where plants would become living sacrifices.

willing or capable of mowing grass, then nothing more than open lawn should be included in the final design. Do not impose a high-dollar landscape when only a shoestring maintenance budget will be provided. Everyone comes out the loser in the end.

Bibliography

Appleton, B. and J. Derr. 1990. Growth and root penetration by large crabgrass and bermudagrass through mulch and fabric barriers. *Journal of Arboriculture,* 8(4):197–199.

Billeaud, L. A. and J. M. Zajicek. 1989. Mulching for weed control. *Grounds Maintenance,* 24(2):16,20–23, 107.

Clarke, A. B. 1979. Designing for low maintenance. *Proceedings of the Second Annual Ornamentals Short Course.* Hawaii Institute of Tropical Agriculture and Human Research, Univ. of Hawaii at Manoa, HI.

Photo 7-24. Learning the operation and needs of the client and site users saves landscape maintenance dollars. Items as simple as strategically placed waste receptacles reduces unsightly trash, debris removal, mowing time, and produces a higher-quality landscape.

Church, B. A. 1991. Cutting time. *Grounds Maintenance,* 26(2):100–103.

Durand, L. C. 1987. How to design landscapes for maintenance economy. *American Nurseryman,* 165(4):51–55.

Fink, M. and D. Hensley. 1992. Let Mother Nature help with landscape design. *Nursery Manager,* 8(5):54–55.

Gogue, G. J. 1978. The correlation between landscape design and maintenance considerations. In: *Manual of Site Management.* Environmental Design Press, Reston, VA.

Hensley, D. 1990. Designers should plan with maintenance in mind. *Nursery Manager,* 6(5):70–71.

Hensley, D. 1990. Designing to reduce costs of maintenance. *Nursery Manager,* 6(7):95–102.

Hensley, D. 1991. Low-maintenance trees. *Grounds Maintenance,* 26(2):36–38, 112.

Koch, J. 1990. Designing for snow removal. *Grounds Maintenance,* 25(11):44, 59.

Niedenthal, A. 1983. *Landscape design for minimum maintenance.* Cooperative Extension Bulletin HO-176, Purdue University, W. Lafayette, IN.

Roche, J. 1992. Mulch: Perfect for beauty in landscapes. *Landscape Management,* 31(4):18.

Squire, J. W. 1978. Initial design as a factor in ultimate site management. In: *Manual of Site Management.* Environmental Design Press, Reston, VA.

Svenson, S. E. and W. T. Witte. 1989. Mulch toxicity. *American Nurseryman,* 169(2):45–46.

Wade, G. L. 1990. Low-maintenance landscaping. *Landscape Management,* 29(10):48–54.

Williams, E. A. 1978. How design should recognize and be influenced by maintenance at public scale today. In: *Manual of Site Management.* Environmental Design Press, Reston, VA.

Chapter 8
Pruning Landscape Plants

Pruning, the removal of plant parts to control size or improve form, is an annual maintenance event for most shrubs and many trees, especially in their early development. Some landscape plants require pruning several times every season. Pruning is the most frequently misunderstood, but critical function in directing the development of plants to fulfill the intent of the landscape designer. Proper pruning requires time and understanding of the plant's habit, it's biology, and it's function in the design.

Why Prune?

The primary reason for pruning is to *maintain the size and natural form* of landscape plants. Correct pruning and training extends the useful life of a plant in the landscape. Pruning also *removes* dead, diseased, or damaged branches. Removing spent flower heads or fruit *encourages* development of flowers and fruits next season, as with *Rhododendron* spp. Pruning also encourages flowers on plants which bloom on their current season's growth, such as *Buddleia* spp., *Hydrangea arborescens*, *Hydrangea paniculata*, *Lagerstromia* spp., and many *Spiraea* spp. by providing additional leaf area, carbohydrates, and blooming sites.

Pruning is necessary to ensure *safety* in the landscape. Prune limbs rubbing against a structure or restricting vision from windows or traffic. Limbs interfering with power distribution lines must be removed to protect the physical safety of the client and others, as well as prevent interruption of service. Trees interfering with electrical distribution lines are the number one cause of power outages. Hazardous limbs must also be removed for safety of the client and passers-by and reduction of owner liability.

Pruning maintains plants in *unnatural shapes* as with hedges and screens, formal gardens, and topiary shaping of plants. Pruning is used to *renovate* old, overgrown plants and restore them to their proper landscape function and size.

Pruning can compensate for *root loss* at planting. Research, however, indicates marked species differences. The benefit of pruning for some species at planting is questionable. Pruning trains young trees to their proper form for future development.

Photo 8-1. Pruning or shearing plants to unusual shapes has long been a part of landscape horticulture. Formal gardens of royalty in Europe and Asia often contained manicured topiary in the form of animals, geometric forms, and other symbols.

Developing and Scheduling a Pruning Program

It is the responsibility of the landscape manager to develop a *program* for the proper timing and pruning of trees and shrubs on each property. A well-managed pruning program requires trained personnel, proper equipment, proper timing (scheduling), and efficient handling of brush.

Schedule pruning when it is required and appropriate. Pruning is an intricate part of landscape management, not an interference with other duties. Problems occur when pruning is postponed until there is a slow-down in other work or until the supervisor is looking for something to keep the crew busy. Allowing plants to grow out of bounds means that extensive cutting will be required later. Remedial pruning is more costly and disruptive to the landscape and will probably not make the client happy. Pruning is an annual maintenance event and even more frequent in some situations.

Site Inventory

The quantity, type, age, general condition, and location of the plants are used to develop and price a pruning program. Some firms classify plants in broad categories based on flowering habit and plant type (deciduous or evergreen, tree or shrub). An example of general categories might include:

A. *Deciduous shrubs*
   1. Inconspicuous flowering (prune any time during the dormant season).
   2. Early flowering (flowers borne on one-year-old wood—prune after flowering).
   3. Late flowering (flowers borne on current season's wood—prune during dormant season).
   4. Shrubs with prized fruit (prune during the dormant season).

B. *Evergreen Shrubs*
   1. Needle-leaf evergreens (prune dormant season).
   2. Broadleaf evergreens (base pruning on flowering).
   3. Pines, spruce, firs, and most cone-bearing species (pinch new candles).

C. *Roses* (require frequent pruning and dead-heading).

D. *Vines* (pruning based upon flowering habit; specialized equipment required for tall-growing vines).

E. *Flowering Trees*
   1. Early flowering (prune after flowering).
   2. Late flowering (prune in dormant season).
   3. Prized fruit (prune lightly in season).

F. *Large or shade trees*
   1. Separate "bleeders and non-bleeders".

G. *Pine or other large conifers.*

H. *Groundcovers* requiring mowing or pruning.

Photo 8-2. Pruning vines on large buildings requires specialized equipment. Schedule vine pruning on flowering habit.

113

This is not the only way to schedule or categorize pruning. Groupings should reflect regional variations in species and timing and crew organization. Select an inventory system complex enough to be worth the effort, yet simple enough to understand, explain, and use. Breaking down the plants on a property within pruning groups provides basic information for determining bids, budgeting personnel and equipment, and scheduling.

Personnel

Pruning is handled differently among professional operations. Some use specialized pruning crews to prune as necessary for all of their properties. Others firms have one or more members of a general crew assigned to prune the sites they are specifically responsible for. With some companies, however, everyone prunes everything. Each method has advantages and disadvantages.

Regardless of the organization, the personnel or supervisor responsible for pruning should know the names and be able to identify the various plants on site. It is impossible to know when or how to prune if no one knows what is to be pruned. Training specialized pruning crews or personnel in plant identification, prescribed pruning techniques, and operation of specialized equipment is more beneficial and profitable. Specialized personnel can also prune more efficiently and profitably; their work is easier to estimate.

Do not assign just anyone to prune or supervise a pruning crew. Select people with interest in, and respect for plants. Such employees respond to training and produce the desired results.

It may be more efficient and cost effective for some in-house operations to contract an outside firm for pruning. Contract pruning eliminates the need to purchase infrequently used equipment and train current employees. High work in trees must only be handled by an arborist with the proper training, experience, and equipment. Trying to do tree work beyond the firm's capabilities is a good way to get someone hurt, make the problem worse, and fall behind in other areas.

Scheduling

Scheduling on a calendar basis, using dates when pruning was done the previous year, is not completely valid. Weather conditions modify blooming dates and growth flushes. However, recording the dates when pruning is accomplished annually serves as a basis or reminder in future seasons. Specific dates are scheduled according to the current year's growth pattern. If practical, all pruning within a site should be scheduled at the same time to avoid return trips and simplify clean-up. Pruning to clear areas for painting, construction, or other "emergency" operations, such as storm clean up, are not part of the normal contracts. Price special jobs separately.

Avoid interfering with classes, meetings, or other activities with noise from chain saws, chippers, and power equipment. Avoiding scheduled events may require special scheduling or overtime work. Understanding the client develops friendly and long-lasting relations.

Brush

Brush or debris disposal is the final aspect of a pruning program. Dealing with brush becomes even more important as the number of public landfills limiting or restricting dumping of organic material increases. Chipping reduces volume, permits recycling of the chips as mulch, avoids a tangled brush pile, and reduces landfill charges or storage space. Chippers are indispensable to large

114

operations, but they are expensive and noisy. They can be rented or leased for the period of greatest use.

Standards

The National Arborists Association and the International Society of Arboriculture have produced standards that may be of assistance in preparing specifications for bids or contracts. The American Standards Institute has also produced standards for tree care operations (ANSI Z133.1-1988). Consult these publications and Chapter 3 of this text, Specifications and Contracts, for assistance in preparing written standards and specifications.

Timing

Proper timing for pruning is extremely important because it affects future flower development. Appropriate pruning times depend upon the plant, it's condition, and the desired results. Remove diseased, broken, or damaged branches anytime. If flowering is not important, then plants can be pruned anytime during the dormant season. To maximize blossoms; however, correct timing depends on the plant's flowering habit.

Prune plants that flower *early in the spring* from buds formed during the past season (one-year-old wood) at the end of their blooming period. Pruning during the dormant season before flowering removes flower buds. Early flowering species include forsythia (*Forsythia* spp.), quince (*Chaenomeles* spp.), magnolias (*Magnolia* spp.) and the majority of other flowering deciduous landscape plants.

Trees and shrubs flowering during the summer or fall do so from *buds formed during the current season's growth.* These species include crape myrtle (*Lagerstromia* spp.), buddleia (*Buddleia* spp., clethra (*Clethra* spp.), rose-of-sharon (*Hibiscus syriacus*), pomegranate (*Punica granatum*), oleander (*Nerium* spp.), frangipani (*Plumeria* spp.), cassia (*Cassia* spp.), jacaranda (*Jacaranda* spp.), and others. Such species should be pruned during the dormant season, generally before growth begins.

Prune plants *prized for their fruit* display (*Malus* spp. and others) lightly during the dormant season. This reduces next year's blossoms only slightly yet allows the site manager to direct and control growth.

Needle-leaf evergreens can be pruned during the dormant season anytime the wood is not frozen. Pruning apparently has the least effect on growth if conducted just before spring growth begins. Juniper and other needle-leaf evergreens should be pruned lightly on an annual basis or somewhat heavier every other year.

Broadleaf evergreens prized for their flowers should be pruned after flowering. Others should be pruned during the dormant season just before spring growth begins.

Avoid pruning during late summer. Pruning during late August or September may force new growth that cannot harden sufficiently before winter. This most commonly occurs during periods of significant fall rain or irrigation, coupled with high nitrogen fertilization and an early winter.

Delay pruning plants routinely susceptible to winter damage until growth begins in the spring. Waiting makes it easier to determine the extent of cold injury and the portions to be removed.

115

Closure of pruning wounds on trees will be somewhat more rapid if cuts are made shortly before or just after growth begins. Research has shown that pruning wounds to ash (*Fraxinus pennsylvanica*), honey locust (*Gleditsia tricanthos*), and pin oak (*Quercus palustris*) were slower to callus when made in the fall [*Journal of Arboriculture* 1979. 5:135]. Pruning during the dormant season also makes it easier to see the operation.

Some trees, known as *bleeders,* lose considerable amounts of sap if pruned in the early spring. This is not particularly harmful to the tree but may be objectionable to the client. Species predisposed to bleeding include maple (*Acer* spp.), birch (*Betula* spp.), yellowwood (*Cladrastis lutea*), walnut (*Juglans* spp.), and elm (*Ulmus* spp.). Prune bleeders in summer, late fall, or early winter instead of late winter and early spring. Sap loss is also minimized if only small cuts are made.

Equipment

Proper tool selection and use minimize injury to the plant and the employee, and complete the task efficiently. There are many brands and types of pruning equipment available in the market place. As with most purchases, the buyer generally receives what he/she pays for. Durable, dependable, quality equipment is expensive. The professional, however, requires more durable equipment than do homeowners. Also purchase extra blades, handles, and parts so repairs and replacements can be made quickly.

Hand pruners

The most frequently used pruning tool is the *hand pruner.* Hand pruners cut limbs or suckers up to one-half inch diameter; cutting larger material damages the shrub and the tool. Two types of hand pruners are available. *Draw-cut* or *scissors-action* hand pruners use a sharpened blade that cuts with a scissors action. *Anvil* or *snap-cut* types feature a sharpened blade that cuts against a broad, grooved head. The scissors-action pruners are preferred because they cut through the twig more easily without crushing tissue.

Ratchet-action hand pruners increase leverage, and thereby reduce the force needed to cut a given branch. Ratchet pruners are useful in cases of a weak grip but they require more time per cut. They also

Photo 8–3. Hand pruners are the most common equipment used by landscape managers. Select professional quality equipment that will last. The top three pruners shown here are *draw-cut* types; the bottom pair is an *anvil* type. Draw-cut pruners will provide a cleaner cut and are the choice of the professional. Hand pruners are available with many different blade sizes and angle for specialized work and comfort.

are not durable enough for the professional. Regardless of type, use of a belt sheath will keep the pruners handy, reduce loss, and increase the life of one's bluejeans.

Another handy tool for pruning small branches is the *pruning knife* with its heavy, hooked blade. Pruning knives require a fair degree of skill to use effectively and efficiently. In the hands of an amateur, the knife can be dangerous to the plant and the employee. In trained hands, it is a versatile tool.

Loppers

Lopping shears or *loppers* prune limbs exceeding the capacity of hand pruners. Loppers are designed to remove limbs up to one inch or so in diameter. Again, hook and blade or scissors-action (parrot beak) heads are preferred to anvil types. The length of the handle determines the leverage and therefore, ease of the cut. Typically, handles range from 24 to 35 inches and are made of wood, steel, or fiberglass, with or without vinyl or rubber hand grips. Better quality units have replacement blades and parts available.

Photo 8-4. Loppers cut limbs and branches too large for a hand pruner, up to one inch or so in diameter. Anvil and draw-cut blades are available. Select a lopper for durability and comfort. Rubber bumpers between the base of the blades cushion the jar caused by closing the handles and increase worker safety and comfort.

Gear-driven and ratchet loppers are available. These modifications increase the force and the size of limbs that can be cut effectively.

Pole Pruners

Pole pruners aid cutting limbs higher in the tree. The pole pruner consists of a pruning head mounted on a handle approximately six feet in length. Extension handles increase the working length of the unit. Although fiberglass is heaviest, it is the safest material for working near electrical wires. Models with telescoping poles add versatility.

The pruning head consists of a heavier scissors-action blade, as found on loppers, operated by a rope. The size of the limb a pole pruner will effectively cut varies between one and 1-1/2 inch, depending on the model and quality. Curved pruning saws for removing larger limbs can be fitted to the pole. Pruning head-saw combinations are available. Cutting large limbs from below with a pole pruner is frustrating, time-consuming, and can be dangerous. Units with chain saw attachments are available and reduce time and anxiety.

Pruning Saws

Pruning saws are essential for removing branches two inches or larger in diameter. Pruning saws are available in a multitude of sizes and types. Each distinct type and size has a particular use. Pruning saws differ from carpenter's saws in two respects; pruning saws have curved blades for working around limbs, and they cut on the draw or pull stroke. Pruning saws are coarse (5 to 6 teeth per inch) and the teeth are arranged in "V" alternately bent to either side when the saw is viewed down the length of the blade. Finer teeth (8 to 10 per inch) are useful for removing small branches.

A *bow saw* with a flat blade of 15 inches or larger is useful for open limbs but cannot be maneuvered among closely growing limbs or into dense shrubs. *Chain saws* have similar limitations but are the most effective and efficient tool when removing large limbs or entire plants.

Another potentially useful tool is a *wire saw* or hand-powered chain saw. These use a short length of special saw chain attached between two lengths of rope or wire. A small weight is attached and the device thrown over the limb to be cut. The wire saw is designed to cut in both directions as it is pulled back and forth over the limb. Wire or rope saws are also useful in removing older stems from tangled shrubs.

Photo 8–5. Three types of pruning saws. The saw on the right is a *limb saw*. Limb saws are curved for better access to limbs and available in many different lengths, widths, and angle. The *bow saw* in the middle makes quick work of limbs but is difficult to maneuver in tight spaces. Several sizes are on the market. The *folding saw* on the right is handy for carrying in the truck, tool box, or work belt to remove the occasional limb.

Hedge Shears

Hedge shears are for pruning hedges, period. Never use hedge shears to prune landscape shrubs. Unfortunately, they are the most common pruning tool used by some landscape managers. Hedge shears feature flat scissors, sometimes serrated, blades eight inches or more in length. For heavy use, hedge shears with neoprene, rubber, or spring shock absorbers between the handles are preferred.

Electric or *gasoline powered hedge shears* have a moving blade resembling a sickle bar mower. Some hedge shearing units can be adapted to chain saws. Gas units avoid the need for a portable generator to power electric shears, extension cords, and the inevitable cut power cord. Power units take much of the drudgery from pruning extensive or tall hedges. The investment can be easily recouped in reduced time and improved morale.

PRUNING TECHNIQUE

Shrubs

Photo 8–6. Shearing is used to shape hedges and topiary, NOT to prune shrubs in the landscape. Power shears take the drudgery out of long hedges or large jobs.

Shrubs, deciduous or evergreen, are most frequently pruned for size control. If extensive and frequent pruning is required to keep the plant in bounds, it is the wrong plant for the particular use or location. Extremely large and fast growing plants are frequently found in home and commercial

118

landscapes due to nursery marketing and production practices (such species can be produced rapidly and inexpensively).

Many landscape architects and designers have little understanding or knowledge of mature plant size or desire a "finished look" as rapidly as possible. These are insufficient reasons to justify continued indiscriminate use of monster plants at the long-term expense of constant and requisite butchering and aesthetics. There are landscape situations where use of large, rapid-growing plants is planned and desirable. The grounds manager, however, most frequently encounters them where smaller plants would better serve the purpose, the client, and the maintenance budget. Replacement with appropriate plant material is the most economical long-term maintenance decision.

Shearing

Too frequently, shrubs, regardless of habit or design intent, are headed back or pruned with hedge shears resulting in "formal," unnatural shapes. *Shearing* results in exceptional growth of branch side shoots, thickening of the interior of the plant to the point where there are no leaves, die back of the branches, and thinning of the base of the plant.

This type of "pruning" is sometimes requested by clients who require their plants to grow as cute little balls or cubes. Sometimes, there is no accounting for taste.

Shrubs are sometimes sheared by untrained, unprofessional hacks. More often, however, the heading back or shearing is the result of the landscape manager or contractor trying to maintain fast growing plants in confined locations, while trying to be financially competitive. More than one landscape contractor has told me that the client wants the work completed as quickly and cheaply as possible; many do not really care what the plants look like. Unfortunate, but too often true.

Photo 8-7. Shearing is not pruning. Distinguish between the two when preparing specifications and maintenance programs for bid by contractors. These pyracantha have been sheared into an unusual shape at the behest of the client. This type of pruning is not acceptable for most landscapes.

Indiscriminate shearing is faster and less expensive than pruning correctly. If a true pruning/thinning program is initiated from installation of the landscape; however, the time to prune each plant is not that much greater than shearing. Also, shearing is not the only way to keep the plant below the windows. If costs and aesthetics are true concerns, removal and replacement of plants requiring frequent pruning is a realistic alternative.

Every landscape manager or contractor professes *QUALITY* work to be their hallmark, rationale for the firm's pricing structure, and their most effective advertisement. Quality workmanship should extend beyond a well-mown lawn to include proper pruning and care of shrubs. Are you a professional grounds manager or a hack? Blame is passed indiscriminately: the client, for his/her lack of budget; the landscape architect or designer, for poor selection and spacing of plants; the nursery, for not having quantities of more suitable plants available; the installation contractor, for planting

119

too close to the building; and the maintenance contractor, for doing the work too quickly and cheaply.

It is the professional and ethical duty of the landscape designer to provide a maintainable landscape, the nursery and the installer to provide the best, even though possibly more costly plants, and that of the landscape manager to consider the design intent before unpacking the gas-powered shears. It is also time for the green industry to educate clients to quality landscape design and help them recover from the "low bid" mentality.

Compact species

Slow growing or compact species, especially broadleaf evergreens, produce most of their growth from terminal buds or buds near terminals. The result is a slowly expanding symmetrical shrub that develops a dense outer layer of foliage. Few leaves develop in the interior. Little pruning is required except occasional removal of a branch that outgrows the general form. Light thinning can open up a compact shrub and stimulate interior foliage, if desired. Such plants should not be sheared.

Photo 8-8. Slow growing or compact shrubs seldom need pruning or shaping.

Thinning technique

Most rapid growing shrubs, especially deciduous species, sprout vigorously from the base. Others develop a main framework from which most new shoots arise. Large growing deciduous shrubs require regular, fairly severe pruning to keep them attractive and reasonably contained.

Deciduous shrubs, except those described earlier as slow growing, should be pruned with a *thinning technique*. Thinning preserves the natural shape, allows internal growth, and reduces shading and, therefore, "leggy" plants (Illustration 8-1). This technique, however, requires more time and training to accomplish correctly. It must be per-

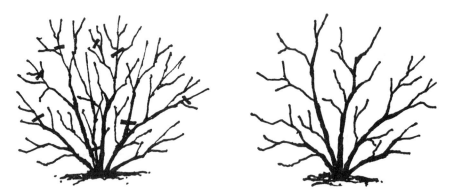

Illustration 8-1. The thinning techniques for pruning shrubs retains the natural form and opens the inside of the plant to light. Make cuts to an out facing bud or lateral at various height throughout the plant. See Table 8-1 for a more detailed pruning sequence. Illustration by Cameron Rees.

formed with hand pruners and each plant must be assessed and pruned individually.

Table 8–1.

The thinning technique ordinarily follows a sequence of pruning decisions and cuts:

1. Remove all diseased, broken, weak branches.

2. Remove all crossing, rubbing branches, and those that lay on the ground.

3. Remove some of the older, heavy growth interior (10–20 percent of the older branches).

4. Reduce length of other various branches varying lengths.

5. Remove some of the new or sucker growth especially from extremely vigorous species and those that tend to develop numerous suckers.

6. Visualize what the plant will look without the branch or cane before each cut.

7. Prune with an eye to the overall health and vigor of the plant. Also consider plant's age and growing conditions especially where weather conditions are extreme.

8. Prune carefully, avoid injury to growth and leave clean cuts without torn edges.

9. When pruning for disease control, such as fire blight or cankers, disinfect after each cut.

Cuts should be made about one-fourth inch above an out-facing bud or lateral branch (Illustration 8-2). Cutting too close to the remaining bud can damage it, while cutting too far away may allow additional buds to break. Buds can be selected to direct growth (Illustration 8-3). When pruning plants with opposite buds, the interior bud should be rubbed off with the thumb or the cut angled to damage or remove it. This results in a single bud becoming the new terminal rather than two, and the subsequent fork.

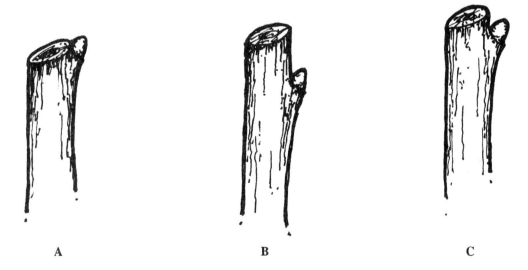

| A | B | C |

Illustration 8-2. *Cut A* is too close; the bud may die resulting in several lower buds braking and twiggy growth. *Cut B* is too high above the target bud; several lower bud may also break. *Cut C* is one-fourth inch above the new terminal bud. It will become the leader on the branch and the natural form is retained. Illustration by Cameron Rees.

Evergreen shrubs can also be pruned with a thinning technique similar to that described for deciduous shrubs. Make cuts to an outfacing lateral branch. Tips can be headed back later if thicker

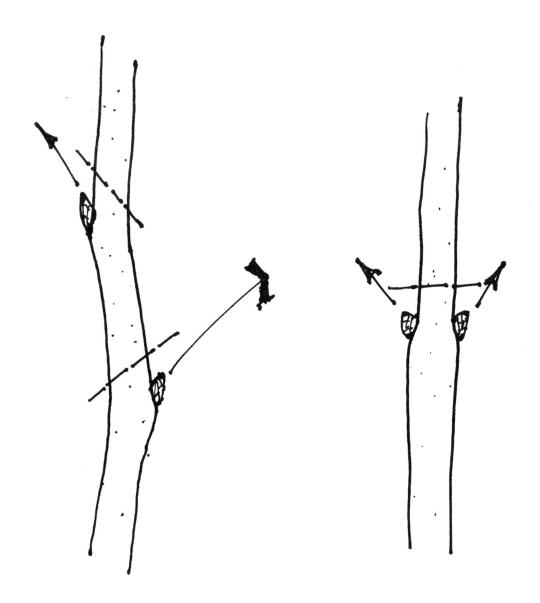

Illustration 8–3. The direction of new growth can be controlled by selecting the new "leader." Cut to an out facing bud to direct the growth away from the center of the plant and to retain the natural shape. For plants with opposite buds, rub off or prune through the inside bud to avoid a fork. Illustration by Cameron Rees.

growth is desired. Non-green portions of arborvitae (*Thuja* spp.), juniper (*Juniperous* spp.), and most other needle evergreens do not have active adventitious buds. Pruning evergreen shrubs severely into this brown, leafless area will not result in new growth. Yews (*Taxus* spp.) and a few species of pine are exceptions.

Shrubs with *colorful canes,* such as red- and yellowed-twigged shrub dogwoods (*Cornus* spp.), are best thinned annually after the shrub is three to five years old. Older twigs lose their brilliant coloration with age and renewal thinning maintains a supply of colorful, new canes.

Photo 8-9. Needle-leaf evergreen can be pruned with a thinning technique to retain their natural shape and control size. Make cuts back to a lateral branch or out-facing bud. Photograph by James Robbins.

Remedial Pruning

Many grounds managers and management firms inherit sites where the trees and shrubs were pruned improperly by their predecessors, or where the plants are terribly overgrown. Ideally, of course, plantings should be designed so that remedial pruning is minimal. If the ideal was commonplace; however, many people would be taller and have considerably more hair.

Some problems with poorly maintained or overgrown planting can be solved with corrective pruning, while others cannot. With few exceptions, conifers will not sprout new growth from their trunks or older branches if they are severely pruned.

Conversely, most (but not all) broadleaf evergreen trees and shrubs will bud out and grow again from even quite old stems and branches. Deciduous plants regenerate most rapidly and will usually be presentable in the first season or two after severe pruning.

Overgrown privet (*Ligustrum* spp.), hydrangea (*Hydrangea* spp.), forsythia, and some spiraeas *(Spiraea* spp.) can be pruned to within four to six inches of the ground. A thick growth of new canes and sprouts will result. The new growth must be thinned severely and proper pruning established the following year. Unhealthy shrubs that are in poor vigor or that

Photo 8-10. Large, overgrown shrubs can be renovated and returned to a useful place in the landscape. The best solutions, however, is to select plants that will not overgrow their space and to prune regularly.

have been long neglected may not respond well to severe measures. These plants should be renovated over two or three years, as described below. Grafted lilac (*Syringa* spp.) or other species should not be cut to the ground. The grafted clone will be removed and replaced by shoots the (undesirable) rootstock.

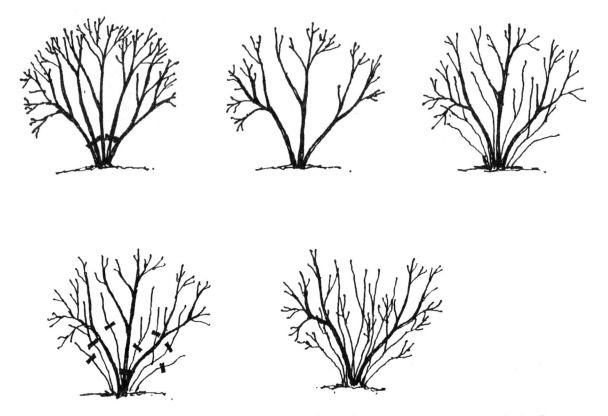

Illustration 8-4. Renovation pruning over several seasons can be used to restore some over grown shrubs. Remove one-third to one-half of the oldest canes or shoots the first year. The second season thin the new growth and remove the next one-half to one-third of the oldest growth. During the third season begin a normal thinning pruning program and remove the remaining one-third of the old growth if the renovation is over three seasons. Illustration by Cameron Rees.

Selective thinning of tops to restore the natural appearance might be preferable to total rejuvenation of a shrub or group of shrubs. Renovation over two to three seasons is successful with lilac, honeysuckle (*Lonicera* spp.), and most deciduous shrubs (Illustration 8-4). Remove one-third to one-half of the oldest growth during the winter of the first year. Prune out the remainder during the dormant season of the second, and possibly third year. The time required to renovate older shrubs depends on their size, age, vigor, and the budget. Growth during and after renovation will be vigorous, so diligent thinning and pruning to remove suckers and re-establish the form and density is absolute. Removal of some of the oldest canes will be required annually or the plant will soon be overgrown again.

Azaleas (*Rhododendron* spp.), camellias (*Camellia* spp.), hollies (*Ilex* spp.), junipers, yews, and other shrubs that have been "globed" can be restored by not hedging back the new growth. Reduce excessive height by shortening several selected branches annually. Remove and thin a number of the oldest branches annually.

Overgrown rhododendrons (*Rhododendron* spp.) can be, but are not frequently rejuvenated by cutting back to 12-inch stubs. A more reasonable approach would be to renovate rhododendrons and other broadleaf evergreens over two to three years by removing a portion of the oldest branches annually as described previously.

Hedges

Hedges serve various functional and aesthetic purposes in the landscape: visual and traffic barriers; backgrounds; formation of "courtyards;" and creation of more formal effects. Hedges may be successfully formed from almost any species. Many old and beautiful hedges from maple, hornbeam (*Carpinus* spp.), beech (*Fagus* spp.), and pine (*Pinus* spp.), species not usually thought of as "hedge plants," can be found in formal gardens throughout the world. Hedges are more commonly established from rapidly growing deciduous species such as privet, or slower growing evergreens such as yew or boxwood (*Buxus* spp.).

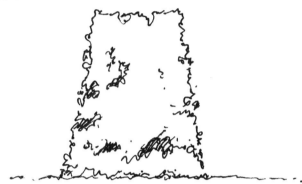

Illustration 8–5. A properly pruned hedge is always wider at the base than the top. Illustration by Cameron Rees.

When establishing a hedge, no pruning except heading back the plants at planting is required the first year. This allows the plants to become well established. During the second year, cut (head) shoots of broadleaf plants to within four to six inches of the height at planting. Evergreens are tip pruned. Until they reach desired height, head back new shoots one-half to two-thirds of their length each time they grow six to 12 inches. This develops a dense, low branching structure and encourages the plants to spread. Hedges, regardless of species, should always be pruned so they are wider at the base than the top (Illustration 8–5).

After the hedge reaches the desired height it is sheared. Timing of shearing is be based on the amount and cycles of growth. Shearing effects last longer if performed after growth has ceased for the season. Shear to one to three new leaves and buds. This forms a dense outer cloak of foliage and reduces growth. Species that grow continuously or produce multiple flushes during the growing season will be pruned several times during the year.

Most broadleaf hedge plants, in contrast to conifers or evergreens, can be pruned back severely. If the hedge has outgrown its desired size or becomes unkempt and ragged, cut back to one-half of the existing height and width. The height and form will redevelop to that desired after shearing a few times. Pruning this heavily is best accomplished just before growth begins so that the hedge is bare for the shortest period of time.

TREES

Pruning at planting

There are several current opinions on pruning at time of planting. Traditional recommendations call for removal of one-fourth to one-third of the branches, and thus potential leaf area, of bareroot and balled and burlapped woody plants at planting. The theory or wisdom behind this advice is to bring the top of the plant into proportion with the roots remaining after harvest.

Barerooting and balling remove a large portion of the functional root system; the larger the tree or shrub, the greater the percentage of active roots removed. Some estimates place root loss at 90 to 95 percent of the original mass. Reduction of potential leaf area would, therefore, reduce water loss via transpiration. Container-grown plants are seldom severely pruned as there is no reduction of the root system at harvest. Post-transplant pruning of container-grown material is limited to clean up of stray or broken branches.

Opponents of pruning at planting suggest there is no benefit and that top pruning reduces photosynthetic capability. Some of the evidence put forth in support of not pruning is based on singular studies and somewhat shaky interpretation of the data.

More reliable work with Newport plum (*Prunus cerasifera* 'Newport') and Sargent crabapple (*Malus sargentii*) by Evans and Klett, Colorado State University [*Journal of Arboriculture* 1984. 10:298], and others indicated no significant differences in root production when leaf:new root ratios of variously top-pruned plants were compared to control trees. Pruning did not appear to improve first-year survival or overall growth of these easily established species. The investigators cautioned that their results cannot be extrapolated for other woody species similarly pruned. In other studies, moderate shoot pruning of Norway maple (*Acer platanoides*) at planting improved structure and did not harm the plants. Research by others with oaks, a significantly more difficult species to transplant, showed advantages in survival when plants were pruned at planting. Many reliable nurseries and plant experts still recommend top pruning of all new transplanted bareroot liners.

A compromise with the existing data and opinions is probably in order. It is doubtful that moderate pruning at planting will benefit survival or growth of relatively easily established species on sites with adequate irrigation and post-plant management. On the other hand, moderate pruning will not harm and will likely benefit more difficult to establish species, or those plants with little or no post-plant irrigation and maintenance.

Pruning at planting does not require the shortening of each and every branch by 25 to 33 percent. All landscape professionals agree that this damages the plant's form. Correct pruning of a transplanted tree is accomplished by removing the least needed branches or those that will interfere with the form or future development of the tree (Illustration 8–6).

Photo 8–11. Begin shaping and training a tree at planting. The top of the tree was apparently damaged, resulting in a fork from the competing opposite buds that assumed leadership. Removing one of these twin leaders at that time would have allowed the tree to resume its normal form. Now a substantial cut must be made to remove one of the competing leaders and the form of the tree is not desirable. Photograph by Larry Leuthold.

Any well-grown tree has several limbs that can be removed, either wholly or in part, without seriously affecting the plant's size or shape. Thin closely-space limbs. Shorten or remove one of any two branches in a weak, V-shaped crotch.

Illustration 8–6. Begin training a tree at planting. Remove unnecessary and injured branches. Illustration by Cameron Rees.

Small trees usually have a number of small side shoots in lower regions of the trunk that will be free of branches in a few years. At least some of these side shoots should remain, but they can be shortened at time of transplanting. Research with pin oak indicated that the tree made greater total shoot growth in the first few seasons after transplanting if some of the side branches were not removed. Selective pruning will establish and likely improve the tree's future form.

Training

Trees should be trained and pruned routinely while they are young, during the first ten or so years after planting, to avoid severe pruning when they are older. Properly pruned younger trees will not likely need to be re-pruned for one to two years. Middle-aged trees can grow for longer periods without pruning.

Train the tree according to its natural form. Plants with *excurrent* or central leader growth habit (pin or Shumard oak (*Quercus shumardii*) are trained differently than those with *decurrent* or multiple leader growth habit (maple or ash).

A tree is a three dimensional object. Train limbs to develop in all directions (*radically*) (Illustration 8–7). Establish *alternate branching* early in the tree's career. Major scaffold branches should develop at least 6 to 12 inches apart to allow for future growth (Illustration 8–8). Damaged, diseased, and broken branches must be removed. Branches that touch or rub against another will cause future problems and should also be removed. Remove interior branches as these receive little light and will grow slowly, eventually dying. Prune away water sprouts and suckers.

Select the broadest-angled branches possible; branches that diverge from the main stem at less than a 40° angle should be removed. Wide crotch-angle branches have greater structural strength and resistance to wind, ice, and snow. Some species

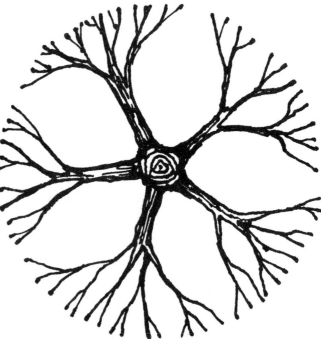

Illustration 8–7. Establish radial spacing of branches. A tree is a three-dimensional object. Illustration by Cameron Rees.

such as halesia (*Halesia* spp), yellowwood, and silver maple (*Acer saccharinum*) are prone to narrow or weak crotch angles. In these cases, prune to direct limbs so they grow more laterally, rather than upright.

The lowest branches will be removed over time, as the tree develops. Do not remove all branches that ultimately need to be taken out at one time. Trees limbed-up too soon develop weaker trunks. The crown height of the tree should be proportional to the trunk. A ratio of crown to clear trunk of 3:1 is sometimes used as a guide. Under city conditions, branches lower than seven to ten feet should be removed, particularly along major streets. This height may be increased to 15 feet to provide truck body clearance.

Illustration 8-8. Establish alternate branching. Branches should emerge throughout the radial plane of the tree and be spaced far enough apart so they will not cause problems as the increase in size in the future. Illustration by Cameron Rees.

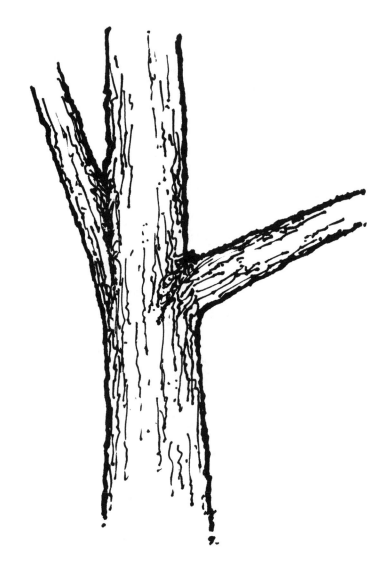

Illustration 8–9. Remove branches with narrow branch angles if possible. Narrow branch angles are weaker and more likely to break under a snow load or during high winds. Illustration by Cameron Rees.

Photo 8-12. Prune to establish a crown to trunk ratio of 3:1. Photograph by James Robbins.

Photo 8-13. Poor trunk to crown proportion. Prune limbs of trees along roadways to accommodate traffic and to avoid injury to the trees and vehicles. These trees, however, have been awkwardly pruned. Prune with the future of the tree in mind, select a framework for future limb and branch development. Proper training eliminates the need for large or drastic cuts later.

Special consideration and training are required for 'Bradford' flowering pear (*Pyrus calleryana* 'Bradford'). This cultivar possesses many attributes that have resulted in its widespread use. It is one of the most popular flowering trees in the country. Branch arrangement and angle are not some of its better characteristics, however. The plant develops four or more major scaffold branches at the same level on the trunk. The tragic result is loss of entire sections of the plant due to wind or snow after the plant is 10 to 15 years old. This can be corrected by proper training, but unfortunately training is not frequently accomplished during nursery production. As a result, many 'Bradford' flowering pears established in landscapes are too large to successfully remove some of the scaffolds and establish alternate branching.

An alternative to this dilemma is specification of properly pruned 'Bradford's in installation specifications and contracts, or selecting other flowering pear cultivars with superior branching habit. A number of such cultivars including 'Aristocrat', 'Chanticleer', 'Trinity', and 'Autumn Blaze' are available in the trade.

Photo 8–14. 'Bradford' callery pairs tend to form major scaffolds at one level. In 15 to 20 years major portions of the tree will be lost to wind and snow load. Train the trees to alternate branching in the nursery or landscape while they are small or select cultivars with better branch architecture. Photograph by Robert McNiel.

Removing Limbs

Previous recommendations have been to remove tree branches as close as possible to the stem or lateral branch. This process is known as "flush cutting". Research by Dr. Alex Shigo, US Forest Service, indicated that this practice delays closure of the pruning wounds.

Branch collars

A branch of a woody plant is joined to the stem only on the underside of the branch, not as a continuous sheath of wood. The stem forms a collar over the branch. Remove branches so that the branch collar is not injured. Cutting into the collar destroys natural defense mechanisms, creates a larger wound, and opens the tree to infection.

Some species have prominent and easily detectable branch collars while others are not so easily discernible. Shigo has developed guidelines to determine where a cut should be made. These *natural target pruning* (NTP) procedures are:

- Locate the ridge of bark formed above the branch at the union, or crotch, of the stem and branch.

132

Photo 8-15. Limbs are only truly joined to the stem on the underside of the branch. This photograph courtesy of Lawrence Hensley and Ernest Hensley and their chain saw and wood splitter.

Photo 8-16. Branch collars are prominent in some species but difficult to discern in others.

- Locate the stem collar surrounding the branch, usually a slight swelling near the main stem or trunk.
- Remove the branch by cutting outside both the bark ridge and the branch collar.
- Where an obvious swelling or collar is not present, cut outside the branch bark ridge and at an angle opposite that formed by the ridge.
- Limbs over two inches in diameter or long, heavy branches should be removed by the three-step method described below.

Old stubs resulting from previous natural damage or poor pruning methods should be removed carefully. In many cases, callus tissue may have begun to form near the stub base. This can be identified by an enlarged area enclosing the lower portion or remainder of the stub. Remove the stub just outside the swollen callus region. If an enlarged callus area is not visible or the stub is recent, remove it at the branch collar.

Three-step Removal for Large Branches

Remove branches larger than two inches in diameter with a *three-step process* to avoid tearing of the bark beneath the limb (Illustration 8-10). The first cut is made on the underside of the branch one to two feet from the crotch. Cut the branch one-fourth to one-third of the way through or until the saw begins to bind. The second cut is made from the top of the limb and two or three inches further out on the limb than the first. Saw until the limb breaks off; the break will occur at the first, lower cut.

133

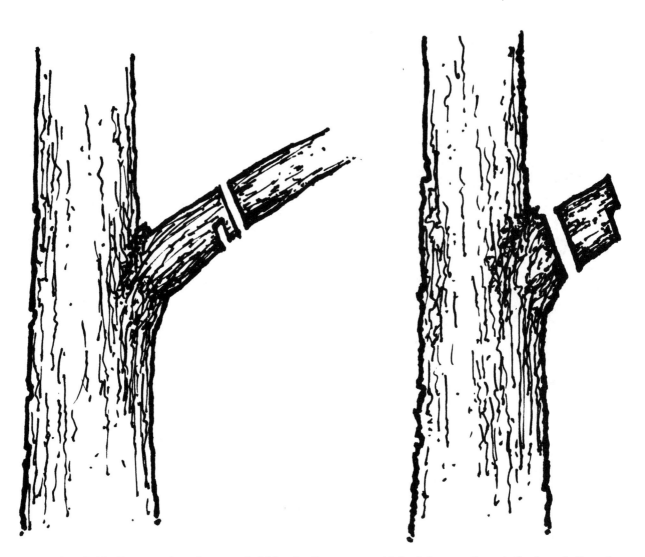

Illustration 8–10. Three-cut branch removal. Make the first cut one-third of the way through the branch from the underside. Make the second cut a few inches further out the branch from the top. The branch will break and drop at the first undercut. Remove the stub with the third cut. Support the stub to avoid tearing the bark. Illustration by Cameron Rees.

The third and final cut is made at the branch collar or crotch. Do not leave the stub as it will be slow to callus or will decay. Scribing or breaking the bark on the lower side of the branch with the saw before making the final cut through reduces the possibility of bark tearing should the limb slip. Large limb stubs should be removed with 2 cuts; the first from the bottom and the second from the top. A heavy stub can be supported with a rope sling to aid the cutting operation and prevent bark tears.

Shaping pruning cuts

Some publications refer to shaping or paring the pruning wound with a sharp knife. *Paring* is cutting the thick bark around the pruning wound and rounding the edges of the cut to provide a smooth, even surface. Although the wound may appear neater, paring does not aid closure or callusing and requires additional effort. Rounding of the edge of a pruning wound may actually delay callus formation and wound closure.

Pruning Paint and Wound Dressings

The practice of painting pruning cuts and tree wounds has been recommended for centuries. Many sources persist in advising to cover any pruning cut larger than one inch diameter with asphalt-based pruning "paints". This counsel is in spite of research showing that wound dressings are of limited benefit in wound closure and of no value in abating infection. Some materials delay callus formation and growth. Research dating back to 1934 and repeated by numerous scientists has shown conclusively that tree wound dressings and pruning paints do not prevent decay in woody plants. There should remain no controversy over this topic; the purpose of pruning paint is cosmetic rather than practical.

Photo 8–17. Pruning paints are strictly cosmetic. They do not promote wound closure, in fact they may delay it and promote decay beneath the coating.

Pruning paint and wound dressings should only be used at the insistence of the client or manager who cling to the old habits without regard to, or possibly knowledge of, published findings. If required to apply a dressing by the contract, client, or manager, then apply only enough to change the color of the wound surface. Aerosol formulations are especially useful for a small, quick application.

Naphthaleneacetic acid (NAA) products can be applied to pruning cuts or in a "pruning compound" to reduce regrowth of tree sprouts following pruning. These materials are labeled for use on many species prone to suckering.

Photo 8–18. Water sprouts are produced by adventitious buds as a result of heavy pruning. Some species, such as crabapple and silver maple are prone to sprouting. Water sprouts can be reduced by avoiding heavy pruning and using cultivars that have been produced on their own roots rather than grafted onto a seedling rootstock. At least two sprout-control products containing NAA are available for after pruning application.

Topping

Unsuspecting clients are too frequently "conned" by less than reputable "tree surgeons" into having their tree topped. *Topping* is the indiscriminate cutting of major limbs to stubs without regard to their location. It is an ill fated attempt to control the size or "shorten" large-growing trees. Topping ruins the form of the tree and results in the development of a vigorous, upright thicket of

135

Photo 8–19. Indiscriminate topping of trees ruins their natural form and produces large amounts of growth that is poorly attached and more prone to loss from wind or snow than the original. NEVER TOP TREES. Photograph by James Robbins.

Photo 8–20. This sycamore (*Platanus occidentalis*) has been *pollarded*. Pollarding is not topping. It is a training system in which the shoots are cut back each year to the same point. An enlarged knob develops at the branch ends. The tree pictured is in Williamsburg, VA. Pollarding was common during the colonial period. Trees have been maintained at the same height by pollarding for hundreds of years in Europe. Pollarding, however, is labor intensive and potentially injurious to the tree. Photograph by James Robbins.

water sprouts. The branches formed by the new shoots are weakly attached and break readily in storms.

In addition, the large, unprotected surfaces of the stubbed branches are vulnerable to decay. This leads to hollowing-out of the trunk and eventual death of the tree.

The end result of topping is loss of function for the tree in the landscape and drastic reduction of its life span. Future problems resulting from topping will be enormous.

Unfortunately, topping is standard operating procedure for some "arborists". A 1992 survey of Yellow Pages advertising by PlantAmnesty showed that 53 percent of the display ads in 10 cities advertised "topping". This practice is reduce by training and education. Only 22 percent of firms displaying membership in the International Society of Arboriculture or the National Arborist Association listed "topping" as a service.

Growth of large-growing or notoriously weak-wooded trees can be controlled and their height reduced with proper arboricultural techniques. Selective thinning of large or high branches or "drop crouching" (removal of branches at laterals) may not be within the realm of all grounds managers.

Photo 8-21. High work and drop crotching of trees to reduce height must only be attempted by a trained, certified arborist. The operation pictured is a *take down* or removal. The tree is taken down in small sections to avert damage to people and property below. Photograph by James Robbins.

Photo 8-22. Upright species seldom require pruning. When they do, remove the limb entirely or prune back to an upward or inward facing bud. Photograph by James Robbins.

High work requires specialized lifts, equipment, climbing techniques, and knowledge. Large tree operations are best subcontracted to certified and experienced professional arborists.

Fastigiate, columnar and upright forms

Fastigiate, columnar, and upright trees and shrubs are narrowly upright in silhouette. Such forms occur in many species, including arborvitae, birch, chamaecyparis (*Chamaecyparis* spp.), crabapple, hawthorn (*Crataegus* spp.), hornbeam, juniper, maple, pine, oak, and yew. Upright and fastigiate are used in formal, home, and commercial landscapes, and as screening plants. Branches of these forms turn sharply upward. Branches grow parallel with little or no horizontal development. Some columnar plants maintain a dominant main trunk with stubby, twiggy side branches.

True fastigiate, columnar, and upright forms seldom need pruning. Remove occasional branches that grow laterally. When shaping and thinning, always prune to a bud on the *inside* of the plant. This is the opposite of normally accepted pruning practices. In the case of upright-growing forms, direct growth inward, rather than outward. Specimens may require an infrequent thinning; remove branches at their origin and cut some small branches at various heights.

Weeping Specimens

Another specialized group of plants used in landscapes have *decumbent* or weeping forms. Young weeping trees gradually build height by arching shoots that develop somewhat above the trunk. These grow into heavier branches that eventually support another layer of central arches. If an upright shoot appears, it should be removed or the weeping habit will be lost. Allow weeping branches to grow to the ground. Trimming the branches to a uniform height above the ground, an artificial "hem line", destroys the effect of the plant.

Weeping trees sometimes spread too wide. In this case, remove outreaching branches at a crotch. Encourage closer-to-the center branches to develop by pruning away young branchlets at an inside bud.

Photo 8–23. Prune weeping cultivars and species to maintain their arching form. Remove upward growing branches; allow the weeping branches to grow to the ground. Photograph by James Robbins.

Large Conifers

Most *large conifers* such as pine, spruce (*Pices* spp.) and fir (*Abies* spp.) have a strong excurrent growth (central leader) habit, especially when young. Large-growing conifers require little training unless an atypical effect is desired. Conifers are pruned to increase the density or thickness between branches, to shape young plants, and reduce the size of older trees.

Pines produce definite whorls of branches marking the point at which the annual growth began. They do not normally produce buds along the entire stem. Therefore, if the annual growth is cut back after growth has matured, the cut terminal will remain a non-growing stub.

In vigorous trees, branch whorls are sometimes spaced further apart on the main trunk than desired. The density of the tree (the space between new whorls) is increased by pinching or cutting off part of the new growth (candle) after it has approached full length and the needles have begun to elongate. Pinching is preferred since cutting with shears causes the needles to develop brown tips. The amount of growth suppression is directly related to the severity of the pinch. The tree will set a new terminal bud, retain the excurrent form, and the distance between the next whorl is reduced.

Photo 8–24. Pinch the candles of pine when the new needles are approximately one-fourth inch in length. The distance between the whorls of branches will be reduced and a new bud will form to retain the excurrent form.

138

Pinching candles will also control the size of mugo pines (*Pinus mugo*). Misshapen or lopsided mugo pines can be repaired over time by pinching the candles on the taller side more severely than those on the shorter side.

Spruce and *fir* also produce a customary whorl of branches that marks annual growth. These species, however, form some buds between annual whorls. Some of the buds remain dormant indefinitely but others form twigs or side branches. Because of these lateral buds, spruce and fir may be pruned at any time of the year. Prune back to a bud, which will break dormancy and continue to grow upward or outward. Do not cut back further than the previous year's growth as the buds beyond that point may not break dormancy.

If the terminal bud of pine, spruce, or fir is destroyed, then the plant will try to replace the leader with two or more shoots from the whorl of buds just below the destroyed leader. All but one of these shoots should be removed to retain the excurrent habit. The remaining shoot may require staking to a more upright position for a season.

Palms

Palms are pruned to remove old and unsightly leaves or fronds and fruiting clusters. Dead fronds of Mexican fan palm (*Washingtonia robusta*) and others can harbor insects and rodents or be a fire hazard. Fallen leaves and fruit are a nuisance and dangerous to passers-by and property.

A palm normally maintains only a certain number of fronds, depending on species and growing condition. As new leaves develop from the terminal, the older leaves die or senesces. Palms can be *self-cleaning*, that is the dead leaves drop naturally, such as Royal palm (*Roystonea regia*). Self-cleaning palms require little pruning maintenance unless they are growing in an area where falling fronds will cause damage or a danger to people. Most palms, however, such as coconut palm (*Cocos nucifera*), queen palm (*Arecastrum romanzoffianum*), and desert fan palm (*Washingtonia filifera*) retain their dead leaves.

Photo 8–25. This coconut palm is in dire need of pruning. The fruit can become lethal weapons if they drop on people or objects. Lower fronds should also be removed. Photograph by Fred Rauch.

Another danger from some palms, particularly coconut palms, is the fruits. The fruit is large, heavy and can do serious damage to people and property when they come tumbling down.

In Hawaii, Florida, and parts of Texas, *hurricane pruning* is commonly performed. Hurricane pruning is the same as any other palm pruning, but it is done just before hurricane season, usually June through October. Although palms are very wind-resistant, violent storms can rip leaves off. Fruits become dangerous missles in high winds.

Palms in high maintenance landscapes are pruned twice a year, spring and fall. Species such as coconut palms that produce large, hazardous fruit or that frequently drop old fronds in high traffic areas are pruned three times per year. If trees are under less maintenance or if semi-annual pruning is not possible, then they should be pruned at least once a year, in the spring.

Palms are monocots. Wounds in the trunk of palms do not callus so climbing spurs should be avoided. Palms cannot be girdled either. Many old coconut palms that have been climbed by arborists with spurs three times every year for decades, however, do not show any ill effects from the experience. Continuous spiking, however, is unsightly and can open the tree to disease invasion. The best way to prune a palm is using a bucket truck.

When pruning a single-stem palm, remove the flowers and all stages of maturing fruit. Remove one-third to one-half of the lower leaves in their entirety. Think of the entire top of a palm tree as a clock. Remove the lower leaves from eight o'clock to four o'clock if pruning two or three times per year. Remove the leaves from nine o'clock to three o'clock if pruning once per year.

Do not remove too many leaves creating "feather dusters". Over pruning at the growing point limits the amount of energy produced through photosynthesis to maintain the terminal. Excessive pruning results in palm decline and "pencil pointing".

Leaves can be removed with a machete, heavy knife, or chain saw. Chain saws are useful for date palm (*Phoenix* spp.) or armored palms (those with spikes) unless there is a danger of transmitting Fusarium wilt.

Take care as not to damage the trunk when removing leaves or fruit. The wounds do not callus. Palms grow only from the terminal. Never remove or damage the terminal growing point.

Multi-stemmed palms form new shoots below ground so entire stems can be removed. There is little need to prune multi-stem palms unless individual stems are too close to a building or internal growth is too thick. Some palms are *monocarpic*, that is the old stem dies after fruiting. Remove these dead stems after final fruiting.

WOUND CLOSURE AND TREATMENT

Wounds, from natural or man-made causes, provide entrance of decay organisms into a tree. The traditional concept of wound closure was developed in the 1800s. Decay fungi were theorized to move unchecked through the stem or trunk because wood is primarily dead, unresponsive tissue. Research by Dr. Alex Shigo and others have conclusively demonstrated that woody plants actively resist the spread of infectious microorganisms throughout the plant through compartmentalization. The model for tree response to external wounds has been dubbed "**CODIT,**" *Compartmentalization Of Decay In Trees.*

Photo 8-26. Properly pruned wounds close quickly. This limb removal wound is covered with *woundwood.*

A bark penetrating injury to a plant is contained with a two-step process. The first response is the accumulation of plant produced *anti-microbial substances* at the edge of the infection. This active plant reaction is not completely understood. Phenolic and other compounds develop in deciduous species and terpenes are produced in conifers. These materials have anti-microbial capabilities. This reaction zone is not static; new zones form in advance of the movement of infection organisms. Tree species vary in anti-microbial production.

In addition to an active reaction zone, vertical movement of decay organisms is *physically hindered* by *plugging of the vascular tissue* by tyloses and accumulation of plant products. This vertical barrier is the weakest of the four found in trees and explains why decay will spread up and down (usually down) in trees. Movement of decay radially and tangentially (toward the interior) is much less.

Inward movement of decay organisms is compartmentalized by the *last intact annual growth ring*. Annual rings result from the change in cell size and density as growth slows each year. There may be production or accumulation of anti-microbial compounds in this area.

Radial spread (around the stem) of decay is held in check by *ray cells*. Ray cells transport sugars across the stem. There may also be some phytochemicals involved in containment.

The fourth and strongest wall is formed by production of *woundwood* from callus. Woundwood prevents movement of the organisms into tissue formed later. Formation of wound-wood by the plant is not analogous to healing of wounds by animals or man, although tree wounds are often said to "heal". Plants do not heal wounds in the sense of regeneration or restoration. They close over defects and compartmentalize them in layers of new tissue.

Compartmentalization has been observed, although sometimes unknowingly, by anyone who has felled a partially hollow tree. Staining of the wood from infection or "hollowing" of the tree can sometimes be seen to be contained or compartmentalized into pie-shaped wedges or distinct zones surrounded by healthy tissue.

The ability to compartmentalize varies greatly among species and between individuals within a species. A tree must have the genetic ability to resist invasion by decay organisms. A tree's response to wounding is also controlled to some degree by environment and tree vigor. The more vigorous growth for the plant, the stronger and more effective the containment of decay.

Photo 8–27. Woundwood ridge formed on thornless honeylocust. The woundwood is formed from *callus* produced by meristematic tissue at the edge of the wound. The age of some wounds can be determined by the number of woundwood ribs; these form annually. Photograph by James Robbins.

Treating wounds

Despite the best intentions, wounds will occur to trees in the landscape. Wounds may be caused by equipment, vandals (two- and four-legged), or accidents.

If bark wounds to trunks or limbs are discovered soon after the incident then the bark can be successfully re-attached. The bark must be torn cleanly and the cambium moist and not discolored. The bark can be held in place by a small nail or with rubber or plastic strips or twine. Wound dressings should not be applied. Remove the ties in about three weeks. The nail can remain in place without harm.

An alternate procedure prescribed in one source is to wrap about two inches of moist, clean sphagnum peat moss over the bark after nailing. The area is then covered with white polyethylene that can be sealed against the trunk at the top and bottom with tape or asphalt paint. The "poultice" is removed in two or three weeks.

If the cambium is injured or if the wound is old, the damaged area should be cleaned and dead or loose bark removed from the edges. Avoid cutting into healthy tissue. Some sources recommend *"tracing"* the wound, that is cutting back to healthy tissue to form an oval or ellipse. It does not seem prudent to enlarge an existing damaged area. Jagged or damaged bark and cambium should be removed but give careful consideration before enlarging the wound for the sake of cosmetics.

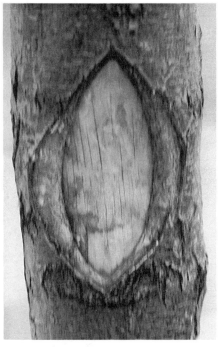

Photo 8-28. A traced or scribed wound. Remove soil and debris from wounds and trace or cut to remove dead or hanging bark. Make cuts as shallow as possible.

Research by Dr. Dan Neely, Illinois Natural History Survey [*Journal of Arboriculture.* 1979. 5:135-140], resulted in some interesting discoveries in plant responses to wounds. He studied the effect of wound shape, direction, time of year, and species. Wounds in the shape of circles, squares, "D's," and ellipses were deliberately imposed. Square wounds were wider than the others and closed slightly more slowly than the others. The "squares" formed an ellipse during closure. There was no difference in rate of closure among the other shapes.

The aspect or *compass direction* of a wound had no effect on the amount of closure. This is in deference to some who claim wounds with southern or western exposure close more slowly because of increased temperatures. This "wife's tale" is not supported by research.

Dr. Neely found that late winter and early spring wounds closed more rapidly than late summer or early fall wounds. The delay may be due to desiccation and to initiation of the growth cycle. Mercer [*Annals of Applied Botany,* 1983. 103:527] found no effect of season on callus development by beech (*Fagus* spp.). Such findings serve as a basis for developing pruning schedules.

Neely showed that wound closure rates were *species dependent* and somewhat based on the rate and amount of radial growth. Mercer also found that callus growth varied with species, but was more rapid for young, vigorous trees or those receiving fertilizer applications.

Drs. Martin and Sydnor, The Ohio State University [*HortScience* 1987 22:442-444], found green ash and sweet gum closed wounds more quickly than 'Bradford' callery pear and river birch. They also compared wound closure of the same species in an urban and rural lawn environment. Wound closure was more closely correlated to species than to common growth parameters. Martin and Sydnor suggested the possibility of selecting trees for urban use based, at least in part, on the basis of response to mechanical damage.

Bibliography

Abrahamson, S. 1982. The right tools make pruning a snap. *Grounds Maintenance,* 17(4):24–32, 122.

Anonymous. 1981. Pruning, winter protection promotes year-round plant health. *Grounds Maintenance,* 16(2):66–67.

Anonymous. 1988. Pruning and trimming ornamental trees and shrubs. *Arbor Age,* 8(9):12–22.

Anonymous. 1989. Safety in pruning palms. *Arbor Age,* 9(9):41–46.

Anonymous. 1990. Retaining natural tree shape critical to pruning. *Lawn & Landscape Maintenance,* 11(5):62–64.

Anonymous. 1990. Tree trimming equipment. *Arbor Age,* 10(9):12–14.

Anonymous. 1992. Pruning tools. *Arbor Age,* 12(9):38–39.

Anonymous. 1993. Your yellow pages tell the story. *PlantAmnesty,* 5(2):8

Anonymous. 1993. Strategies for maintaining trees. *Lawn & Landscape Management,* 15(5):32–36.

Baumgardt, J. 1985. Custom-tailored pruning. *Grounds Maintenance,* 20(4):58–62, 66–68.

Chapman, D. 1981. Keys to pruning evergreens and deciduous shrubs. *Weeds, Trees, and Turf,* 20(2):52–54.

Chapman, D. 1982. Pruning: A key to integrated plant management. *Weeds, Trees, and Turf,* 21(1):52–54, 58.

Code, C. 1988. Tree pruning & staking. *ALA,* 9(9):24–26.

Doughty, S. C. 1990. Pruning properly. *American Nurseryman,* 172(1):103–119.

Evans, P. S. and J. E. Klett. 1984. The effects of dormant pruning treatments on leaf, shoot and root production from bare-root *Malus sargentii. Journal of Arboriculture,* 10:298–302.

Feucht, J. and J. Butler. 1988. *Landscape Management,.* Van Nostrand Reinhold Co., NY.

Fizzell, J. 1984. How to increase your skill at pruning. *Landscape Contractor,* 25(10):8–9.

Flemmer, W., III. 1989. Correcting pruning mistakes. *Grounds Maintenance,* 24(6):10–17.

Gadd, D. 1989. Effective management of tree pruning. *Golf Course Management,* 57:28–34, 38.

Gilman E. F. and R. J. Black. 1990. *Pruning Landscape Trees and Shrubs.* Florida Cooperative Extension Circular 853. University of Florida, Gainesville, FL.

Hagan, B. W. 1994 Tree pruning: Refreshing vital techniques. *Arbor Age,* 14(1):10–12.

Harris, R. 1992. *Arboriculture.* 2nd edition. Prentice-Hall, Englewood Cliffs, NJ.

Harris, R. W. 1994. Clarifying certain pruning terminology: thinning, heading, pollarding. *Journal of Arboriculture,* 20(1):50–54.

Hensley, D., R. McNiel, and M. Hotze. 1979. *Pruning Landscape Trees.* Cooperative Extension Service Publication, University of Kentucky, Lexington, KY.

Hendricksen, J. (Committee Chair) 1988. *American National Standard for Tree Care Operations.* American National Standards Institute, Inc., New York, NY.

Iles, J. 1989. The case against tree topping. *Grounds Maintenance,* 24(6):51, 74.

Kemmerer, H. 1979. Pruning programs require accurate schedule, management. *Weeds, Trees, and Turf,* 18(12):35–36.

Kemmerer, H. 1983. Pruning for design. *Grounds Maintenance,* 18(4):64, 68.

Klett, J., P. Evans, M. Pratt, and M. Schnelle. 1989. Routine pruning may not be warranted. *American Nurseryman,* 169(3):99–101.

Lanphear, W. P. (Committee Chair) 1979. *Pruning Standards for Shade Trees*. National Arborist Association, Wantagh, NY.

Martin, J. M. and T. D. Sydnor. 1987. Difference in wound closure rates in 12 tree species. *HortScience,* 22:442–444.

Mercer, P. C. 1983. Callus growth and the effect of wound dressings. *Annals of applied Biology,* 103:527–540.

McNiel, R. E. and D. L. Hensley. 1980. Determining the damage from tree wounds and decay. *American Nurseryman,* 151(11):15, 104–112.

Neely, D. 1979. Tree wounds and wound closure. *Journal of Arboriculture,* 5:135–140.

Neely, D. 1989. Tree wounds and how they heal. *Grounds Maintenance,* 24(11):40, 42, 46.

Ossenbruggen, S. 1985. A properly placed cut crucial to healthy pruning. *American Nurseryman,* 161(6):132–136.

Ossenbruggen, S. 1985. Tree wounds: to paint or not to paint? *Grounds Maintenance,* 20(6):46, 50, 52.

Phillips, R. 1993. Hand tools. *Arbor Age,* 13(7):9.

Santamour, F. S., Jr. 1986. Wound compartmentalization in tree cultivars: Addendum. *Journal of Arboriculture,* 12(9):227–232.

Shigo, A. 1982. Tree health. *Journal of Arboriculture,* 8:311–316.

Shigo, A. 1986. *A New Tree Biology*. Shigo and Trees, Associate. Durham, NH.

Shigo, A. 1989. *Tree Pruning. A Worldwide Photo Guide*. Shigo and Trees, Associate. Durham, NH.

Shigo, A. 1991. *Modern Arboriculture*. Shigo and Trees, Associate. Durham, NH.

Shigo, A. and H. Marx. 1977. *Compartmentalization of Decay in Trees*. USDA Forest Service Bulletin 405.

Shigo, A. and W. Shortle. 1983. Wound dressings: results of studies over 13 years. *Journal of Arboriculture,* 9:317–329.

Stamen, T. and J. Chambers. 1990. A hard look at future tree pruning standards. *Arbor Age,* 10(1):42–44.

Troy, T. 1991. Tree pruning: start young to avoid problems later. *Lawn & Landscape Maintenance,* 12(4):42–44.

Trusty, S. and S. Trusty. 1992. Pruning with a purpose. *Lawn & Landscape Maintenance,* 13(2):60–63.

Vidic, T. 1992. Tree pruning essentials. *Lawn & Landscape Maintenance,* 13(12):50–54.

Chapter 9
Water Management

Water is the most important environmental factor in establishing plants. Water is the most frequently limiting factor to growth encountered in landscape management. In the majority of the nation, especially the arid and semi-arid regions, irrigation is a constant need and a major responsibility of the landscape manager. Even in the more humid, high rainfall areas of the country, supplemental irrigation is necessary for quality landscapes.

The availability of water or ability to irrigate a landscape sets the pace for the rest of the management and determines the quality of the landscape. The full utilization

Photo 9–1. Water determines the quality of the landscape and sets the pace for landscape management.

of the fertilizer applied cannot be achieved if water is limiting. Likewise, rain and irrigation determine the number and frequency of mowings. It is impossible to maintain quality turf, sensitive ornamentals, seasonal color, or newly planted landscapes in most areas of the country without supplemental irrigation.

Irrigation programs

Irrigation programs must account for the equipment available, climate, and soil conditions, plant needs, and sometimes other considerations, such as water rationing.

Soil factors

The *soil* is the reservoir of water for landscape plants. The soil water reserve is regulated by soil texture and structure, compaction, moisture supply, and soil depth. Irrigation must be applied slowly or in short cycles to clay soils or compacted sites to prevent run-off. Water can be applied more rapidly to coarse textured soils.

Water infiltration and run-off are affected by the topography and the cover of the site. Steep slopes result in rapid run-off and reduced infiltration. Irrigation schedules must be shortened and more frequent to compensate. Soil covered with turfgrass or a mulch increases water infiltration into the soil and reduces run-off.

Plant factors

Water is lost from *plants* by transpiration. Transpiration moves nutrients and other material from the root to the leaves and cools the plant. Plant available water is also lost through evaporation from the soil. These combined losses are termed *evapotranspiration* or *ET*. Evapotranspiration rate is determined by light, relative humidity, temperature, wind, and season.

Water loss is also influenced by plant type, size, and population. *Large plants* lose more water than smaller plants or turfgrass, depending on their shape and sun exposure. A single plant uses more water than a plant in a grouping because of greater exposure to sun and wind. Plants in a mass, however, provide more competition for the available moisture. Plants vary in size, shape, and extent of the root system, the water reservoir potential of the plant, and leaf and branch arrangement and size.

Determining When and How Much to Irrigate

Specific irrigation recommendations are difficult to make because of plant and soil factors, but also because of differences in equipment, expertise, and philosophy. The *objective* of any irrigation program is to balance plant performance and water use. Apply water to supplement rainfall in such a way to avoid run-off and insure wetting of the upper six to ten inches of the root zone. This may require one to two inches of water per week applied in one or more applications.

Manager experience

Most irrigation regimes are determined by the experience and expertise of the manager. This requires experience, knowledge, and observation. Many plants present some signal when too little water is available. Wilting, especially of the new growth, is the most obvious water stress signal. In addition, shiny leaves will take on a dull appearance and some species, such as bluegrass, develop a bluish color. Other turfgrasses develop an uneven color. Wilting of impatiens is sometimes used as a signal that watering is needed. These annuals are sensitive to water stress and wilt before other plants show drought symptoms.

The moisture content of the soil can be estimated by *feel.* Take a soil sample with a probe or trowel four to six inches deep. Roll or squeeze a small sample of soil into a ball. If the soil will not mold into a ball, it is too dry to supply adequate water to the plants. If the ball formed will not crumble when rubbed with the thumb, the soil is too wet. If the soil can be molded into a ball that crumbles when rubbed, the moisture content is about right for plants. This highly unscientific method is influenced by soil texture; sandy soils will crumble even when wet.

Photo 9-2. The dial of a tensiometer calibrated from 0 to 100 centibars.

146

Tensiometers

Tensiometers, properly installed, provide accurate readings of plant available soil moisture. A *tensiometer* is a tube filled with water with a hollow ceramic tip at one end. A gauge for measuring vacuum is attached to the other end. As moisture in the soil decreases, water moves out of the clay tip, creating a partial vacuum inside the tube. The tension is measured by the gauge.

Readings are calibrated in gradations from 0 to 100 *centibars* (cb; 100 centibars = 1 bar = 1 atmosphere). Tensiometers provide an accurate picture of soil moisture status within this range. The permanent wilting point of some plants is 1,500 cb (15 bars), but this varies with species. Drought tolerant

Table 9–1. Soil-moisture relationship to measured soil moisture tensions.

Soil Water Condition	Centibars (cb)
Saturated	0
Limited Soil Air	0–10
Field Capacity	30
Reduced Water Availability	80–90
Permanent Wilting Point	1,500

species typically have higher permanent wilting points. Many plants undergo water stress when soil-water tension exceeds 30 to 40 cb. Up to 90 percent of available water is held between 30 cb (field capacity) and 80 cb. A reading of 0 indicates saturated soil. Available air is limited at less than 10 cb.

Using two tensiometers at different depths gives an indication of the moisture level between these points. The depth of each tensiometer depends on the primary plant of interest. For grass, the primary absorbing root zone is in the upper six inches of the soil. For trees and shrubs, the water status of the upper 6 to 18 inches of soil is important.

Turfgrass managers routinely use tensiometers to schedule irrigation with improved plant growth and water use efficiency. Tensiometer readings are measured to determine the point where plant stress to the turf is first observed. Irrigation is then commenced at some point before this benchmark.

Tensiometers with electric contacts are used with irrigation controls. In this way the irrigation system is automated based upon predetermined soil moisture levels.

Tensiometers, however, are not free of problems or maintenance. Clay cups are fragile and can become clogged. Tensiometers are limited to shallow depths and are expensive. They have a limited operating range and can not measure moisture tensions greater than one bar. They are subject to vandalism unless they are buried. Tensiometers must be removed during freezing weather.

Photo 9–3. Correlating irrigation and tensiometer readings of soil moisture saves water.

Table 9–2. Some firms offering soil moisture sensing equipment for grounds managers.

Automata, Inc.
Grass Valley, CA 95945

Buckner, Inc.
Fresno, CA 93722

Irrometer Co., Inc.
Riverside, CA 92516

Lang Penetrometer
Gulf Shores, AL 36542

LESCO, Inc.
Rocky River, OH 44116

National Research and Chemical
NACCO/Grow More
Gardena, CA 90248-2140

Rain Bird Sprinkler, Mfg.
Glendora, CA 91740

Soilmoisture Equipment Corp.
Santa Barbara, CA 93105

Soiltest, Inc.
Lake Bluff, IL 60044

Spectrum Technologies, Inc.
Plainfield, IL 60544

Systematic Irrigation Controls, Inc.
Costa Mesa, CA 92626

Electrical Resistance Meters

Soil moisture can be measured as the *electrical resistance* between electrodes embedded in fiberglass, nylon, or gypsum blocks. Blocks can be buried at various depths in the soil. Soil moisture readings are made with a calibrated resistance meter. Resistance measurements for soil moisture are most accurate between 100 and 1,500 cb, but are not as sensitive as a tensiometer to tensions less than 100 cb. The majority of plant available moisture, as discussed earlier, occurs between 30 and 80 cb. Therefore, electrical resistance devices have limited adaptation to turfgrass and landscape

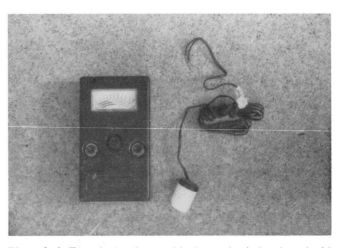

Photo 9–4. Electrical resistance blocks are buried and read with a resistance meter. This equipment is not sufficiently accurate at less than 100 centibars.

148

irrigation determination. Models more sensitive to plant active water tensions (< 100 cb) are on the horizon.

Water Budgets

Irrigation can be planned and scheduled, or "*budgeted*" if the water-holding capacity of the soil is known and evapotranspiration (ET) reports are available. The amount of water lost daily through ET is reported in many regions. *ET rates* are adjusted for different landscape compositions and microclimatic differences. In theory, the specific amount of water lost can be replaced at appropriate intervals. Replacing only the water lost daily provides maximum conservation of water. Irrigation using ET rates requires reasonable records but is used by golf courses and other turfgrass intensive sites.

Developing irrigation programs for landscape plants using water budgets is more complex. Landscapes offer a great deal more diversity of species within a single-value irrigation zone. Planting densities affect irrigation requirements and vary in sections of a landscape. There are also complex combinations of canopy coverage beneath trees and shrubs in a developed landscape. There has been a great deal of research, especially in California, to determine the water use coefficients of landscape plants and plant combinations. The K_L method [University of California Cooperative Extension Leaflet 21493] considers environmental factors, species differences, and plant densities to estimate the amount of water a given landscape needs to maintain acceptable quality. This water budget model can be used to estimate water for new and existing landscape projects. Mathematical models require adjustment and refinement to compensate for local conditions. Models will become more accurate and use will increase as additional knowledge is gained about plant water use.

Measuring Foliage Temperature

Exposed leaves of plants with sufficient soil moisture have temperatures equal to or slightly below air temperature. As soil moisture becomes limiting, transpiration, and thus evaporative cooling, is reduced and leaf temperatures increase. Landscape plants in dry soil have leaf temperatures from 10 to 25° F above ambient temperatures.

Using infrared sensing instruments, the *temperature* of exposed and unexposed leaves can be measured and compared to the air temperature. These instruments resemble a police radar gun and are pointed at the object in question.

At present, this technique is in the research and development stage. Research in turfgrass management, however, indicated that irrigation frequency was reduced when irrigation was based on leaf temperatures, compared to irrigation on queue from a tensiometer. In a few years, evaluating surface temperature may provide an efficient method of determining irrigation needs and plant stress. Infrared temperature instruments presently cost several thousand dollars.

IRRIGATION METHODS

Basin Irrigation

Water can be applied to basins constructed around individual plants, beds, or entire landscapes, by fixed bubblers, hoses, or tanks. The area must be reasonably flat. Infiltration characteristics of the soil must be such that the water moves into the root zone before it evaporates. Basin irrigation is used for newly planted trees in many places, and entire landscapes in the Southwest. Mulches reduce evaporation between waterings.

Sprinkler Irrigation

Sprinklers are the most common method of applying water to landscape turfgrass and plantings. The uniformity and effectiveness of the system depend upon its design and installation. Irrigation system design

Photo 9–5. Basin irrigation for a street tree planting.

must accommodate varying water pressures, wind conditions, and topography. Application rates are determined by soil type, infiltration rates, and soil covering. Proper design, installation, and maintenance determine the utility of the system and the quality of the landscape. Design and installation professions are licensed or certified in many states and for good reason.

When designing and operating an irrigation system for turfgrass, take special care so that woody and herbaceous ornamentals will not be over-watered. Turfgrass will probably be irrigated more frequently than ornamentals. Woody and herbaceous beds should be zoned for separate control. The plant beds should be constructed so water from the turf area does not drain into them.

Some landscape supervisors prefer to control the rate and frequency of water application manually. Automated systems that water for set periods on given days are particularly useful where site or soil conditions limit infiltration or on contract properties. Automated systems can be further sophisticated by adding *rain sensors* that prevent operation or turn the system off in the event of rain. Other refinements include the addition of *freeze sensors* that prevent operation when the outside temperature is below a set point (e.g., 45° F.).

Irrigation can be initiated by tensiometers, as discussed earlier. Using tensiometers increases moisture conservation and makes the system more responsive to soil moisture levels. A new control system [The Toro Company] takes advantage of rainfall by irrigating turf only when needed. Instead of

Photo 9–6. Sprinkler is the common type of irrigation for managed landscapes.

telling the system when to start, the ceramic soil moisture sensor and controller tell the system when to stop. This control system has shown cost savings in recent tests and may become popular. Computer controlled systems are also available and should improve in the future.

The landscape manager or contractor must *control the irrigation scheduling.* The quality and pace of other landscape operations, such as mowing, are in large part established by the irrigation schedule.

Drip or Trickle Systems

Drip or *trickle irrigation* has become a popular and practical addition to landscape sites, especially in areas where water conservation is paramount. Drip irrigation applies water slowly for long periods to only a portion of the root zone. Drip irrigation operates at very low pressures, (10 to 50 pounds per square inch (psi)). It allows for precise, controlled applications of water that save water and labor, and produce quality plant growth.

Several different delivery systems are available. *Drip tapes* are thin-walled polyethylene, or similar material, hoses with periodic holes (every 12 inches more or less) for water to drip or ooze out. Drip tapes are primarily used in vegetable production but have application in annual and perennial flowers or groundcovers beds. The tapes are more applicable to trees and shrubs in nursery rows than to landscape plantings.

Line source systems disperse water all along its length. Soaker hoses are line source systems. Drip irrigated groundcovers often use line-source irrigation products.

Photo 9-7. Drip irrigation emitter.

Most commonly, landscape drip irrigation systems deliver water via *emitters* inserted in the lateral or on the end of small plastic tubes. Emitters can be selected to apply water at rates as low as 0.5 gallons per hour (gph) and up to two or more gph. The number of emitters that serve an individual plant can be adjusted as its water needs increase with the season and growth.

Drip irrigation requires a good filtration system to reduce maintenance and ensure proper operation. Pressure regulating valves or pressure compensating emitters will be necessary. The drip system can be automated with timers, tensiometers, and other moisture sensors. Drip can be added as part of an overall site irrigation plan. Design and installation information for trickle irrigation are widely available from manufacturers and other sources.

Drip systems dramatically increase water conservation and supply the plant a more constant moisture level compared to

Photo 9-8. Drip irrigation ring.

151

overhead systems. The cost is less and drip systems offer flexibility. A Northern California landscape architect estimated sprinkler systems installation at $.90 to $1.25 per square foot (1990 dollars). Installation cost for drip system was estimated to be $.60 to $.75 per square foot.

Laterals and emitters can be added or removed as necessary. Laterals and main lines can be buried and concealed, and emitters can be buried if necessary for aesthetics. Operation of the system is more difficult to monitor if the emitter discharge is underground. Above ground systems are subject to vandalism, fire, and chewing by animals.

The most common problem for drip irrigation is plugging of lines or emitters by soil particles, water deposits, bacterial slimes, and algae. Drip systems are more difficult to monitor since there is no spray; each emitter much be checked individually. Self-cleaning emitters are available but more expensive. These emitters require less maintenance, but are not fool-proof.

Clogging by mineral deposits from the water or algae can be compensated for by acid and chlorine injection. Cleaning emitters and periodically flushing the system are simpler and less expensive solutions, according to some managers. Other common mistakes with drip irrigation include failure to install adequate numbers of emitters per plant or locating them too close to tree trunks.

Drip systems are sometimes considered temporary irrigation systems, except in confined areas. However, the plant's water needs need not eventually outgrow the potential supply with good planning and provisions for expansion. Emitters should be added or changed to a higher discharge volume as plants grow and their needs increase. Research has indicated that 50 to 65 percent of the plant's root system needs to be wetted to supply adequate moisture.

Mini-sprinklers

Mini- or *micro-sprinklers* are relatively new entries into the irrigation market. Water is applied slowly and uniformly to the root zone as with drip irrigation. The wetted zone, however, is expanded by the sprinklers to a more practical range for landscape applications. The wetting diameter ranges from six inches to 25 feet. Discharge rates vary from four to 40 gph. The shape of the zone can be circular, angular, or rectangular. The heads are placed on plastic risers of varying length and connected to the lateral by small diameter tubes. Sprinklers, nozzles, or emitters can be mixed or changed and also moved to meet changing water requirements.

Photo 9-9. Mini-sprinklers combine the best of sprinkler (wider coverage) and drip irrigation (water conservation) technology.

These small sprinklers have utility for bedding plants, trees, shrubs, and groundcovers. Mini-sprinklers are not acceptable for use in turfgrass. They work well near pedestrian ways, in median strips, and in other locations where over-spray and run-off are undesirable.

Sub-surface Irrigation

There is considerable interest in the use of porous rubber pipes buried four to six inches underground to irrigate lawns and landscapes. *Subsurface irrigation* of ornamentals or vegetables is by no means new. Articles in trade and popular press have appeared for the past 15 or 20 years. Distribution of an underground irrigation supply is severely limited by soil texture, structure, compaction, and saline content. There are many problems with water quality, efficacy, and longevity of the sub-surface systems.

Research is underway on another new generation of subsurface irrigation techniques and products. The long-term effects of sub-surface drip irrigation are not yet known. Hopefully problems can be solved and a true, no-waste irrigation system may be on the horizon.

General Irrigation Recommendations

Sprinklers are best used early in the morning. Water pressure is greater, there is minimal wind, operation will not interfere with other site activities, and the foliage dries quickly. Evaporation in hot, windy areas is reduced.

If the landscape is irrigated with *movable sprinklers,* variations in the distribution pattern will be minimized if settings are made so they are equal to the radius covered by the sprinkler. This produces an overlapping pattern similar to that used in in-ground systems.

Design or amend the irrigation system to reflect the exposure and microclimate of

Photo 9–10. Hand watering is expensive but sometimes required to supplement irrigation in new intensive planting.

the plants (north versus south sites, sunny versus shady locations, and wind). This may mean entirely different irrigation equipment in some sections of the landscape and many more separate controls.

Schedule regular inspections of the system. Overhead systems should be checked weekly, preferably right after mowing. Inspect and clean filters frequently, especially if the system uses non-city water. Flush drip lines twice per year. Inspections and repairs will be discussed in detail later.

Apply enough water to soak the soil to a depth of six inches or more but do not over-water. Apply irrigation at a rate to minimize run-off.

Newly planted material must be watered more frequently because of its smaller root zone. Newly planted container-grown plants require frequent monitoring and irrigation. The sole source of water for container-grown plants is limited to the container soil until new roots grow into the surrounding soil.

When scheduling irrigation for mixed plantings, water to meet the needs of the least tolerant species. Monitor the soil water supply and irrigate based upon actual need. This will require use of tensiometers or other sensors.

Table 9-3. Water Quality

The *quality* of irrigation water applied to landscape plants and turfgrass is extremely important. New landscapes are often forced to irrigate with lower quality water. In some areas landscapes and turf must use brackish or brackish/standard water mixtures.

Irrigation water containing moderate to high levels of soluble salts may initiate a soil salinity problem or worsen an existing problem. The quality of foliage of many plants is damaged by moderately salty water.

Salts in water can be inexpensively and accurately measured with a *solubridge*. This instrument gives a measure of conductivity of a current passed through a solution. The unit of measurement are in *millimhos* (mmhos) or *millisiemen per square cm* (mS/cm). The value of the two units of measurement is identical; only the name has changed. To covert mS/cm or mmhos to ppm, multiply by 700.

Solubridge readings for classifying quality of irrigation water.

mS/cm	Salinity level	Irrigation value
<0.25	Low	Excellent quality for irrigation on most soils.
0.25 to 0.75	Moderate	Satisfactory for irrigation.
0.75 to 2.25	High	Avoid on poorly drained soils. Salt tolerant plants recommended.
>2.26	Very high	Not recommended for irrigation. Only a few salt-tolerant species can be grown using this water.

Table 9-4.

Normally, soluble salts are the greatest concern for irrigation water for landscape use. In some instances, however, landscape managers must also be concerned with concentrations of other elements. This concern is greatest when the landscape is regularly irrigated with "*gray water*," industrial water, water from drainage ponds, or any questionable sources. The following are acceptable levels determined by Ohio State University for irrigation water.

Desirable ranges for specific elements in irrigation water.

Element	Level (ppm)
Aluminum (Al)	0–5.0
Ammonium (NH$_4$)	undetermined
Boron (b)	0.2–0.8
Calcium (CA)	40.0–120.0
Chloride (Cl)	0–140.0
Copper (Cu)	0–0.2
Fluoride (Fl)	0–1.0
Iron (Fe)	2.0–5.0
Manganese (Mn)	0.5–2.0
Magnesium (Mg)	6.0–24.0
Molybdenum (Mo)	0–0.2
Nitrate (NO$_3$)	0–5.0
Phosphorous (P)	.005–5.0
Potassium (K)	0.5–10.0
Sulfates (SO$_4$)	0–414.0
Zinc (Zn)	1.0–5.0

Irrigation System Maintenance

Irrigation maintenance and installation are two of the fastest growing services for the landscape industry. Most full-service landscape management contractors offer irrigation system checks and repair. Irrigation can also add a new dimension to the company. Quality service is an excellent way to obtain consideration for later installation contracts by the same client or general contractor.

Irrigation service is usually billed as a *fixed-fee* for checks and evaluations. Irrigation checks or monitoring may be conducted weekly, bi-weekly, or monthly, depending on the client, and the budget. The frequency of inspections and the amount of service depends on the age of the system, how well it was designed and installed, its level use, and traffic.

Photo 9-11. Portable irrigation systems increase water efficiency where automated or underground systems are unavailable. Traveling irrigation systems are very effective for large turf sites and athletic fields.

Irrigation repair is usually billed *per hour*. If the contractor uses a production rate estimating system, then irrigation labor is billed at a higher rate than general labor. The higher rate is because of the expertise required by irrigation technicians and cost of inventory and equipment necessary. Irrigation technicians require licensing or certification in some areas.

Irrigation maintenance and service require knowledge of irrigation equipment, installation, and trouble shooting. An inventory of irrigation products and parts is necessary. Special equipment includes a voltage meter, wire tracer, and a small manual pump. Trenchers can be rented or leased. Licenses and permits may also be required. Licensed electricians are sometimes required to install or repair low voltage controller wiring.

Most distributors conduct seminars on basic irrigation design, installation, marketing, and service. Videos are available for training or refresher programs. Irrigation distributors are a valuable source of information and knowledge.

Irrigation System Evaluation

The most common maintenance procedure is what is termed a "*check*" or "*walk-through*" while the system is operating. Set the controller to a minimum time (two, three, or five minutes) per zone so that the system can be checked efficiently. Some

Photo 9-12. Irrigation management adjusts timing to reflect the season, weather conditions, changes in plant growth, and soil factor.

155

systems have remote control devices that advance the controller and speed the procedure. Check drip irrigation emitters to make sure they are not plugged; the filter should also be checked and cleaned as necessary.

Irrigation servicing adjusts irrigation programs and station times as necessary. All regions of the country operate with a spring, summer, and fall schedule reflecting plant water requirements. The number of days of operation and run times increase as water needs increase during the summer. Winter irrigation is done in the deep South, Southwest, California, and Hawaii.

Schedule "walk-throughs" to follow mowings to catch any damage from the machinery. Commercial irrigation systems should be checked at least every other week. Since commercial sites are usually irrigated at night, problems may go unnoticed. Residential systems require the least maintenance from the contractor's point of view. Problems are usually spotted and reported by the client. Systems using marginal water quality or frequent problems require more frequent cleaning.

Winterization

In the northern states (usually USDA zone 7 and north) irrigation systems are *"winterized"* annually. More southerly areas, USDA zones 8 and 9 (minimum temperatures 10 to 30° F) require freeze sensors and draining pumps and all above-ground components. Zone 10 and warmer do not require winterizing. They will be adapted to a winter watering schedule.

The water in the system is evacuated with pressure for full winterization. Tow-behind air compressors can be rented in most localities. Adequate air volume and proper air pressure are important. The recommended minimum air compressor

Photo 9-13. Blowing out an irrigation system in the fall. Photograph by James Robbins.

volume is 60 cubic feet per minute (cfm). It requires a lot of air to push out a large column of water. Undersize compressors will not provide enough air to completely blow out a large system. Blow the system out with 60 to 80 psi; higher pressures can damage the piping and equipment.

Shut off the irrigation supply valve before blowing the system. Always have one zone *on* while the compressor is operating. Air is compressible and can build up pressures sufficient to cause many problems if not handled correctly. Begin with the most distant zone and flush each zone twice.

In addition to blowing out the system, shut off and unplug the controller and remove the battery. If the controller is located outside or installed in a moist area, it may be advisable to leave the controller plugged-in. The heat generated by the transformer helps keep the cabinet dry. Set all watering times to zero. Remove or inactivate any sensors.

The average residential system will require 30 to 45 minutes to winterize. Large commercial systems may require an entire day or longer.

156

Spring Start Up

Part of irrigation servicing is turning the irrigation system on every spring. The water supply is turned on and the controller activated. Walk through the system to check for damage to heads during the winter. The system should be re-checked after any major repairs.

Re-set all sprinklers and valve boxes to the proper grade. Check the controller, batteries and fuses, reset contacts, and clean the controller box. Check the backflow preventer connections and make sure rainouts and other sensors are operating.

Water Conservation

Conservation of water by the green industry cannot wait. Water use, supplies, and quality have become critical throughout the nation. There is a flurry of interest in any product that promises any assistance in conserving water. Western states have become leaders in realistic water conservation. The rest of the nation must learn from their efforts to conserve this limited, precious, and increasingly expensive resource.

General techniques to conserve water

When watering, water well and infrequently. Try to fill the entire root zone profile, whether the target is turfgrass or trees, but do not overwater. Light frequent waterings encourage shallow rooting and greater water stress later.

One school of thought suggests mowing as low as the particular turf will handle. This supposedly reduces the transpiring leaf surface. Another school points out that low mowing of turf encourages shallow rooting. They suggest raising the mowing height for cool-season grasses during the summer. Higher mowing heights increase rooting depth and water reserve. The taller grass blades shade the soil and reduce evaporation.

Zone irrigation systems according to sun, shade, turf, and plant areas. Though more costly, the practice allows separate control of watering and increased efficiency. Use automatic irrigation controllers with sensors that shut off during natural rain. Water between midnight and 8:00 am when water loss through evaporation is lowest.

Xeriscapes

Nowhere is the emphasis on water conservation as critical as it is in the West and the Southwest. Mandatory conservation programs are often controversial, hard to implement, and often rejected by the public. Out of this concern the *XERISCAPE* concept was initiated by the Denver Water Department in 1981. Xeriscape™ is a coined and trademarked word combining the Latin *xeri-*, for dry and *scape* from landscape. Xeriscape has come to represent a positive, creative approach for water conservation without the sacrifice of beauty.

Xeriscape concepts include and build upon: *Education* of the public in water-conserving measures; *Demonstration* of water conservation landscape principles; and *Cooperation* between industry, citizens, and government. Xeriscape programs are currently promoted in Arizona, California, Colorado, Florida, Georgia, Hawaii, Kansas, Oklahoma, and Texas. Training programs have been directed to the public and green industry professionals. Several botanic gardens and municipalities have initiated demonstration projects. These numbers will grow as the concept gains attention, legitimacy supported by research, and acceptance from landscape designers, architects, nurserymen, and landscape managers.

Photo 9–14. The Xeriscape™ garden at the Denver Water Department.

The basic premise behind the concept is to save water. Figures from water departments and suppliers indicate that nearly 50 percent of residential water is used for the landscape. Water savings between 30 and 60 percent can be achieved by implementing Xeriscape elements. Water savings are achieved without sacrifice of aesthetic values of the landscape. The landscape does not consist of a sea of gravel more suitably known as "zero-scape."

The Xeriscape program has not developed any new or novel approaches to water conservation. Many current landscape norms in semi-arid regions were adapted. Most Xeriscape concepts are solid, age-old horticultural principles that, when combined, provide maximum water savings. The real solution requires much more than just a plant list; Xeriscape has provided a positive forum for change.

Xeriscape is based upon seven elements or water conservation guidelines: 1) follow good design principles; 2) appropriate use of turf; 3) efficient irrigation; 4) soil improvements; 5) mulches; 6) lower water-demand plants; and 7) appropriate maintenance.

Photo 9–15. Water conservation landscapes demonstrating low water use plants and irrigation technology are becoming popular additions to botanic gardens, arboretums, and for water departments. This garden on Oahu, Hawaii is provided by the Board of Water Supply.

Low Water-Demand Plants

Research has identified several low water-use plants [*HortScience,* 19:856]. Appendix 5 lists several *low-water requiring species* or "Xeriscape" plants for temperate areas developed from several sources. This list and others serve only as a broad basis for plant selection.

Few trees and shrubs have actually been *quantitatively* assessed for water-use rates. Many low-water-use plant lists have assumed that plants capable of surviving in arid regions are low water users. The physiological mechanisms by which plants control water-use rates and resist drought vary considerably among and within species. Individual selection must consider site specific conditions, the intent of the design, and aesthetics. Future research will further quantify water use rates by plants under landscape conditions.

Unique tags to bring low water use plants to the consumer's attention have resulted from combined efforts between garden centers, the National Xeriscape Council, and other marketing organizations. The number of drought tolerant species available for landscape use is increasing as they gain popularity and acceptance.

Proper Design and Planning

Planning is the most important step in creative water conservation. The planning process is no different from that of conventional landscapes. Designers consider the activity and desires of the owner, the site, and use design principles to develop a final concept. Special note is made of microclimates and design takes advantage of these features. The time and capital expenditures for installation and maintenance are thoroughly considered and reflected in the final plan.

Mixing plants of different water needs is the most water inefficient way to design any landscape. Too many people, including landscape professionals, feel that if they use low-water demand plants among other ornamentals in the landscape, then they will reduce the need to irrigate. (Wouldn't it be nice?) Ideally, the landscape bed should be irrigated to meet the needs of the least drought tolerant species included in the composition. If mixed with conventional water-use plants, there is no savings realized from drought-resistant species. They may even suffer from over-watering.

The key to water conservation is *hydrozoning*. Hydrozoning groups plants according to their water needs or irrigation scheduling preferences. The plants can be irrigated effectively and efficiently.

Table 9–5. Examples of hydrozones or water zones for water conserving landscapes
Designers and managers in Denver work with three defined *water zones* or *hydrozones* to develop water conserving landscapes. The following zones are the amounts of water, in inches of water, required for a sandy loam soil in midsummer during a rainless period.
High-water use zone: Area uses 18 to 20 gallons of water per square foot for a 20-week growing season. Without rainfall, apply 0.5-inch of water three times per week.
Moderate-water use zone: Area uses approximately 10 gallons of water per square foot through a 20-week growing season. Without rainfall, the plants require 0.75-inch of water once a week.
Low-water use zone: Area uses 3 gallons or less water per square foot during a 20-week growing season. Without rainfall, irrigate with 0.5-inch of water every other week.

A water-efficient landscape does not require that *all* plants be drought tolerant. High-water use plants can be efficiently used in a water conserving landscape if they are grouped together and managed appropriately. Use higher water use plants in high visibility, high impact, or critical areas where the increased consumption of water is justified.

Medium-use plants should likewise be grouped together so they may be irrigated efficiently. Low-water use plants can be used in appropriate areas. Low-water use plants may be effective as screens and barriers and in lower-management areas. Many drought tolerant plants offer outstanding aesthetic attributes and warrant use as specimens or accents. Group low water-use species together so that irrigation can be reduced drastically.

Reduced Turf

The major portion of the water used to support a traditional landscape went to support the *turf,* according to Xeriscape literature. The recommendation to eliminate or limit turf to conserve water has sparked some controversy. Some municipalities have restricted use of turf and encouraged specific turfgrasses in new landscapes. Many woody plants, however, actually use more water than turfgrasses. I am sure that more will be written on this subject as legislation, lobbyists, and water shortages become more numerous.

Turfgrass has a definite and important place in commercial and residential landscapes. Base selection and management of grass on sound scientific and design strategies. Locate grass where it provides functional benefits. Turfgrass is used for recreation and entertainment. In some areas, however, turf serves no function and little purpose, except to be maintained. In these instances, grass could be replaced with less water demanding materials such as groundcovers, low water-use plants, mulches, or hard surfaces.

Select appropriate low water use turfgrasses for moderate- and low-irrigation landscapes. Studies have quantified the water use rates of most turfgrasses. There are significant differences in water use rates between turf species. Bermudagrass possesses significantly more drought tolerance than bluegrass, for instance. There are also wide differences on drought tolerance and resistance among commercially available cultivars within a grass species. Consult the local Cooperative Extension Service for regionally specific recommendations.

The lawn must be zoned separately from landscape plantings so that both can be irrigated individually and efficiently.

Efficient Irrigation

If *irrigation* is to be installed, design water saving measures into the system. Design the system to accommodate the microclimates. Northern and eastern exposures require less water, while slopes should be irrigated more slowly to reduce run-off. Drip irrigation aids water conservation in shrub and tree plantings, but it is not cure-all for conserving water.

Photo 9-16. A poorly designed irrigation system. Heads on standards in turf prevent effective mowing and irrigation.

Proper management of the irrigation system reduces water use from 10 to 25 percent. Monitor and irrigate different water-use zones of the landscape independently. Zone high demand areas and other plantings separately from low water demand areas. Check irrigation systems to eliminate leakage from damaged heads, excessive overlap, overthrow onto hard surfaces, and clogged emitters.

Do not water areas according to a rigid schedule or time clock. Water according to needs of the individual plant zones. Monitoring the water needs of the plants and irrigating manually, or on the basis of soil moisture measuring devices, saves a great deal of water. Deep infrequent waterings encourage deep roots and drought tolerance.

Soil Improvement

Soil improvement before planting improves water infiltration and retention. The exact nature of amendments, if necessary, depend on the site. Soil structure and aggregation are the key to proper soil water relations.

Mulches

Mulches reduce water loss by reducing evaporation. In addition, mulches reduce weed competition, slow erosion, and regulate soil temperatures. Mulches are also aesthetically pleasing. Mulch material may be either organic (bark and wood chips) or non-organic (rocks and gravel). Either type of mulch should be applied to a depth of three to four inches. Organic mulches improve soil structure over time, but will require periodic replenishment as they decompose. Inorganic mulches do not decompose, but will require periodic raking and refreshing.

Photo 9–17. Rain sensors shut off the irrigation system during precipitation. They can save calls from the client. Rain sensors are required by law on irrigation systems in some cities.

Photo 9–18. Mulches conserve water and improve irrigation efficiency.

However, excessive layers (over 6 inches) of organic mulch placed or building-up on a bed may result in anaerobic decomposition of the material. The products of anaerobic respiration are alcohols and aldehydes; both are harmful to plant roots. The greatest problem occurs when too much mulch is applied to soggy sites, or where there is an overabundance of irrigation. The problem is alleviated with careful management.

Appropriate Maintenance

Correct management techniques and timing are important to maintain the water conservation features of a landscape. Proper fertilization, pest control, pruning, and irrigation system maintenance enhance water conservation. A well-designed water-conserving landscape consisting of well-adapted plants can reduce maintenance by up to 50 percent.

Other management factors must reflect the water conservation mode of the landscape. Reduce nitrogen rates of turf and woody plants. High fertilization rates result in excessive turf and woody plant growth that cannot be supported by the water budget. Mow at a somewhat higher setting. Be diligent in mulching beds and controlling weeds.

Antitranspirants

Antitranspirants or antidesiccants are chemicals that reduce transpiration. Although antitranspirants are most useful at transplanting, they have been used to reduce water requirements and plant loss during drought. Antitranspirants have also been applied to reduce irrigation in semi-arid areas, protect from aerial salt damage, and to protect conifers from winter burn with varying success. They have been around

Photo 9-19. Proper and appropriate maintenance is critical to obtain maximum water conservation benefits from every landscape. Photograph by James Robbins.

since the early 1960s. Antitranspirants may reduce transpiration by:

1. *Reflective Materials.* Application of reflective materials to a plant leaf reduces absorption of light and leaf temperatures, thereby reducing transpiration. Reflective materials are light colored or

Product	Manufacturer
Blanket, Nufilm	VAP Special Products, Inc. Fremont, NE
Cleary's Clearspray	W. A. Cleary Chemical Corp. Somerset, NJ
Cloud Cover	Easy Gardener, Inc. Waco, TX
Folicote	Aquitrols Pennsauken, NJ
Natures' Touch Leaf Coat	Natures' Touch Division Agro Chemical, Inc. Franklin Park, IL
Moistruin-4	Burkes Protective Coatings Washougal, WA
Preserve	Precision Laboratories, Inc. Northbrook, IL
Transfilm	PBI Gordon Corp. Kansas City, MO
VitaCoat	Green Pro Services Hempsted, NY
Wilt-Pruf	Wilt-Pruf Products, Inc. Essex, CT
Winter Shield	Rockland Corp. West Caldwell, NJ

Table 9-6. Some antitranspirants and antidesiccants and their manufacturers

silvery films. Although effective, the color change may not be acceptable for landscape use. Reflective coverings also reduce photosynthesis and plant growth.

2. *Film Coverings.* Film-forming wax, latex, or plastic coverings sprayed onto leaves block the stomata and thus reduce water loss. Film-forming antitranspirants are the most common types found in the green industry. They are useful as transplant aids.

3. *Physiological Means.* Research during past few years has sought chemicals that restrict the opening of the stomata without coating the leaf. Some materials identified are potentially environmentally damaging or incredibly expensive. Some day there may be abscisic acid (ABA) derivatives or other materials that reduce plant water loss during excessive stress periods without affecting growth or breaking the budget.

Film-forming antitranspirants

The effectiveness of the film-forming antidesiccants vary with species, stage of development, and atmospheric conditions. The duration of the water loss reduction varies with individual products, environmental conditions, application accuracy and coverage, and the amount of new foliage produced after application.

Films, regardless of brand, provide only limited protection. Under the best conditions, the manager can anticipate reduced transpiration from only a few days up to possibly 14 days. Cracks in the film resulting from leaf growth, movement by the wind, incomplete application, expansion of the leaf, and the environment soon result in near normal water loss rates.

Antitranspirants have been helpful in transplanting plants in full leaf. When transplanting during the off season a few days respite from water loss may be critical to the plant's success. Antidesiccants have also reduced water loss during shipping of bareroot nursery plants.

Film-forming materials are sometimes applied to conifers to reduce winter burn or drying. These materials have not shown any consistent practical protection against winter burn in several studies.

Wetting Agents

Wetting agents are surfactants that lower the tension between soil particles and water. Wetting agents enhance the ability of water to moisten solid substances; they make water wetter. They vary considerably in their effects on different soils. For general use, landscape managers should look for a non-ionic material with a high residual activity and a high concentration of active ingredients. Many different wetting agents are available in liquid or granular formulations under several trade names.

Wetting agents have enhanced water penetration through thatch and into soil. Golf courses frequently use these products to combat dry spot on greens. The net result is a more efficient, uniform use of natural or applied water. Run-off is also reduced because of increased infiltration.

Wetting agents are not cure-alls for turf, thatch, or drought problems. They are one of several practices available for use in improving water penetration and movement into hydrophobic (water repelling) soils, thatch, and localized dry spots. Wetting agents are effective in correcting these conditions for one or two weeks after application. They are too expensive for general maintenance use. The majority of soils where turfgrasses are grown are hydrophilic (wettable). The benefits of wetting agents on normal, wettable soils, have not been consistently documented by research. There are few reasons, according to some turfgrass experts, to believe any significant benefits would occur.

Water-Holding Compounds

Hydrophilic gels are known as hydrogels, moisture-holding compounds, cross-linked polymers, super-sluppers, and other jargon and tradenames. These water-holding materials absorb many times (30 to 1,500 depending on product) their weight in water and then release it as the environment becomes dry. There are three types of absorbent polymers in the trade. The first is *starch-graft copolymers*. The starch materials are rapidly decomposed by soil bacteria and fungi. Their life-span in the soil varies from a few days to a few months.

Further refinements in absorbent compounds resulted in development of synthetic *cross-linked poly-acrylamides* (polyacrylates) and *acrylamide-acrylate co-polymers.*

Table 9–7. Wetting agents for irrigation management in turfgrass and landscapes.

Company	Product
Arborchem Products Co. Fort Washington, PA	Arborchem Aquatic Surfactant
Aquatrols Cherry Hills, NJ	AquaGro
Goldschmidt Chemical Co. Hopewell, VA	Break-Thru
O. M. Scott and Son Co. Maryville, OH	Scott's Hydrozyme Wetting Agent
Grace-Sierra Milpitas, CA	Hydraflo
Kalo, Inc. Overland Park, KS	Hydor-Wet
Lesco, Inc. Rocky River, OH	Accu-Wet and Lesco Wet
Loveland Industries, Inc. Greeley, CO	L1700 and Silwet L-77
PBI/Gordon Kansas City, MO	Aqua-Zorb
Precision Labs, Inc. Northbrook, IL	Paragon
Roots, Inc. New Haven, CT	Noburn
W. A. Cleary Somerset, NJ	Super-Wet and Super Wet 15G

Synthetic polymers usually remain active for one year or more, according to manufacturers. Most of the gels presently being considered for use in agriculture are acrylamide-acrylate co-polymers.

Manufacturers suggest hydrogels may increase available water, improve media aeration, reduce compaction, improve drainage, increase plant survival and growth, enhance germination and survival rates, and provide safer athletic playing surfaces. These properties would be very advantageous in plant production and landscape management. Water-holding compounds are used for gel seeding of vegetable seeds and as packing material for shipping bareroot nursery plants.

Interest in these materials in the landscape industry has waxed and waned several times during the past 20 years since their introduction into the agronomic and horticultural markets. Unfortunately, managers seeking information about the effectiveness of hydrophilic polymers encounter conflicting "facts" from sales representatives and horticulturists alike. It is up to the manager to digest the available information and make an informed decision. These materials are expensive and present certain advantages and disadvantages.

Research on the use of hydrogels as a medium amendment in plant production, landscape, and turfgrass management has increased, but remains conflicting. The studies differ widely in products, plants, procedures, and test conditions. The quality of product performance also varies widely.

Results from any given study cannot be universally extrapolated to every plant species, material, or situation.

Incorporation of gels at manufacturer's rates does sometimes appear to be advantageous in improving plant water status for some species under limited moisture conditions. There have been several *bona fide* research projects indicating that addition of some gel products to container medium has reduced water stress and increased time to wilt. Other plants and reports, however, have shown no advantage, in fact some indicate damage from use of the materials.

Studies to determine the value of these materials as transplant aids are also variable. Dipping bareroot plants in gel solutions before planting has not been highly rewarding. There was no benefit to plant water relations from dipping plants in a hydrogel or planting them in a media other than pure sand [*HortScience*, 1986. 21:991–992.]. The gels may cause the roots to cling together, actually reducing the potential water-absorbing area for several days. No research reports, beyond testimonials, have indicated any positive effect on plant survival or growth resulting from sprinkling small quantities of hydrogels in the bottom of planting holes, adding them to the planting backfill, or from watering-in the plant with gel containing water.

Currently, there is insufficient information available to predict which plant species may be aided by use of gels. Similarly, the effect of various environmental conditions on hydrogels is just beginning to be published.

One interesting study evaluated the amount of water actually absorbed by one product [*Soil Science News and Views*, 1989. 10(7):3]. The manufacturer indicated the product could absorb 500 times its weight in water. The maximum amount of distilled water it absorbed after six hours was slightly over 350 percent of its weight. This was less than promoted but still significant.

The researcher soaked the material in a solution of 0.01 molar $CaCl_2$, which is similar in salt content to an average soil solution. This reduced the amount of water absorbed by 90 percent.

Other studies [*Journal American Society Horticultural Science*, 1990. 115:382; *Journal of Environmental Horticulture*, 1990. 8(3):113.] indicated that fertilizer salts and overall salinity of the soil solution dramatically reduce absorption by hydrophilic gels. Divalent ions such as Ca and Mg inhibit cross lining and "lock" the polymer in place, restricting expansion and reducing water absorption by 90 percent. Monovalent ions, K and NH_4, reduced hydration of several gels by 80 percent.

The role of hydrophilic gels in turfgrass management has received a great deal of recent interest. Many articles have been published about the water conserving and irrigation reducing potential of co-polymer gels. The calculated increase in water stored in the soil by one author was 0.25 inches of water from 320 pounds of soil-incorporated hydrogel. This was equivalent to one day of water for a summer ET for the region. Unfortunately, this increase in water holding was *calculated*, rather than *measured*. A sales representative calculated that it required 1,300 pounds per acre of his/her product to store water equaling a four-day supply for turfgrass. Again, this publication referred to potential water savings on paper, not in the field.

An agronomist, however, calculated that if the dry hydrogel is applied into the seed zone at the rate of 10 pounds per acre (apparently the maker's recommendation), it would hold 5,000 pounds of water, based on manufacturer's claims [*Soil Science News and Views*, 1989. 10(7):3]. This assumes no influence from salinity or fertilizer ions and 100 percent of potential hydration.

Although this may appear to be a great deal of water, an actively growing crop can be expected to use about 40,000 pounds of water per acre per day. The 5,000 pounds of water accounts for only 12.5 percent of the crop's daily water use and this could conceivably be used up in less than one day. An acre of silt loam soil (six inches deep) could hold approximately 400,000 pounds of plant available water. The material's contribution would be less than 1 percent of the total, at the rate applied.

Research concerning the potential role of hydrogels in turf management has been less positive than published testimonials. Butler and Fry [*HortScience*, 1989. 24(1):79] extrapolated from greenhouse studies that 80x rates (7,000 pounds/A) would be needed to enhance field establishment of tall fescue. Dr. Tony Koski, Colorado State University, has been unable to reduce irrigation on bluegrass or tall fescue with incorporation of gels into the soil, even at 80 pounds per 1,000 square feet. One place where polymers may provide a benefit is very gravely soil where water normally passes through very quickly. Fertilizer ion and salinity concentration of irrigation water and the soil solution may dramatically affect water-holding capacity of hydrophilic gels in turf.

While hydrophilic gels may have some advantages in some limited situations, they are not a panacea. Gels cannot substitute for good management. Each manager must determine if these effects are real or truly economical in their situation. Much of the published literature from promoters represent testimonials, rather than hard scientific facts. A glowing testimonial, in most instances, should not be taken as the gospel. *Caveat Emptor.*

Bibliography

Anonymous. 1989. New moisture sensor reduces water consumption by 50 percent. *ALA/ Maintenance*, 10(4):20.

Anonymous. 1989. Water absorbents increase transplant survival. *Lawn & Landscape Maintenance*, 10(8):44.

Anonymous. 1990. The role of polymers in water management. *Golf and Sports Turf*, 6(6):11–19.

Anonymous. 1990. "Micro" irrigation: An alternative low volume watering method. *Lawn & Landscape Maintenance*, 11(10):10.

Anonymous. 1992. Use wetting agents, cultural procedures to reduce dry spots. *Landscape Manager*, 31(11):31.

Anonymous. 1992. Trees or turf? *Grounds Maintenance*, 27(10):13–14, 68.

Anonymous. 1993. National xeriscape council disbands. *Landscape and Irrigation*, 12(6):37.

Arpin, R. J., J. Borland, J. Reber, and S. Wynn. 1985. Plant Lists. In: *Mile High and Dry Xeriscape Symposium.* Denver Water Dept., Denver, CO.

Beard, J. B. 1973. *Turfgrass: Science and Culture.* Prentice-Hall, Inc., Englewood Cliffs, NJ.

Billeau, L. 1988. Landscape the xeriscape way-mulching. *National Xeriscape News*, Mar./Apr.:3.

Bisconer, I. 1988. Successful drip irrigation. *Grounds Maintenance*, 23(7):3–12, 18.

Black, R. and D. Rogers. 1989. *Soil Moisture Measurements.* Cooperative Extension Bulletin L-795, Kansas State University, Manhattan, KS.

Borland, D. 1986. Xeriscape. *Nursery Manager*, 2(3):82–84, 88.

Borland, J. and G. Weinstein. 1989. Mulch: Is it always beneficial? *Grounds Maintenance*, 24(2):10–14, 120–122.

Bowman, D. C., R. Y. Evans, and J. L. Paul. 1990. Fertilizer salts reduce hydration of polyacrylamide gels and affect physical properties of gel-amended container media. *Journal American Society for Horticultural Science,* 115(3):382–386.

Carpenter, P. L., T. D. Walker, and F. O. Lanphear. 1975. *Plants in the Landscape.* W.H. Freeman and Co., San Francisco, CA.

Carrow, R. N. 1985. Getting back to basics. *Weeds, Trees, and Turf,* 24(7):44, 48–50.

Cline, H. 1993. Turf vs. ornamentals: Which uses more water? *Western Turf Management,* 4(7):12.

Cline, H. 1993. Soil amendments can provide many benefits. *Western Turf Management,* 4(8):21.

Costello, L. R., N. P. Natheney, and J. R. Clark. 1991. *Estimating Water Requirements of Landscape Plantings.* Univ. California Cooperative Extension Service. Leaflet 21494. Davis, CA.

Cox, R. A. and J. E. Klett. 1984. Evaluation of some indigenous western plants for xeric landscapes. *HortScience,* 19(6):856–858.

DeYoung, J. 1991. Low-volume drip. *Lawn & Landscape Maintenance,* 12(5):28–30.

Dunn, G. 1989. Test with a product having alleged value for increasing plant available water in soil. *Turfgrass Topics,* 10(3):3–4.

Evans, J. 1992. Selling the benefits of irrigation. *Lawn & Landscape Maintenance,* 13(4):32–38.

Evans, R. Y., I. Sisto, and D. C. Brown. 1989. The effectiveness of hydrogels in container plant production is reduced by fertilizer salts. University of California Cooperative Extension Service. *Flower and Nursery Report,* Summer:5–7.

Fonteno, W. C. and T. E. Bilderback. 1993. Impact of hydrogel on physical properties of coarse-structured horticultural substrates. *Journal American Society for Horticultural Science,* 118(2):217–222.

Foster, W. J. and G. J. Keever. 1990. Water absorption of hydrophylic polymers (hydrogels) reduced by media amendments. *Journal of Environmental Horticulture,* 8(3):113–114.

France, V. and D. Welch. 1987. Landscaping the xeriscape way-limiting turf areas. *National Xeriscape News,* Sept./Oct.:3.

Fry, J. D. and J. D. Butler. 1989. Water management during tall fescue establishment. *HortScience,* 24(1):79–81.

Gibson, H. 1988. Irrigation training schools. *Grounds Maintenance,* 23(11):28–30.

Gibson, H. 1990. Irrigation with wetting agents. *Grounds Maintenance,* 25(7):22,66–70.

Harris, R. W. 1983. *Arboriculture.* Prentice-Hall, Inc., Englewood Cliffs, NJ.

Hartin, J. and L. Frank. 1993. Hydrozoning: An innovative way to reduce water waste. *Landscape and Irrigation,* 17(7):50–54.

Henderson, J. and D. Hensley. 1986. Hydrophilic gels can influence nutrient retention in media. *American Nurseryman,* 162(9):107–113.

Henderson, J. C. and D. L. Hensley. 1986. Efficacy of a hydrophilic gel as a transplant aid. *HortScience,* 21:991–992.

Henderson, J. and D. Hensley. 1987. Do hydrophilic gels improve germination and survival? *American Nurseryman,* 166(4):189–194.

Henderson, J. C. and F. T. Davies. 1987 Effect of a hydrophilic gel on water relations, growth, nutrition of landscape roses. *HortScience,* 22:114.

Hensley, D. 1989. Mulching by the side of the road. *Nursery Manager,* 5(5):76–77.

167

Hensley, D. 1990. Creative landscaping for water conservation. *Nursery Manager*, 6(9):83–86.

Hensley, D. 1990. Gels may improve water availability in some cases. *Nursery Manager*, 6(11):65–66.

Hensley, D. 1991. Make the most of mulches. *Nursery Manager*, 7(3):96.

Hensley, D. 1993. How to save money, water by using drip irrigation. *Nursery Manager*, 9(7):104–105.

Hensley, D. 1993. Irrigating to conserve water. *Hawaii Landscape*, 7(3):14–15.

Hensley, D. L. and C. F. Fackler. 1984. Do waterholding compounds help in transplanting? *American Nurseryman*, 159(3):93.

Hummel, R. 1993. Effect of antitranspirant sprays on water relations of container-grown woody and herbaceous plants. *The Digger*, June:48.

Klett, J. and R. Cox. 1986. Xeric landscapes need well-chosen plants. *American Nurseryman*, 163(10):58–59, 61–65.

Latta, M. 1988. Landscaping the xeriscape way-use of lower water-demand plants. *National Xeriscape News*, May/June:2.

Lehmann, D., W. Cline, and D. Hensley. 1991. Making the most of mulches. *Nursery Manager*, 7(3):96–97.

Lynch, B. and B. Vinchesi. 1989. Regular maintenance prevents need for urgent repair service. *Lawn & Landscape Maintenance*, 10(7):20–24, 26.

Kauck, D. L. 1986. Water-absorbing compounds: what can they do for you? *Greenhouse Grower*, 4(11):54–56.

Knopf, J. 1991. Xeriscaping. *Grounds Maintenance*, 26(2):78, 80.

Knowles, S. D. 1990. Choosing an irrigation system. *Landscape Management*, 29(3):80–86.

MacNair, J. 1993. Estimating water use and irrigation schedules for ornamental landscapes. *Landscape and Irrigation*, 17(4):40–45.

Major, M. 1990. Misconceptions contribute to slow wetting agent acceptance. *Lawn & Landscape Maintenance*, 11(5):56–60.

Marcellino, M. 1989. Stop water shortages from evaporating your landscapes. *ALA/Maintenance*, 10(6):28–31.

Milford, M. H. 1988. Landscaping the xeriscape way-soil amendments. *National Xeriscape News*, Jan./Feb.:3.

Maloney, K. and J. Wright. 1993. Subsurface irrigation: The solution when overspray brings criticism. *Landscape and Irrigation*, 17(5):84–86.

Neely, D. and E. B. Himelick. 1968. Fertilizing and watering trees. Circular 52. Illinois Natural History Survey, Urbana, IL.

Nus, J. 1993. Water-absorbing polymers. *Golf Course Management*, Special International Edition:54–60.

Pellett, H., R. Hummel, and L. Mainquist. 1980. Relationship of fall watering practice to winter injury of conifers. *Journal of Arboriculture*, 6(6):146–149.

Pirone, P. P., J. R. Hartman, M. A. Sall, and T. P. Pirone. 1988. *Tree Maintenance*. Oxford University Press, New York, NY.

Polhemus, D. 1992. Soil polymers for turf areas: A technical review. *SportsTURF*, 8(6):14–17.

Pollard, E. 1992. Protecting irrigation systems through winterization. *Landscape and Irrigation,* 16(10):74–76.

Pryor, W. C., Jr. 1991. Designing a water conserving landscape on a large site. *Lawn & Landscape Maintenance,* 12(2):20.

Riccardi, T. J. 1989. Tricks of the irrigation trade. *Grounds Maintenance,* 24(11):26–28.

Rogers, D., L. Stone, and R. Black. 1989. Tensiometer use in scheduling irrigation. Cooperative Extension Service Bulletin L-796, Kansas State University, Manhattan, KS.

Sarsfield, A. C. 1985. Drip and minis in the commercial landscape. *Grounds Maintenance,* 20(10):34–36.

Severson, L. J. and B. C. Mart. 1989. Is there such a thing as solid H$_2$O. *Arbor Age,* August:12–16.

Shurtleff, M. C. 1993. Trees and drought. *Grounds Maintenance,* 28(4):49–54.

Sloan, M. and D. Hensley. 1987. Xeriscape: Creative landscaping for water conservation. *Grounds Management Forum,* 11(2):6–7.

Solomon, K. H. and G. Jorgensen. 1992. Subsurface drip irrigation. *Grounds Maintenance,* 27(19):24–26.

Spaid, T. H. and D. Hensley. 1986. Mulch selection guide. *Nursery Manager,* 2(3):113–114.

Swearengin, R. 1987. Water savings flow with efficient irrigation, good practices. *National Xeriscape News,* Nov./Dec.:1, 6.

Vinchesi, B. and B. Lynch. 1990. Winterizing irrigation systems can avoid pipe stress. *Lawn & Landscape Maintenance,* 11(10):33–34.

Welch, D. F. 1988. Landscaping the xeriscape way-appropriate maintenance. *National Xeriscape News,* Sept./Oct.:1.

Welch, D. F. 1991. Xeriscape guidelines and turfgrass use. *Grounds Maintenance,* 26(2):79.

Westrick, D. 1989. N.J. Irrigation contractors fight to install low voltage wiring. *Lawn and Landscape Maintenance,* 10(9):12.

Chapter 10
Fertilizing the Landscape

Fertilization of landscape plants is the most discussed topic in landscape management. Fertilizer is applied regularly and in copious quantities. The timing and rates vary with region, climate, species, and recommendations of individual authors and managers.

Some grounds managers believe that fertilizer possesses mystical quality, curing all ills; "When in doubt, fertilize." Fertilizer maintains the health and vigor of woody and herbaceous plants. Research has equated proper levels of plant nutrients with reduction in winter bark splitting of trees, reduced severity of drought damage, and increased insect and disease resistance. Aesthetically, proper nutrition will increase the size and number of fruit and flowers, as well as increased size, color intensity, and amount of foliage.

Fertilizer is not a magic powder. It will not "take care" of all of the problems encountered by the plant or grounds manager. No amount of added nutrients can make up for lack of water, poor drainage, or other limiting site factors. Excessive fertilization, especially nitrogen, increases some problems. Fireblight is more severe when there is excessive succulent new growth. Excessive nitrogen can increase the density of shade trees; understory plants may suffer from reduced sunlight. Fertilizer pollution is a genuine problem, one that every landscape professional must be concerned with.

Landscape plants rely on man to provide the majority of their nutrients. They do not have the advantage of century-old, humus-rich forest soils. Landscape sites are frequently stripped of top soil or filled with poor quality material. Landscape sites are often low in critical nutrients. Landscape plants do not have the advantage of natural nutrient recycling; leaves and grass clippings are collected before their nutrients can be returned to the soil. Fertilization is a routine but very important part of the management of every landscape site.

The Essential Elements

Sixteen essential elements are necessary for plant growth. An element is classified as *essential:* if the plant fails to complete its life cycle in its absence; the action of the element in the plant is specific (it cannot be replaced by another element); and it has a direct effect on the plant (as opposed to indirect, such as repelling animals or insects).

The essential nutrients are divided into "*Macro:*" carbon (C); hydrogen (H); oxygen (O); nitrogen (N); phosphorus (P); potassium (K); calcium (Ca); magnesium (Mg); sulfur (S). And, into "*Micro*" elements: iron (Fe); manganese (Mn); zinc (Zn); boron (B); copper (Cu); molybdenum (Mo); and chlorine (Cl). Recent work has indicated that Nickel (Ni) may also be an essential element. Classification as macro- or micronutrients does not refer to their importance, but to the relative amounts of the materials found in a plant.

Carbon (C), hydrogen (H), and oxygen (O) are obtained from air and water; they are not manageable, that is, they cannot be added as a "fertilizer." Nitrogen, phosphorus, and potassium are referred to as the *fertilizer elements* for obvious reasons. Iron (Fe) is frequently referred to a *border element,* it is classed as a macronutrient by some sources and a minor element by others. Iron is required in greater amounts and deficiency problems are encountered more frequently than for other microelements.

Macronutrients

Nitrogen

Nitrogen is the most important fertilizer element, the most frequently limiting nutrient in landscape soils, and of the greatest concern to landscape managers. Nitrogen is supplied to plants through decomposition of organic matter, nitrogen fixation by soil microbes and some higher plants, and the addition of fertilizers. Nitrogen is rendered unavailable to plants due to absorption by weeds and other non-target plants, utilization or denitrification by soil organisms, volatilization, and leaching.

Addition of nitrogen results in the greatest response in plant growth of any fertilizer element. There is no additive effect when nitrogen is applied in association with other nutrients.

Specifications and recommendations

Nitrogen is the most common nutrient applied to any landscape site. It will be applied at least annually and most likely several times during the year for the benefit of the turf. Turf fertilization is discussed in detail in Chapter 12.

Nitrogen fertilizer rates for turfgrass and woody plants should be specified and recommended as *pounds of nitrogen,* rather than pounds of a specific fertilizer. This allows the contractor freedom of choice in fertilizer material based on price, site, and handling considerations. If a slow release material is required, the percent nitrogen necessary as slow release or water insoluble nitrogen (WIN) should be specified. For instance, *"The fertilizer shall contain 60 percent slow release nitrogen."*

If other fertilizer nutrients are necessary or required, specify these in pounds of element (e.g. two pounds phosphorus per 1,000 square feet) or their inclusion can be indicated as a ratio. For instance, *"Two pounds of nitrogen per 1,000 square feet shall be applied as a 3:1:1 fertilizer."* This indicates that one-third pound of P_2O_5 and K_2O will be applied for each pound of nitrogen. This recommendation might be used where phosphorus and potassium levels are marginal. Allowing the contractor freedom to choose specific products to accomplish the fertilization program results in more profit for the contractor and a better price for the client.

Calculating fertilizer rates

The number of pounds of any fertilizer to yield the required rate of nitrogen or other element specified is easily calculated. Divide the pounds of nitrogen required by the percent of nitrogen (as a decimal) in the fertilizer analysis.

> *For Example:*
>
> You wish to apply 2 pounds of nitrogen (N) per 1,000 square feet as urea. Urea (45-0-0) is 45 percent (0.45) N.   Therefore, 2 (pounds of N desired) divided by 0.45 (% N in urea) equals 4.4 pounds of product.
>
> To apply 3 pounds of N, it would require 9 pounds of ammonium nitrate (33-0-0) (3 ÷ 0.33 = 9).
>
> Ten pounds of superphosphate (0-20-0) to apply 2 pounds of P_2O_5 per 1,000 square feet (2 ÷ 0.20 = 10).

And on, and on, nothing magical, no need for a computer. Fertilizer rates can be calculated in the dust on the hood of the pickup.

Nitrogen Fertilization of Trees

Rates

An all-purpose recommendation for most soils and moderate rates of tree growth is two to four pounds of nitrogen per 1,000 square feet of *crown area*. The crown area is considered the inside of the *dripline* or edge of the canopy (or slightly beyond). This is not an enchanted area; the roots of trees are known to extend beyond the dripline in all directions. A general figure frequently discussed is that the roots extend twice the radius of the crown. Another is that the roots extend outward a distance approximately equal to the height of the tree. The extent of a tree's roots vary species and soil.

Measurements of sugar maple (*Acer saccharum*) indicated that the root area was 1.75 times greater than the radius of the crown. The root area of tuliptree (*Liriodendron tulipifera*) was 2.5 times greater than the crown area. The root area and crown area of pin oak (*Quercus palustris*) were about the same. Sandy soils are more conducive to larger root systems than fine-textured soils.

Regardless, the dripline makes a convenient area to measure. It is easy for most employees to find and is a concept the client understands. If fertilizer is applied within the dripline of the tree, there are more than enough active roots to adsorb the material. Some arboriculture texts recommend calculation of nitrogen rates based on the estimated root zone (two times the crown radius) and application of the material to the same area. This figure may involve the entire front yard of small residential lots and application beyond the dripline has not been advantageous.

Experimentally, trees have responded to a variety of nitrogen rates. Whitcomb, in Oklahoma, found maximum growth with four pounds of nitrogen per 1,000 square feet. Good growth was achieved by Neely, in Illinois, with six pounds nitrogen per 1,000 square feet. In Ohio, Dr. Elton Smith found maximum growth of trees in a nursery from three to six pounds nitrogen per 1,000 square feet per year applied in three applications. The majority of these and other studies, however, have involved nursery production and did not consider turf response. The quality of turf in a maintained landscape is of equal importance to that of the trees and shrubs.

The two to four pound rate recommended in this discussion provides a guideline for reasonable growth within the figures used experimentally. Soils with high levels of organic matter may need less nitrogen. Sandy soil, especially in high rainfall areas, will require more. Evergreens need lower

172

levels of nitrogen than deciduous trees. Rates for trees in turfgrass should be calculated to include the amount of nitrogen supplied to the turf.

In most situations, trees in managed turf with a reasonable fertility program will not require additional nitrogen. If the contract, specific problems, or the desire to promote additional tree growth require the use of additional nitrogen, it should be applied in two or more applications (usually spring *and* fall) or as a deep root feed application to not burn the turf. Never surface apply more than two pounds of rapidly available nitrogen per 1,000 square feet per application beneath trees in turf.

Caliper recommendations

There are various formulas for computing the amount of nitrogen needed to fertilize a tree based upon trunk diameter or caliper at *dbh* (diameter breast height or 4 1/2 feet). Caliper calculations have been historically used by arborists. In most managed landscapes, however, the contractor or grounds manager is dealing with several trees of different sizes, turf, shrubs, herbaceous perennials, annuals, and bulbs. It is more efficient to calculate nitrogen rates on a square foot basis, rather than measuring each tree annually.

A common recommendation is one-half pound nitrogen per inch dbh. Work by Dr. Jim Robbins while at Kansas State University found that rates based on crown area of open-growing trees typically provided more nitrogen than did rates based on trunk diameter for a wide variety of species.

Special situations

Trees in *confined areas,* such as parking lot islands, street trees, or planters, have restricted root systems and limited clear surface area. Base nitrogen fertilization rates on *open root area,* not crown spread. Normal rates of nitrogen applied to the few feet of surface not covered by pavement will result in high salt accumulation problems, damage to the roots, and top growth in excess of that which can be supported by the roots. In root-confined situations, the nitrogen applied should be on the low side of recommended rates and this should be divided into split applications made several times per year as foliar sprays, limited surface applications, or other alternative methods. Each case must be evaluated individually by a competent professional.

Upright, columnar, or *fastigiate trees* should be fertilized based on estimated root spread rather than upon their actual crown area. Calculate the area of the root zone using a radius equal to the tree's height for rate and application purposes.

Be aware of potential problems for turf growth and vigor under trees, especially when higher nitrogen rates are required. Some sources recommend reduction of nitrogen rates to turf under dense stands of trees because of the change in morphology and physiology of the grass plant resulting from the reduced light.

Over-fertilization of trees can over-stimulate foliage, exposing understory plants to heavy shade and the associated growth responses and problems. Soil and water pollution problems may result. Be careful with recommendations and application methods; keep the environment in mind. Higher rates of nitrogen for the tree's benefit should be applied as a deep (6 to 12 inches) root or soil injection application in these situations.

Timing

Timing of nitrogen and other nutrient applications for maximum benefit varies with research study and location. Several researchers have found fall better than or equal to spring application. Neely found greatest stimulation from nitrogen applied in April in Illinois. All studies agreed that application should be timed so there is nitrogen available for the new flush of growth in the spring. Timing is not as important for applications of phosphorus, or most other nutrients, including micronutrients.

In general, preferred application time for trees and shrubs in the Midwest and North is October to November. Soil temperatures in the fall are favorable for root activity and nutrient absorption; roots are active as long as soil temperatures remain above 40°F. Moisture conditions are conducive for work and movement of the material into the root zone. Fall is also the preferred time for application for the majority of nitrogen used in cool-season turf programs.

Early spring, four to six weeks before bud break, appears to be nearly equal in benefit to fall application. Some authors have speculated that loss from leaching would be less for spring applications and, therefore, more nitrogen is available for plant absorption. However, this has not been demonstrated experimentally.

In regions with milder conditions, growth begins earlier in the spring and continues later in the fall. Nitrogen applications in late winter or early spring are appropriate. In areas of high rainfall or coarse-textured soils, a second, midsummer application may be beneficial. In subtropical and tropical areas, fertilize in advance of major flushes of growth.

In all cases where winter damage is a possibility, avoid heavy late summer and early fall applications of nitrogen to trees. These can result in a late flush of growth that may fail to acclimate (develop cold hardiness) before the severe autumn freezes.

Split applications of fertilizer, late fall and spring, may be considered. Split applications to trees are more costly since the site must be visited twice. Some research has reported growth increases with spilt applications in nurseries. If high nitrogen rates are used, split applications should be made to preserve the turf. Never apply more than 2 pounds readily available nitrogen per 1,000 square feet per broadcast application for landscape plants in turfgrass. Higher nitrogen rates can be used with soil injection methods.

Shrubs

A rate of two to four pounds of nitrogen per 1,000 square feet of bed area is the most common figure used in the trade. A four pound application is not excessive in shrub beds where there is no turf or groundcover. If groundcovers are present, consider lower rates or sweeping or irrigating granules from the leaves. Rhododendrons, azaleas, and other ericaceous species have shallow roots that are injured by higher rates of quickly available nitrogen. Use lower rates or split applications. In addition, ericaceous species should be fertilized using an acid material to help maintain an acidic soil reaction.

Needle evergreens, such as pine, fir, and spruce respond to lower fertilization rates than deciduous species. Research has shown that rates above a certain minimum do not translate to increased growth. There is no need to try to segregate them, however, as the additional nitrogen used for deciduous species will not harm evergreens.

Frequency

Fertilization frequency depends on the *type* and *age* of the tree or shrub, the *objective* of the fertility program, *soil conditions, maintenance level,* and the *budget.* Most trees and shrubs will respond to annual applications of nitrogen. Neely found, however, that growth increases from fertilization persisted only one to two years after application. *Nutrient deficiencies* require successive applications until the problem is corrected. Soil and foliage tests tell the manager the effectiveness of the fertilizer program. Foliar applications of micro-nutrients are required annually to alleviate the symptoms.

Fertilize recently established landscapes annually until the plants reach sufficient size. Established woody landscape plants require less fertilization, only enough to retain good color and reasonable vigor. Fertilize these on a biennial basis, although annual fertilization will not cause any plant problems. Again, a good turf fertilization program may supply all of the nitrogen necessary for established woody landscape plants.

Older, mature trees, especially in lower maintenance situations, such as parks, can be fertilized less frequently. Application of nitrogen every three to four years is usually adequate. These recommendations will vary with specific circumstances.

Fertilization at planting

There are as many different recommendations for fertilizing trees and shrubs at planting as there are trees planted. Research has not helped solve this dilemma. In fact, some published reports have added to the controversy. Recommendations vary from none to 0.1 pound of nitrogen mixed in the backfill or applied to the surface after planting. One researcher reported no response of bareroot landscape trees to soil nitrogen levels during the first 3 years after planting.

Other research [*Journal of Arboriculture,* 1988. 14:204] found that container-grown magnolia (*Magnolia grandiflora*) grew more if a small amount of fertilizer (12 percent N) was added at planting. Table 10–1 illustrates that this increase in growth occurred regardless of where the fertilizer was placed (in the bottom of the hole, in the backfill, or on the surface after planting). Also, the increase in growth was evident three years after planting and fertilizer application. Container-grown plants are more likely to utilize and respond to nitrogen added at planting than are bareroot plants or possibly balled and burlapped plants. Container-grown material is transplanted with a full compliment of roots, whereas the root systems of bareroot and balled and burlapped stock is severely reduced (up to 90 percent, depending upon plant size) at harvest.

Consider incorporating fertilizer when planting in low fertility soils or where subsequent fertilizer applications are unlikely, such as roadsides, or other low budget landscapes. If the contract calls for application of fertilizer at planting, the decision has already been made. Regardless, use low levels of a low salt-index nitrogen fertilizer, with phosphorus and potassium included, if needed. Slow release materials are expensive, have low salt levels, and provide a source of nitrogen for several months. The material may be buried beneath the plant's root system or ball, mixed thoroughly into the backfill, or applied to the surface immediately after planting.

Table 10–1.

Percent increase in height and stem diameter of container-grown *Magnolia grandiflora* as influenced by fertilizer placement at transplanting into the landscape.

Sampling date	Height				Stem Diameter			
	Fertilizer placement				Fertilizer placement			
	none	top	backfill	bottom	none	top	backfill	bottom
7/80	18.9a[y]	25.7b	27.0b	22.4ab	—	—	—	—
12/80	20.3a	29.7b	31.1b	27.2b	24.1a	26.4ab	33.6b	35.3b
5/82	73.6a	92.6b	92.3b	91.2b	93.6a	109.3ab	119.1b	116.2b

[y]Mean separation by Tukey's HSD (0.05). Means in each row under height or stem diameter that are followed by the same letter are not statistically different.

Adapted from: D. L. Hensley, R. E. McNiel, and R. Sundheim. 1988. Management influences on growth of transplanted *Magnolia grandiflora*. *Journal of Arboriculture*, 14:204–207.

Bring shrub and turfgrass areas to recommended soil test levels before planting. Nitrogen is usually incorporated during bed or soil preparation but should not exceed two pounds nitrogen per 1,000 square feet.

Phosphorus, and sometimes potassium, are revered for stimulating root growth if included in the planting hole. Phosphorus and potassium should be brought up to proper levels based on soil tests before planting, since these elements are not readily mobile in the soil. Mixing them into the planting hole incorporates the nutrients into the root zone. Addition of phosphorus or potassium to the planting hole in soils where they are not limiting has no effect on top or root growth of woody landscape plants. The use of high-phosphate, vitamin-fortified, root "enhancers" or stimulators has as much effect on woody plant root growth as snake oil for growing hair. Marketing is still more powerful than science, or common sense.

Phosphorus

Most soils contain adequate *phosphorus* for trees and shrubs. Phosphorus will occasionally be limiting or unavailable at soil *p*H above 7.0 where it can complex with calcium. At low soil *p*H, phosphorus may precipitate out of the soil solution as iron and aluminum phosphates. The amount and availability of phosphorus to landscape plants can be estimated by soil tests indicating the amount of phosphorus in the soil and the soil *p*H. Foliar analysis determines the amount of phosphorus in the plant.

Routine addition of phosphorus-containing fertilizers has shown no benefit or growth response to woody plants unless phosphorus is limiting in the soil. Sources proclaim enhanced root development of woody plants, especially in urban and other difficult sites, if additional phosphorus is added at planting and during annual fertilization. There is no experimental evidence, however, that addition of phosphorus in non-deficient situations increases root growth in woody plants. There is evidence, however, that high phosphate "starter" fertilizers aid establishment of vegetable and other herbaceous transplants.

Phosphorus does not move readily in the soil; broadcasting concentrates it near the surface. This is fine for turfgrass but limits availability of supplied phosphorus to deeper-feeding trees. For efficiency, amend the soil based on a soil test before planting. Deep root applications places nutrient sources in the zone of the majority of feeder roots of established trees. Excessive levels of phosphorus will not harm woody species, but overuse of phosphorus containing fertilizers contributes to water pollution.

Potassium

Most landscape soils contain adequate *potassium* for plant growth. Deficiencies have been reported in areas of Florida, Hawaii, and other localized situations. Soil tests can confirm visual symptoms. Foliar analysis may be misleading since potassium is readily mobile in the plant and is also leached from leaves by rain and irrigation.

Potassium is not mobile in soil. It is best incorporated in planting areas before plant establishment or applied to existing trees and shrubs by deep root applications or soil injection methods.

Potassium possesses almost mystical benefits for plants according to some authors, such as increasing drought resistance, reducing winter damage and disease severity, and enhancing flower color. There is little published research to support these attributes for woody plants or that potassium affects plant responses more than other elements. Addition of potassium will not promote a growth response in woody plants unless it is deficient. Large amounts of potassium may cause magnesium deficiency, especially in sandy soils.

Calcium

Calcium is seldom restricting in most soils. It may be limiting is acid soils, sandy soils in high rainfall regions, acidic peat soils, and soils derived from serpentine rock. Calcium can be added as agricultural or dolomitic limestone to acid soils and as gypsum to alkaline sites using surface applications. It should only be applied on the basis of a soil test. As with phosphorus and potassium, calcium is most efficiently supplied by incorporation before planting.

Magnesium

Magnesium can be leached from acidic sandy soils and tied-up in unavailable forms in calcareous soils, but is sufficient for growth of landscape plants in most areas. Add dolomitic limestone as a magnesium source for acid sites and Epsom salts ($MgSO_4.7H_2O$) in neutral or alkaline soils. As with the other nutrients, except nitrogen, it is most expedient to correct magnesium deficiencies before planting and then only on the basis of a soil test.

Iron

Iron is the most common micronutrient problem and probably the second most common nutrient deficiency occurring in landscape plants. Iron deficiency may be due to low iron content of the soil, but more commonly it is the result of unavailability due to high (alkaline) soil *p*H. Symptoms (interveinal chlorosis, yellow between green veins) occur most frequently in cold, wet soils, during periods of drought, or in situations where the root system has sustained damage. Plant species vary widely in the ability to scavenge iron from the soil and their susceptibility to iron chlorosis. Pin oak (*Quercus palustris*) and ericaceous species are notable in their susceptibility.

Photo 10–1. Iron is the most common micronutrient problem. Many species, such as oak and azaleas are prone to iron problems in alkaline soil.

Horticulturists have attempted to correct iron deficiency for over 100 years with every iron compound conceivable in every manner imaginable. Even today, there is considerable research underway in this area.

If the problem is due to low amounts of iron and other soil conditions are adequate to permit plant utilization, then iron levels can be successfully increased. In areas where the problem is due to alkaline soil reaction, a permanent solution is to avoid use of susceptible species, such as pin oak. Select only plants that tolerate the local conditions contributing to iron chlorosis.

Soil acidification with sulfur or aluminum sulfate in small planting areas is feasible; however, this solution is not economical or permanent for large sites. A large amount of material will be required and the soil must be amended deeply (at least 12 to 18 inches). Specific rates follow in the section on *Soil Reaction.*

Constant leaching of alkaline material in limestone-based soils increases the *p*H of acidified soils over time. The problem is aggravated when the site is irrigated with alkaline water. The duration of soil acidification projects increases if substantial amounts of organic matter are incorporated.

Iron compounds can be applied to the soil surface, sprayed onto plant foliage, injected into tree trunks, or injected into the soil. Application of large amounts of *iron sulfate* to the soil surface has provided mixed results. The *p*H change is temporary and the iron is immobilized in a short period of time. Several authors have reported reasonably long-term, semi-permanent success in treating iron chlorosis by deep root application of iron sulfate/sulfur mixes. Mixtures of 1:1 or 3:1 sulfur:iron sulfate have relieved iron chlorosis for several years. Theoretically, sulfur reduces the *p*H in localized areas around the hole making the iron in the iron sulfate available.

Surface application of *iron chelates* to soil is less affected by soil *p*H. Chelates do, however, vary in their relative stability at high soil *p*H. Since the material is mobile in the soil, the treatment must be repeated periodically. Iron chelates can be included in liquid soil injection mixes and have been reported effective for two or more years.

Spray applications of iron sulfate or iron chelates to the foliage have given irregular response with different species (effective with oak to ineffective with citrus). Foliar applications are effective for only a single season. Since iron is not mobile in the plant, new foliage emerging after an application will be chlorotic. Other disadvantages include problems in coverage, staining of walks, cars, and buildings, foliar residue, and potential foliar burn under certain conditions. Foliar applications correct only the symptoms, not the problem, but may be useful in correlation with other, longer-term treatments.

Organic iron salts have been *injected* or *implanted* into tree trunks since 1930 and this process can correct iron deficiency for up to three years. Several systems are commercially available. Gelatin capsules of ferric ammonium citrate, ferric citrate, or other organic salts are inserted into holes drilled into the trunk. Pressurized injection is also utilized commercially. The Mauget® system offers iron and other micronutrient injection treatments.

Another injection system, Medi-ject®, uses iron sulfate with water as a carrier, gravity-fed into holes drilled in the lower trunk or root flare. I have observed several trees treated with the Medi-ject® system in Kansas; these were free of iron chlorosis symptoms for four to six years and grew normally after treatment. Tree injections will be further discussed under application techniques.

Manganese

Manganese (Mn) is another commonly deficient micronutrient, second only to iron. As with iron, deficiency may be due to low manganese levels in the soil, or unavailability of existing supplies due to soil *p*H. At *p*H values above 6.5, manganese is converted to a low solubility form and sensitive plants will show deficiency symptoms. Symptoms are difficult to distinguish from those of iron (interveinal chlorosis) and the two are often mistaken for each other. Red maple (*Acer rubrum*), citrus, several species of palm, apple, cherry, and many other species are especially troubled by manganese deficiency. Symptoms are more likely under drought conditions.

Acidification of alkaline soils will usually correct the deficiency, however, the potential problems and economics make this an unattractive alternative. Manganese sulfate has been used as a soil treatment but manganese chelate may be more successful. Foliar sprays provide annual relief of the symptoms and trunk injections have been successful.

Zinc

Zinc (Zn) deficiency is most common on heavily-graded areas and in alkaline soils of the western United States. It is also a problem in Florida and other areas along the Gulf coast. Zinc deficiencies are aggravated by heavy or long-term use of high-phosphate fertilizers. Leaves of zinc deficient plants are yellow and small and internodes may be short.

Surface application or soil injections of zinc sulfate are more successful below soil *p*H of 6.0. Zinc chelates have been more successful in other situations. Annual foliar applications can be used. Trunk injections of zinc solutions are effective. Some people have resorted to driving zinc nails into the trunks of trees, but I have seen no reports on the success of this treatment.

Other nutrient deficiencies

Any nutrient can occur in insufficient quantities for plant growth due to supply or other factors mitigating uptake. Deficiencies of sulfur (S), molybdenum (Mo), boron (B), and copper (Cu) are rare and isolated. Sulfur is supplied to landscape plants via decomposition of organic matter, as part of many pesticides and, unfortunately, by air pollution. Problems with boron, copper, and molybdenum are isolated and managers should consult local authorities. Chlorine (Cl) and nickel (Ni) have not been reported in deficient levels under field conditions.

FERTILIZATION PRACTICES

Fertilizer recommendations are cloaked in secrecy and tradition. There are wide variations in amounts, timing, materials, and other facets of current fertilization techniques. Many grounds managers and landscape maintenance contractors have basic misunderstandings of soils, nutrients, and plant growth. Landscape fertilization programs are complicated by different plant types, sizes, and nutrient requirements of plants growing in immediate proximity.

The manager must be sure the *plant symptoms* are due to a nutrient deficiency or toxicity before applying corrective fertilizers. Foliage discoloration, chlorosis, and other classic "nutrient deficiency symptoms" are mimicked by pesticides, drought, excessive moisture, temperature, soil and air pollutants, compaction, and physical injury.

The plant's *location* impacts the fertility program and plant response. Plants growing in low-stress pastoral settings, such as many home backyards, require less crucial attention to nutrition than plants growing in parking lots or urban situations.

The physical properties of the *soil* influence the amount of nutrients held, and to an extent, their availability. Be cognizant of the influence of soil texture, soil structure, and soil depth on nutrient retention.

Not all plants respond to fertilizers in the same way. Faster growing species respond more rapidly and dramatically than slower growing species. Growth of some deciduous and evergreen species, such as oaks and pines, respectively, is limited by the number of preformed initials in the buds. The first year after fertilization they may show improved leaf color, but will not show increased growth until the following season.

The greatest growth response of landscape plants results from *nitrogen* (N); there will be no growth response to added phosphorus (P) or potassium (K) unless the soil is deficient in these elements. There is no additive or synergistic effect if either phosphorus or potassium are included with nitrogen in a fertilizer program.

Some *plants* have specific nutritional problems. Pin oaks (*Quercus palustris*), sweet gum (*Liquidambar styraciflua*), and birch (*Betula* spp.) develop iron chlorosis in alkaline conditions. Red maple (*Acer rubrum*) frequently suffers from manganese deficiency.

The manager must also consider the strategy or reason for applying fertilizer. The goal for young trees may be to increase their growth rate. With mature trees, however, fertilizer is applied to maintain foliage color and health. Growth rate is less important.

Photo 10–2. Palms are especially sensitive to potassium, magnesium, manganese, and nitrogen deficiencies.

Palms

Palms present special nutritional problems for landscape managers. Palms quickly suffer from insufficient or inappropriate fertilization. They are slow growing plants

180

so they take longer to recover from nutrient disorders. Nitrogen, potassium, magnesium, and manganese are the most frequently encountered nutrient deficiencies. Soil nutrient deficits are best corrected prior to planting.

Controlled-release nitrogen forms are preferred to rapidly available sources. Fertilizers should be formulated to release for long periods at higher temperatures; palms grow in sub-tropical and tropical regions.

The fertilizer ratio of 3:1:3 (N:P:K) is recommended by several palm experts. The fertilizer should also contain magnesium at one-third the rate of potassium. Micronutrients should also be included. "Palm specials" produced by several fertilizer formulators are available with these general specifications. Consult the fertilizer label and local Extension Services for rates. Broadcast materials beneath the crown (palm roots are not wide spreading); do not place fertilizer against the stem or where newly emerging roots can be injured.

Table 10–2. Nutrient element deficiency symptoms of woody plants	
Nutrient	**Symptoms**
Nitrogen (N)	Young leaves small, pale. Uniform yellowing beginning with older leaves. Abscission of older leaves may occur.
Phosphorus (P)	Leaves small, dark-green with bronze to purple tinge.
Potassium (K)	Marginal and interveinal chlorosis of recently matured leaves; beginning at tips, followed by necrosis.
Magnesium (Mg)	Marginal and interveinal chlorosis of older leaves; leaves thin.
Calcium (Ca)	Death of terminal buds, tip dieback and chlorosis of young leaves.
Sulfur (S)	Uniform yellowing of new leaves. Older leaves usually not affected.
Iron (Fe)	Interveinal chlorosis of young leaves.
Manganese (Mn)	Interveinal chlorosis, usually beginning at margins and progressing toward midribs, followed by necrotic spots between the veins.
Zinc (Zn)	Whorls of small, stiff, and mottled leaves near the tip of current season's growth.
Boron (B)	Terminal growth dies; lateral growth sparse foliage. Leaves are small, thick, misshapen, and brittle.
Copper (Cu)	Terminal growth dies, preceded by rosetting. Veins lighter than blades.
Molybdenum (Mo)	Leaves sometimes cupped; interveinal chlorosis preceded by marginal chlorosis.
From: E. M. Smith. 1986. *Fertilizing Landscape and Field Grown Nursery Crops.* Ohio State University Cooperative Extension Service Bulletin 650.	

Determining Deficiencies or Toxicities

Grounds managers have a number of tools at their disposal to determine deficiencies or toxicities of plant nutrients and to monitor nutritional programs.

181

Visual analysis

Many experienced managers can adequately gauge the nutritional needs of plants by appearance. Appearance cannot reveal intricate problems, but deficiencies of nitrogen, iron, manganese, and magnesium produce definable foliage symptoms. Tables 10-2 and 10-3 list common deficiency symptoms for landscape plants.

Shoot growth and *leaf size* are common indices of the nutritional status in trees and shrubs. If a young, moderately-fast growing shade tree has twig growth of less than nine to 12 inches per year, it will respond to application of additional nitrogen. Mature

Photo 10–3. Some nutrient deficiencies provide distinct visual symptoms, however, foliar discoloration can also be the result of chemicals, environmental, and man-made problems.

trees producing less than six inches of new growth per year will also respond. These growth rates will vary with species and site.

Table 10–4.	
General symptoms of nutrient *toxicities* for specific elements. Further examination and soil and foliar analyses should be conducted before definitive actions are taken.	
Nutrient Element	**Symptoms**
Nitrogen (N)	In some plants (e.g. azalea), excess *nitrates* result in iron deficiency symptoms (interveinal chlorosis) because of iron poor metabolism. Toxicity results in injury and death of the root system. Yellowing or bleaching of new foliage may occur.
Phosphorus (P)	Variable responses, including iron or zinc deficiency. Chlorosis of the older foliage may appear. Chlorotic areas are irregular as contrasted to regular symptoms of potassium and magnesium deficiencies.
Boron (B)	On older leaves, chlorosis is followed by necrosis at the tips of the serrations or irregularities along the leaf margin. Abscission of the foliage usually follows.
Manganese (Mn)	Chlorosis and yellowing of the new foliage may appear because of the increase of free Mn in highly acid conditions or poor aeration.
Aluminum (Al)	Death of the plant is usually preceded by variable chlorosis and necrosis of the foliage, which usually results from highly acid conditions. Pink hydrangea flowers become blue when aluminum is present.
Adapted from: Swanson, B. T., C. Rosen, R. Munter, and C. Lane. 1986. *Soil Testing and Fertilizer Applications for Nursery Management and Production.* University of Minnesota Agricultural Extension Service Bulletin AG-BU-2830.	

Problems associated with using visual symptoms are obvious. A slight deficiency may reduce growth without noticeable foliar symptoms. Once symptoms appear, plant growth has been impaired. Although some nutrient deficiencies produce distinct traits, others are generalized. It is usually impossible to determine the specific cause of a problem based solely upon visual observations. Also, it is often difficult to separate deficiency symptoms from those produced by pesticides, compaction, toxic nutrient levels, air and soil pollution, and biotic factors.

Soil Analysis

Soil tests are inexpensive guides to soil nutrient and *p*H levels. Soil tests typically indicate levels of phosphorus (P), potassium (K), and *p*H. Some will also include calcium (Ca), magnesium (Mg), lime requirement (based on a buffer *p*H test), and local problem elements, such as iron (Fe), or zinc (Zn). Additional tests are usually available upon request and for a price. Nitrogen is seldom determined because soil levels change rapidly. Some tests determine soil organic matter content and use this to make recommendations for nitrogen additions; this is common for home garden and agronomic crop reports.

Sampling procedures

Soil tests are of the greatest value when establishing a landscape. Deficiencies can be determined and corrected before planting. After planting, soil tests should be taken every three to five years; more frequently if the site has a history of nutritional problems, or if it contains excessive cuts or fills.

Professionals sample the area with a soil core probe. A hand trowel or shovel can be used to remove samples but make a larger hole. Take 20 to 30 cores per area and remove the turf and debris from the core. Collect a total of about a pint of soil per sampled area. Generally, samples will be taken from the upper six to 12 inches of soil. A few sources suggest sampling two to four feet deep for trees, but there is minimal opportunity to change the nutrient status at this depth. The majority (90 percent according to some research) of the feeding roots of trees and shrubs are concentrated in the upper six to 18 inches of soil. For turf or annual flowers, the depth of the soil cores can be limited to six inches.

Sample atypical areas separately. Cuts or fills will have a different soil nutritional status and potential needs. Separate excessive slopes, open flat areas, and areas that are distinctly different. Be reasonable. Twelve different fertility programs cannot be developed for the same site. The manager, however, should be cognizant of where problem areas are.

Dry the samples at room temperature before sending to the lab. Soil test services are available through most county Cooperative Extension offices and private laboratories. University soil testing laboratories in each state are listed in Appendix 4. The Extension Service is less expensive than private labs but the turn around is longer. The wait is even longer during planting season when the university or county lab will be backlogged with farm samples. Unfortunately, most soil analysis labs are geared to agronomic crops and not landscape plants. Private and a few public labs have developed specific tests and recommendations programmed for turf, but few have recommendations for established woody species.

Interpreting soil test results

Results should be interpreted by someone with experience in evaluating laboratory data in relation to plants and soils in the given region. The test results reflect *soil levels*. Just because the nutrient level appears adequate does not mean that it is available to the plant. This is especially true for minor nutrients.

The soil nutrient levels in Table 10–5 are *guidelines*. Soil test levels below these ranges are deficient and corrective action should be taken. Soil test levels at the lower end of the ranges will probably not result in deficiency symptoms but may limit growth. Corrective measures are, therefore, advisable.

Soil test results are reported in *pounds per acre* for the macronutrients and *parts per million* (ppm) for micronutrients. One part per million equals around two pounds per acre at plow depth (six to eight inches). Soil test results for phosphorus and potassium, and more importantly their recommendations, may be described as *nutrient elements* (P or K) or as the fertilizer elements (P_2O_5 and K_2O) per acre or other given unit area.

Table 10–5.	
Soil test values for most landscape plants should be within or above the following ranges for adequate growth and vigor.	

Soil *p*H:
    5.0-7.5

Soil nutrients:

Available P	30–100 pounds per A
Exchangeable K	200–400 pounds per A
Exchangeable Ca	800–3000 pounds per A
Exchangeable Mg	150–2000 pounds per A
Available Mn	20–40 pounds per A
Available B	0.5 pounds per A
Available Zn	3 pounds per A

Soluble salts:

< 2.0 millimhos per cm:	no growth problems
2.0–4.0 millimhos per cm:	expect injury to sensitive plants
4.0–8.0 millimhos per cm:	widespread injury to many landscape plants

Adapted From: E. M. Smith. 1986. *Fertilizing Landscape and Field Grown Nursery Crops.* Ohio State University Cooperative Extension Service Bulletin 650.

Convert recommendations in P to P_2O_5 and K to K_2O to calculate amounts of specific fertilizers necessary. The conversion from the elemental to the fertilizer form (and vice versa) is:

$$P = P_2O_5 \times 0.44 \qquad K = K_2O \times 0.83$$

$$P_2O_5 = P(2.3) \qquad K_2O = K(1.2)$$

For example,
    If a soil test indicated that site contained 20 pounds of P per acre, and the manager wished to increase this to 80 pounds phosphorus (P) per acre, how much P_2O_5 would be required?
        80 pounds P − 20 pounds P = 60 pounds P required.
        60 pounds P (2.3) = 138 pounds of P_2O_5 required.

    To apply 100 pounds of potassium (K) per acre would require:
        100 (1.2) = 120 pounds of K_2O

Foliar or Tissue Analyses

Foliage, tissue, or leaf analyses determine the mineral element content within a plant. It is an important tool for establishing and maintaining a proper nutrition program and for diagnosing suspected mineral deficiencies or excesses. Foliar analysis can be used over a wide range of soils and climatic conditions. It should be used in coordination with soil tests to develop a better nutritional picture of the site. Foliage can be analyzed at university laboratories through the local Cooperative Extension office or by private laboratories. Each laboratory has specific sampling procedures, but the following suggestions apply:

1. Samples should be taken between mid-June to mid-September (mid growing season) from the most recently matured leaves. These occur midway on the current season's growth. If sampling for problem diagnosis, be sure to sample both affected and healthy plants for a comparison. Collect soil samples in the same area for analysis.

2. Take 30 to 100 leaves from deciduous species or 50 terminal cuttings from narrow-leafed evergreens. Do not collect diseased, injured, or dead foliage.

3. Wash samples with a 0.1 percent detergent solution to remove dust and residues. Rinse thoroughly and dry the samples. Send samples to the testing laboratory in the mailer supplied. Follow the directions specified by the testing laboratory.

4. Obtain professional assistance to interpreting the results of tissue tests.

Interpreting foliar analysis results

Table 10–6 serves as a *guideline* for levels of various elements typically found in normal and deficient woody species. This information was collected after extensive evaluation of "healthy" and abnormal plants. Consult with the Cooperative Extension Service or other local experts for specific regional information or peculiarities.

FERTILIZERS

The fertilizers used to maintain or correct the soil or plant nutritional levels vary in content, application method, and cost. Fertilizer selection should be based on more than just price. The specific use, application equipment and firm's operation, as well as price, affect fertilizer selection. Consider the following when selecting or purchasing fertilizers.

a. *Analysis* is the percent (%) of N-P_2O_5-K_2O in the material. A 20-10-5 fertilizer contains 20% N, 10% P_2O_5, and 5% K_2O. Fertilizer is sold as the oxides of phosphorus and potassium, not the amount of actual element available. The conversion from elemental to oxide (fertilizer) is presented on page 185. A fertilizer containing all three major fertilizer elements, nitrogen, phosphorus, and potassium, is a *complete fertilizer*.

b. *Ratio* is the mathematical relationship of one fertilizer element to another within the analysis. A 20-10-5 has a 4:2:1 ratio; 12-12-12 is a 1:1:1 ratio fertilizer. Fertilizers are sometimes specified or recommended as ratios, especially for turfgrass management. Ratios higher in phosphorus or potassium are used to correct deficiencies while controlling nitrogen rates.

c. The *source of nutrients* is important. The percent of fast versus slow release nitrogen affects duration, results, and price of the material. *Acid-based* fertilizers are preferred for acid-loving plants and to lower soil *p*H.

d. *Handling ease, method of application* (dry or liquid), and *labor requirement* obviously affect purchase decisions. It is possible to purchase fertilizer and herbicide or insecticide combinations for use in turf. Combination products reduce application labor but these materials are more expensive.

Table 10–6.

Foliar element ranges for woody plants.[a] These serve as guidelines for interpreting tissue analyses of landscape plants.

Macronutrient	Low (%)	Sufficient (%)	High (%)
Nitrogen			
Evergreen	1.0–1.5	1.5–3.5	3.5–5.5
Deciduous	1.5–2.0	2.0–4.5	4.5–7.0
Phosphorus	0.1–0.2	0.2–0.6	0.6–1.0
Potassium	1.0–1.5	1.5–3.5	3.5–6.0
Calcium	0.2–0.5	0.5–2.5	2.5–4.0
Magnesium			
Evergreen	0.1–0.2	0.2–2.0	2.0–2.5
Deciduous	0.2–0.3	0.3–1.0	1.0–2.5

Micronutrient	Low (ppm)	Sufficient (ppm)	High (ppm)
Manganese	20–30	30–800	800–1,000
Iron	30–50	50–700	700–1,000
Boron	20–30	30–50	50–200
Copper	4–6	6–50	50–200
Zinc	25–30	30–75	75–100
Molybdenum	0.4–0.6	0.6–6.0	6–20

[a]Based on recently matured leaves midway on shoots of current season's growth for deciduous plants and on terminal cuttings from evergreens.

Adapted from: E. M. Smith. 1986. *Fertilizing Landscape and Field Grown Nursery Crops*. Ohio State University Cooperative Extension Service Bulletin 650.

More importantly, determine if the combination product delivers the proper amount of nutrients *and* the necessary pesticide rate for the maintenance program. Separate applications of fertilizers and pesticides provide better options than combination materials.

Bulk fertilizer is much less expensive than bagged material. I remember one young manager who decided to save a great deal of money and ordered two tons of fertilizer in bulk. It made quite a nice pile in the middle of his garage. He had no place to properly store it and lost more in handling, labor, and waste than was saved.

e. *Price* varies with manufacturer, distributor, and brand. Price depends on source of nutrients, quantity purchased, transportation costs, incorporation of other materials (pesticides), and the distributor's markup. Calculate the cost of fertilizer elements by dividing the price per pound by the analysis percentage (as a decimal).

Example:

    If ammonium nitrate (33-0-0) costs $15.50 per 100 pounds; then $0.1550 per pound ÷ 0.33 (33% N) = $0.47 per pound nitrogen.

    If urea (45-0-0) costs $16.00 per 100 pounds, then $0.16 per pound ÷ 0.45 = $0.36 per pound of nitrogen.

Table 10-7.

Nutrient content (%, analysis), reaction, solubility, and salt index of common in organic fertilizer used in landscape management.

Fertilizer	N	P$_2$O$_5$	K$_2$O	MgO	CaO	S	Other	Salt Index[a]	Acidic or Basic[b]	Water Solubility
Nitrogen source materials										
Ammonium nitrate	34	—	—	—	—	—	—	105	A	High
Calcium nitrate	17	—	—	—	4	—	—	53	B	High
Potassium nitrate	14	—	47	—	—	—	—	74	B	High
Sodium nitrate	16	—	—	—	—	—	—	100	B	High
Ammonium sulfate	21	—	—	—	—	24	—	69	A	Medium
Mono-ammonium phosphate	12	62	—	—	—	—	—	30	A	Low
Di-ammonium phosphate	21	54	—	—	—	—	—	34	A	Very Low
Urea	47	—	—	—	—	—	—	75	A	High
Phosphorus source materials										
Mono-ammonium phosphate	12	62	—	—	—	—	—	30	A	Low
Di-ammonium phosphate	21	54	—	—	—	—	—	34	A	Very Low
Mono-potassium phosphate	—	52	35	—	—	—	—	8	B	Medium
Superphosphate, single	—	20	—	—	23	9	—	8	N	Very Low
Superphosphate, triple	—	45	—	—	20	2	—	10	N	Very Low
Potassium source materials										
Potassium chloride	—	—	60	—	—	—	—	116	N	High
Potassium nitrate	14	—	47	—	—	—	—	74	N	High
Mono-potassium phosphate	—	52	35	—	—	—	—	8	N	Medium
Potassium sulfate	—	—	54	—	—	18	—	46	N	Medium
Sulfate of potash-magnesia	—	—	22	18	—	22	—	43	N	Medium
Magnesium source materials										
Dolomite	—	—	—	22	31	—	—	1	B	Very Low
Magnesium ammonium phosphate	6	29	—	—	—	—	16-Mg	8	A	Low
Magnesium sulfate	—	—	—	16	—	13	20-Mg	44	N	High
Sulfate of potash-magnesia	—	—	22	18	—	22	—	43	N	Medium
Calcium source materials										
Dolomite	—	—	—	22	31	—	—	1	N	Very Low
Lime-calcium	—	—	—	—	57	—	—	5	B	Very Low
Superphosphate, single	—	20	—	—	23	9	—	8	N	Very Low
Gypsum	—	—	—	—	30	16	—	8	N	Very Low
Calcium Nitrate	17	—	—	—	3	—	—	53	B	High

188

Other[c]

Boric Acid	—	—	—	—	—	13-B	—	—	Soluble
Copper sulfate	—	—	—	—	12	25-Cu	—	—	Soluble
Ferrous sulfate	—	—	—	—	—	20-Fe	—	—	Soluble
Iron chelate (EDDHA/DPTA)	—	—	—	—	—	6-10 Fe	—	—	Soluble
Manganese sulfate	—	—	—	—	13	25-Mn	—	—	Soluble
Zinc sulfate	—	—	—	—	12	23-Zn	—	—	Soluble

[a]Salt index is a measure of the effect of fertilizers on the salt concentration of the soil solution. The concentration of the soil solution is compared against an equal weight of sodium nitrate, which was assigned a value of 100.

[b]A = Acid Reaction, B = Basic Reaction, N = Neutral

[c]These nutrients are applied in such minute quantities that any effect on soil acidity is negligible except for iron sulfate which can be applied in quantities large enough to increase acidity.

Adapted from: Swanson, B. T., C. Rosen, R. Munter, and C. Lane. 1986. *Soil Testing and Fertilizer Applications for Nursery Management and Production*. University of Minnesota Agricultural Extension Service Bulletin AG-BU-2830.

Nitrogen is the *least expensive* fertilizer element. The cost of nitrogen increases in blended and slow release materials. Phosphorus, especially in a completely soluble form, is the *most expensive* macronutrient. Micronutrients are very expensive on a per-pound basis, but are used in small quantities per acre.

Types of Fertilizers

The most familiar products are dry *inorganic* fertilizers. These are chemical salts that provide readily available plant nutrients. Inorganic fertilizers are often salts impregnated onto a carrier. The nutrients are put into solution by water. Inorganic fertilizers may provide specific elements, such as ammonium nitrate (33-0-0) or urea (45-0-0), or several elements when they are combined as blends, such as 27-3-3.

Liquid or *water-soluble* fertilizers are used in the greenhouse and turfgrass industries. The carrier is eliminated making the product completely water soluble. Water soluble formulations may be sprayed on plant foliage or injected into the soil. In the soil, soluble nutrients act similar to those from dry formulations; there is no difference in the source of nutrients to the plant. Water soluble forms of phosphorus and potassium are expensive but are valuable for providing nutrients when conventional application methods are unavailable.

Acidic fertilizers are available in dry and soluble formulations. These products use a sulfur-based or other acidic sources of the nutrient, such as ammonium sulfate or ammonium phosphate. Acidic materials slightly lowers soil *p*H. They are used for fertilizing rhododendrons, azaleas, and other ericaceous species or where high soil or irrigation water *p*H is a problem. These materials may be more expensive than other nutrient formulations but are worth the additional cost in specialized situations.

Slow release formulations reduce nutrient loss due to leaching and provide controlled release of nutrients over time. Depletion of phosphorus and potassium is relatively slow, therefore, there is little need for slow release formulations. Slow release forms of potassium, however, are used in turf management. Depletion and loss of nitrogen, however, is rapid. Controlled-release products are expensive but offer advantages, especially in turf management. Their use may not be justified in ordinary tree and shrub care, however, they have advantages in low fertility and high rainfall areas, or where economics or inaccessibility dictate infrequent fertilizer applications.

Release of nitrogen may be controlled by:

1) *Low permeability coatings* of plastic or wax over soluble fertilizer [Osmocote® (Grace-Sierra) and sulfur coated urea (SCU)]. Nitrogen loss is regulated by particle size and coating thickness. There is some temperature effect and a very large moisture effect on nutrient release. Sulfur coated urea has no appreciable effect on soil *p*H. It should not be relied upon to reduce alkaline soil reactions.

2) Nitrogen formulations that require *microbial action* to release the elements, such as ureaformaldehyde (UF). Ureaformaldehyde was the first synthetic organic fertilizer. Urea is soluble, but complexing with formaldehyde produces a slow release nitrogen. The release rate is based upon formaldehyde content and environmental factors that influence microbial action (temperature, moisture, and *p*H). The nitrogen fractions from UF products are classified as *cold water soluble* (immediately available), *cold water insoluble* (microbially available over a moderate period); and *hot-water insoluble* (microbially available over a long period and unavailable).

Ureaformaldehyde is widely used for turfgrass. Nitrogen application rates can be reduced as a result of residual nitrogen if this material has been used for a period of time. Ureaformaldehyde is also available in micro-fine powders for soil injection. Ureaformaldehyde is formulated with phosphorus and potassium into tablets for use at planting.

Methylene urea is made by the same process but contains a great percentage of cold water soluble and insoluble fractions. Nitrogen is available over a shorter period than UF.

3) *Low solubility* formulations of nitrogen. IBDU (isobutylidene diurea) is a synthetic-organic fertilizer containing 31 percent nitrogen. The nitrogen is released slowly by hydrolysis to urea and is controlled largely by the size of the granule. Dissolution depends on moisture, but there are also temperature and *p*H effects.

Table 10–8.				
Approximate nutrient content (%, analysis) of several organic fertilizers.				
Fertilizer	**N**	**P_2O_5**	**K_2O**	**Comments**
Blood, dried	12.0	1.5	0.5	Rapidly available source of nitrogen.
Bat Guano	6.0	9.0	3.0	Partially decomposed bat manure from caves in southwest U.S.
Bird Guano	13.0	11.0	2.0	Partially decomposed bird manure from islands near South America.
Kelp or Seaweed	1.0	0.5	9.0	Good source of potassium
Manure Cattle Chicken Horse Sheep Swine	 0.5 1.0 0.6 0.9 0.6	 0.3 0.5 0.3 0.5 0.5	 0.5 0.8 0.6 0.8 1.0	Manure is typically low in fertilizer elements, but when used in large amounts as a soil conditioner, adds significant nutrients. Nutrient content varies, particularly with bedding materials used. Avoid fresh manure. Uncomposted animal manure often contains weed seed.
Raw bone meal	4.0	20.0	0.0	Phosphorus very slowly soluble.
Steamed bone meal	2.0	27	0.0	Phosphorus is soluble, some nitrogen lost by steaming.
Cotton seed meal	6.0	2.5	2.0	Acid in reaction, good for ericacous plants
Hoof and horn meal	14.0	0.0	0.0	Good source of organic nitrogen.
Peanut Hulls	1.0	0.0	1.0	Low in nutrients
Sewage sludge	2.0	1.0	0.5	Variable. Check source. Avoid those possibly contaminated with heavy metals.
Activated Sewage sludge	6.0	3.0	0.5	
Tobacco stems	1.5	1.0	6.0	Good source of potassium; alkaline reaction.
Wood ashes	0.0	2.0	6.0	Source of potassium; very alkaline.
Adapted from: Swanson, B. T., C. Rosen, R. Munter, and C. Lane. 1986. *Soil Testing and Fertilizer Applications for Nursery Management and Production.* University of Minnesota Agricultural Extension Service Bulletin AG-BU-2830.				

4) *Natural organic* fertilizers (blood, bone and fish meal, sewage sludge, manures, and others) are low in nitrogen, usually less than 6 percent, and other elements (Table 10–8). Nutrient availability depends on microbial release. Nitrogen is in an organic form and available slowly over a long period. Natural organics are expensive per pound of plant nutrient, difficult to handle, and may produce unpleasant odors. A manure spreader may also be a little noisy and leaves tracks in the client's petunia bed. Research has proven conclusively that there is no difference in plant absorption and uptake of nutrients, regardless of whether they originate from chemical salts or from natural organic materials.

Organic fertilizers, however, are making significant inroads in the landscape and turfgrass management markets. Technology continues to improve. Composting and digestion have become environmentally feasible methods to dispose of organic wastes that were once buried in landfills. Waste handling operations have also increased in scale so that the quantities of material have increased and the price has decreased. Organic fertilizers, however are still expensive. The attitudes of contractors and clientele are also changing. New emphasis is being placed on "non-chemical" alternatives and for ecologically sound management. Marketing of organic materials has become fierce; confusion and misconceptions have resulted.

Several claims have been made for organic fertilizers, with and without research support. Some organic fertilizers have been shown to suppress some soil-borne pathogens. Research is continuing in this area. Some organic fertilizer marketers claim their products reduce thatch in turfgrass. Fertilizer source, however, has not had any effect in that accumulation according to research. Natural organic fertilizers do add small amounts of organic matter to the soil. The effect may become significant over a period of time. Organic fertilizers do reduce nitrate movement; however, this same benefit is accorded synthetic slow release nitrogen sources.

Table 10–9.
The increase in the number of organic fertilizers on the market has resulted in confusion and misconceptions for marketers, professionals, and clients. There are no universally accepted terms or legal definitions. Several cases involving lawn care and landscape management advertising are pending before the Federal Trade Commission. The Professional Lawn Care Association of America (PLCAA) has provided some definitions to standardize marketing and to reduce misunderstandings. The following are not legal definitions, but guidelines for landscape professionals.
Natural: Products derived from animal, biological, mineral, or plant source in a form substantially the same as it occurs in nature. The materials may be altered or manipulated to improve distribution.
Organic: Any substance containing carbon is "organic." Organic materials may be naturally occurring or man-made.
Natural-based: A mixture that includes natural materials. The portion is not generally defined. Some sources feel that the material should contain at least 50 percent natural material by weight or volume to deserve the term "natural-based."
Organic-based: A mixture including some portion of organic materials. Some sources feel that the material should contain 50 percent or more organic material by weight or bulk to deserve the term "organic-based."
Natural fertilizer: A substance composed only of natural organic and/or natural inorganic fertilizers and fillers.
Natural organic fertilizer: Fertilizers derived from plant or animal products containing one or more essential elements for plant growth. These materials may be subjected to biological degradation.
Natural inorganic fertilizer: A nutrient source produced by or existing in nature. It may be altered from its original state for distribution.

One commercial source, Milorganite® (6-2-0), is comprised of dried and processed sewage sludge from Milwaukee. It has long been and is still used as a non-burn, slow release fertilizer in some segments of the turf and golf course industries. The nitrogen content of natural organic fertilizers is seldom greater than two to three percent. Natural organic fertilizers with a nitrogen analysis greater than this are supplemented or fortified with organic or inorganic chemical fertilizers.

APPLICATION METHODS

Surface application of dry fertilizer

Application of dry fertilizer to the soil surface is the most economical and fastest delivery method. Surface application is appropriate for nutrients that move readily in the soil, notably nitrogen and most chelated micronutrients. Research has shown no difference in plant response if nitrogen was surface applied, applied as a deep root application, or liquid injected into the soil. Soil applied methods were all superior to foliar application of nitrogen.

For an individual tree or groups of trees, surface apply fertilizer to the approximate crown area. This can be calculated as

Photo 10–4. Surface application is the most cost effective method of applying nutrients that are relatively mobile in the soil.

a circle or rectangle. The crown area is a convenient area to calculate and apply fertilizer. Tree roots extend beyond the drip line, however, there are more than sufficient roots beneath the crown to absorb the surface-applied material.

Fertilizer can be surface applied with drop or impeller (cyclone-type) spreaders. Divide the amount of material to be applied in half and apply the two halves separately. Make the second application perpendicular, at a right angle, to the first. Irrigate the area to remove granules from the turf and begin moving it into the root zone.

Surface application to shrub beds is made over the entire bed. Be careful of the turf if applying high rates of nitrogen or at times other than scheduled turf fertilization. Most managers do not schedule separate applications for shrub beds. They make sure that the material applied to turf is also applied to shrub areas. Irrigate after surface fertilizer applications to prevent damage to groundcovers in shrub beds.

Turf beneath trees in under- or non-fertilized turf may be stimulated resulting in an "oasis" effect. This can be compensated by extending the treatment area past the drip line. Fertilized turf may be over-stimulated if high rates of nitrogen are surface applied. Split-surface, deep root feed applications, or soil injection will reduce damage if additional nitrogen over and above that applied to the grass is required.

Surface drenches of soluble fertilizer

Soluble fertilizers are sometimes incorporated in irrigation water and surface applied. This is referred to as *fertigation*. Fertigation can be effective for soil-mobile nutrients, however, it requires a rather expensive proportioner to accurately inject fertilizer into the irrigation system. Soluble nutrient formulations are readily available but offer no other special advantages over dry formulations. They are usually more expensive.

Fertigation is most frequently used for summer applications of nitrogen to warm season turf on golf courses in the South. It has severe limitations for cool season turf and will not likely be adapted in the majority of the nation. Wholesale application of soluble nutrients is an environmentally questionable practice in light of concerns about water and groundwater pollution.

Deep Root Application Methods

Punch or drill method

Application of fertilizers into the root zone of the tree assures availability of non-mobile nutrients such as phosphorus or potassium. Historically, this has been the method for applying all fertilizers to trees. Holes are punched on two-foot centers with a steel bar or drilled (by a manual or power soil auger) under the crown, starting two to three feet from the trunk. This requires 250 holes per 1,000 square feet. The holes should be eight to 12 inches deep.

The fertilizer is divided into equal increments and placed into each hole. Dry fertilizer can be mixed with sand or other material for easier application. The holes

Photo 10–5. Soil augers can be used to add fertilizers to the root zone. Augers also relieve compaction and provide air channels. Photograph by James Robbins.

are filled with the original soil, sand, calcined clay, perlite, or other granular material.

This method is expensive and time consuming. Punching 12-inch holes deep every two feet with an iron bar makes for a *very* long day. Use of a punch bar may also compact the sides of the holes, reducing air and fertilizer movement. Soil augers are preferred for deep root fertilizer applications as they avoid compacting the holes and are much more rapid.

Deep root application avoids the "oasis" of surface applied nitrogen. The operator can use higher rates of nitrogen in a single application with no damage to the turfgrass. It may, however, produce tufts of green grass in the spring. It is an effective method to move phosphorus and potassium into root zone if they are required. This method is also used to successfully apply sulfur:iron sulfate mixtures to combat iron chlorosis. It is seldom used in shrub beds as it can damage the root systems of many species.

Drilling holes with an auger also relieves compaction beneath established trees. Filling the holes with sand, perlite, vermiculite, calcined clay, or other aggregate produces long-term air channels to the root system. Research in Ohio showed trees in poorly drained silt and clay-loam soils benefited as much from drilled holes with no fertilizer as they did from drilled holes with fertilizer.

Soil Injection

Dry material

Injection of dry material, usually mixed with sand or other solid carrier, with high-pressure air requires specialized and expensive equipment and is not widely utilized in the industry. Injection of dry fertilizer can use any source of nutrients, including slow release formulations. The blast fractures soil and relieves compaction; the sand or other aggregate may further alleviate compaction.

Liquid material

Liquid injection of fertilizers for tree and shrubs has become common. It is more rapid and economical than punch and drill methods. The high-pressure hydraulic sprayers used by lawn service and pesticide applicators can be easily adapted to soil injection. Fertilizer solutions are corrosive, but stainless steel or plastic lined tanks reduce equipment maintenance. Pump, lines, and non-protected tanks must be cleaned thoroughly after fertilizer application.

Injection sites should be two to three feet apart, somewhat wider than recommended for punch or drill deep root applications, and eight to 12 inches deep. Limit pressure to 150 to 200 psi. The fertilizer is apportioned equally among the holes. Delivery can be calibrated by meters, or more commonly, by timing each injection to determine the total amount of fertilizer solution, and therefore nitrogen, applied. Soil injection can also improve aeration and water penetration.

Numerous brands and types of soluble complete and specialized fertilizers are available. Many managers mix their own, adding expensive soluble phosphorus and potassium only if the situation warrants. Urea is frequently used as an inexpensive soluble nitrogen source. A micro-fine ground

Photo 10-6. A soil-injection lance used to liquid inject fertilizers into the root zone of trees and shrubs.

ureaformaldehyde product is available to provide slow release nitrogen. This material can be used in soil injection systems without damage to equipment, according to the manufacturer. Soluble iron and other micronutrients, as well as acidifying agents, are also available.

Liquid soil injection is an efficient method of incorporating fertilizer into the soil and becoming the most popular method of providing supplementary fertilization for landscape trees.

Tree spikes

Tree spikes, available from several manufacturers, are solid, bullet-shaped chunks of fertilizer that are implanted into soil. The spikes contain a complete fertilizer with a slow release nitrogen source, with or without micronutrients. They are marketed as different formulations for trees, shrubs, fruit trees, and broadleaf evergreens. The number of spikes driven into the ground depends on the size of the tree to be treated.

As a fertilizer, they are probably the most expensive source of nitrogen available. The spikes are also probably the least effective method of fertilization. The salt content of the fertilizer material is very high; I have seen turf killed in areas surrounding soil implanted spikes. It requires several months for the fertilizer salts from the spikes to dissolve and disperse in the soil to a level low enough to allow effective absorption without potential damage to the roots. The few point sources of fertilizer are inadequate for effective adsorption by trees.

"Palm spikes" containing manganese, potassium, and magnesium have been used for correcting deficiencies of these elements. Some landscape managers that I have spoken with have been pleased with the results of these products in palm nutrition programs.

Foliar application

Application of nutrients to leaves is not as effective as soil treatment. Nutrients are absorbed by leaves, however, the absorption may be limited. Foliar sprays can be used to apply macro- and micronutrients in situations where traditional soil application is difficult or impossible, such as trees in parking lots, above- or below-ground planters, or plants where the root zone is covered by a surface.

Fertilizers used in aerial sprays are soluble and dilute. Addition of a surfactant increases nutrient foliar absorption, however, excessive surfactant may cause the fertilizer to "burn" the leaves. Foliar fertilization must be repeated more frequently, up to six or more times per year in some situations. Thorough coverage is essential and plant absorption and damage are influenced by temperature, moisture, and relative humidity. Leaf and over-spray residues may not be desirable.

Photo 10–7. Foliar application of soluble nutrients is the only way to fertilize some plants where the root zone is inaccessible.

Trunk implants and injections

Trunk implants or injections of nutrients are effective ways to supply micronutrients that would be tied up if soil applied, notably iron, manganese, and possibly zinc. Neither method should be considered for nitrogen nor other macronutrients. The amount that can be supplied via injections or implants is negligible compared to the plant's requirements and the possibility of defoliating the tree is very high.

One implant system available from several companies uses dry water-soluble micro-element salts or chelates of micronutrient in gelatin capsules (see Photo 10–11). These gelatin capsules are inserted into holes drilled into the tree trunk; they dissolve and the "payload" is delivered to the leaves via the transpiration stream. Some implants require the hole to be sealed, others do not. Insecticides and other materials are also available as implant capsules.

Pressure injection systems using bottled nitrogen, compressed air, or adapting a pressure sprayer are used to inject micronutrients, growth regulators, insecticides, and fungicides into a tree. Most species can be successfully treated in this manner, however, it appears butternut (*Juglans cinerea*),

Photo 10-8. Power injection to trees can result in bark splitting and trunk cracks to some species and if the injection is improperly done.

Photo 10-9. The Mauget® system inject minor nutrients under low pressure. Photograph by James Robbins.

shagbark hickory (*Carya ovata*), white ash (*Fraxinus americana*), some maples, fir, some pine, and a few others do not readily accept injection solutions.

The Mauget® system uses a small volume of concentrated nutrient or other solutions injected into trees under slight pressure using plastic reservoirs. This system makes the smallest wound of any of the injection or implant systems discussed.

A gravity-fed system is used to inject iron sulfate for iron chlorosis (Medi-ject®). Iron sulfate and water are placed in a reservoir elevated above and connected to the several injection sites at the base of the tree trunk. The material enters the trunk and is carried via the transpiration stream. Time required for emptying the reservoir varies and is much more rapid under conditions where the tree is rapidly transpiring (Photo 10-10).

Objection to all injections and implants centers around the wounding of the tree. Injection wounds provide potential entry to decay and disease organisms, discoloring of the wood, and possible weakening of the trunks of small trees. Other potential problems include sap leakage from holes, damage to the cambium at insertion points, and leaf burn and defoliation when too much nutrient is applied at the wrong time to sensitive species. Research in this area has not provided consistent findings.

To minimize potential injury: 1) use the smallest injection holes possible; 2) inject as low on the trunk or root flare as possible; 3) space sites in a spiral around the trunk; and 4) always follow label directions for recommended rates and materials.

Trunk injections and implants are effective and efficient methods of providing some micro-nutrients and other materials to a tree that could not be accommodated in other ways. Trunk

Photo 10-10. The Medi-ject® system infuses iron sulfate for control of iron chlorosis in trees. Results last for up to 5 or more years.

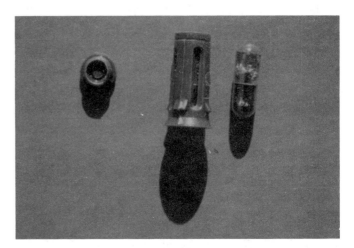

Photo 10-11. A solid implant of an iron compound for relieving iron chlorosis in trees. Treatments last for up to two to three years.

treatment with micronutrients will last up to several years. Certain precautions should be taken, however, to reduce potential plant injury. I know of no situations where injections or implants have been recommended for or applied to shrubs.

Soil Reaction (*p*H)

Soil reaction, or *p*H, refers to the *acidity* or *alkalinity* of the soil. It is a measure of the relative proportion of hydrogen (H+) and hydroxide (OH−) ions. Soil *p*H is measured on a 14 point scale. The middle, *p*H 7.0, is neutral. Values greater than *p*H 7 are alkaline and those below are acidic. The scale is logarithmic. A soil *p*H of 6.0 is, therefore, ten times more alkaline (less acid) than a *p*H of 5.0. A *p*H of 7.0 is 100 times more alkaline than *p*H 5.0, a *p*H of 8.0 is 1,000 more alkaline, and so on.

Soil reaction information is necessary for determining soil fertilizer requirements and for developing fertilization programs. The *p*H of a soil affects the availability of nutrients to the plant and the activity of microorganisms. Soil *p*H is not the only factor governing nutrient availability but it has a tremendous impact (Figure 10-1). All micronutrients, except molybdenum and chloride, become less available as soil alkalinity increases. Phosphorus also becomes less available in high *p*H soils. Iron and manganese can become seriously deficient in alkaline soils. The *p*H at which iron and manganese deficiencies affect growth or elicit symptoms varies among plant species and individuals within a species. Conversely, manganese and aluminum can reach toxic levels under highly acid conditions.

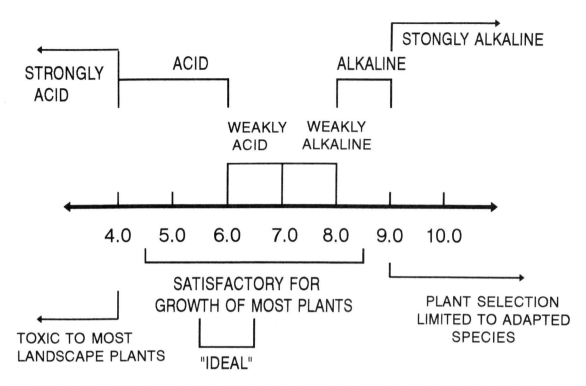

Figure 10–1. Relative alkalinity and acidity (*p*H) of soils. The scale is logarithmic. A soil *p*H of 4.0 is 10 times more acid than a *p*H of 5.0 and 100 times more acid than a *p*H of 6.0.

Most plants will tolerate a range of *p*H, usually from 5.0 to 8.3. A *p*H of 8.3 is as high as calcium-based soils can go. Soils with higher *p*H values involve sodium or other salts and growth is limited to tolerant species. Soil *p*H below 4.0 are toxic to all but a few of the most tolerant species. The "best" or "ideal" soil *p*H for ornamental plant growth is between 5.5 and 6.5.

Adjusting Soil *p*H

Soil *p*H can be adjusted by addition of *lime* or *sulfur*. The amount of material necessary depends upon the level of change desired, soil texture, organic matter, and the material used. Fine-textured soils or those high in organic matter require more lime or sulfur to attain a given change in *p*H than coarser-textured soils.

Acid soil *p*H is moderated by addition of ground or *agricultural limestone* (calcium

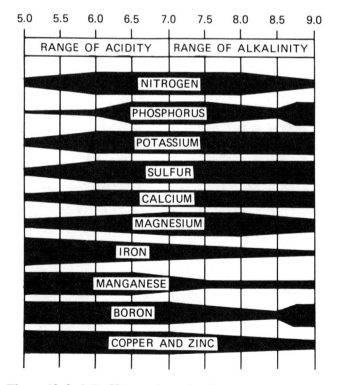

Figure 10–2. Soil *p*H has a dramatic effect on many nutrients. Availability of most decrease as soil *p*H increases.

199

carbonate) or *dolomite* (calcium magnesium carbonate). *Quicklime* (calcium and magnesium oxides) and *slaked lime* (calcium and magnesium hydroxides) act more quickly than limestone but they are more expensive and difficult to handle. The duration of the change in *p*H is shorter than from limestone.

Soil *p*H should never be adjusted except under the guidance of a soil test. The amount of amendment necessary is determined by a separate soil test using a buffer to measure the potential soil acidity or alkalinity. Table 10-10 indicates the *approximate* amounts of ground limestone or dolomite lime necessary to achieve a change in *p*H. These amounts are based upon water *p*H.

To be most effective, lime should be spread evenly over the soil surface soil and incorporated. Ideally, *p*H adjustment should occur before planting. Lime can be surface applied over existing turf and around ornamental plants with no damage. The change in *p*H by surface applied material will take longer to occur since the limestone must dissolve and leach into the soil.

Alkaline soils are acidified by applying *agricultural sulfur*. The amount of sulfur required to lower *p*H is greatly influenced by the buffering capacity of the soil. Limestone-based soils are difficult to successfully acidify for long periods. The carbonate in the soil provides a constant source of neutralizing material. It is much easier to raise than lower soil *p*H. Again, sulfur should be added on the basis of a soil tests. Table 10-11 provides *approximate* rates of agricultural sulfur based upon water *p*H for three soil types. Modification by sulfur is most effective when it can be incorporated prior to planting.

Sulfur can be applied to turf and existing ornamental plantings. Foliar burn can occur during periods of temperature over 80°F and high humidity. Do not apply more than five pounds of sulfur per 1,000 square feet per application over turf.

Finely-ground dusting and spray sulfur can also be used to lower soil reaction. These work more rapidly than agricultural sulfur but are much more expensive and difficult to handle. *Aluminum sulfate* is frequently recommended for lowering soil *p*H. It is more expensive but acts more rapidly. The duration of change is not as long as with sulfur. Excessive amounts of aluminum sulfate can result in potential aluminum toxicity at low soil *p*H. Additions of sulfur or lime do not prompt permanent changes in soil *p*H; periodic re-treatment will be necessary.

Table 10-10.					
Amounts of agricultural limestone needed to increase soil *p*H to approximately 6.5 in upper 6 to 8 inches of several soils.					
Desired increase in *p*H	**Limestone (pounds/1,000 square feet.)**				
	Sand	**Sandy loam**	**Loam**	**Silt loam**	**Clay loam**
4.0 to 6.5	60	115	165	200	230
4.5 to 6.5	50	100	135	165	195
5.0 to 6.5	45	80	110	130	155
5.5 to 6.5	30	60	80	95	110
6.0 to 6.5	15	35	40	50	60
Dolomitic limestone containing both calcium and magnesium is preferred in areas where magnesium deficiencies exist.					

Table 10–11.

	Sulfur (pounds/1,000 sq. ft.)		
Change in *p*H desired	Sands	Loams	Clays
8.5–6.5	50	60	70
8.0–6.5	28	35	50
7.5–6.5	12	20	25
7.0–6.5	3	4	7

Amount of sulfur (pounds per 1,000 square feet) needed to reduce soil *p*H of several soils to approximately 6.5.

Fertilizer Pollution

Concern about contamination of ground and surface water is increasing among the general public and professional grounds managers. Agriculture is a major contributor to fertilizer and pesticide pollution. The landscape management industry is highly visible. A great deal of public concern has been directed toward it. Some of this criticism is warranted, some is not. Regardless, concern over fertilizer and pesticides will continue in the future. The green industry must police itself, otherwise, someone else will.

Nitrogen will move through the soil and enter ground and surface water primarily through leaching. Phosphorus loss is almost entirely due to erosion, although phosphorus can leach from sandy soils.

The following are some guidelines that can minimize the impact of nutrient pollution:

Photo 10–12. Take special care when developing nutrient program and making fertilizer application around water.

1. Do not regularly over-water. Excessive irrigation leaches nitrates.

2. Keep erosion to a minimum, especially near bodies of water.

3. Apply only the amount of nitrogen fertilizer needed. Apply it at the optimum time for plant utilization and apply it in a manner to minimize loss. Use slow release fertilizers where economically and ecologically practical.

4. Avoid using phosphate fertilizers to landscape plantings unless required. Be careful of phosphate applications to turfgrass and landscape beds in sandy soils or sites with surface run-off or erosion.

Bibliography

Agnew, M. 1993. Natural organic nitrogen sources. *Golf Course Management,* Special International Edition:39–42.

Anonymous. 1991. PLACCA offers guideline on advertising. *LESCO News,* 23(5):16–1.

Anonymous. 1991. Tree fertilization. *Arbor Age,* 11(2):32–38.

Barnard, B. 1990. Methods and materials. *Tree Care Industry,* 1(3):8–10.

Carpenter, P. L., and T. D. Walker. 1990. *Plants in the Landscape.* W. H. Freeman, New York, NY.

Carrow, R. N. 1982. Efficient use of nitrogen fertilizer. *Grounds Maintenance,* 17(7):10–18.

Chapman, D. J. 1982. Timing and methods for landscape trees. *Weeds, Trees and Turf,* 19(3):66,68.

Chase, A. R. and T. K. Broschat. 1991. *Diseases and Disorders of Ornamental Palms.* APS Press, St. Paul, MN.

Copley, K. 1981. Soil testing. *Grounds Maintenance,* 16(6):22–26.

Doughty, S. C. 1988. The basics of tree fertilization. *Landscape Contractor,* 29(9):11–14.

Ferrandiz, L. 1990. Tree fertilization techniques. *Grounds Maintenance,* 25(6):10–14.

Feucht, J. R. and J. D. Butler. 1988. *Landscape Management.* Van Nostrand Reinhold Co., NY.

Fischbach, J. E. and B. Webster. 1982. New method of injecting iron into pin oaks. *Journal of Arboriculture,* 8(9):240.

Funk, R. 1990. How trees take up nutrients. *Grounds Maintenance,* 25(6):16–22.

Funk, R. 1990. Fertilizer basics. *American Nurseryman,* 172(11):55–63.

Gerstenberger, P. 1990. Soil *pH* and nutrient availability. *Tree Care Industry,* 1(3):12–13.

Gibson, H. 1990. Fertilizer spreaders. *Grounds Maintenance,* 25(9):10–20.

Gitlin, B. 1993. Organic fertilizers. *Lawn & Landscape Maintenance,* 13(5):52–59.

Good, G. 1989. Fertilizing shade trees. *Landscape Contractor,* 30(5):20–21.

Hall, R. 1991. Natural organic fertilizers. *Landscape Management,* 30(12):8–9.

Harris, R. W. 1992. *Arboriculture. Integrated Management of Trees, Shrubs and Vines in the Landscape.* Prentice-Hall, Inc., Englewood Cliffs, NJ.

Harris, R. W., J. Paul and A. Leiser. 1977. *Fertilizing Woody Plants.* University of California Agricultural Science Leaflet 2958.

Hensley, D. 1989. How to study for a soil test. *Nursery Manager,* 5(7):104–105.

Hensley, D. and G. Aldridge. 1990. The effect of nitrogen fertilization on spring and fall Scotch pine. *Nursery Manager,* 6(5):60–61.

Hensley, D., R. McNiel, and R. Sundheim. 1988. Management influences on growth of transplanted *Magnolia grandiflora. Journal of Arboriculture,* 14(8):204–207.

Hensley, D., R. McNiel, and R. Sundheim. 1989. Magnolia grandiflora. *Nursery Manager,* 5(2):62–67.

Hodel, D. R. 1992. An update on the mineral nutrition of palms. *Pacific Coast Nurseryman,* May:55–60.

Hoehn, C. 1993. Slow-release fertilizers: When is the price right? *Lawn & Landscape Maintenance,* 14(8):24–32, 68.

Kelsey, P. 1990. Salt in fertilizer. *Tree Care Industry,* 1(3):18.

Kvaalen, R. V. and P. L. Carpenter. 1978. *Fertilizing Woody Plants.* Purdue University Cooperative Extension Bulletin HO-140.

McIver, T. 1990. Liquid vs. dry: The pendulum swings. *Landscape Management,* 29(8):26–27.

Morris, R. L. and B. T. Swanson. 1990. Iron chlorosis in trees. *Journal of Arboriculture,* 16(10):279–280.

Mugaas, R. J., M. L. Agnew, and N. E. Christens. 1992. Fertilizing to protect surface water quality. *Landscape Management,* 31:38–40.

Neely, D., E. B. Himelick, and W. R. Crowley, Jr. 1970. Fertilization of established trees: A report of field studies. Illinois Natural History Survey Bulletin, 30(4):235-266.

Peck, T. R. 1981. What to expect from soil tests. *Journal of Arboriculture,* 7(1):11-12.

Pirone, P. P., J. R. Hartman, M. A. Sall, and T. P. Pirone. 1988. *Tree Maintenance.* 6th edition. Oxford University Press, New York, NY.

Rao, B. 1990. Iron chlorosis. *Grounds Maintenance,* 25(6):44-49, 65-66.

Rogers, M. 1993. Slow-release nitrogen. *Grounds Maintenance,* 28(7):12-22, 70.

Schwartz, J. W. and R. F. Follett, 1979. Liming Acid Soils. USDA Fact Sheet AFS-4-5-4.

Smith, E. M. and C. H. Gilliam. 1980. Soil fertility practices are vital for growing healthy landscape plants. *American Nurseryman,* 151(3):15, 78-81.

Smith, E. M. 1978. Fertilizing trees and shrubs in the landscape. *Journal of Arboriculture,* 4(7):157-161.

Smith, E. M. 1986. *Fertilizing Landscape and Field Grown Nursery Crops.* Ohio State University Cooperative Extension Service Bulletin 650.

Smith, E. 1988. Systemic fertilization of trees. *ALA,* 9(9):32-34.

Smith, E. 1990. Tree fertilization. *Tree Care Industry,* 1(3):4-5.

Steele, B. 1991. Liquid vs. dry fertilizers: Perception and reality. *The Landscape Contractor,* 32(3):16-17.

Stevens, R. H. 1993. Different fertilizers for different applications. *The Landscape Contractor,* 34(7):12-15.

Stevens, R. H. 1993. Organic fertilizers: Some comments. *The Landscape Contractor,* 34(7):16-17.

Stevens, R. H. 1993. Soil testing for best results. *The Landscape Contractor,* 34(7):18-19.

Swanson, B. T. and C. Rosen. 1984. *Tree Fertilization.* University of Minnesota Cooperative Extension Bulletin AG-FO-2421.

Swanson, B. T., C. Rosen, R. Munter, and C. Lane. 1986. *Soil Testing and Fertilizer Applications for Nursery Management and Production.* University of Minnesota Cooperative Extension Service Bulletin AG-BU-2830.

Tatter, T. A. 1992. Recommendations for liquid soil fertilization of trees and shrubs. *Arbor Age,* 12(2):28-30.

van de Werken, H. 1984. Why use obsolete fertilizer practices? *American Nurseryman,* 159(7): 65-71.

van de Werken, H. 1984. Fertilization practices as they influence growth rate of young trees. *Journal Environmental Horticulture,* 2(2):64-69.

Vidic, T. F. 1993. Fertilizing woody landscape plants. *Landscape Management,* 32(6):30, 34.

Watson, G. 1992. Tree and shrub fertilization. *Grounds Maintenance,* 27(1):42-46.

Watson, G. W. and P. Kelsey. 1993. Soils: The root of tree problems. *Arbor Age,* 13(8):14-18.

Westrick, D. 1991. Perception vs. reality: How much fertilizer do trees need? *Lawn & Landscape Maintenance,* 12(1):52.

Whitcomb, C. E. 1987. *Establishment and Maintenance of Landscape Plants.* Lacebark Publications, Stillwater, OK.

Whitworth, D. 1989. Mediocre growing conditions accentuate need for fertilization. *Lawn and Landscape Maintenance,* 10(10):50-51.

Williams, D. J. 1984. *Fertilizers for Landscape Plants.* University of Illinois Cooperative Extension Service Bulletin NC-10-84.

Yeager, T. H. and E. F. Gilman. 1990. *Fertilization of Trees and Shrubs in Home and Commercial Landscapes.* University of Florida Cooperative Extension Service Special Series ORH-05.

Chapter 11
Color in the Landscape

Color, the most striking component of any landscape, has taken on new meaning in the realm of commercial landscapes. Home gardeners have long used annuals, perennials, bulbs, and other seasonal plants to produce continuous and changing colorful accents in their landscapes. Color, in the form of seasonal displays, has become important to many corporate landscapes and to many landscape managers. Beds of annuals, groundcovers, and perennials are used to brighten and accent corporate headquarters, office buildings, hotels, shopping centers, apartment and condominium developments, parks, and metropolitan areas.

Color has become an important selling tool in the competitive game of office and apartment leasing. Beds of flowering plants provide the competitive edge to persuade people to patronize one restaurant, hotel, mall, or apartment complex over another. Some commercial property managers consider the cost of annuals as an advertising expense rather than site maintenance. Many companies base their success and "uniqueness" on the visual quality of their environment. Flowers make large residential complexes seem more like individual "homes."

Color has universal appeal. People prefer to live, work, and shop in pleasant environments and colorful flowers certainly contribute to the "atmosphere." A summer survey of campus employees at Kansas State University asked about various aspects of the campus. The most frequent positive comment concerned the beds of annual flowers around the campus. This astounded the "powers that be;" they had never considered the impact of annual flowers beyond decoration and a budget expenditure.

Success with annual color requires selection of the appropriate plants and sites, as well as adequate bed preparation and post-planting management.

Photo 11–1. Color from herbaceous and woody plants are an important part of commercial landscapes. Color adds interest, definition, and identity to the landscape. Large residential complexes seem more like home. Photograph by James Robbins.

Annuals

Annuals or *bedding plants* are general names applied to true botanical annuals and tender perennials that are unable to survive winter except in the mildest areas of the nation. Innumerable species in endless sizes and colors are available. Annuals are one of the most inexpensive ways to brighten a dull landscape and to attract attention.

Photo 11–2. Annuals or bedding plants are the mainstay of landscape color plantings. Petunia is one of the five species that make up the majority of bedding plants used in residential and commercial landscapes.

Photo 11–3. Use annuals and other color plantings in high visibility areas. Entry signs and areas where people congregate or view are prime locations.

Design

Annuals can be used in beds, borders, to create special effects, in containers, and as subtle additions to passive areas. Select colors carefully; the design need not be a collection of color nor species. Large massed beds of single-color annuals are attractive, sophisticated, and appropriate for many particular situations.

If limited because of spatial, environmental, or budgetary restrictions, concentrate on the critical areas. Key impact areas include entry areas, signs, outdoor eating areas, and other places where people congregate or view. Be imaginative! A relatively few species, impatiens (*Impatiens wallerana*), begonias (*Begonia* spp.), marigolds (*Tagetes* spp.), petunias (*Petunia* × *hybrida*), and annual vinca (*Catharanthus roseus*), account for the vast majority of the annual flowers in commercial landscapes. The accompanying lists in Appendix 6 provide suggested favorites, and tried-and-true annuals for several regions of the country.

Consider maintenance when designing annual beds. Although some flowers qualify as truly low-maintenance plants, most do not. Place beds away from street and parking lot curbs to reduce stress. Avoid small beds of less than 50 square feet. Locate color beds a minimum of six feet from the base of shallow-rooted trees to reduce competition for nutrients and water. Be sure that there are water hookups near the bed. Even if there is an irrigation system, hand watering will be necessary during establishment and times of stress.

Photo 11–4. These pansies and snapdragons are a fall-winter color display for this Southern California landscape.

Photo 11–5. Mums are a favorite fall display in the Midwest.

Commercial clients want extended landscape color, 12 months per year if possible. Beds are re-planted or "changed" with new, fresh plants. The number of *color changes* depends on the environment and budget. In milder climates, year-round color is relatively easy to achieve. In colder climates, however, the choices for late fall, winter, and early spring color are limited.

Pansies (*Viola × wittrockiana*) and spring-flowering bulbs are favorites for spring color and are usually followed by a summer display of flowering annuals. Fall displays of mums (*Chrysanthemum × morifolium*), flowering cabbage (*Brassica oleracea*) or kale, pansies, wallflowers (*Erysimum* spp.), or snapdragons (*Antirrhinum majus*) can follow summer annuals. Christmas rose (*Helleborus niger*), an evergreen perennial, may be planted for December and January bloom in much of the South.

Seasonal color must be *cost effective*. Some publications refer to a *cost:bloom* ratio. This is simply the cost per plant, including maintenance, divided by the days of effective floral display. This number allows comparison of the different alternatives available. Mums are a favorite fall flower in many areas; however, some landscape managers have found their limited floral time difficult to justify in light of cost. Other managers use marigold, petunias, or ornamental cabbage or kale for fall displays. Although more cost effective, transplants of these species are difficult to find in the autumn.

The humble pansy is one of the most cost effective bedding plants in the milder areas of the nation. Planted in the fall, they provide sporadic color throughout the winter, join with spring-flowering bulbs in the spring, and provide their own exhibition up to the time for planting summer annuals.

207

Photo 11-6. Pansies are one of the most versatile fall/winter/ spring color plants for milder areas of the country. Photograph by James Robbins.

Plant selection

There are many species of flowering annuals and perennials grown throughout the country. Within these, there are innumerable cultivars that vary in size, color, form, season of bloom, pest resistance, and environmental tolerance. Foremost, choose plants that tolerate the environment of the site. No amount of management can counteract the wrong plant for the site. Appendix 6 provides lists of annuals tolerant to various environments.

Select and use only quality plants. Bedding plants should have healthy roots extending to all sides of the pot. The top should be deep green and well proportioned to the size of the container and character of the plant. Plants with excessive tops use more water than their small root systems can supply upon planting. Plants should be free of insects and diseases and hardened-off to prevent scorching in the full sun.

Plants grown in *cell packs* are the most important component of the retail bedding plant market. Commercial landscape managers generally want larger, better established plants. Commercial sites typically use plants grown in large cell packs and four- and five-inch pots. Some managers prefer six-inch or even larger material. Plant prices increase in direct proportion to the pot size. Large plants, however, provide immediate effect. The client sees the results of his/her expenditure at once. In actuality, the individual cost of the plant is small when compared to labor and equipment for preparing, planting, and maintaining the bed. The firm can offer the client instant gratification with only a moderate increase in actual cost.

Most management firms purchase bedding plants from local or regional wholesale greenhouses. Contact the greenhouse grower far enough in advance to be sure that the quantities of the specific plants needed will be available and ready on the prescribed date. Choice is limited to what the grower has or will produce, however, special-order crops are possible with adequate notice. Some growers have begun producing plants for summer and fall planting, in addition to the traditional spring market. This has added to the variety of autumn color that the landscape management firm may offer.

Many landscape management firms have found it advantageous and profitable to produce their own transplants. This assures quantities and delivery dates and allows flexibility in species and cultivar selection. Consider all of the facility and material costs, as well as the special labor requirements before plunging into the greenhouse business. Running a greenhouse is like running a dairy; it requires daily commitment.

Bed Preparation

Proper soil preparation is critical for the success of annuals and other color plants. The area should be tilled to a depth of eight to 16 inches. Most floriculturists recommend incorporation of organic matter such as leaf mold, compost, peat moss, or sterilized manure. Organic matter improves moisture retention, drainage, aeration, and structure of the soil. Incorporate organic matter at a rate of approximately 20 to 25 percent of the volume of the root zone. This will require 2 inches of material if tilled to an eight inch depth.

Fertilizer is also incorporated during be preparation. Most summer annuals do not require a high level of fertilization. The fertilizer applied assures establishment, vigorous initial growth, and subsequent flowering. Apply one to two pounds of nitrogen per 1,000 square feet of bed as a complete low-nitrogen material with a ratio of 1:2:1, 1:1:1, 1:2:2, or similar. Higher rates are sometimes used, however, excessive nitrogen results in leggy plants, rank vegetative growth, and reduces flowering. Some managers incorporate slow release products such as Osmocote® [Grace Sierra] or sulfur coated urea at planting to reduce supplemental additions of nitrogen. I have read no recommendations for use of high-nitrogen material such as ammonium nitrate or urea with annuals; all have employed a low-nitrogen complete fertilizer.

Most annuals tolerate a soil pH range from 5.0 to 7.0 or slightly higher. Use tolerant species for alkaline sites. Addition of lime, sulfur, or other pH adjusting materials should not be made except on the basis of a soil test. Several managers also incorporate fungicides, wetting agents, and water-holding compounds. Their cost and dubious benefits should be carefully evaluated and justified before increasing project costs.

After incorporating organic material and other amendment and thoroughly tilling, the beds should be raked smooth and slightly mounded. Remove sticks, roots, clods, and debris from the bed and the site.

Planting

Do not plant summer annuals until danger of frost is past. Some species are relatively cold-hardy and can be planted in the early spring or even the fall in some areas. Store annuals that cannot be planted immediately due to scheduling or weather in a lightly shaded area. Be sure they are watered as necessary.

Photo 11-7. Annuals require diligent watering and care while awaiting installation.

209

Keep plants moist during the planting operation. They may dry out quickly in the open. Carefully remove plants from the pot, including those made of peat. Gently crush the root mass with the fingers to stimulate root growth into the surrounding soil. Begin planting in the center of the bed and keep traffic in the worked soil to a minimum. Make the hole slightly larger than the root ball and set the plant at the same depth or slightly higher than it was growing in the container. Smooth out the soil around the plants after planting, including footprints. Planting aids and mechanical planters speed large scale operations.

Mulching

Some landscape managers *mulch* annuals immediately after planting, others wait until the plants have "set-up" for a few days, and others (probably the majority) do not mulch at all. Mulch aids water conservation, weed control, and gives the bed a "finished" look. Apply two inches of organic mulches such as pinestraw, bark, compost, fumigated or composted hay or straw. Incorporating the organic mulch from the previous year or planting adds organic matter to the bed. Some additional fertilizer should be incorporated at planting if an organic mulch is used or a small amount of a low-nitrogen material spread on top of fresh organic mulch. This compensates for nitrogen loss during decomposition of the mulch.

Watering-in

Water the newly planted bed immediately after planting or mulching. Use a water wand, breaker, or sprinkler to water the base of the plants. Water until the bed is wet to a depth of three inches for transplants from two-inch containers and deeper for those from larger pots. Keep the wand or breaker in motion to reduce washing of the soil or mulch.

Some managers water-in with or inject a "starter" solution containing a soluble, high-phosphate fertilizer such as 10-52-17. The benefit from this may be questionable especially if adequate amounts of nutrients are incorporated prior to planting.

Summer Fertilization

Summer annuals will require one or two additional applications of a 1:2:1, 1:1:1, or similar ratio fertilizer at the rate of one-half to one pound of nitrogen per 1,000 square feet of bed (one to two pounds of 5-10-5 per 100 square feet) during the growing season. An alternative is to water with a dilute solution of 20-20-20 or similar soluble fertilizer every four to six weeks.

Irrigation

The water needs of summer annuals are similar to those of turfgrass. Deep, less frequent irrigation encourages deeper rooting. Incorporation of organic matter during bed preparation increases water holding capacity and drainage. Beds surrounded by turf should be slightly raised to prevent ponding of surface water from the lawn. Annuals may be watered with soakers, by hand, or with sprinklers. Drip emitters and mini-spray heads can be easily added to existing drip systems. Overhead sprinklers can damage large or fragile blossoms and wet foliage predisposes some annuals to increased disease problems. Schedule overhead irrigation early enough during the day to allow rapid drying of the leaves.

Physical Care

Faded flowers of calendula (*Calendula officinalis*), dahlia (*Dahlia* spp.), geraniums (*Pelargonium* x *hortorum*), marigolds, some petunias, and a few other species should be periodically removed, or *deadheaded*. Deadheading keeps the plants vigorous, reduces disease problems, and increases subsequent flowering. Blossoms can be pinched or removed with hand pruners. Dead leaves of summer annuals should be removed as prudent.

Petunias, snapdragons, and pansies frequently need to be pinched back after transplanting or following the first flush of bloom to control size and increase later flowering. Pinching requirements are less for some newer hybrids. Alyssum (*Lobularia maritima*), phlox (*Phlox subulata*), and other creeping annuals can be pruned if they encroach upon walks or other surfaces.

Weed Control

Weed control is often the most expensive maintenance item for seasonal color beds. Mulching helps to physically control weeds until the plants grow together or "canopy over."

Black plastic is sometimes used as a physical barrier to weeds in low maintenance situations. The plastic is spread over the prepared bed and the edges buried to secure them. Annuals are planted through holes made with a bulb planter or other device. Decrease the spacing between plants to be sure that the plants will grow to a solid bed hiding the plastic. The edges can be hidden by covering with a mulch. Punch additional holes through the plastic between plants to increase water movement to the soil.

Few herbicides have been specifically developed for seasonal color species. Most herbicides were developed for other purposes and adapted for use in these ornamentals. The number of materials and the quantity of herbaceous annuals and perennials included on their labels is somewhat limited. Labeling and the number of available materials are improving, however, as the market potential for "flower" herbicides is realized.

Chemical weed control in an annual bed is complicated by the number of different species planted in one area. A herbicide tolerated by one annual may be deadly to another. Many of our annual flowers are close relatives to some of the targeted weeds. When developing the plant palette for a site, consider herbicide tolerance as well as aesthetic parameters.

The irregular shape and size of annual beds often make calculating the amount of herbicide necessary difficult. Irregular bed shapes make proper herbicide application troublesome or impossible if the material must be kept off of the surrounding turf or ornamentals.

Preemergence herbicides, those that prevent weeds from germinating or growing, provide the most effective chemical control of weeds. There are several preemergence materials that are safe and effective over a wide array of bedding species. *Before applying any pesticide, always read and understand the label.*

In recent years, several *postemergence herbicides* that selectively remove annual grasses from seasonal color plantings have been introduced. The materials, most notably fluazifop (Fusilade

211

2000®) and sethoxydim (Poast®), can be applied over-the-top or as a directed spray to many different species. However, they will damage and kill certain species [*HortScience*, 1987. 22(6)].

Pest Control

Pest problems (bacteria, fungi, insects, or mollusks) are minimal with most annuals and other color plants. Prevention is always the best control. Insect and disease potential can be reduced by proper site selection, proper planting techniques and spacing, and removal of dead leaves and flowers. In short, good management reduces problems.

Some species, however, such as calendula, grandiflora petunias, and zinnias (*Zinnia* spp.) are prone to diseases. Disease incidence and severity are compounded by poor air circulation, moderate shade, and overhead irrigation. Fungicides are effective for reducing or controlling diseases and may be necessary. Avoid problematic species if difficulties persist or for questionable sites.

Aphids, white flies, thrips, and mites are the most common insect pests. Insect problems increase with the stress of summer; pesticide applications may be warranted. Use chemicals as infrequently as possible to insure the greatest benefit.

Slugs and snails can be a serious problem for young annuals and other herbaceous plantings. They are especially fond of marigold, petunia, salvia (*Salvia* × *superba*), and hosta (*Hosta* spp.). Poisonous baits placed in the planting are about the only effective means of control. Bait must be placed where they cannot be consumed by animals or children.

Containers and Hanging Baskets

Movable or stationary containers add color to areas where planting beds are not feasible. Containers can be moved into critical impact areas when they are at their peak and then moved out as they wane. Although management of color plantings in containers is more exacting than for ground beds, many companies have found this an ideal way to dress up entrances, pool-sides, and amenity areas.

Hanging baskets provide unique appeal when filled with trailing annuals or foliage plants. They can be used to brighten or soften pool-sides, patios, entries, and public and private landscape areas. Chains used to display hanging baskets must be sturdy and should not rust. Locate containers and hanging baskets with traffic and safety, as well as display, in mind. Consider the size of the hanging basket and its ultimate weight when filled with media and water. One-gallon of water weighs eight pounds.

The type of pot used as a container depends on the landscape setting, amount of decoration desired, and budget. Regardless

Photo 11-8. Containers of various design make mobile and interesting color displays for residential, commercial, and public landscapes.

of construction material, drainage is essential. If drainage holes are not provided then they should

212

be installed. Some grounds managers use a thick layer of gravel in the bottom of the undrained containers. This should be done *only* if drilling drainage holes is impossible.

Hanging baskets are also available in a variety of materials and come in every imaginable configuration. The most common materials are plastic and sphagnum moss. Reservoirs can be added to the bottom of solid hanging baskets to reduce drainage onto surfaces and store water.

Avoid soil as a container medium. Most firms purchase pre-packaged soilless medium of bark or peat mixed with aggregate materials such as perlite and vermiculite. Some companies mix their own container medium but pre-packaged materials are often more economical considering material, labor, storage, and handling costs. Also, most commercially available media contains adequate nutrients for annuals. Fill containers to within one inch of the rim for easier watering. Leave additional space if mulch is added. Fill hanging baskets to within one-half inch of the rim. Plant annuals, foliage, and other plants as usual. Water-in until water begins to run out of the drainage holes of the container.

Select plants tolerant of the environment they will be placed in. Several popular container and hanging basket plants are listed in Appendix 6.

When replanting previously used containers the old medium should be completely removed. Some site managers, however, only replace the upper six or so inches of large containers with fresh medium during the second year. Re-using old container media increases the chance of soluble salt toxicity and nutrient deficiency, and soil borne insects and diseases. In most situations, complete replacement of the planting medium provides economical and aesthetic insurance.

Containers require more frequent watering than ground beds since the growing area and water reservoir are limited. Containers and hanging baskets often require daily irrigation. Larger pots provide easier moisture management than small containers. Those placed in an exposed environment (sun and wind) lose water even more rapidly. Keep this in mind when planning, locating, and bidding maintenance of containerized color. Drip irrigation can be adapted to containers and hanging baskets.

Because of the frequency of irrigation and therefore leaching of nutrients, containers require more careful monitoring of plant nutrient levels. Fertilize containerized plants with a dilute water-soluble fertilizer during irrigation. Some managers irrigate regularly with a dilute fertilizer solution, however, most fertilize with a water-soluble material only once every week or two. Incorporation of slow-release nitrogen sources in the planting media can provide a nutrient reservoir. Considering the amount of irrigation that containers and hanging baskets receive, there is a fine line between adequate nutrition from long-term sources and over-indulgence. Too much nitrogen causes rank growth and reduced floral display.

Containerized annuals require the same deadheading and monitoring for pest problems as those in ground beds. Containers should be turned occasionally to keep the composition more symmetrical in growth. Hanging baskets may require occasional pruning to keep the cascading growth uniform. Some work on hanging baskets may require step ladders; a factor that should be considered when bidding and budgeting.

SPRING-FLOWERING BULBS

Spring flowering bulbs are favorite color plant in many areas of the country. Post Properties, Atlanta, Georgia plants 1,000,000 spring bulbs annually. Tulips (*Tulipa* spp.) are the most popular

Photo 11–9. Spring-flowering bulbs are an exciting awakening to spring.

bulb used commercially. Tulips should be thought of as an annual, rather than a perennial color crop. The bulbs are usually destroyed during preparation for subsequent plantings of annuals. Transplanting spent bulbs is expensive and re-establishment success is limited. Bloom of "permanent" tulips planted among established landscape ornamentals declines in a few years.

Hyacinths (*Hyacinthus* spp.) are also planted for color and provide a recognizable and subtle fragrance. Hyacinth bulbs are more expensive than tulips. They too should be considered as a one-time plant.

Daffodils and narcissus (*Narcissus* spp.) are hardy, prolific, and persistent spring-flowering bulbs. They are valuable additions to permanent landscape beds, wooded areas, or naturalized landscapes. Daffodils and narcissus will persist many years with little maintenance.

Crocus (*Crocus* spp.) is actually a corm rather than a bulb. Crocus makes an attractive, low maintenance color plant for naturalizing or permanent landscape beds. Narcissus and crocus are best used in mass plantings or drifts.

Photo 11–10. Tulips are the most popular spring-flowering bulbs for professional and home gardeners.

Photo 11–11. Crocus are corms rather than bulbs. They provide long-term inexpensive color for naturalized areas and planted beds. Photograph by James Robbins.

214

Planting Bulbs

Spring flowering bulbs should be planted in the fall; therefore, they require planning, preparation, and early sales to clients.

Label crates and boxes of bulbs carefully upon receipt. Lost tags lead to strange color combinations; a yellow tulip cannot be distinguished from a red one without a label. Store bulbs in a cool, dry area until planting.

In most areas, spring flowering bulbs are planted in the autumn before the ground freezes. Previous color plants are removed and the bed tilled and prepared as discussed earlier. In the South and Southwest (roughly South Carolina to southern California southward) cold-treated bulbs can be planted in mid-January. Store bulbs in reliable commercial storage at 40°F. until planting time. Bulbs require a physiologically predetermined number of hours of cool temperature (below 40°F.) for good flowering. The should bloom eight to ten weeks after planting.

Incorporate fertilizer into spring bulb beds at the same rate described for flowering annuals. The amount to be applied may be reduced if the annuals or fall color planting received substantial or a late side-dressing of fertilizer. Many recommendations suggest that bonemeal be added at planting for all bulbs. Bonemeal is simply a very low nitrogen (and expensive) slow release fertilizer. It imparts no protection for the bulbs and possesses no special attributes.

Space the bulbs four to six inches apart, tip to tip. Lay-out the entire bed before planting, especially if pansies or another cold-tolerant annual is to be added as a companion planting later. Bulbs may be planted with a bulb planter, trowel, or in a pre-dug trench. The depth of planting depends on the type of bulb utilized (Table 11–1). Plant bulbs with the flat side (basal root plate) down and the pointed side up. In higher budget sites, beds are raked to level the area and one to two inches of mulch, such as pinestraw or bark, spread for appearance and to reduce erosion during the winter. Nature will supply the watering-in moisture necessary for fall-planted bulbs, although irrigation should be supplied if the site or season is dry.

Maintenance

Bulbs will sometimes sprout or show foliage during early or mid-winter warm periods. This is not usually a problem; spring-flowering bulbs are very cold tolerant. Extreme temperatures occasionally may yellow the foliage and flowers can be damaged under drastic conditions. Mulching reduces fluctuations in soil temperatures.

For bulbs used as a one-time color display, no maintenance procedures are necessary. If quality bulbs and planting procedures have been used, nature will do the rest. The plants can be deadheaded after the blossoms fade for a neater appearance. Allow foliage to remain if there will be a delay before bed preparation for annuals. Remove the bulbs when preparing the beds for annuals.

Remove the faded flowers of tulips, narcissus, or daffodils that will remain in place to prevent seed formation. Seed production uses carbohydrates that would otherwise be stored in the bulb. Keep the leaves intact as long as possible. Ideally, the leaves should be allowed to turn yellow before they are removed. Delay mowing of the turf in areas containing naturalized bulbs and crocus as long as possible.

Table 11–1. Planting depth and spacing for some common landscape bulbs and corms.

Flowering time	Planting Depth (inches)	Spacing (inches)	Flowering Height
very early			
Galanthus (Snowdrops)	4	1	vl
Eranthis (Winter aconite)	4	1	vl
Iris reticulata	4	2	vl
Crocus	4	2	vl
Chionodoxa (Glory of the snow)	4	2	vl
Puschkinia libanotica	4	2	vl
Fritillaria meleagris	4	4	l
early			
Kaufmanniana tulip	6–8	6	vl
Fosteriana tulip	6–8	6	vl
Single and double early tulips	6–8	6	l
Muscari (Grape hyacinth)	4	2	l
Miniature daffodil	6–8	4	l
Trumpet daffodil	6–8	6	mh
Hyacinth	6–8	6	l
mid-season			
Greigii tulip	6–8	6	l/mh
Mendel and Triumph tulip	6–8	6	mh
Darwin hybrid tulip	6–8	6	mh
Fritillaria imperialis	6–8	12	h
Daffodil and Narcissus	6–8	6	mh
late			
Scilla campanulata (Spanish quill)	4	3	l
Parrot tulip	6–8	6	mh
Double late tulip	6–8	6	mh
Lily-flowered tulip	6–8	6	h
Darwin and Cottage tulips	6–8	6	h/vh
very late			
Dutch iris	6–8	4	mh

vl = very low, up to 6 inches
l   = low, 6–12 inches
mh = medium high, 12–20 inches
h   = high, 20–28 inches
vh = very high, over 28 inches

Plantings of bulbs in permanent beds with other ornamentals will receive adequate nutrition from fertilizer applications. Bulbs are seldom troubled by insects and diseases.

HERBACEOUS PERENNIALS

Perennials have enjoyed a tremendous surge in interest in home and commercial landscapes. A few companies have specialized in designing, planting, and maintaining landscaped perennials. *Perennials* are broadly defined as plants that will survive for three or more years in the landscape (as opposed to annuals or biennials). These species enter dormancy each winter and re-emerge the next spring. The tops generally die down. The term "herbaceous" is frequently appended to perennials to distinguish the soft and fleshy stems of these plants from woody shrubs and trees.

Perennials are especially useful in apartment, condominiums, and corporate landscapes where color is desired throughout the season. They provide a succession of bloom with moderate management and do not require replanting annually.

Herbaceous perennials offer a wide range of color, form, texture, and flowering

Photo 11-12. Perennial plantings are gaining popularity for commercial color plantings. A large selection of species and cultivars are available.

season. Many herbaceous perennials offer striking winter interest. There are perennials suitable to every soil, moisture condition, and light situation. Perennials can be adapted to formal, informal, or naturalistic landscapes. Popular perennials for different regions of the country and others adapted to stressful sites are listed in Appendix 7.

Perennial gardens or beds are not without problems. Deadheading is necessary to maintain plant vigor and flowering and to control re-seeding by certain species. Perennial beds require a large area relative to annual color beds because of the greater mature size and growth rates of the perennials. A variety of plants are required to maintain flowering over the season. Some perennials must be divided and replanted on a three- or four-year cycle (some require annual division). A few perennials are extremely invasive and can become serious weeds.

Quality maintenance of perennial beds and gardens requires understanding and knowledge of the individual plants. This text is too limited in scope to attempt to address the requirements and maintenance techniques of the vast number of species used across the country. Before bidding or engaging in the perennial management business, collect and study some of the informative texts available in the field. As with everything in life, a great deal of the knowledge in the field comes from experience. Be prepared to make and to learn from mistakes.

Photo 11-13. Proper irrigation of perennial and annual color plantings is essential for quality growth and reasonable maintenance.

ROSES

Roses, the "Queen of the flowers," are popular in home gardens. Roses are being used increasingly in commercial landscapes. Roses are most frequently found in apartment, condominium,

217

Photo 11–14. The rose is one of the best loved landscape plants in the world. Unfortunately, they also require more care than most every other landscape ornamental.

and residential communities, rather than corporate landscapes. Roses are best enjoyed where people have time to relax, enjoy, and "stop and smell the roses."

Roses provide incredible diversity in color, form, and texture. Climbing roses can be trained on fences to add another dimension and sense of quality to the landscape. Shrub and miniature roses can be used as groundcovers. Some of the newer "shrub" cultivars make striking and effective bank covers, especially in the milder regions of the nation. Roses, however, are also one of the most demanding and exacting plants in the landscape. They require an enormous expenditure of time, capital, and dedication to keep them presentable. Roses ranked number one among all shrubs in the amount of hours required per 100 square feet of bed in a survey conducted by the University of California. Limit roses to landscapes that can afford them.

Photo 11–15. Several new cultivars of shrub roses are entering the market. These plants require much less care than Hybrid Tea roses and make excellent additions to many landscapes as accents, masses, and tall groundcovers.

Site selection and planting

Select a well-drained site with a minimum five to six hours of full sun. Soil *p*H should be adjusted to 6.0 to 7.2; however, roses are reasonably adaptive. Roses are sometimes susceptible to iron chlorosis in alkaline soils. A soil test provides a true picture of the nutrients that should be incorporated before planting. In the absence of a soil test, incorporate one pound of nitrogen as a 1:2:1, 1:1:1 or similar complete fertilizer per 1,000 square feet. Organic matter (approximately 25 percent of the root volume) may be incorporated prior to planting to improve the water and nutrient reserve, internal drainage, and soil structure. Most rose beds are constructed to be higher than the surrounding soil surface to improve drainage.

Planting holes for roses are the same as those for any other ornamental. Position the bud union (the knob-like area where the scion is grafted or budded to the rootstock) two inches below the soil surface. This will provide additional protection against cold temperatures. Organic mulches aid in water conservation and weed and temperature control. Mulches provide a finished appearance, aid growth and development of the rose, and are always recommended by home and commercial rose growers.

Management

Roses should receive one to two inches of rainfall or supplemental irrigation per week. Irrigate to moisten the soil to a depth of six to ten inches. Drip irrigation or soaker hoses are preferred since wetting the foliage encourages disease. If overhead watering is necessary, irrigate in the early morning so the foliage will dry rapidly.

Fertilize established roses when they begin to leaf out in the spring. Fertilizers incorporating systemic insecticides help reduce some of the inevitable pesticide applications that will be necessary. Insecticide-fertilizer combinations are used by commercial and home gardeners and are probably worth the additional expense in the case of roses. Follow label directions for rates and timing. Fertilizers with a 3:1:1, 2:1:1, or similar complete fertilizer applied once every four weeks is sufficient for proper growth and flowering. A small amount (four to eight ounces) of fertilizer is spread around individual plants. Fertilizer can be broadcast over the entire bed at the rate of one-half to one pound nitrogen per 1,000 square feet.

Insect and Disease Control

Roses are plagued by a variety of diseases and insects. They require a weekly or bi-monthly spray program beginning with the first five-leaflet leaf. Disease pressure can be reduced by proper site selection (full sun and good air circulation) and by avoiding wetting the leaves during irrigation. Remove fallen leaves that host Blackspot and other diseases. Alternate fungicides in the spray program for the best control.

Insect feeding can be reduced by application of fertilizers containing a systemic insecticide. Regardless, monitor the plants carefully and be especially heedful of aphids, mites and thrips.

Pruning

Roses must be pruned frequently during the growing season, often once per week. When pruning, first remove all dead, diseased, and weak (thin and spindly) growth. Remove all branches with stem disease or cankers at least one inch below the diseased portion and disinfect the pruner with a 70 percent or greater alcohol or a weak bleach solution before making another cut. Sucker growth originating from below the bud union must be removed. Make cuts at a 30 to 45 degree angle and one-fourth inch above an out-facing active bud or branch. This keeps the center of the shrub open.

Prune faded flowers to prevent setting of seed and reduction in future flowers. Remove flowers by cutting back to above a five-leaflet leaf. For vigorous-growing cultivars or to control the size of the plant, count down to the third to fifth five-leaflet leaves before removing the faded flower. New shoots will form quickly below this cut and produce the next flower in the shortest possible time. Do not deadhead after September in areas where winter damage can occur.

Miniature roses require only a light pruning to shape them in the early spring. Remove dead, diseased, and damaged wood as necessary during the growing season. Miniatures also require periodic deadheading during the summer.

Climbing roses

Climbing roses bloom only on one-year-old or older canes. Climbing roses are not usually pruned during the first two or three years after planting except to remove dead, diseased, or damaged canes, and to train them. Climbing roses that bloom periodically throughout the summer should be pruned in the spring. Those that flower only in the spring are pruned after flowering.

During annual pruning of climbing roses remove the weakest of the new canes. Also remove the old flowering canes that have lost vigor. Retain five to six of the most vigorous new canes.

Winter protection

Hybrid Tea roses require some form of winter protection in most regions of the country. Most climbing, shrub, and miniature roses are reasonably cold hardy except in extreme northern regions. Winter protection usually consists of mounding eight to ten inches of soil or bark mulch over the center of the plant in late fall, following the first hard freeze. Rose canes can be pruned back to 10 to 14 inches to facilitate covering. Some rose growers cover this soil or bark mound with an additional layer of straw, hay, or bark mulch. The greater the danger of winter injury, the greater the protection required. Straw and hay, how-

Photo 11–16. Roses put to bed for the winter under a blanket of hardwood mulch. The mulch is spread over the bed when the plants are uncovered after danger of frost.

ever, serve as an excellent winter abode for rodents. Styrofoam or plastic rose "cones" are used to cover roses. These, however, provide minimal protection and are not adequate where serious danger of winter injury is prevalent.

The soil or mulch should not be removed until just before growth resumes in the spring and danger of extremely cold weather is past. Bark mulch has an advantage in that it can be spread over the bed. Prune out winter damage after the roses initiate growth and further possibility of low temperature injury is past. Retain four to six healthy canes.

In areas where mounding or additional protection is not needed, Hybrid Tea roses are pruned to three to four feet in the late fall. Plants are again pruned in early spring to remove dead and winter-damage canes. Four to six healthy canes are selected as the main branches of the plant for that season. These are pruned back to 18 to 20 inches; all cuts are made to an outside facing bud.

Bibliography

Anonymous. 1981. *Labor Requirement Analysis for Landscape Maintenance.* Cooperative Extension Leaflet 21232, University of California, Berkeley, CA.

Anonymous. 1986. Perennials mean easier-not forgotten maintenance. *Landscape Contractor,* 27(9):16–17.

Anonymous. 1989. *The Professional Guide to Flowering Annuals.* Professional Plant Growers Association, Lansing, MI.

Armitage, A. M. 1989. *Herbaceous Perennial Plants.* Varsity Press, Inc., Athens, GA.

Bryant, D. 1993. Spring color. *Western Turf Management,* 4(3):6–7.

Cathy, H. M. 1977. *Spring Flowering Bulbs.* USDA-ARS Home and Garden Bull. No. 136.

de Vroomen, R. 1984. Bulbs in the landscape design. *Landscape Contractor,* 25(10):12–13.

Ferguson, S. 1992. Bulbs offer many choices for spring color. *Landscape and Irrigation,* 16(10):22–24.

Graber, D. and D. Hensley. 1987. Evaluation of postemergent grass herbicides for use in annual flower and groundcover plantings. *HortScience,* 22(6):1281–1283.

Hensley, D. and F. Gibbons. 1985. Tolerance of some garden flowers to selected preemergence herbicides. *Transactions Kansas Academy of Science,* 88(3-4):146–153.

Hensley, D., M. Witte, J. Hartman, and R. Scheibner. 1980. *Roses and Their Care.* Cooperative Extension Service Fact Sheet HO-53. University of Kentucky, Lexington, KY.

Leuthold, L. D. and M. Albrecht. 1989. Flowering perennials. Cooperative Extension Service Circular MF-707 Revised, Kansas State University, Manhattan, KS.

Leuthold, L. D. and M. Albrecht. 1989. Flowering annuals. Cooperative Extension Service Circular MF-706 Revised, Kansas State University, Manhattan, KS.

Lewis, A. J. 1988. Commercial color. *American Nurseryman,* 168(12):24–29.

McGarigle, C. 1990. Ravishing roses have a past, present and great future in landscape plans. *Landscape Contractor,* 31(2):24–25.

Peppler, K. 1990. Colorful landscape uses of popular plant materials. *Lawn & Landscape Management,* 11(4):54–56.

Professional Plant Growers Assn. 1989. Keeping the landscape colorful with flowering annuals. *ALA/Maintenance,* 10(6):52.

Reilly, A. 1988. Here today . . . here tomorrow. *Landscape Management,* 27(3):42–46.

Sinnes, A. C. 1981. *All About Annuals.* Ortho Books. San Francisco, CA.

Smith, S. L. 1989. Flower power. *American Nurseryman,* 170(8):69–75.

Stack, L. 1990. Flower power on the golf course. *Landscape Management,* 29(3):72–76.

van der Hoeven, G. A. 1990. Learn to design perennial flower gardens. *Grounds Maintenance,* 25(4):102–106.

Williams, D. 1981. Fertilizers for nonwoody ornamentals. *Grounds Maintenance,* 16(1):14–18, 27.

Chapter 12
Turfgrass Management

by Roch Gaussoin[1] and David Hensley

Turfgrass is the nations' most popular groundcover. Turfgrass management represents a significant portion of the labor expended for landscape management and profit margin of many firms. Full service landscape management companies report that turfgrass maintenance represents 70 percent or more of their effort and gross sales. Any successful landscape management firm must offer some facet of turfgrass management. Programs range from simple chemical applications to full-service site management, including cultural and physical management. Every landscape manager must understand the fundamentals of turfgrass management. The intent of this chapter is to provide a rudimentary understanding of turfgrass management techniques. Refer to the references at the end of this chapter or the introduction of this book for further information.

Introduction

Turfgrass is the surface layer of vegetation used to stabilize the soil, provide a recreational surface, and to enhance the aesthetics of a landscape. Grasses are categorized as *cool* or *warm* season. As this classification implies, *cool season grasses* are best adapted to the cooler regions of the US; *warm season grasses* are better adapted to warmer environments. The *Transition Zone* (Illustration 12–1) is the area where both warm and cool season grasses may be grown, but conditions are ideal for neither. This region presents the greatest challenge to turfgrass managers. Cool season grasses are susceptible to summer stresses and warm season grasses are prone to winterkill.

Illustration 12–1.

Establishment and Renovation

Turfgrasses can be established from seed or vegetatively propagated using sod, sprigs, or plugs. Establishment methods depend on species, availability, and economics. The basics of establishment for cool and warm season grasses are identical, except for timing. Cool season grasses are best

---

[1]Extension Turfgrass Specialist, Department of Horticulture, University of Nebraska, Lincoln, NE.

established in the late summer or early fall, whereas warm season grasses are best installed in the late spring or early summer. Proper site preparation is critical for long-term success of a the lawn and its perpetual management. Greater numbers of customer complaints are received about poor or spotty lawns than any other facet of landscape installation or management.

Table 12–1. Characteristics of commonly used turfgrasses.							
		Environmental Tolerance*					
COOL SEASON		Heat	Cold	Shade	Drought	Wear	Recuperative Potential
Creeping Bentgrass	*Agrostis palustris*	VG	VG	G	P	P	VG
Kentucky Bluegrass	*Poa pratensis*	G	G	F	G	F	G
Rough Bluegrass	*Poa trivialis*	P	G	VG	P	F	F
Chewings Fescue	*Festuca rubra* ssp. *commutata*	F	F	VG	VG	F	F
Hard Fescue	*Festuca longifolia*	F	F	VG	VG	F	F
Creeping Red Fescue	*Festuca rubra*	F	F	VG	VG	F	F
Tall Fescue	*Festuca arundinacea*	VG	P	G	VG	VG	F
Perennial Ryegrass	*Lolium perenne*	F	P	F	P	G	F
Annual Ryegrass	*Lolium multiflorum*	P	P	F	VP	G	P
WARM SEASON							
Bahiagrass	*Paspalum notatum*	VG	P	F	F	G	G
Bermudagrass	*Cynodon dactylon*	VG	F	VP	VG	G	VG
Improved Bermudagrass	*Cynodon* spp.	VG	F	P	G	VG	VG
Buffalograss	*Buchloë dactyloides*	VG	VG	P	VG	F	VG
Carpetgrass	*Axonopus* spp.	VG	P	F	VP	P	G
Centipedegrass	*Eremochloa ophiuroides*	G	P	F	VP	P	P
St. Augustinegrass	*Stenotaphrum secundatum*	VG	P	VG	P	F	VG
Seashore paspalum	*Paspalum vaginatum*	VG	VP	F	P	G	VG
Zoysiagrass	*Zoysia* spp.	VG	G	G	G	VG	P

*VG = Very Good; G = Good; F = Fair; P = Poor; VP = Very Poor
    All characteristics are relative to tolerances within each grouping (i.e., cool vs. warm season). Within species considerable variation exists among cultivars. Check with local seed companies or the county extension office concerning specific cultivars.

New Turf Installation

The steps for successful turfgrass establishment are:

1. *Soil Test*. At a minimum, tests for phosphorous, potassium and *p*H should be conducted. This serves as the basis for pre-plant and post-plant nutrient applications.

2. *Weed Control.* Weed populations can be significantly reduced if proper steps are taken during establishment.

Before seeding, an irrigation, followed by a light, mechanical cultivation will alleviate weed pressure prevalent in a new site. This approach is more successful for annual than for perennial weeds. Perennial weeds require application of a systemic, non-selective herbicide such as glyphosate at a suitable interval before cultivation.

A more aggressive but expensive approach to weed control is sterilization of the area before seeding. Sterilization, when done properly, eliminates soil-borne plant pathogens and insects, as well as weeds. Sterilization is, however, expensive and requires the services of a certified and experienced applicator. It is not an operation for the novice.

3. *Rough Grading.* Fill low spots and level high areas. Contour grade according to landscape installation specifications. Install supplementary drainage if required. If rough grading is extensive, remove and stockpile topsoil for use in establishing the final grade. Avoid adding or removing more than two inches of soil around existing trees. Extensive excavation around prized trees requires use of tree wells and other specialized techniques to insure survival.

4. *Addition of soil amendments.* After establishing the rough grade, add any required or desired soil amendments. The soil pH (obtained from the soil test) may indicate the need for lime or sulfur. Consider lime if the soil pH is below 5.5. *Starter fertilizers* are added or incorporated before seeding. Starter fertilizers usually have a ratio of 1:1:1 or 1:2:1, and are important in the early growth and establishment of new turfgrass plantings.

5. *Final Grade.* Final grading should be done immediately before seeding, sodding, or sprigging. Remove rocks and other debris. Rake or drag the area with a piece of chain-link fence or wooden drag to smooth the area for seeding.

6. *Apply seed, sprigs, plugs, or sod.* The choice between seed and vegetative propagation material depends on several management factors. Establishment by seed is the least expensive method, but it is also the slowest and most postplanting labor intensive. See Table 12-2 for seeding rates.

Sodding is the most expensive initially, but establishment time is greatly diminished, compared to seeding. Subsequent management following sodding is less costly than for seed-

Table 12-2. Recommended seeding rates (pounds of seed per 1,000 square feet) for major turfgrass species			
Species	**High***	**Medium****	**Low*****
Cool season			
Kentucky bluegrass	2–3	2–3	1–2
Perennial ryegrass	6–8	6–8	4–6
Tall fescue	8–10	8–10	8–10
Creeping bentgrass	1–2	1	not recommended
Fine Fescues	not recommended	4–6	3–4
Warm season			
Bahiagrass	not recommended	6–8	4–6
Bermudagrass (hulled)	1–2	1–2	1
Buffalograss (burs)	not recommended	1–2	1
Centipedegrass	not recommended	1	1
Zoysia	not recommended	2–3	2–3

*Relatively high management inputs, such as golf course greens and fairways and sports turfs.
**Golf course fairways, home lawns, or showcase grounds.
***Utility turfs, parks, or general grounds.

ing. Time to establishment and cost for sprigging and plugging fall between seeding and sodding, depending upon species.

Use only certified seed. Sod is certified in some states. Certification assures that the grass is true to name and free of weeds and pathogens.

7. *Rake and/or Roll.* Seed and vegetative materials must be in intimate contact with the soil for successful establishment. Raking is necessary to facilitate good soil contact after broadcast seeding. Rolling sod with a light roller firms the soil and eliminates air pockets.

8. *Irrigation.* Moisture is most critical factor for new turfgrass installations. Frequent, light irrigation is necessary until the new root system develops from seed or sprigs. Sod and plug installations must be thoroughly soaked so that the underlying soil is wet. Roots will not grow into dry soil.

10. *Mowing.* During initial establishment, the turf should be mowed frequently. Mowing promotes lateral growth and spread, and can significantly speed establishment. The first mowing after planting should occur as soon as the grass is high enough to mow at optimal height. See the mowing section of this chapter for height recommendations for various turfgrass species.

Photo 12–1. Moisture is the most critical factor for new turfgrass installations. Photograph by Roch Gaussoin.

Renovation

Turfgrass declines over time. Clients or managers may also be interested in changing existing turf to an improved or less management-intensive species or cultivar. The overseeding or conversion of a species is referred to as *renovation*. Many of the steps described for establishment plantings are used in renovation, with minor exceptions.

For conversion from one cultivar to another within a single species stand it is not necessary to eradicate the existing planting. For changing from one species to another and retaining a solid stand, it is essential to eradicate the existing turf with a non-selective herbicide. Vegetation control is also not necessary for overseeding bare or thin spots in an existing turf. Renovation with sod or sprigs requires more aggressive site preparation, similar to that required for establishment of a new turf. The existing cover is killed and the site tilled and ordered.

Winter Overseeding

Overseeding of dormant warm season turfs, usually bermudagrass, with a cool season species is common in the southern United States. Annual or perennial ryegrass are the most commonly used for winter overseeding, but rough bluegrass and fine fescues have become acceptable overseeding choices. All of the perennial grasses offer improved quality, stress tolerance, pest resistance, and greater manageability than annual ryegrass. Winter overseeding success depends on the cool season grass used, seed bed preparation, timing, and post planting maintenance.

Overseeding of warm season turfgrasses is done in the fall, approximately one month before the grass goes off-color. The warm season turf is scalped (mown as low a possible) and the seed is broadcast at 5 to 10 pounds per 1,000 square feet. Slit-seeding provides a more even stand and is preferred if the equipment is available.

Developing A Turfgrass Nitrogen Fertility Program

Turfgrass fertility programs determine the pace and requirements for other management practices. Differences in geographic location, soil, climate, turfgrass species, and maintenance level strongly influence application timing. These general recommendations for timing and rates should only be used as a guideline. Adjustments for individual site and programs should be made as necessary.

Timing

Application timing is determined by turfgrass species. Warm season turfs, like bermudagrass, buffalograss, or zoysiagrass, are fertilized at a different time of year than cool season turfs, like tall fescue and Kentucky bluegrass. Differences in timing fertilizer applications are related to the period when the turfs are actively growing. Warm season turfgrasses go off color in early fall and, depending upon location, will not green-up until late spring, as late as April or May, in some regions. The most active growth period for warm season grasses is summer. Cool season turfs, on the other hand, grow actively in the spring and fall but minimally during late summer. Fertilizer is applied to an actively growing turf. There are, however, exceptions to this guideline.

Cool season turfgrass

Cool season turfgrasses should receive the majority of their annual application in the fall. University research and practical experience have shown that turf that is fertilized in the late fall has better root growth, fewer weeds, disease and thatch, green color later in fall, and earlier spring green-up than cool season turf that is heavily fertilized in the spring. A demonstrated disadvantage of heavy spring fertilization is the promotion of a top-growth flush, at the expense of root growth, prior to the summer stress period. In general, cool season turfs should receive two-third's of their total annual nitrogen (N) application in the fall and one-third in the spring. For example: if the desired annual nitrogen application was 3 lb./N/1,000 ft.^{2}, 1 pound should be applied in the spring and 2 pounds in the fall. How these applications are applied (i.e., single or split application) will depend on fertilizer carrier (slow or quick release) and length of growing season.

Warm season turfgrass

Warm season grass fertility programs should begin in the early spring, as the turf becomes active, and continue through the active growing season. Over stimulation of warm season grasses in late fall should be avoided. Succulent growth is more susceptible to frost damage or winterkill.

Rates

Application rates of nitrogen fertilizers depend on species, as well as the level of maintenance desired. Turf that is abundantly fertilized requires more frequent mowing and irrigation, but the turf is higher quality. Other management practices also influence fertility rate. For example, if clippings are removed, higher rates of fertilizer need to be applied to compensate for the nutrients lost in the removed clippings. Additionally, if the turf is irrigated frequently or grown on sandy soils or in a high rainfall region, higher nitrogen levels should be used. See Table 12-3 for monthly nitrogen requirements for most turfgrass species.

To use Table 12-3, locate the turfgrass species in Column 1 and the level of management appropriate for the site in column 2, 3, or 4. The rate represents a range of the *monthly* nitrogen requirement per month of the growing season. For example, if you are maintaining *bermudagrass* at a *very high level of manage-*

Table 12–3. Monthly nitrogren requirements for different turfgrasses at three management levels.

Higher ends of ranges are suggested for sites that are irrigated frequently, in high rainfall areas, with sandy soil, or if clippings are regularly removed after mowing.

Low maintenance levels are used for sites with low management inputs, such as parks or other general turfs. Medium to high maintenance levels are used for general and home landscape turfs with regular management inputs (water, mowing, and other care). Very high maintenance fertilization levels should be used only for highly maintained recreational turf sites, such as golf courses or athletic fields.

Turfgrass	Pounds of Nitrogen per 1,000 sq. ft. per growing month Level of Management		
	Low	Medium to High	Very High
Cool Season			
Chewings Fescue	0.2–0.3	0.4–0.6	not adapted
Red Fescue	0.2–0.3	0.4–0.6	not adapted
Kentucky Bluegrass (common)	0.3–0.4	0.5–0.6	0.7–0.8
Kentucky Bluegrass (improved cultivars)	0.4–0.5	0.6–0.7	0.8–1.5
Perennial Ryegrass	0.3–0.4	0.5–0.6	0.7–0.8
Tall Fescue	0.3–0.4	0.5–0.6	0.7–1.0
Colonial Bentgrass	0.3–0.4	0.5–0.6	0.7–0.8
Annual Bluegrass	0.3–0.4	0.5–0.6	0.7–1.0
Creeping Bentgrass	0.3–0.4	0.5–0.6	0.7–1.5
Warm Season			
Bahiagrass	0.0–0.1	0.2–0.4	not adapted
Bermundagrass	0.3–0.4	0.5–0.7	0.8–1.5
Buffalograss	0.0–0.1	0.2–0.4	not adapted
Centipedegrass	0.0–0.1	0.2–0.4	not adapted
Carpetgrass	0.2–0.3	0.4–0.6	not adapted
St. Augustinegrass	0.3–0.4	0.5–0.7	0.8–1.0
Zoysiagrass	0.3–0.4	0.5–0.7	0.8–1.0

ment, the monthly nitrogen requirement would be *0.8 to 1.5 pounds of nitrogen* per 1,000 square feet *per growing month*. If the growing season in this example is 11 months, then the total annual nitrogen requirement would be 8.8 to 16.5 pounds per 1,000 square feet. Obviously this amount would not be applied in a single application nor necessarily in monthly applications. The number of applications and application timing depends on carrier, scheduling, fertility program, and other restrictions within the operation.

As another example, suppose the managed property is *Kentucky bluegrass*. Home lawns are managed at a *medium to high maintenance* level. The corresponding monthly nitrogen fertility requirement would therefore be *0.6 to 0.7 pounds* of nitrogen per 1,000 square feet per month of the growing season. As with the bermudagrass example, the number and timing of applications depends on site specific circumstances and the fertility program.

Mowing

Mowing is the most frequent maintenance event occurring on a landscaped site. Mowing strongly influences the development of the turfgrass plant. It results in a temporary decline in root growth, reduces carbohydrate production, creates entry ports for disease-causing organisms, and upsets plant water relations. Mowing also has a tremendous impact on management budgets and profits. Since this most basic, and often mundane, maintenance procedure is conducted so frequently and expansively, small changes can significantly influence mowing time and costs. Mowing is also one of the most frequent topics of client complaints. Mowing should never be taken for granted but viewed with a serious eye toward efficiency and profit.

Equipment selection

Landscape managers have a seemingly infinite choice of mowing products, sizes, brands, and accessories. Choosing the wrong mower can be an expensive mistake. Every type of mower has its optimum performance areas and limitations. Before buying, carefully consider your needs. No two operations or sites are identical.

The type, size, and number of mowers required for economical and efficient operation depends upon:

Table 12–4. Determine your needs before buying a mower.
Mowers, like all equipment, are expensive. The large number of options and differences among the brands available can be confusing. Before committing to a purchase, consider the following:
• What are the present and anticipated acreage requirements? • Who are your primary mowing clients: small sites, large commercial, utility turf, manicured turf, or others? • How many different types of mowing units are required? • What types of topography (slopes, ditches, berms) are most prevalent on the sites? • How often will mowing of wet or soggy turf be required? • Will the equipment be required or useful in other operations, such as snow removal, parking lot cleaning, etc.? • What brands are presently used and how do you like them? • Are service and parts readily available?

A. The *area* to be mown;
B. The turf *species;*
C. The *management intensity* and type of use for the site;
D. The numbers and type of *obstacles;*
E. The *topography;* and
F. The available *labor force.*

Regardless, the unit selected must be maneuverable, adequately powered, easily adjusted, readily serviced, and efficient in fuel, dollars, and labor.

Mower types

Rotary mowers are the most versatile and popular type available to the landscape manager. The 36-inch walk-behind rotary mower is probably the mainstay of most landscape maintenance companies. Rotary mowers can be used for quality turf, for rough areas, to remove seed heads, and to pulverize fallen leaves. They are best suited for cutting turf to heights between one to five inches.

Blades of a rotary mower travel at high speeds on a horizontal plane and cut the leaf blade upon impact, like a scythe. This results in some tearing of the blade. The quality of the cut depends upon the sharpness and balance of the blade and the type and condition of the turf. Scalping of the turf can be a problem, especially on

Photo 12-2. The thirty-six inch walk behind mower is the workhorse of most landscape and turfgrass management firms. Note the operator is wearing ear protection, long pants, and steel-toed boots for his protection. Also note that the clipping are blown away from the street to reduce clean up. Photograph courtesy of Mr. Mark Yahn, Ground Control™ Landscaping and Maintenance, Orlando, FL.

uneven terrain. Cutting width varies from 18 inch "trim" mowers to multiple blade units that mow up to 27 feet or more. Rotary mowers have a high power requirement. When selecting rotary mowers, pay special attention to safety features. Ejection of stones and debris offers potential injury to operators and bystanders.

Reel mowers are the preferred machine for quality turf situations, especially for turfs mowed at one-inch or less. They are the standard mowers for greens, tees, and for high-quality residential or commercial turf. Reel mowers are preferred for dense turf such as zoysiagrass and bermudagrass. The power input is very low, only about one to one and one-half horsepower per foot of cut. Ground-driven reel gangs are the most economical method of mowing large acreage.

Reel mowers cut by a scissors action of the reel against a bedknife. Reel mowers cut, not rip, the turf blade. They provide a

Photo 12-3. The quality of cut for reel mowers depends on the number and hone of the blades. Photograph courtesy of James Robbins.

quality cut from two inches down to 3/32 inches but have problems dealing with tall grass. The quality of cut depends upon the number, speed, and hone of the blades and the type and height of the turf. A quality sharpening machine or service must be available. Reel mowers require a relatively level surface for effective and efficient operation. Reels, rocks, and other hard debris do not mix

229

well. Self-powered or pulled units offer from as little as few feet in cut to over 26-feet wide swaths at a single pass.

Flail or *vertical mowers* cut by the impact of a fixed or free-swinging blade in a vertical plane. They are not used for quality turf situations but are commonly utilized for large-scale mowing and vegetation control situations such as roadsides, parks, and utility turf. Flail mowers may actually cut more acres than any of the other types, despite their "rough" reputation. The quality of the cut varies with the sharpness, number, and spacing of the blades. Wider blades provide fast and efficient cutting of vegetation where appearance is not a prime concern. Smaller blades result in a higher quality cut in more visible areas.

Photo 12–4. Flail mowers cut with a swinging blade on a vertical axis. They are widely used for mowing rough areas.

Throwing rocks and debris is not a great problem with flail mowers, so they work well along roadsides. Flail mowers are available as self-powered units or can be tractor-mounted and powered by the Power Take-Off (PTO). Cutting width varies from five feet to 20 feet with multiple unit machines.

Sickle bar mowers are used for cutting hay and mowing tall grass and weeds such as along roadsides. Sickle bars cut by the action of a reciprocating knife across a plate. They require less power than flail mowers but must be attached to a tractor. They are relatively inexpensive and maneuverable, but require frequent adjustment for efficient operation. Sickle bar mowers are slower than other types. They are primarily adapted to coarse bunch-type grasses and may clog frequently in fine-textured, dense grasses. They also produce an undesirable swath of cut grass that may smother remaining cover.

Special situations

Mulching mowers are receiving renewed interest due to present and anticipated restrictions on dumping clippings and other landscape wastes in public landfills. Thirty-three percent of the respondents to a 1990 trade publication survey used mulching mowers in their commercial mowing operations. Of these, 38 percent began using them less than three years ago.

Mulching mowers have been around for several years. They are designed to direct the clippings around the deck and back into the blade(s) to cut and re-cut them into small pieces before forcing them into the turf. The technology varies from providing additional blades and adjusting the pitch of the blades, to re-designed and re-engineered decks. Kits are available to retro-fit present rotary mowers for use as mulching units. Mulching mowers vary from 21-inch trim mowers to 70-inch riders.

Mulching mowers avoid collecting clippings and contributing to landfill overuse. They can reduce mowing time. Mulching clippings is also valuable in returning nutrients to the turf. The clippings do not contribute to thatch build-up or to disease or insect problems.

Use of mulching mowers may require mowing the site more frequently or at a regular cutting schedule. The concept and practicality of the units allow less leeway for letting the turf go one or two days past the normal schedule. Mulching mowers have higher power and energy requirements. Lastly, they cut the clippings more finely, but they do not make them disappear completely.

The use of mulching mowers will increase in the future, as will their efficiency and economy. Technology and competition among major and new manufacturers will undoubtedly make improvements on the design and effectiveness of these machines.

Zero-turning radius mowers or ZTR's can literally turn on a dime and give you a nickel in change. Such machines provide incredible maneuverability with an experienced operator and can increase productivity in open turf. These units also feature a hydrostatic drive that eliminates belts and chains in the drive system. ZTR's present superior traction and drive in wet situations, the capability of running the mower in reverse, and increased speed. They also require larger power units and are much more sophisticated machines than the "common" mower. Repairs are more costly and cannot be made in the field. Mowers featur-

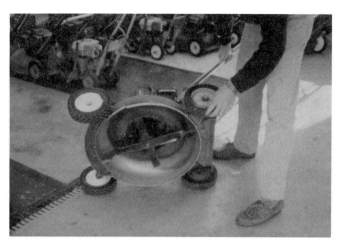

Photo 12–5. Mulching mowers cut and re-cut grass clippings forcing the small pieces into the turf. Mulching mowers use multiple blades and a different frame to assure clippings are finely cut. Mulching mowers make smaller clippings and help hide them; however, they do not eliminate clippings.

Photo 12–6. Zero-turning radius mower with grass catcher and edger. Photograph courtesy of Excel Corporation, Hesston, KS.

ing hydrostatic drives and zero-turning radius have made steady increases in market share. Some estimates place them at a 30 percent share of the mower market.

Slopes

Mowing excessive slopes productively and safely presents a challenge. More than one manager has employees mow steep slopes with cleats instead of boots or lower rotary mowers down steep grades with ropes. There are several specialty mowers on the market designed to make frequent slope mowing profitable and safer. These may utilize: self-leveling features to keep the engine and operator level, dual-hydrostatic or all-wheel drives, tilting decks, roll-over protection systems providing operator safety in case of accident, and/or automatic seat leveling to keep the operator upright

231

reducing fatigue and accidents. These features do not come free, but can be justified if sufficient areas of steep grades (over 25 percent) require servicing.

Some simple modifications aid in adapting conventional mowers for occasional slope use. A low center of gravity and wide tires improve stability. Machine weights or weighting the tires increases traction, but they also increases compaction and fuel consumption. Power steering and hydrostatic drive increase the machine's maneuverability. Adding roll-over protection and seat belts to riding units improve rider safety. Slopes are ideal locations to consider establishing slow-growing turf species or groundcovers and to use growth regulators to reduce the number of required mowings.

Photo 12-7. Heavy-duty rotary mowers are used for utility turfs and rough terrain. This unit has all drive/all wheel steering, a 65-horsepower engine, and safety equipment. Photograph courtesy of Excel Corporation, Hesston, KS.

Hovering Mowers

My wife still talks about seeing mowers that floated during a trip to the Magic Kingdom in Florida several years ago. Until she married me, she assumed that they too were part of the magic or a manifestation of the advanced technology prominently on exhibit. I hope I was worth that minuscule bit of education.

Hovering, floating, or Fly mowers are actually string trimmers floating on a cushion of air. The operator guides the mower over the top of the turf. They are used, but not in large measure, because of their ability to glide over rocks, wet areas, and slopes. Floating mowers are more than a novelty and are used commercially by some golf courses to mow bunker edges and slopes and by commercial managers with problem sites. Disadvantages include their small, 15- to 21-inch cutting width, potential cost, and the difficulty in finding one to purchase.

Photo 12-8. A floating mower that rides on a cushion of air. Useful for maintaining turf on slopes or near water.

Mowing Height

Mowing height depends upon the kind of grass, the intensity of culture, climate, stress, and the time of year. Each grass has a lower and upper tolerance limit for mowing. Close mowing reduces tolerance to environmental stresses, diseases, weeds, and requires more careful management of other factors. Cool season grasses are mowed taller than warm season grasses because of their erect growth habit. Bermudagrass and zoysiagrass build up excessive thatch if mowed too tall. Table 12–5 lists recommended mowing heights for common landscape turfgrasses.

Most managers of cool season turfgrasses cut the lawn higher in the summer than in the spring and fall. The additional foliage improves the grass's environmental tolerance by increasing carbohydrate-producing area, maintains deeper roots, improves turf competition with weeds, and increases shading of the soil. Similarly, managers of warm season turfgrasses will sometimes raise the mowing height in the early and late portions of the growing season as a compensation measure for cold stress and reduced photosynthetic activity.

Table 12–5. Recommended Mowing Heights

The mowing height depends upon the type of turf, use, and management of the area. The following are general guidelines for common landscape turfs. The mowing height for cool season turf is commonly raised during the summer to compensate for heat and drought stress. Warm season turfs are typically mown at the same height year round. Some managers will raise the height of warm season turf slightly in early and late season to compensate for cooler temperatures.

Warm season turfgrasses	Mowing height (inches)		
Bahiagrass	2.5–3.0		
Bermudagrass	0.5–1.5		
Buffalograss	2.0–3.0		
Carpetgrass	1.0–2.0		
Centipedegrass	0.75–1.5		
St. Augustinegrass	1.5–3.5		
Seashore paspalum	0.5–1.0		
Zoysiagrass	0.75–2.0		

Cool season turfgrasses	Spring	Summer	Fall
Chewings and red fescue	1.5–2.0	2.0–2.5	1.5–2.0
Kentucky bluegrass	1.5–2.0	2.0–2.5	1.5–2.0
Perennial ryegrass	1.5–2.0	2.5–3.0	1.5–2.0
Tall fescue	2.0–2.5	2.5–3.0	2.0–2.5

Regardless of the mowing height, sharp blades are essential to a quality operation. Dull blades bludgeon the leaf, leaving frayed tips that give the lawn a whitish cast. Sharp blades also improve efficiency and save fuel. Most operations keep extra sets of sharpened, balanced blades and make one or more exchanges for dull blades per week, depending on the quantity and type of turf mown. Sharp blades are especially important for quality mowing of zoysiagrass, ryegrasses, and tall fescue.

Mowing Frequency

Turfgrass may be mown from once a day on golf greens, to once per season along roadsides. High quality landscapes are usually associated with frequent, consistent mowing. For most landscape turfs, a generally accepted guide is not to remove more than one-third of the total leaf surface at any one mowing. Waiting too long between mowings results in an imbalance between the shoot and roots and retards growth. In addition, mowing

---

Table 12–6. Adaptation to mowing height of some common turfgrass species.

Turfgrasses vary in their adaptation to close mowing. The highest quality turf and most efficient management results from cutting the grass at the proper height. The following indicates the relative preferences of different turfgrasses for high or low mowing heights.

High mowing height

Cool season species	Warm season species
Tall Fescue	Bahiagrass
Chewing and Red Fescues	St. Augustinegrass
Perennial Ryegrass	Centipedegrass
Kentucky Bluegrass	Carpetgrass
Bentgrasses	Zoysiagrass
	Bermudagrass

Low mowing height

grass that is "too tall" requires more time and fuel, produces a great deal of "hay" that must be removed, and can result in sun scald during the summer.

Seed head formation also influences mowing frequency. Bahiagrass, bluegrass, buffalograss, carpetgrass, St. Augustinegrass, centipedegrass, and some bermudagrasses produce excessive numbers of seed heads that disrupt an otherwise uniform lawn. Mowing operations may be primarily to remove these and flowering structures of several weeds during certain times of the year.

Table 12–7. Mower Safety

• Mowers can be dangerous. In 1988, more than 60,000 people were injured due to power mowers. Mowers should never be taken for granted.
 • The following can help you and your employees mow safely.
  • All safety features should be in place and in working order.
  • Make sure all bystanders, especially children and pets, are removed from the mowing area. Debris thrown from a power mower can travel at lethal speed, sometimes over 200 miles per hour.
  • Dress properly, avoid loose fitting clothing that can become tangled in moving parts. Also avoid shorts, sandals or other open shoes; keep exposed skin covered if possible. Shoes and boots should provide solid footing. Several firms require or supply steel-toed boots for their mowing employees.
  • Gasoline is extremely explosive; treat it with respect. Never refuel with the engine running.
  • Unattended mowers should not be left running. Do not disable automatic kill or cut-off switches.
  • Take special precautions on slopes.
   – Mowers are designed to be pushed, rather than pulled.
   – Mow across the slope.
   – Start at the top of the grade and work down the slope.
   – When changing directions, turn so that the mower is always downhill to the operator.
  • Check the area before mowing, especially when the grass is tall, for rocks and other potential missiles.
  • Watch where you are mowing. You should have a clear field of vision for 3 to 4 feet in front of the machine.
  • Stop the engine and disconnect the spark plug wire before working on the engine or blade.

Ideally, mowing schedules, specifications, and contracts should be based upon the growth rate of the grass, rather than a set time schedule. This is difficult to schedule and bid. Mowing may be required twice a week in the spring, every two weeks in the summer, and once a week in the fall. Weather conditions, irrigation schedules, and fertility practices all affect the amount of mowing that must be accomplished. Unfortunately, most clients and contracts are attuned to a set number of mowings per season. Fortunately, turfgrass is less vulnerable to damage from removing more than one-third to one-half of the foliage during non-stress periods. Violations of the one-third rule to cool season turfgrasses are of less consequence to the plant during the spring and fall than during the heat of the summer.

If mowing frequencies in specifications and contracts cannot be established on the growth rate of the turfgrass, then some compensation should be added. Many managers establish 5-day or twice-a-week mowing schedules during the fastest-growing part of the season. This can help meet the needs of the turfgrass, as well as those of the client and manager to have a set number of mowings to budget and schedule.

Photo 12-9. Clippings blown onto the street and left to be removed by the wind are unattractive and unprofessional. In this situation, the clippings on a wet street are dangerous and a liability to the property owner and maintenance crew.

Photo 12-10. Graining in turf is reduced by changing mowing direction, alternating mowing equipment, with brushes, and by double-cutting.

Mowing Pattern

Mowing patterns affect efficiency and the end result. Perimeters should always be mowed first so that trimming and blowing work can commence. The property can be "squared-off" with bagging mowers to keep walks, drives, and pools free of clippings. Another method used to reduce clipping clean-up without bagging is to discharge clippings away from critical areas and into the uncut turf. Mowers will rarely blow clipping further than a distance equal to four times the width of the mower deck. If the first four passes are discharged away from walks, then few, if any, clippings will be blown onto them when the mower changes directions for the fifth pass. If all clippings are to be collected, then the discharge direction is of little consequence.

When grass is mown in the same direction repeatedly, it tends to lean and grow horizontally in that direction. This is referred to as *grain* and is a special problem on golf greens. Mowing landscape turf constantly in the same direction has similar consequences. This phenomenon is common in home lawns. In addition, turf wear and compaction from the mower wheels is accentuated by mowing repeated in the same pattern and direction.

The direction and pattern for mowing landscape turf should be alternated to minimize formation of a grain. Further, many managers mow landscape turf diagonally to the street or longest property line (diagram). They, and many clients, feel that this provides a "baseball field" stripping and increases curb appeal. The direction of the diagonal is alternated each mowing.

Turf can be mowed more rapidly, according to some sources, by mowing constantly around the site and inward. This eliminates sharp turnarounds and backtracking. However, the same, continuous pattern results in graining, even if the mowing direction is alternated. The wheels also run in the same area each mowing and establish compacted "tracks."

Some managers double-cut, mow the property a second time in the opposite direction, so that the turf stands tall. This obviously increases the cost, but if the client requests and is willing to pay for this "quality" look, then why not. It will not damage the grass. Other firms alternate the size of equipment used on a site to keep from establishing tracks. They may use 36-inch walk-behinds one week and 52-inch riders the next.

Brushes or combs are sometimes attached to the front of mowers to assist in straightening or lifting turf for more effective mowing if grain is a particular prob-

Photo 12–11. Mowing when the soil is saturated from rain or irrigation compacts the site and damages the turf, in addition to looking awful.

lem. Brushing turf with a power broom will also lift the turf and dispel clumps of grass. This may be especially useful if the turf must be mowed when it is wet.

Clipping Removal

Collecting and removing clippings adds 15 to 25 percent to mowing time. Grass clippings also account for 20 to 50 percent of the residential solid waste added to municipal landfills each week of the growing season. Several municipalities and some states have banned dumping of clippings and landscape waste in their public landfills. Unfortunately, some clients demand that clippings be bagged and removed.

Clipping removal is largely dependent upon mowing frequency. Short clippings from frequent mowings filter down into the turf and need not be removed for any organic reason. The reasons for removing clippings are purely aesthetic and contractual. The contribution of clippings to thatch is minimal, if any, since the leaf blades decompose rapidly. There is also no increase in the incidence of disease as a result of not collecting normal clippings. On the positive side, clippings are a source of plant nutrients, especially nitrogen.

Excess or long clippings that remain on the top of the grass should be removed.

Photo 12–12. Removal of clippings should be efficient. This mower has a large capacity catcher and dumps into a truck for removal or in a composting area on-site. Photo courtesy of Excel Corporation, Hesston, KS.

These will be unsightly and elicit a call from the client. They also exclude sunlight and favor disease development. They are not the mark of high quality mowing or management.

If clippings are to be collected, then it should be done efficiently. Baggers and catchers should hold a significant amount to reduce the number of dumpings required. The catchers should not be so large that they become too heavy to handle or affect mower operation. Keep the receptacle or truck for holding clippings as close to the mowing operation as possible.

Some firms do not catch the clippings but rake them into piles and onto canvas for loading. The raking works many of the small clippings into the turf and reduces the bulk that must be removed. These managers feel that the time and cost of raking are no greater than that required for catching the clippings and emptying the catchers. Raking may actually be more efficient in the case of wet or very tall turf.

Photo 12–13. A light, hand-held, power edger. Edging removes grass growing over walks and curbs. Edging frequency depends on turf type. The St. Augustinegrass in this photo requires edging less frequently than bermudagrass or other rhizomatous species. Photograph courtesy of Mr. Mark Yahn, Ground Control™ Landscaping and Maintenance, Orlando, FL.

Photo 12–14. String or line trimmers have become the standard equipment for trimming grass around signs and other objects in turf. Photograph courtesy of Mr. Mark Yahn, Ground Control™ Landscaping and Maintenance, Orlando, FL.

Trimming and Edging

Edging and trimming provide crisp edges that improve the appearance and curb appeal of the landscape. Both operations put the finishing touch on maintenance operations. *Edging* is the cutting of turfgrass along a sidewalk, curb, or planted bed to create a delineating edge. It may be done by hand, or more typically with a power edger using a vertical blade. Edging should not expose a wide strip of soil that can be invaded by weeds. *Trimming* is the horizontal cutting of grass around buildings, signs, trees, and other obstacles in the lawn area. Trimming is typically conducted with a power string or spin trimmer.

The frequency of edging and trimming depends on the maintenance level of the site, turf species and growth rate, and budget. Both operations may be conducted every mowing, sometimes needlessly. Trimming around objects in the landscape will require attention to keep the tufts of turf from being noticed. Sidewalks, on the other hand do not generally require edging every week. Bermudagrass, bluegrass, and other "creeping" grasses require more frequent edging, possibly every second or third mowing. Tall fescue and other bunch-type grasses do not rapidly encroach upon walks and may only require edging two or three times per season. Reducing weekly edgings on the site is one way to reduce or negotiate a budget without dramatically affecting visible quality.

Photo 12–15. A trimmer with a covered reciprocating blade cuts grass and protects trees. Girdling by string trimmers operated by inexperienced or careless employees are a major cause of loss of landscape trees and shrubs.

Some managers profess to using growth regulators on stoloniferous turf along walks, parking lots, and landscape beds. This, supposedly, reduces the growth rate, invasive nature, and edging and trimming required. Growth regulators can cause discoloration of turf and affect the appearance. Obtain full information and realize the consequences before embarking upon this venture.

Mowing aids reduce trimming around trees and objects in the landscape. Mowing aids range from brick or other permanent mowing strips along buildings and curbs, to weed-free bands around trees and sign posts. Many landscape management firms spray narrow bands of non-selective post-emergent herbicides, sometimes tank-mixed with preemergents, around obstacles that require trimming. These narrow bands prevent the grass from growing up to the object. All necessary trimming can be done with the mower; string trimming is eliminated entirely. I have known of companies that offer banding around trees and other obstacles at little or no charge to the client in order to reduce trimming operations.

Photo 12–16. Mowing aids maintained around trees and other objects in turf eliminate the need for trimming. Photograph courtesy of Mr. Mark Yahn, Ground Control™ Landscaping and Maintenance, Orlando, FL.

In some landscapes the turf is removed around trees, signs, buildings, or other obstacles and replaced with a mulch. This again keeps grass from growing up to the object and eliminates hand-trimming. Small mulched beds around trees also add a quality appearance to the landscape. The use of steel, plastic, or wooden edging around all mulched landscape beds prevents encroachment of bunch-type grasses, but does not prevent growth of rhizomatous or stoloniferous species into the beds.

Blowing

Typically, the final task in landscape mowing-edging operation is use of a power blower to remove unwanted clippings from walks and parking lots. Power blowers have become indispensable utensils in management operations, replacing the push broom. They serve many functions and add to the professional appearance of managed landscapes.

Use professional manners with power blowers. Several municipalities, neighborhood associations, and condominiums have limited or banned their use because of noise.

Turf Irrigation

Irrigation is essential for growing high-quality turf in most areas of the country. Seasonal distribution of precipitation is inadequate to maintain uniformly green, vigorous grass throughout the growing season. Irrigation is costly in terms of the capital investment, as well as labor, if the system is not automated. The cost of water is a significant portion of many landscape budgets, especially in arid and semi-arid regions. The cost and availability of water are an increasing concern for landscape and turf managers. Landscape managers must contend with the many problems associated with too little and too much water. Chapter 9 details water management and irrigation for landscape sites. A few particulars of turfgrass irrigation should be addressed separately, however.

Photo 12-17. Cleaning up with a power blower is the final step in mowing. Clippings are blown back into the cut grass or collected and removed from the site. Photo courtesy of Mr. Mark Yahn, Ground Control™ Landscaping and Maintenance, Orlando, FL.

Performance of turfgrass, and plants in general, are influenced by soil, weather, and plant growth characteristics. The water requirements must be considered during planting design and planning for irrigation. Many grasses perform well under extended drought or with reduced irrigation (Table 12-8). These turfgrasses may be installed initially or as a renovation in water-critical situations.

Table 12-8. Relative tolerance and performance of common turfgrasses under extended drought or reduced irrigation stress.		
Performance Rating	**Cool Season**	**Warm Season**
Excellent		Bermudagrass Buffalograss Zoysiagrass
Good	Tall Fescue Canada Bluegrass	Bahiagrass Seashore paspalum
Fair	Red Fescue Kentucky Bluegrass	St. Augustinegrass
Poor	Annual Bluegrass Bentgrasses Perennial Ryegrass	Centipedegrass

239

Irrigation Scheduling

A single, all encompassing irrigation schedule cannot be specified because of variances in sites, soils, turf species, management practices, growing season, climate, and requirements of the client. Careful irrigation scheduling, however, is critical for quality turfgrass.

Frequent, shallow irrigation of established turf causes the grass plants to be shallow rooted. The turf is thereby more susceptible to the effects of drought and less able to exploit water reserves in the soil. Frequent, shallow irrigation also encourages disease, weed infestation, thatch accumulation, and soil compaction. Shallow-rooted turf is more sensitive to injury from high and low temperatures, as well as winter desiccation. A similar situation can be found in heavy soils that are continuously over-watered. The turfgrass rooting depth is reduced by inadequate oxygen deeper in the soil and problems synonymous with shallow rooting are found.

Generally, watering once a week is adequate except during periods of severe stress. More frequent watering is needed on sandy soils, on south-facing slopes, berms or mounds, where competition for water from trees and shrubs is severe, in areas bordering pavement, and under more intense management. Compaction and thatch complicate irrigation scheduling and rates.

Irrigation scheduling can be facilitated by soil water measuring devices such as tensiometers. Typically, the more sophisticated the site, the more sophisticated soil and/or plant water measurements will be required to assure quality. Managers of golf courses and other heavily managed, intensive use sites make greater use of evapotranspiration calculations for irrigation scheduling than do managers of more typical landscapes.

Apply adequate water to thoroughly wet the upper six to eight inches of the turfgrass root zone. It is preferable to apply sufficient water to penetrate to the subsoil moisture avoiding a dry layer in between that would restrict rooting. The rate of application should allow maximum infiltration without run-off, depending on soil texture, structure, compaction, and degree of slope.

Newly-seeded Areas

A newly seeded lawn is the exception to these ideas for watering frequency and quantity. Frequent, shallow irrigation is required for seed germination and to promote growth of newly emerged seedlings. As the seedlings grow and mature, watering interval should become less frequent but the soil soaked deeper, until normal irrigation management is achieved. Spring-seeded, cool season or late season planted, warm season turf will mandate careful and continued water management during the initial season.

Other management influences on irrigation

Landscape management and non-management factors affect irrigation scheduling. Water loss from run-off is reduced by aerating. Aeration holes catch and hold water as well as increase infiltration. Removal or breaking of the thatch layer by aeration or verticutting speeds water movement into the soil.

Where disease is a factor, the best time to irrigate turf is in the pre-dawn morning. Golf courses, athletic fields, and high traffic public and corporate areas are frequently irrigated at night, so as not to impede play or daytime traffic. Nocturnal watering is also common in arid and semi-arid regions to reduce loss to evaporation on sunny, windy days, and to improve irrigation efficiency.

240

Shady areas require less water than those in sun or partial shade. Irrigation of shaded sections on the same schedule as sunny areas increases disease and weed problems. If possible, turf in shade should be irrigated and managed separately than that in full sun.

Irrigation of turf in winter is not often practiced in northern areas because of the time and cost of charging and re-draining the irrigation system. However, cool season turf in northern areas may require irrigation during dry, open winters, especially when associated with extended warm periods. Winter watering may be necessary for grasses with low levels of drought tolerance on exposed dry areas, compacted sites, extreme slopes, or on southern and western exposures of highly reflective buildings. It may be possible to install ample automatic drain values and design zones to accommodate winter irrigations of critical areas, if necessary. Typically only one or two irrigations are required; these can be done anytime the soil is not frozen. Irrigation of frozen soil is not beneficial and can have harmful effects.

Mowing and fertilization practices greatly affect irrigation practices and vice versa. While the transpiration rate of low-cut turf is less than that of taller-cut turf, taller grass has deeper roots. A more extensive root system allows for greater water harvesting from the soil. It is common to raise the cutting height of cool season turf during the peak water use periods of the summer. It is easier to manage water use and irrigation of taller turf during dry periods.

The fertilization program should reflect the potential and realistic irrigation expectations of the site and the manager. High levels of nutrients, especially nitrogen, used for heavily managed and high quality sites are wasted if the grass does not have the water resources to utilize these fertilizer additions for growth.

Aeration

Mechanical aeration or cultivation is a common management practice for golf courses, sports fields, and other intensive use sites. It has become a standard and annual management procedure for commercial and residential sites suffering from heavy soils, significant thatch, compaction, or traffic problems. Several companies specialize in mechanical aeration as a major portion of their business. Mechanical aeration is one of the few maintenance practices that can actually improve soils under perennial turfgrass.

Photo 12–18. Small core aerators are useful to aerate and manage residential properties.

Coring

Core aeration or *coring* uses hollow tines or spoons to extract cores from the turf. The depth of the core depends upon the capabilities of the machine and the physical constraints (bulk density and moisture content) of the soil. Core depths of three inches are common and possible with modern equipment and reasonable soils. To maximize effectiveness, core as deeply as possible.

Coring is preferred to spiking or slicing for aerifying turf. Coring provides a physical channel through surface layers due to topdressing, surface compaction, and thatch. Water and air infiltration are vastly improved. While the aeration of the soil between and below the actual core holes may not

241

METHOD	PENETRATION DEPTH (INCHES)	TINE SPACING (INCHES)	SOIL LOOSENING (0 TO 10[1])	AMOUNT OF SOIL BROUGHT TO SURFACE (1 TO 5[2])	BEST SOIL MOISTURE FOR OPERATION	COMMENTS
Table 12–9. A comparison of different turf aeration methods.						
FORKING	6	2 to 4	3 to 4	2	Field capacity	First aeration method.
HOLLOW TINE CORING						
Spoons or tine-tractor drawn or self-powered	3 to 6	6	4	2 to 4	Field capacity	Several types and brands; some with changeable spoons. Spoons enter soil at an angle.
Drum type (hollow tine)	2 to 3	2 to 3	2	2 to 4	Field capacity	Several types and brands available.
Vertically operated tines	3 to 5	2 to 6	4	3 to 5	Field capacity	Most common form of aeration.
Verti-drain®	10 to 12	1 to 8	8 to 10	2 to 4	Field capacity or drier	Hollow tine.
SOLID TINE CORING						
Vertically operated shatter-core	3 to 5	2 to 6	4 to 8	1	Less than field capacity	
Rotary pattern solid core units	3	4	4 to 10 (variable)	2	Field capacity or drier	
Verti-Drain®	12 to 16	1 to 8	9 to 10	1	Drier than field capacity	
SLICING						
Solid tines or blades						
Straight-line tines	3 to 7	6 to 12	2	1	Field capacity	Many types and brands. Most common type of sliding unit.
Straight-line blades	2 to 4	4	2	1	Field capacity	
Off-set tines	6 to 8	7	4 to 8	1	Drier than field capacity	Aerway®
SPIKING	1/2 to 2	1 to 2	2	1	Field capacity	Pulled or motorized. Several brands.
HIGH PRESSURE WATER INJECTION	4 to 20	3 to 6	4 to 6	1	Field capacity	At least 2 brands. Uses high pressure water jets.

[1]Degree of soil loosening. 1 = none; 10 = most effective
[2]Amount of soil brought to surface by operation. 1 = none; 5 = large amount

be improved, significant benefits in the soil air content do occur. Root growth within the holes is stimulated and shoot growth on top of the holes is increased. The holes serve as major root development areas for many years. Drying of incessantly wet soils is also increased as a result of coring.

Coring increases turfgrass response to fertilizers, particularly those nutrients that are relatively immobile in the soil such as lime, phosphorous, and potassium sources. Coring prior to fertilization provides a means of inserting these materials into the root zone.

Photo 12-19. Innovations in aeration equipment has resulted in equipment capable of depths up to 12 inches. Photograph by Roch Gaussoin.

Cool season grasses are best core aerated during the spring or fall. Aeration in the fall is preferred. Areas with intensive problems or traffic may be core aerated spring and fall if necessary. Warm season turfs are commonly aerated in early summer. Spring coring may open the turf to increased pressure from annual grassy weeds if a pre-emergent herbicide is not used. Aerating after application of a preemergent herbicide does not reduce the chemical's effectiveness. Avoid coring during periods of stress as the holes allow the soil to dry more rapidly.

In taller-cut turf the cores are normally left on the surface. Irrigation, rain, or mowing breaks up the cores. The soil from the cores will work its way into the thatch layer, aiding in its control. A power rake or verticut mower can be used to break up the cores quickly if necessary. Set the height of the blades so that they hit the cores without damaging the turf. The cores can also be broken up by dragging. If the soil is of poor quality, it may be best to collect and discard the cores. Topdressing with a good quality soil or soil mixture is standard practice in golf course management but is not often feasible, economical, or necessary for large or common landscape sites.

Photo 12-20. A spike aerator pokes holes in compacted soil and thatch layers. Weights are added over the drum of this pull-behind unit to increase penetration. Photograph courtesy of James Robbins.

Slicing and Spiking

Slicing and *spiking* are less intensive aeration or cultivation practices. Slicing uses V-shaped knives mounted on disks to penetrate the turf and soil. Spiking makes shallow perforations in the turf with small knives and is primarily practiced on golf greens and tees. Both procedures do not remove cores; therefore, there is little disruption of the turf or its use. Slicing or spiking improve infiltration, relieve surface compaction, and help control thatch. Many grounds managers core aerate severely compacted or problem areas in spring and fall, and also slice the turf periodically during the

Photo 12–21. Thatch is the intermingled layer of living and dead roots, stolons, rhizomes and stems between the green vegetation and the soil surface. Photograph courtesy of "Thatch in Turfgrass"—Crop Sci. Soc. of Am. 1982.

Photo 12–22. Species differ in their thatching tendency. Photograph courtesy of "Thatch in Turfgrass"—Crop Sci. Soc. of Am. 1982.

summer. Slicing athletic fields during the playing season is preferred since there is less disruption of play. Slicing also makes the field more impact-absorbing and increases the safety of play, according to some managers.

Thatch

Thatch is a common problem of many landscape sites. *Thatch* is an intermingled layer of living and dead roots, stolons, and stems between the green vegetation and the soil surface. Thatch contains material that is largely undecomposed and some in an advanced stage of decomposition. What causes the thatch layer to develop is not completely understood. A typical explanation is that thatch accumulates because the production of stems, crowns, and roots exceeds the rate of decomposition. Factors that suppress the rate of organic matter decomposition or promote excessive plant growth are thought to trigger the event.

Certain turf species and cultivars are more prone to thatch problems. Species with a high lignin content, a component of plants that resists decomposition, are more prone to thatch accumulation

244

(Table 12–10). Turfgrass species that produce rhizomes or stolons such as zoysiagrass and creeping bentgrass build up thatch faster than bunch-type grasses, such as perennial ryegrass or tall fescue. Pesticides that adversely affect earthworms and other decomposing organisms also promote thatch.

Despite the common belief of some clients, grass clippings do not contribute to thatch. Clippings are 75 to 85 percent water and decompose quickly. They also contain little lignin. Research at the University of Missouri by Doug Soper and John Dunn found no more thatch in closely mown zoysiagrass plots than in controls where clippings were collected every mowing.

The extent of a thatch problem is determined by removing a pie-shaped wedge of grass and soil and measuring the amount of organic matter accumulated. Sample several areas over the site, especially if the management program differs. A small layer of thatch, less than one-half inch, is actually beneficial. It increases the grasses' resiliency, improves its tolerance to traffic, and insulates against abrupt changes in soil temperature. If the thatch layer exceeds one-half inch in cool season turf, steps should be taken to reduce it.

The turf's susceptibility to heat, cold, and drought damage increase with increasing amounts of thatch. Scalping during mowing and insect and disease problems also increase because of thatch. Thatch is difficult to rewet after it has dried, so irrigation efficiency decreases and localized dry spots increase. Movement of fertilizer, herbicides, and other chemicals is impeded by a thatch layer.

Table 12–10. Relative tendency of several turfgrass to produce thatch.

Cool season species	Warm season species
High Tendency	
Bentgrasses	Zoysiagrass
Kentucky Bluegrass	Bermudagrass
Fine Fescues	St. Augustinegrass
Perennial Ryegrasses	Centipedegrass
Tall Fescue	Carpetgrass
	Bahiagrass
	Buffalograss
Low Tendency	

Removing thatch

Excessive thatch, over one-half inch, should be physically removed. This process can moderately to severely injure the turf. It should be accomplished during active growth and when there is a long period available for recovery. Cool season turfgrasses may be dethatched in the fall or spring. Fall is preferred since the area can be efficiently fertilized to hasten recovery. The area can also be over-seeded if necessary.

If thatch is removed from cool season grass in the spring, applications of preemergent herbicides and a light fertilization should be planned to reduce weed infestations and to enhance recovery. As a rule, schedule thatch removal from cool season species when at least 30 days of favorable growing conditions are anticipated afterward.

Remove thatch from warm season turf after it has obtained 100 percent green-up in the spring. Make a regular application of fertilizer after mechanical removal. Avoid removal of thatch during summer or when the grass is under stress. High temperatures and water stress reduce growth and recuperation and encourage weed infestation.

Even though mechanical dethatching produces a tremendous volume of material on the surface, it only removes a portion of the thatch in the turf. Some sources claim that power raking removes as little as 25 percent of the organic material where there has been substantial build-up. The cause of the thatch accumulation must be determined and solved or the problem will return.

Photo 12-23. Dethatching or power-raking brings large amounts of organic material to the surface. This operation, however, only removes a portion of the true amount of thatch present on a site.

Mow the site closely before dethatching. Bag or rake clippings and remove the debris resulting from hand or power raking immediately. Soil moisture should be at or slightly less than field capacity for best results. Dethatching wet soil severely damages the turf and greatly reduces efficiency.

Equipment

Thatch is removed by hand or *power-raking*. Hand raking is laborious and only practical in very small areas. Power rakes or vertical mowers use wire tines or steel blades to lift the thatch and usually a small amount of soil to the surface.

Photo 12-24. A power rake removes by combing up the material with wire tines. Photograph courtesy of James Robbins.

Core aeration

Core aeration or cultivation can be used to reduce thatch accumulation. Soil cores removed during core cultivation create a channel through the thatch layer to improve water and chemical penetration. Cores should be allowed to remain on the surface if acceptable to the client. The cores will breakdown and redistribute soil throughout the thatch, thus inoculating it with microorganisms that aid decomposition.

Biological control of thatch

Several biological dethatching materials are available. These materials usually contain specific microorganisms that theoretically may increase the rate of thatch decomposition. Research trials on the efficacy of these materials have not been extensive; preliminary results have shown that irrigation and environment have a significant effect on thatch decomposition.

246

Management solutions and prevention

Good turf management minimizes thatch accumulation. Proper cultural practices are the most efficient and least expensive method to control thatch. Proper mowing frequency and height reduce the amount of grass stem cut and deposited upon the soil surface. Fertilizer should be applied at times and in amounts to meet, but not to exceed, the nutritional needs of the grass. Avoid light, frequent irrigations that encourage shallow rooting.

Apply pesticides only as needed. Pesticides can affect microorganism and earthworm populations. Earthworms, in addition to feeding on decaying grass tissue, provide channels that mix soil into the thatch and improve aeration and drainage.

Pest Management

The key to successful control of turfgrass pests, whether they are weeds, insects, or diseases, begins with cultural programs that promote healthy, vigorous growth. A properly managed turf outgrows many diseases or insect infestations, and competes against weeds.

Correct identification of the pest is also critical to successful pest management. Pest identification guides are available from State or County Extension offices. Many universities offer diagnostic services for turf and landscape problems. This service is normally offered free or for a nominal charge.

Disease Control

Over watering, improper fertilization, heavy thatch, susceptible species or cultivars, improper mowing practices, and environmental extremes contribute to disease incidence and severity. Chemical disease control is more expensive than chemical weed and insect control. Except for very high maintenance turf such as golf courses or sports fields, disease incidence is often tolerated or managed by subtle alterations in cultural practices.

The majority of turfgrass diseases are caused by fungi. Fungicides used to control these pathogens are classified as *preventive* or *curative*. *Preventive* treatments are applied when conditions are favorable for development but disease symptoms are not evident. *Curative* treatments are applied after disease symptoms are evident. Disease symptomology is variable among pathogens and regions of the country. Consult local experts or regional publications for up-to-date disease descriptions and management strategies.

Insect Control

Identification of insect damage and the specific pest is less complex than for disease management. Insects damaging turfgrass may feed on the leaves *(surface feeders)* or roots *(sub-surface feeders)*. The larval stage of most turfgrass insects is the most damaging.

Surface Feeders. Armyworms, cutworms, and sod webworms are larvae of moths or butterflies feeding on grass leaves. Sod webworms and cutworms are nocturnal feeders. An unusual amount of bird activity often indicates severe infestations of these insects. Chinch bugs damage grass plants by sucking plant sap. The damage is drought-like in appearance.

247

Effective control with insecticides requires correct identification and timing. Managers should thoroughly understand the target pest's life cycle and feeding habits before attempting chemical control.

Sub-surface Feeders. The larval stage of May/June beetles, Japanese beetles, and chafers are usually white or grayish with brown to dark brown heads and six true legs. The larvae appear "C shaped." Injury appears similar to turf that needs irrigation. In some cases, where roots are severely damaged, the sod can be rolled back like a carpet. Mole crickets, a potentially serious pest in the southern US, and the larvae of several billbug species also feed on grass roots. Wireworms, larvae of click beetles, bore into the buried portion of a stem to feed on the roots.

Table 12–11. Feeding characteristics of common turfgrass insects.			
Insect		**Feeding Location**	**Life Cycle State that Damages Turf**
Billbug	*Spenophorous* spp.	above ground	Larvae
Chinch Bug	*Blissus* spp.	above ground	All
Cutworm	Noctuidae family	above ground	Larvae
White Grub	Numerous Genuses	below ground	Larvae
Mites	Order Acarina	above ground	All
Mole Cricket	Gryllotalpidae family	below ground	All
Sod Webworm	*Crambus* spp.	above ground	Larvae
Wireworm	Elateridae family	below ground	Larvae
Ataenius Beetle	*Ataenius* spp.	below ground	Larvae
Greenbug Aphid	Aphididae family	above ground	All

Weed Control

Of the major pests in management of quality turfgrass, weed control offers the most rapid gratification. In most cases, once the weed is eradicated the turf is capable of rapidly filling-in the void. In some cases, however, weeds are indicative of a more serious site or cultural problem. Effective control requires altering the management or site to alleviate the original problem. For example, many weeds persist in conditions where soils are poorly drained. Solving the "weed problem" requires correction of the drainage problem. Herbicides may temporarily relieve the symptoms, but the turf will be weak and the weeds will return.

Weed control is a service expected by all clients. While some lawn care companies offer disease and insect control as an option to clients, all landscape and lawn maintenance firms offer weed control.

Two pieces of information are critical to successfully control turfgrass weeds: weed type (whether the weed is a *grass, broadleaf,* or *sedge*) and its life cycle. The correct choice of herbicide depends on the type of plant represented by the weed.

Grassy weeds (monocots) are easily distinguished from *broadleaf weeds* (dicots) by the orientation of the leaf veins. In grassy weeds the veins are parallel to each other along the entire length of the leaf. The veins of broadleaf weeds are "netted" or web-like.

A third group of weeds is the *annual and perennial sedges.* Sedges are often incorrectly referred to as grassy weeds because of their grass-like appearance and parallel veination. Sedges can be easily distinguished from the grasses by their triangular or three-sided stems.

Weeds in turfgrass can be classified by two life cycles types. *Perennials* live from year to year. Many perennial weeds have vigorous taproots or other below-ground storage organ (tubers, corms, or rhizomes). Perennial weeds can propagate by these underground storage organs or by seed.

Annuals are plants that complete their life cycle (seed to plant to seed) in one year. Annual weeds can be further classified as either *winter* or *summer* annuals. *Winter annuals* germinate in the fall, overwinter as a seedling, and set seed and die in late spring or early summer. *Summer annuals* germinate in the spring, set seed in late summer and are normally killed by the first frost.

Application Timing

Herbicides are classified as *preemergence* (applied before weed germinates) or *postemergence* (applied after the weed emerges from the soil) materials. Some, but not many, herbicides act as both pre- and postemergence chemicals. Timing of applications depends on the type of herbicide used and the target weed. Obviously, preemergence herbicides must be applied before germination of the weed seed to be effective. Table 12–12 lists examples of life cycles and optimal application timing for several common lawn weeds.

Turfgrass Plant Growth Regulators

Synthetic *plant growth regulators (PGR's)* have been available for use in turfgrass management for several years. PGR's are used with varying success in golf courses, public parks and grounds, cemeteries, highway roadsides, and more recently home lawns.

Managers must consider the cost effectiveness, longevity, and possible problems before including these materials in their programs. Turfgrass plant growth regulators are not fool proof and do not eliminate mowing. Environmental and management factors influence efficacy of the materials. PGR's may, if used properly, reduce mowing and suppress seed head formation.

Plant growth regulators are classified as either Type I or Type II regulators. *Type I regulators* control growth and suppress development (such as seedhead formation) of turfgrass plant. *Type II regulators* control only the growth of plants. If seedhead suppression is one of the management goals, only Type I regulators are recommended.

A factor to consider in PGR selection is *phytotoxicity,* or potential discoloration of the turf resulting from application. Many PGR's exhibit some degree of phytotoxicity, however, this is highly species dependent. There has been some success in masking discoloration with nitrogen or iron fertilizers.

Application timing and absorption site are critical to PGR success. *Root absorbed compounds* must be watered in to be effective. The activity of *foliar absorbed compounds* is reduced by rainfall or irrigation following application.

PGR's applied during dormancy or prior to green-up delay initial green-up and reduce the size of emerging leaves. Root absorbed regulators can be effectively applied at this time, however, foliar absorbed materials are ineffective. They require green leaves for absorption.

249

Table 12–12. Common turfgrass weeds, life cycle examples, and optimal herbicide type and application timing.

WEED	OPTIMAL APPLICATION TIMING

PERENNIAL GRASSES
Quackgrass
    Agropyron repens
Nimblewill
    Muhlenbergia schrebi
Smooth Brome
    Bromus enermis
	Postemergence, late summer to late fall

PERENNIAL BROADLEAFS
Dandelion
    Taraxacum officinale
Yellow Wood Sorrel
    Oxalis stricta
Plantain
    Plantago spp.
Ground Ivy
    Glechoma hederacea
Wild Violet
    Viola spp.
Mouseear Chickweed
    Cerastium vulgatum
Mallow
    Malva spp.
White Clover
    Trifolium repens
Yarrow
    Achillea millefolium
	Postemergence, late summer to late fall

SUMMER ANNUAL GRASSES
Crabgrass
    Digitaria spp.
Goosegrass
    Eleusine indica
Foxtail
    Setaria spp.
Barnyardgrass
    Echinochola crusgalli
Sandbur
    Cenchrus spp.
	Preemergence, Jan/Feb in southern U.S., March/April in Transition Zone, April/May in northern U.S.

SUMMER ANNUAL BROADLEAFS
Spurge
    Euphorbia spp.
Purslane
    Portulaca oleracea
Carpetweed
    Mollugo verticillata
Black Medic
    Medicago lupulina
Prostrate Knotweed
    Polygonum aviculare
	Postemergence, when weeds are young and actively growing (Feb–Mar) or preemergence with similar timing as summer annual grasses.

WINTER ANNUAL BROADLEAFS
Henbit
    Lamium amplexicaule
Common Chickweed
    Stellaria media
Speedwell
    Veronica spp.
	Postemergence, when weeds are young and actively growing (Sept–Dec) or preemergence in early fall.

Type I regulators applied during spring green-up reduce the number of seedheads by about 80 percent. Root absorbed Type I regulators applied at this time will suppress plants but delay green-up Foliar active regulators only suppress those plants that have greened-up.

The greatest benefits from PGR's occur when applied during the rapid vertical growth period. Mowing requirements can be reduced by as much as 50 percent. Seedhead control at this application time is usually 90 percent. This application timing, however, often results in a slight loss of grass quality from the second to fourth week after application The turf's green color, however, is enhanced during the seventh to tenth week.

The most detrimental time to apply PGR's is when seedheads begin to appear and elongate. The plant is internally producing its own growth inhibitor. The combination of the natural and applied plant growth regulators can severely retard growth retardation and thin the stand.

Table 12–13 summarizes some of the information available on PGR's. No specific recommendations are intended.

Table 12–13. Plant growth regulators labeled for turfgrass use.					
Trade name	**Common name**	**Absorption Site**	**Type**	**Phytotoxicity**[a]	**Source**[b]
Embark	Mefluidide	Foliar	I	M	PBI Gordon
Embark Lite	Mefluidide	Foliar	I	M	PBI Gordon
Limit	Amidochlor	Root	I	M	PBI Gordon
Cutless	Flurprimidol	Root	II	M	Lesco
Scott's TGR	Paclobutrazol	Root	II	M	O.M. Scott's
Primo	Cimectacarb	Foliar	II	None	Ciba-Geigy
Slo-Gro	Maleic Hydrazide	Foliar	I	M/S	Uniroyal
Maintain	Chlorflurenol	Foliar	I	M/S	U.S. Borax

[a]Phytotoxicity can depend on environmental conditions, plant health and cultural practices. M = Moderate and S = Severe phytotoxicity, respectively.
[b]Commercial companies are mentioned in this publication for the purpose of providing specific information. Mention of a company does not constitute a guarantee or warranty of its products or an endorsement over products of other companies not mentioned.

Bibliography

Abrahamson, S. 1990. Guidelines for establishing turf. *Grounds Maintenance,* 25(8):10–14.

Abrahamson, S. 1991. Bidding lawn renovations. *Grounds Maintenance,* 26(8):42–44.

Baxendale, F. and R. Gaussoin (ed.). 1992. *Integrated Management Guide for Nebraska Turfgrass.* Cooperative Extension Publication No. EC92-1557. Univ. of Nebraska, Lincoln, NE.

Beard, J. B. 1986. Thatch. *Grounds Maintenance,* 21(11):36–40.

Buckingham, F. 1982. Controlling thatch and soil compaction. *Grounds Maintenance,* 17(8):10–11, 38–42.

Buckingham, F. 1987. One solution: aeration. *Grounds Maintenance,* 22(6):7, 52–53.

Carrow, R. 1987. The problem: compaction. *Grounds Maintenance,* 22(6):6–8.

Carrow, R. N. 1990. Developing turfgrass cultivation programs. *Golf Course Management,* 58(8):14–22.

Cook, T. 1989. Good judgment, proper timing needed for renovation. *ALA/Maintenance,* 10(4):56–59.

Daniel, W. H. and R. P. Freeborg. 1987. *Turf Managers Handbook.* Harvest Publishing Co., Cleveland, OH.

de Shazer, S. A., T. P. Riordan, F. P. Baxendale and R. E. Gaussoin. 1992. *Buffalograss: A Warm Season Native Grass for Turf.* Cooperative Extension Publication No. EC92-1234-C. Univ. of Nebraska, Lincoln, NE.

Decker, H. F. and J. M. Decker. 1988. *Lawn Care: A Handbook for Professionals.* Prentice Hall, Englewood Cliffs, NJ.

Feucht, J. and J. Butler. 1988. *Landscape Management.* Van Nostrand Reinhold Co., New York.

Gaussoin, R. E. 1990. Influence of cultural factors on species dominance in annual blue-grass/creeping bentgrass. *Golf Course Management,* 58(8):24–43.

Gaussoin, R. E. 1990. Early season fertilization. *Landscape Management,* 29(3):69–72.

Gaussoin, R. E. 1991. Estimating *Poa annua* populations. *Golf Course Management,* 59(8):40–42.

Gaussoin, R. E. 1991. Pre-emerge control of broadleaf weeds. *Northern Turf Management,* 2(8):8, 42.

Gaussoin, R. E. 1992. Selecting traffic-tolerant turfgrass varieties. *Landscape and Irrigation,* 16(8):9–11.

Gaussoin, R. E. 1992. Understanding preemergence herbicides. *Golf Course Management,* 60(12).

Gaussoin, R. E. and T. P. Riordan. 1992. *Warm Season Turfgrasses for Nebraska.* Cooperative Extension Publication No. G85-767-A (Revised). Univ. of Nebraska, Lincoln, NE.

Gaussoin, R. E. and T. P. Riordan. 1992. *Thatch Prevention and Control.* Cooperative Extension Publication No. G85-751-A (Revised). Univ. of Nebraska, Lincoln, NE.

Gaussoin, R. E. and R. Shearman. 1992. *Lawn Weeds and Their Control.* North Central Regional Extension Publication No. 26 (Revised). Univ. of Nebraska, Lincoln, NE.

Gibeault, V., J. Meyer, M. A. Harivandi, M. Henry, and S. Cockerham. 1991. *Managing Turfgrasses During Drought.* Leaflet 21499 Cooperative Extension, University of California, Davis, CA.

Halterman, D. 1988. Selecting core cultivation equipment. *ALA,* 9(9):28–30, 45.

Harivandi, A. M. 1993. Thatch: The hidden enemy. *Landscape and Irrigation,* 17(6):8–12.

Hensley, D. 1991. Easy money, tough sell. *Northern Turf Management,* 2(9):6–7.

Hensley, D and G. L. Davis. 1992. Cool-season sod, "Instant turf." *Northern Turf Management,* 3(8):1–2.

Jedrzejek, S. 1991. Thatch accumulation can retard growth and cause erratic fertilizer, pesticide response. *Lesco News,* 23(5):4–5, 8.

Knoop, W. E. (ed.). 1992. *Turf Management Digest.* Farm Press Publications, Clarksdale, MS.

Kronenberg, J. 1989. The choice is yours: Improve the old or start anew. *ALA/Maintenance,* 10(4):26–27.

Landry, G. 1993. Success with overseeding warm-season grasses. *Landscape and Irrigation,* 17(9):8–10.

Landry, G. and T. Murphy. 1990. Overseeded turfgrass in transition. *Grounds Maintenance,* 25(1):80–86, 136.

Leuthold, L. D. 1982. *Watering Your Lawn.* Cooperative Extension Service Bulletin MF-440, Kansas State University, Manhattan, KS.

Leuthold, L. D. and R. E. Gaussoin. 1990. *Lawn Weed Control.* Cooperative Extension Publication No. C-685 (Revised). Kansas State University, Manhattan, KS.

Mace, A. E. (ed.). 1985. *All About Lawns.* Ortho Books, San Francisco, CA.

Mello, J. 1987. Bringing back the grass. *Landscape Management,* 26(8):22-24, 26.

Murdoch, C. 1985. Adaptation of turfgrasses in Hawaii. *Fertility and Ornamentals Short Course.* Dept. of Horticulture, University of Hawaii, Honolulu, HI.

Murphy, J. and P. Rieke. 1990. Comparing aerification techniques. *Grounds Maintenance,* 25(7):10-12, 76-79.

Murphy, J. and P. Rieke. 1991. Update on aerification. *Golf Course Management,* 59(7):6-7, 10-16, 20-28.

Riordan, T., R. E. Gaussoin and G. L. Horst. 1992. *Tall Fescue Lawn Calendar.* Cooperative Extension Publication No. G81-558-A (Revised). Univ. of Nebraska, Lincoln, NE.

Roche, J. 1993. Minimizing compaction on athletic fields, golf courses. *Landscape Management,* 32(8):22-30.

Shane, W. W. 1989. Rain, stress result in varied turfgrass problems. *Lawn & Landscape Maintenance,* 10(9):44-46.

Steenbock, A. and D. Hensley. 1991. Disposal options reshape lawn care. *Northern Turf Management,* 2(7):22, 30.

Steinegger, D., R. Gaussoin and G. Horst. 1993. *Evaluating Your Landscape Irrigation System.* Cooperative Extension Publication No. G93-1181.

Stougaard, B. and R. Gaussoin. 1991. *Lawn Weed Prevention and Management.* Cooperative Extension Publication No. G91-1045. Univ. of Nebraska, Lincoln, NE.

Street, J. 1988. Properties of thatch. *ALA,* 9(5):18-19.

Smiley, R. W., P. H. Dernoedon, and B. B. Clarke. 1992. *Compendium of Turfgrass Diseases* (2nd Edition). APS Press, St. Paul, MN.

Tashiro, H. 1987. *Turfgrass Insects of the United States and Canada.* Cornell Univ. Press. Ithaca, NY.

Turgeon, A. J. 1988. Thatch. *Landscape Management,* 27(3):58-61.

Turgeon, A. J. 1991. *Turfgrass Management* (Third Edition). Prentice Hall, Englewood Cliffs, NJ.

Vargas, J. M. 1981. *Management of Turfgrass Diseases.* Burgess Publishing Co., Minneapolis, MN.

Vengris, J. and W. A. Torello. 1982. *Lawns* (3rd Edition). Thomson Publications, Fresno, CA.

Watkins, J. E. and R. Gaussoin. 1992. *Rust Diseases of Turfgrass.* Cooperative Extension Publication No. G92-1119. Univ. of Nebraska, Lincoln, NE.

Watkins, J. E. and R. Gaussoin. 1993. *Stripe Smut Disease of Turfgrass.* Cooperative Extension Publication No. G93-1149. Univ. of Nebraska, Lincoln, NE.

White, R. 1991. Turfgrasses: They're more than blades and roots. *Lawn & Landscape Maintenance,* 12(6):32-38, 69.

Chapter 13
Pesticide Management and Use

Roch Gaussoin[1]

Pest management is an extensive and essential part of landscape management. Pest management requires careful and judicious use of chemical pesticides or alternative means to reduce damage to the environment. Application of pesticides is a financially lucrative facet of most landscape management operations. Pesticide applications are the landscape manager's greatest risk and liability. Safe and prudent pesticide use requires knowledge of pesticide regulations, the chemicals, environmental and human toxicology, and application technology. It is not within the scope of this chapter to comprehensively cover every aspect of pesticide use and application. References listed at the end of this chapter and Chapter 1 of this text are recommended for a more thorough dialogue on specific topics.

Photo 13–1. The proper identity of the pest must be determined before effective controls can be initiated. Treatment for the mites causing the galls on this maple at this point of the season will be ineffective. Improper diagnosis wastes time and capital, pollutes the environment, and does not solve the problem. Photograph courtesy of James Robbins.

Pesticide Regulations

Certification

The Federal Insecticide, Fungicide, and Rodenticide Act (FIFRA) was amended in 1972 to initiate a program to certify individuals who apply pesticides. These amendments to FIFRA include the following:

All pesticides must be classified as either *"General"* or *"Restricted"* use. *General Use* products present little or no hazard to the applicator and have no adverse effect on the environment when used according to label directions. Toxicity of *Restricted Use* materials presents a potential hazard to the

---

[1]Extension Turfgrass Specialist, Department of Horticulture, University of Nebraska, Lincoln, NE.

applicator or other persons. Use of these products without additional regulatory restriction may cause adverse effects to the environment.

Persons applying Restricted Use Pesticides (RUP) are required to be *certified* in their safe and appropriate use.

Provisions for civil and criminal penalties (up to $5,000.00 and one year in prison) were established for people violating FIFRA.

The Federal Government granted regulatory "primacy" to the states. This meant that individual states had jurisdiction over all pesticide matters as long as the state's regulations met the minimum Federal standards. Because pesticide certification became the responsibility of each state, certification requirements and pesticide regulations often differ significantly from state to state. In most states, however, pesticide regulations and certification requirements are more stringent than the minimum Federal requirements. Check with the pesticide regulatory board in the state(s) the firm will be applying pesticides for more information (see *Appendix 8* for addresses of each state's pesticide agency). Companies applying pesticides in more than one state must meet the requirements in each.

Right to Know Legislation

In 1986, the *Superfund Amendments and Reauthorization Act* (SARA) was signed into law. Title III of this legislation or the *Emergency Planning and Community Right to Know Act* directly affects landscape managers. Employers are required to inform and train employees of potential hazards associated with products and chemicals they may use or come in contact with. Companies are also required to obtain *Material Safety Data Sheets* (MSDS) for all chemicals, not just pesticides, used in the operation.

The MSDS provides information on physical and chemical characteristics, physical and health hazards, routes of entry, exposure limits, carcinogenicity, safe handling, first aid, and medical procedures for the chemical. The MSDS, at the very minimum, must be stored in a conspicuous location in the workplace. If chemicals are carried in a vehicle and applied elsewhere, then the vehicle must carry the appropriate MSDS. Chemical MSDS's are available from chemical distributors or manufacturers. Addresses of sources of MSDS of many materials used in landscape and turfgrass management can be found in Appendix 9.

Additionally, the legislation requires firms to maintain an *inventory* of chemicals based on their hazard rating. If the inventory exceeds a certain level then the quantity must be reported. Further information concerning SARA can be obtained from any regional Environmental Protection Agency (EPA) office (addresses in Appendix 10).

The Pesticide Label

The *pesticide label* is the written, printed, or graphic matter on, or attached to the pesticide or any of its containers or wrappers. The pesticide label constitutes a *legal and binding contract* between the applicator and the chemical company prohibiting the use of the pesticide in any application or procedure not consistent with the label. A thorough understanding of the components of the pesticide label is critical for proper pesticide use and application, as well as circumvention of potential liability for pesticide misuse. A generic pesticide label is shown in Figure 13-1.

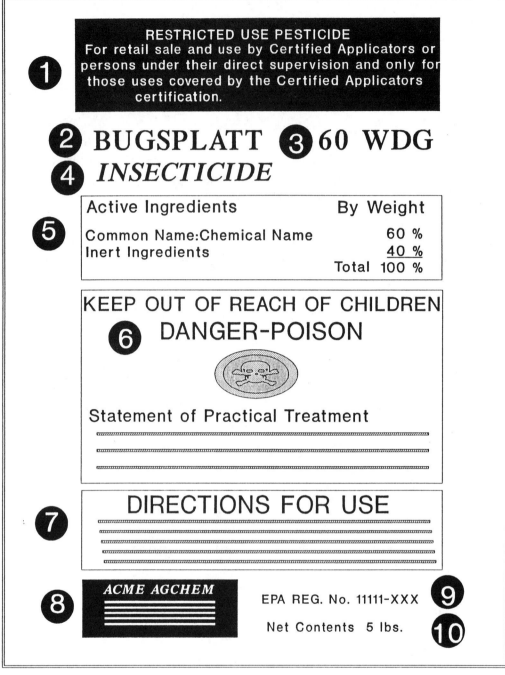

Figure 13–1.

By Federal law, every pesticide label must contain certain specific information. The numbered sequence on Figure 13–1 allows for explanation of each label component. Many of the components are self-explanatory.

1. *Restricted use block.* If the pesticide labeled is a *Restricted Use Pesticide* it is always designated as such in a block at the top of the label. Appropriate certification is required to purchase and use restricted use materials. *General Use Pesticides* do not require such designation.

2. *Trade name.* This is the name chosen by the manufacturer or distributor for marketing purposes. The trade name is prominently displayed in large print and may not be used in the *active ingredient* section. In this generic example the trade name is *BUGSPLATT*.

3. *Type of formulation.* Pesticides are seldom marketed as 100 percent active ingredient. Pesticides usually contain from 1 to 70 percent active ingredient. The remainder of the product is solvent and materials to facilitate application and/or increase safety. The resulting product is called a *formulation.*

Not all pesticides are available in all formulations. When faced with a choice, the information in Table 13-1 will aid the decision making process. The amount of active ingredient in dry formulations is normally expressed as a *percentage*. Bugsplatt (Figure 13-1) is formulated as a *60 WDG*. This means it is a *water dispersible granule* and contains 60 percent active ingredient.

In liquid formulations the active ingredient is expressed as *weight per unit volume*. For example, a pesticide designated as a *7 EC* is an emulsifiable concentrate formulated with 7 pounds active ingredient per gallon of formulation. Metric formulations are usually expressed in kilograms active ingredient per liter of formulation.

4. *Type of pesticide.* The type of material is based on target species. In this example Bugsplatt is an *insecticide*. Other common types used in landscape management include herbicides, fungicides, bactericides, and plant growth regulators.

5. *Ingredients.* The *official common name* is a name suggested by the manufacturer and approved by the Pesticide Regulation Division of the EPA. Regulations require that officially approved common names appear in the active ingredient section unless no common name has been approved.

The *chemical name* is the name designating the contents or formula of the actual toxin in the formulation. When an accepted common name is not available, the chemical name normally appears in the active ingredient section. If a pesticide contains more than one active ingredient, as is the case in pesticide combinations, all active ingredients are listed by both common and chemical name in decreasing order based on percentage.

The remainder of the pesticide formulation is classified as *inert ingredients*. This may be water or an organic solvent in liquid formulations or talc or clay in dry formulations. If *surfactants* or *wetting agents* are added as part of the formulation then their content is not expressed explicitly. They are lumped together with the inert ingredients. Although technically considered inert, many of these ingredients exhibit biological activity.

6. *Hazard statements.* All pesticide labels contain the statement "*Keep Out Of Reach From Children.*" Additionally, pesticides may contain "*signal words.*" These group pesticides based on their toxicity to people, animals, and the environment.

Toxicity is based on scientific evaluations that determine the relative hazard of various compounds. The results of these investigations determine the LD_{50} (Lethal Dose, 50 percent) or LC_{50} (Lethal Concentration, 50 percent). Routes of exposure for toxic substances are *oral* (the toxin is ingested), *dermal* (the toxin comes in contact with the skin), or *inhalation* (the toxin is breathed in through the mouth or nose). Briefly, the LD_{50} represents the amount of toxic substance relative to the weight of an organism that will cause death in 50 percent or more of the test organisms exposed to that amount.

Table 13–1. Comparison of pesticide formulations commonly used in landscape management.

Formulation	Label Abbreviation	Mixing/ Loading Hazards	Phytotoxicity	Effect on Application Equipment	Agitation Required	Visible Residues*	Compatible with other Formulations	AI Expressed as**
Dry Formulation Applied as Sprays								
wettable powers	WP	Dust inhalation	Safe	Abrasive	yes	yes	Very good	Percent
Dry flowable/ water dispersible granules	DF WDG	Safe	Safe	Abrasive	yes	yes	Good	Percent
Liquid Formulations								
Flowables	F	Spills and splashes	Maybe	May affect rubber pump parts	yes	yes	Fair	Pounds per gallon
emulsifiable concentrates	EC	Spills and splashes	Maybe	May affect rubber pump parts	yes	no	Fair	Pounds per gallon
Dry Formulations, applied dry								
Dust	D	Severe inhalation hazards	Safe	—	yes	yes	—	Percent
Granules and pellets	G	Safe	Safe	—	no	no	—	Percent

*Some formulations, upon drying, will leave residues which can be aesthetically unacceptable on some ornamental plants.
**Active ingredient.

258

The LD$_{50}$ is expressed in milligrams of toxic substance per kilogram of body weight (mg/kg). To convert LD$_{50}$ values to units easier to comprehend multiply the LD$_{50}$ by (1.6×10^{-5}) to determine ounces of toxic substance per pound of body weight. For example, if a 200 pound individual ingested 1.6 ounces of a toxin with a LD$_{50}$ of 500 mg/kg, then the person would have a 50 percent chance of dying $(500 \times 1.6 \times 10^{-5} \times 200$ pounds = 1.6 ounces).

Inhalation toxicity is expressed as milligrams toxin per liter of air (mg/liter) and represents a concentration of airborne toxin that would be lethal to 50 percent or more of a test population breathing that concentration.

All toxicity evaluation is done on surrogate animals, such as rats, mice, or guinea pigs, and represents an *estimate* of potential hazard to humans.

Table 13–2. Pesticide label signal words and associated toxicities.

Category	Signal Word	Toxicity	Equivalent Toxic Quantity for 200 pound human
Highly toxic I	**Danger** A skull and crossbones graphic, in red, is required for all Category I pesticides.	Oral LD$_{50}$ 0–50 mg/kg Dermal LD$_{50}$ 0–200 mg/kg Inhalation LC$_{50}$ 0–0.2 mg/liter	0–0.16 oz 0–0.64 oz
Moderately toxic II	**Warning**	Oral LD$_{50}$ 50–500 mg/kg Dermal LD$_{50}$ 200–2,000 mg/kg Inhalation LC$_{50}$ 0.2–2.0 mg/liter	0.16–1.6 oz 0.64–6.4 oz
Low toxicity III	**Caution**	Oral LD$_{50}$ > 500–5,000 mg/kg Dermal > 2,000–20,000 Inhalation. LC$_{50}$ > 2.0–20 mg/liter	1.6–16 oz 6.4–64 oz
Relatively non-toxic IV	**No statement**	Oral > 5,000 mg/kg Dermal > 20,000 mg/kg	> 16 oz > 64 oz

Categorization of pesticides based on their toxicity and associated signal words are shown in Table 13–2. This categorization also determines specific recommendations for equipment required by the applicator for safe handling, application, and possible medical treatment requirements for exposure victims. This information must also be included on the pesticide label.

7. *Directions for use.* This is normally the longest section on the label and includes the following minimal information: storage and disposal precautions; specific pests controlled; product rate and application carrier recommendations; application procedures; nontarget protection; compatibility with fertilizers or other pesticides; any additional information critical to proper use; and environmental protection. Additional information and directions can be listed.

8. *Name and address of chemical company.* This is the name and address of the manufacturer and phone number to contact for questions or emergencies.

9. *Environmental protection agency registration number.* The number under which the product is registered with the EPA.

10. *Net contents.* The total amount of material in the package, including inert ingredients.

Pesticide Adjuvants

Pesticide *adjuvants* are substances added to a pesticide formulation or spray solution to enhance effectiveness. Most formulations contain some sort of additive to improve its delivery or solubility. The landscape manager can also purchase adjuvants to add to a pesticide mixture to enhance pesticide performance.

While pesticides are formulated to be suitable over a wide variety of application conditions, they cannot be synthesized for all possible situations. The addition of a suitable adjuvant allows the applicator to customize the spray mixture for a specialized need or to compensate for different environmental conditions. Adjuvants are added to pesticide or spray solutions to:

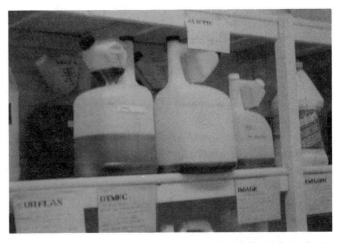

Photo 13–2. Store pesticides properly and safely. Consult the label for storage precautions. Always store pesticides in their original container in a secure, ventilated area. Photograph by David Hensley.

Photo 13–3. Store dry formulations of pesticides in a dry, ventilated area. Do not store any chemicals in areas where the crew works, eats, or takes breaks. Photograph courtesy of James Robbins.

1) Improve the wetting ability of the spray solution.
2) Control evaporation of spray droplets.
3) Improve pesticide persistence.
4) Increase foliar or insect uptake.
5) Adjust the *p*H of the spray solution.
6) Improve spray droplet coverage.
7) Increase safety of the spray to nontarget plants or animals.
8) Correct spray tank incompatibility problems.
9) Reduce spray drift.
10) Mark spray pattern (dyes, colorants).

Many spray applications benefit from the use of adjuvants, however, they should not be added haphazardly or without specific reasons. Check the pesticide *and* adjuvant labels to make sure these materials are suitable to the application site, target pest, and application equipment. Often a single

Photo 13–4. Spreaders are spray adjuvants that increase the spread or contact area of the pesticide on the target's surface. Photograph by Roch Gaussoin.

Photo 13–5. Defoamers can be added to the spray tank to limit foam to limit drift and improper application. Photograph by Roch Gaussoin.

product will accomplish two or more separate adjuvant functions, such as spreader-sticker, spreader-activator, or spreader-sticker-drift retardant. Some manufacturers also produce a blend of chemicals to accomplish multiple functions.

Problems often result from the misuse of adjuvants. Using the wrong type or amount of additive can result in loss of selectivity or an increase in phytotoxicity of a spray material. For example, the addition of a surfactant to some 2,4-D formulations results in significant stand loss in Kentucky bluegrass. Once again, check all labels for proper use directions and adjuvant compatibility. A summary of adjuvants commonly used in landscape management and their functions are shown in Table 13–3.

Pesticide Application Equipment

Pesticides used in landscape management are normally applied either as a *liquid* through spray equipment, or as a *granular* formulation through dry application equipment. Each method or type of equipment has advantages and disadvantages. Selection of specific application equipment depends upon economics, availability, and suitability for the particular use attempted.

261

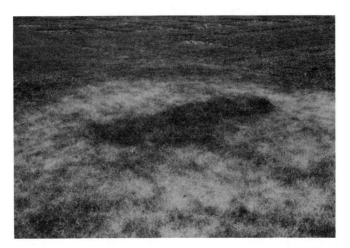

Photo 13–6. Even though spray adjuvants are listed on the label as inert, many possess biological activity. The damage on this Kentucky bluegrass turf was the result of a spreader-sticker applied at a very high rate. Photograph by Roch Gaussoin.

Liquid Application Equipment

Over 75 percent of all agricultural pesticide applications are made as liquid sprays. Spray equipment range from simple, hand-operated, non-powered applicators to complex, multi-nozzle, powered boom sprayers. Landscape managers must balance pesticide application needs, efficiency, and economics when selecting equipment. There is no single machine that provides for every specific need for a site manager. Several types and sizes of applicators will be necessary for safe, effective, and efficient application of the various landscape chemicals.

Hand-operated, non-powered sprayers

This equipment requires no power source to pressurize the unit. Most of the following are inexpensive, require minimal maintenance, and are simple to operate.

Hose-end sprayers. A small container containing pesticide is attached to a garden hose and pressurized from the water source. Hose-ends are suitable for application to landscape turf, shrubs, and small trees.

Hose-ends naturally require access to a water source. They are suitable for most formulations, but are most effective for soluble materials or those miscible in water. Formulations requiring agitation, such as wettable powders, must be frequently shaken. Hose-ends are not effective or suitable for large areas. They cannot be used on tall trees because the sprayer will not operate at or near vertical. Changes in water pressure can significantly alter output. Hose-end sprayers are difficult to calibrate.

Hose-ends are not the best choice for routine pesticide application but are appropriate for some situations.

Compressed air sprayers consist of a small container (1 to 5 gallons in volume) attached to a short hose and spray wand. The wand normally contains a single nozzle but multi-nozzle sprayers are available. Nozzles adjusting from a fine mist to a solid stream are common for small or homeowner oriented, compressed air sprayers.

262

Table 13–3. Adjuvants commonly used in landscape management.

PURPOSE	SURFACTANT	STICKER	SPREADER STICKER	COMPATABILITY AGENT	BUFFER	ACIDIFIER	DEFOAMER
Reduce surface tension	yes		yes				
Increase pesticide uptake	yes		yes			yes	
Improve sticking	yes	yes	yes				
Protect against wash-off/abrasion	yes	yes	yes				
Reduce volatilization	yes	yes	yes				
Improve mixing				yes	yes	yes	
Lower pH					yes	yes	
Slow breakdown					yes	yes	
Deduce drift							yes
Eliminate foam							yes

The unit is pressurized with a hand-operated pump and is capable of developing fairly high pressures. Compressed air sprayers are suitable for small landscapes, shrubs, small trees, and spot-spraying in turf. These sprayers are suitable for applying most formulations. Pesticides requiring agitation such as wettable powers need frequent shaking. Small units are useful for spot spraying and applications to areas inaccessible to larger equipment.

Compressed air sprayers require frequent pumping to maintain constant pressure. Pressure loss during spraying significantly alters output. Pressure limiting valves and pressure gauges increase accuracy and reduce pressure fluctuation during operation. Regular maintenance is required for continued operation and to prevent corrosion of metal parts. Compressed air sprayers are available as hand-held or backpack units.

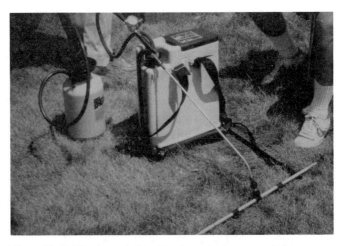

Photo 13–7. Hand-carried and back-pack compressed air sprayers are inexpensive and versatile in landscape maintenance operations. Note the gauge on the back-pack sprayer allowing accurate calibration and the multi-nozzle boom for rapid application to turf or ornamental bed areas.

Wick applicators are specialized applicators used to apply postemergent herbicides to weeds. The herbicide is gravity fed from a reservoir to a sponge or rope wick. The wick is wiped on the weed leaving a thin film of herbicide. Wick applicators are an excellent way to apply broadleaf herbicides around or under trees and shrubs because drift to the nontarget plant is eliminated. Wick applicators must be cleaned frequently and can only use water soluble herbicides.

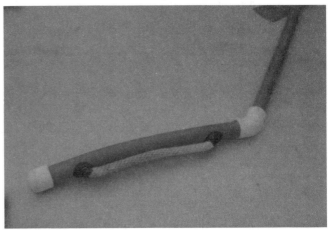

Photo 13–8. A home-made wick applicator. Photograph by David Hensley.

Powered Sprayers

Powered sprayers, as per their name, require an auxiliary gas or electric power source to pressurize and deliver the liquid. Powered sprayers also require a pump. Most powered sprayers are equipped with tank agitators to constantly mix the spray solution and pressure regulation systems to eliminate pressure fluctuations. Many contain elaborate nozzle manifold systems. The expense and complexity of powered sprayers depend on their size, accessories, and ultimate use. They require frequent maintenance but are necessary for applying pesticides to large area.

Powered backpack sprayers are similar to non-powered backpack sprayers except that the sprayer is powered by a small 2-cycle gas engine. Powered backpack sprayers are suitable for all pesticide formulations. Their greatest disadvantage is the additional weight from the gas motor and fuel.

264

Photo 13-9. A high-pressure mist blower applying pesticides to mature pecan trees. Smaller versions and back-pack mist blowers are used in landscape management. Carefully consider the cost of the equipment and possible drift before purchasing most blowers for residential and commercial landscapes. Photograph by David Hensley.

Photo 13-10. CDA sprayers offer portability and low volume application. Photograph by Roch Gaussoin.

Mist blowers or *forced-aid sprayers* are specialized tree application equipment. With these sprayers the spray droplets are propelled as a mist into the tree canopy. They are suitable for application of chemical that must penetrate a dense tree canopy or for spraying tall trees. Recent environmental concerns about drift potential of pesticides propelled at high velocity has caused greater scrutinization of their use.

Controlled droplet applicators (CDA). Liquid from a pesticide reservoir is precisely metered to a nozzle assembly that delivers it on to a spinning serrated disk. Centrifugal force throws the liquid out in a

Photo 13-11. Low pressure boom sprayers are ideal for large turfgrass areas such as golf courses, parks, and general grounds. Photograph by Roch Gaussoin.

uniform pattern and droplet size. CDA's are best suited for herbicide and insecticide applications. The resulting tiny droplets are difficult to see. These units have a low output and are advantageous in areas where access to a water source is a problem. Use in landscape maintenance has been limited, but improvements in CDA technology in the late 1980s have increased interest in their application.

Low pressure sprayers are the most common powered sprayer used in landscape management. Sprayers may be equipped with a single, hand-held nozzle or have a multi-nozzle boom for rapid application over a wide area. Low pressure sprayers are versatile, applying material to turf or trees, and suitable for every pesticide formulation. They can also be adapted for liquid fertilizer applications.

Photo 13–12. High pressure sprayers are essential for applying materials to the canopy of trees. Photograph courtesy of Bestway Sprayers, Ritchie Industries, Conrad, Iowa.

High pressure hydraulic sprayers generate high pressures, as the name implies. These units are equipped with a single nozzle and useful for all pesticide formulations. High pressure sprayers are essential for pesticide application to tall trees and to penetrate dense foliage. They may be adapted for soil injection of fertilizers and other materials.

Granular Application Equipment

The selection of equipment to apply granular pesticides or fertilizers is less extensive and the machinery is less flexible than that available for liquid.

Granular spreaders can be used to apply fertilizers and for broadcasting grass

Photo 13–13. A commercial spray truck designed for efficient and profitable chemical application. The unit contains two separate tanks and power hose reels so that two different materials can be carried and applied as appropriate on the route. Also note the storage area for small sprayers, chemicals, and safety equipment. Photograph by David Hensley.

seed. Granular formulations of pesticides are safer to use than their liquid counterparts. Application of granules sometimes results in less chemophobic client resistance than spray applications. Granular formulations are usually formulated with a low percentage of active ingredients, reducing the possibility of serious damage resulting from over application.

Granular applicators also present several limitations. The volume of the carrier cannot be adjusted as with liquid materials, so each product must be calibrated individually. The actual product must be used during calibration resulting in potential exposure and pollution. Fewer products are available in granular form than in liquid formulations. Some granular products, especially postemergence foliar herbicides, are less effective than their liquid counterparts. Despite the disadvantages, however, many landscape firms use only granular applicators and have effectively used this as a marketing advantage to counter client phobia about spraying.

Photo 13-14. A motorized centrifugal spreader for fertilizers and granular pesticide application. Photograph by David Hensley.

Hand operated granular applicators can be carried or strapped to the operator's chest. An adjustable opening at the bottom of the hopper meters the pesticide to a spinning disk operated by a hand crank. The speed at which the operator turns the crank determines the width of application. These spreaders are relatively inexpensive and easy to use. Machines constructed of stainless steel, heavy plastic, or other non-corrosive material provide longer service. Calibration is complicated by walking and cranking speeds of the operator.

Centrifugal spreaders. The granular material is carried in a hopper that feeds a metered amount to a spinning disk. When the pesticide strikes the disk it is thrown, via centrifugal force, in a relatively uniform pattern, around the spreader. The speed of the disk determines the effective spreader width. The disk speed is controlled by ground speed with ground-driven applicators and by crank revolutions with hand-operated machines. Some spreaders utilize an external power source to drive the disk. These powered spreaders are mounted on utility vehicles or tractors and disk speed is independent of ground speed.

Photo 13-15. A large centrifugal spreader. This unit is powered by its wheels as they turn. Motorized units are also available. Photograph by David Hensley.

Drop spreaders contain a box or hopper mounted between two wheels. The width of the drop spreader hoppers used in landscape operations range from three to five feet. Larger models are used in agricultural operations. As the spreader is pushed, the wheels turn a baffled cylinder within the hopper that facilitates dispersion of the granules through adjustable openings at the base of the hopper.

The swath of the drop spreader equals the width of the hopper. Output is controlled by the adjusting the size of the opening on the bottom of the hopper and, to a lesser extent, ground or walking speed. Some drop spreaders can be pulled behind a utility vehicle, but most are pushed by the applicator.

Drop spreaders are useful for application of granular materials in areas where the swath of a centrifugal spreader is too wide. Drop spreaders have a low coverage per unit time (they are slow) because of the narrow swath. They are also prone to skips and overlaps of applied materials. The problem of skips and overlaps is reduced by applying half-rates of the material in two, perpendicular applications. This, however, takes twice as long.

Calibration

Accurate calibration of application equipment is critical. Inaccurate or sloppy calibration has economic, legal, and environmental ramifications. Under-application results in poor pesticide efficacy, increased client call-backs for re-application, and affects profit margin. Over-application increases the possibility of damage to the site, irate customers, replaced landscapes, lawsuits, and is a breach of FIFRA. Over application of pesticides could result in civil and criminal penalties.

Calibration of liquid application equipment

Regardless of the type of equipment used, two pieces of information are necessary to calibrate liquid application equipment These are *sprayer output* and *coverage.*

Sprayer output

The output of a sprayer must be determined. This is usually ascertained in *fluid ounces per minute* (OPM). Materials needed to measure output are a stopwatch, a container to catch the liquid, and an accurate liquid measuring device calibrated in ounces.

Equip the sprayer with the nozzle or nozzles that will be used in the actual spraying operation. Calibrate the sprayer at the same operating parameters (such as pressure, speeds, and terrain, if possible) that will be used on-site. For multi-nozzle boom sprayers, output should be measured for each nozzle. Replace worn and incorrect nozzles before final calibration.

Operate the sprayer in a stationary position for a predetermined amount of time (usually less than a minute) and collect the output in the collection containers. Measure the amount collected and record this number on a piece of paper or in a notebook. Repeat this output measurement a minimum of two more times to ensure an accurate reading. Use the *average* of the three readings to determine output in ounces per minute (OPM).

For example:

The output of each nozzle was collected for 10 seconds and the process repeated three times (Table 13–4). The average output of each nozzle was multiplied by six to obtain the individual nozzle *output per minute* (OPM). The average of the three collections, summed across all nozzles equals the *total output* of this sprayer in OPM.

It is sometimes more convenient to work with sprayer output in *gallons per minute* (GPM). Divide the output in OPM by *128 ounces per gallon* to produce the output in GPM. In this example the output was 364 OPM that, when divided by 128, results in an output of *2.84 GPM.*

This method for determining output can be used for most sprayers. One exception is high pressure hydraulic sprayers used commonly for application of pesticides to tall trees. These sprayers

NOZZLE	Oz./10 seconds	OPM (ounces per minute)	AVERAGE (OPM)
Table 13–4. Determination of output of the 5 nozzle boom sprayer in the calibration example.			
1	13 22 12	78 66 72	72
2	13 22 12	78 66 72	72
3	12 12 13	72 72 78	74
4	11 12 13	66 72 78	72
5	13 12 12	78 72 72	74
		total output	364 ounces per minute

deliver a large volume of material under very high pressures. Collection of the output in a container is impossible.

To determine the output of high pressure sprayers, fill the spray tank with water to a predetermined level and operate the sprayer under actual spray conditions (minus pesticide) for a measured time. Record the amount of water needed to refill the tank back to the original level. Repeat this procedure at least two more times and determine output as outlined in the example of the multinozzle boom sprayer example.

Coverage

The second piece of information required for accurate calibration is *coverage* or the amount of time it takes to spray a given area. For most large scale agricultural spraying operations this is expressed in *minutes per acre* (MIN/A). For landscape applications it is more convenient to express sprayer coverage in *minutes per 1,000 square feet* (MIN/M). M is the Roman numeral for 1,000.

Materials needed to determine coverage are a stopwatch and a tape measure. Measure a straight line between 25 and 100 feet in length and mark the beginning and end points. The calibration distance for self-propelled spreaders should be greater than that used for non-powered sprayers. Run the sprayer at the same speed to be used on site and record the time it takes to go the measured distance. Repeat this procedure a minimum of two more times to assure accuracy. Use the average of these three measurements to determine the coverage of the sprayer.

For example, to determine the speed of the 5-nozzle boom sprayer used in the previous example:

Run	Seconds to travel 100 feet
1	89
2	90
3	91

TOTAL 270/3 = 90 seconds/100 feet

In this example the sprayer takes 90 seconds, or 1.5 minutes, to travel 100 linear feet.

Next, the *effective spray width* of the sprayer being calibrated must be determined. The effective spray with is determined by measuring the distance between the outermost nozzle on each side of the boom.

Let us assume that the 5 nozzle boom in the example has an effective spray width of 10 feet. We already know that this sprayer takes 1.5 minutes to cover 100 linear feet. To determine coverage, multiply the linear feet traveled (100) by the effective spray width (10 feet) to determine the total area covered in the 1.5 minutes. For this example 100 feet × 10 feet = 1,000 square feet.

This sprayer, therefore, requires 1.5 minutes to cover 1,000 square feet. Its MIN/M coverage is 1.5. To determine *minutes per acre* (MIN/A) multiply MIN/M by 43.56 (1.5 × 43.56 = 65.34 MIN/A).

The output in OPM or GPM and the coverage in MIN/M or MIN/A is multiplied to obtain the amount of water applied per unit area. For our example, ounces (oz.) per 1,000 square feet (OZPM) = [362 OPM × 1.5 MIN/M] = 543. Gallons per acre (GPA) = [2.84 GPM × 65.34 MIN/A] = 185.56. Simply put, this sprayer, equipped and operated at the same conditions as calibrated, will deliver 543 OZPM or 185.56 GPA.

Some pesticide labels have specific OPM or GPA requirements. For example a label may read "apply this product in a minimum of 60 gallons of water per acre." If the sprayer, as calibrated, results in an output that is higher or lower than required for a particular pesticide, adjustment will be needed. Sprayer output may be reduced by: 1) decreasing the nozzle orifice size; 2) decreasing the spray pressure; and/or 3) increasing the speed of the sprayer. Conversely, sprayer output may be increased by increasing nozzle orifice size and/or spray pressure, or by decreasing the speed of the sprayer.

Adding the Pesticide

Once a sprayer has been accurately calibrated the operator is ready to add pesticide to the tank. This is often the point at which many applicators make serious errors. Inaccurate measurement of the pesticide or miscalculation of the amount of product to add results in over or under application. As an example, assume that a turfgrass pesticide label requires the material to be applied at the rate of *4 ounces per 1,000 square feet*. Let us also assume that we are applying the material using the previously calibrated 5-nozzle boom sprayer (delivering 4.24 gallons (543 oz.) of water per 1,000 square feet).

270

It should be obvious that the addition of 4 ounces of product in each 4.24 gallons of water in the spray tank is required.

Errors are made when *dry ounces* are not distinguished from *liquid ounces*. Key points to remember to avoid confusion are that there are 16 dry ounces per pound and 128 liquid ounces per gallon. Further, dry ounces are a *weight* or mass measurement, whereas liquid or fluid ounces are a *volume* measurement. Containers used to measure liquid ounces are never appropriate for dry weight measurements. Keeping these simple, but often overlooked, points clear is paramount to accurate addition of pesticides to a spray tank.

Product labels normally list rates in the amount of *product* required for a given area or application. Universities and Federal and State Agencies, however, often express recommendations on an *active ingredient* (AI) basis. Because pesticides are very rarely formulated as 100 percent active ingredients, the amount of product and a recommendation based on AI are not synonymous.

For example, suppose the applicator has been using a product that is formulated as a 50 WP. The label rate is 2 pounds of product per acre. The label was misplaced and no one at the firm remembers the exact rate. An employee who had read this text suggests that the local County Extension Office is always more than willing to help. The agent informs him/her that the product should be applied at 1 pound AI per acre. The specific product is a *50 WP* indicating that the contents of the bag are 50 percent active ingredient or pesticide. The remainder is filler or adjuvant.

To apply the product at 1 pound AI per acre it is necessary to add 2 pounds of product per acre (1 lb. AI per acre ÷ 1 lb. product is 0.5 lb. AI). If the operator had added only 1 pound of the product per acre then he or she would have inadvertently under-applied the pesticide. Make sure when adding a pesticide to a spray tank that the desired rate and what is added to the tank are equivalent.

Calibration of Granular Application Equipment

Calibrating dry application equipment is similar to the process described for liquid applicators with a few subtle differences. The carrier (water) volume for liquid applicators can be increased or reduced depending upon the particular operation. Granular pesticides are formulated with an inert carrier so the pesticide concentration is fixed. It cannot be adjusted. This requires that calibration be performed for each and every granular product used. Also, the actual pesticide (or fertilizer) must be used during calibration since the size and densities of granular products vary. Relative humidity also affects dispersion of granules. Calibration should be repeated under extremes of relative humidity if these vary considerably during the application season.

The first step in calibration of a granular applicator is to calculate the area to the covered (*coverage*) of a particular machine. For drop spreaders, coverage is simply the width of the hopper multiplied by a premeasured distance. For example, coverage of a drop spreader with a 4-foot wide hopper traveling a distance of 25 feet is 100 square feet (4 ft. × 25 ft. = 100 sq. ft.).

The swath width of a centrifugal spreader is controlled by the speed of the centrifugal disk and is altered by changes in cranking speed of hand-cranked spreaders, ground speed of ground-driven spreaders, or motor speed for powered spreaders. Coverage by these spreaders, therefore, is variable and must be determined for the speed used in actual pesticide applications.

Determine the swath of centrifugal spreaders by placing a series of collection vessels on a one-foot spacing perpendicular to the spreader's line of travel. The containers can be cigar boxes, pie tins, or any similar receptacle. Each container used should have the same dimensions. Load the spreader with the pesticide and set the opening on a medium setting. Run the spreader, at the speed to be used in actual operation, over the collection vessels with the output open. This operation should be done at the shop or in an open or paved area, *not* on the client's lawn or driveway.

Check the collection containers for granules. By observing the amount and distribution of the material in the collection vessels, spreader swath can be reasonably estimated. If the material in each container is also weighed, distribution can be checked and adjusted.

Coverage of a centrifugal spreader is swath width multiplied by a premeasured distance. For example, a centrifugal spreader with a swath of 10 feet traveling a distance of 25 feet has a coverage of 250 square feet (10 ft. × 25 ft. = 250 sq. ft.).

The next step is to determine the desired rate of the granular material. For example, the label rate of a pesticide is 180 pounds of *product* per acre. To facilitate calibration and avoid unnecessary waste of pesticide, this quantity is reduced to a much smaller area. In the previous drop and centrifugal spreader examples, coverage was determined to be 100 and 250 square feet, respectively. The amount of material to deliver 180 pounds per acre must be reduced to these smaller areas. This is done by setting up a ratio or proportion problem and solving for the unknown.

For the drop spreader:

$$\frac{180 \text{ pounds}}{43{,}560 \text{ sq. ft.}} = \frac{x \text{ pounds}}{100 \text{ sq. ft.}}$$

$$x = 0.41 \text{ pounds}$$

For the centrifugal spreader:

$$\frac{180 \text{ pounds}}{43{,}560 \text{ sq. ft.}} = \frac{x \text{ pounds}}{250 \text{ sq. ft.}}$$

$$x = 1.03 \text{ pounds}$$

When x is solved correctly, this amount of material should be applied to the calibration areas and is equivalent to the desired 180 pounds per acre.

The final step in calibration is to determine the spreader setting required to apply the desired amount of material, based on calibration, to equal the desired rate. Many granular applicators provide suggested settings for common landscape chemicals in their operations manual. To accurately apply pesticides or fertilizers, however, these settings should be used only as calibration guidelines, not as the accurate and absolute setting.

To determine the *correct* setting the spreader is to be operated at, the machine must be calibrated at the recommended setting, the output collected and weighed, and the setting adjusted as necessary.

Collection of the output from drop spreaders can be accomplished one of two ways. Many commercial drop spreaders come with a *calibration pan.* This is attached beneath the spreader so that when the spreader is pushed over the predetermined calibration course, the output is collected in the pan. If a calibration pan was not included with the spreader (many less expensive and homeowner models do not) one can be made.

Without a calibration pan, the spreader can be pushed over a clean surface, such as a shop floor or hard surface driveway, and the material swept up and weighed. A potential problem with this method is that the spreader is being pushed along a surface that will be very dissimilar to a landscape. Wide variations in speed result in inaccurate calibration. Use of a calibration pan is more efficient and the spreader can be calibrated on a surface similar to the actual operation.

It was determined that the drop spreader in our earlier example needed to drop 0.41 pounds of material in the calibration distance to apply the pesticide at the desired rate. This means that 0.41 pounds or 6.6 dry ounces of material must be delivered over a 25 foot course with a 4-foot drop spreader. If the initial setting chosen does not deliver this amount then appropriate adjustment is needed. If the collected amount is less than the calculated requirement, then the setting can be increased or the applicator speed reduced somewhat.

Conversely, a decrease in the output setting, or an increase in speed results in a lower output. Once a setting is found that delivers close to the desired amount, the output should be collected a minimum of two more times and the average calculated to ensure accuracy.

Use of a calibration pan for centrifugal spreaders has been impractical. I have read recommendations to tape a garbage bag over the bottom of the spreader to collect the output. The bag is removed and the contents weighed. This recommendation was probably made by someone who never tried it personally. It sounds much easier than it is in practice.

The PennPro Collector™ attaches to the bottom of several popular brands of rotary spreaders. The device collects the granules for weighing and direct calibration, according the manufacturer. The apparatus may make rotary spreader calibration quicker and more accurate. I have not used the collector nor seen on data on its efficacy or practicality.

The normal procedure for collecting output from a centrifugal application is to operate the spreader over a tarp or plastic sheet of known dimensions placed in the calibration path. The output is then weighed. If the tarp differs in dimensions from the previously determined calibration area, and it probably will, the operator must recalculate to expected volume for the size of the catch tarp. If the tarp is wider than the spreader swath then coverage is simply calculated as swath width multiplied by tarp length. The additional width has no bearing. If the tarp is narrower than the spreader swath, then coverage is equal to the catch tarp length multiplied by its width.

If the initial setting chosen does not deliver this amount then appropriate adjustments will be needed. If the amount collected is less than the calculated requirement, the setting can be increased.

Because the speed of travel of ground driven centrifugal spreaders affects spreader swath, increasing or decreasing speed affects coverage. Adjusting the speed cannot, therefore, be used to alter output for a ground-driven spreader. For mounted centrifugal spreaders or any centrifugal spreaders whose disk speed is independent of ground speed, then adjusting vehicle speed can be used to alter output.

Applicators should remember that it is extremely difficult, if not impossible, to calibrate a spreader to deliver *exactly* the amount calculated. Granular pesticides contain low concentrations of the active ingredient to compensate for the inherent calibration inaccuracy. The applicator should adjust the settings so that the delivery is as close as reasonably possible to the recommended amount.

The operator, however, should and must be willing to settle for close. If the calibrated amount is within 10 percent of the calculated amount, the applicator should proceed with the application confident that he/she is applying the material within a safe and effective range.

Determining Application Area

The area of an existing or proposed landscape must be determined to accurately calculate pesticide and fertilizer quantities. These calculations are used to determine job costs, material requirements, and inventory necessary. Determining the area of a landscape is not difficult and can be accomplished several ways.

A mechanical device that is sometimes used to measure areas of landscape drawings and maps is called a *Compensating Polar Planimeter* or simply, a *planimeter*. A planimeter is an accurate measuring tool in the hands of an experienced operator, but it is limited to paper plans and maps.

Field and plan measurements of landscaped areas can be accomplished by the use of *geometric figures* or by the *line offset method*.

Geometric Figures

Any site can be divided into rectangles, trapezoids, circles, ovals and triangles of varying size. The area of the entire or individual parts of the site, therefore, can be determined by calculating the areas of the various geometric figures and summing them.

Line Offset Method

If a particular area does not lend itself to the use of geometric figures, then the *line offset method* can be used. This method reduces large irregularly shaped areas to a series of smaller trapezoids spaced along a measured line. It is also useful for measuring areas of bodies of water. When done correctly, the line offset calculations will determine the area to within 5 percent. Determining the area of an irregularly shaped figure involves the following steps. Also, see Figure 13–2 for an example.

1. Determine the *length line*. This is the longest axis of the figure. The endpoints are designated points *A* and *B*.

2. Mark the *offset lines* at right angles (90 degrees) to the length line. These lines should be equally spaced along the length line. The number of offset lines required or distance is somewhat arbitrary. If the shape of the area to be measured is relatively uniform then fewer offsets are needed. The more irregular in shape the area to be measured, the more offset lines will be required. Additionally, the greater the number of offset lines used, then the greater the measurement accuracy.

Choose the number of offset lines to be used so that they divide the length line (line A-B) into equal segments and define areas amenable to calculation. For example, If line A-B equals 50 feet and the figure is reasonably uniform in shape than an appropriate distance between offset lines might be 10 feet. If the figure is irregular in shape, then 5 foot intervals between offset lines would better estimate the area. For very large areas, where the length line may exceed 300 feet, the offsets can be spaced 30 feet (10 yards) or further apart, to facilitate calculations.

Table 13–5.

A *rectangle or square* is a parallelogram with four right angles. The area is calculated by multiplying the length (L) by the width (W).

AREA = (L)(W)

A *trapezoid* is a quadrilateral with only two parallel sides. The area is found by multiplying the average length of the parallel sides (A + B) by the height (H).

$$AREA = \frac{A + B}{2}(H)$$

A *triangle* is a polygon with three sides. The area of a triangle is the base (B) multiplied by the height (H) divided in one-half.

$$AREA = \frac{(B)(H)}{2}$$

A *circle* is closed curve with an equal perimeter radius from the center. The area of a circle is the radius squared (R^2) multiplied by pi (3.14). The radius is equal to one-half the diameter.

$$AREA = (3.14)R^2$$

An *oval* has an egg-like or elliptical shape. The area is the length (L) multiplied by the width (W), multiplied by 0.8.

AREA = [(L)(W)]0.8

3. Measure the length of each offset line. Make sure to measure every offset line from A-B, including the offset lines on each edge, if appropriate.

4. Add the lengths of all offset lines together and multiply by the distance between offset lines on the length line.

Public Relations and Pesticide Application

High visibility is one means used by landscape contractors to generate new business. One unfortunate aspect of this visibility is the perception by many consumers that the application of pesticides is a *life-threatening* and perilous operation. The application of pesticides to a landscape

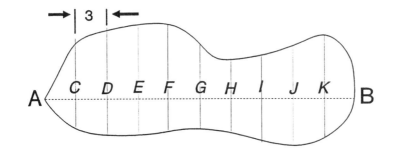

All measurements in feet

| 3 |

A C D E F G H I J K B

Length of Offset Lines

A = 0   I = 10
B = 0   J = 12
C = 10 K = 12
D = 12
E = 11
F = 10
G = 9
H = 7

Sum of offsets = 93

Area =
Sum of Offsets X Distance Between Offsets
=
93 ft X 3 ft = 279 square feet

Figure 13–2.

is necessarily a visible operation. Examples of employees who have had to stop applying pesticides because of queries from homeowners are commonplace. If the person applying pesticide can competently and politely respond to questions from the public, then down-time experienced can be minimized and public relations are vastly improved.

Much of the bad press pesticides and the green industry have received is not justified. Some of it is, however. The unscrupulous, unknowing, and uncaring actions of a few less-than-professionals in this industry have resulted in a black eye for all landscape professionals.

Photo 13–16. Improper pesticide application may result in client loss, negative public relations, and criminal and civil liabilities. Employees must be adequately trained to deal with the unexpected. Photograph by Roch Gaussoin.

It is paramount that every landscape management firm presents a positive public image. This surpasses snappy uniforms and clean vehicles and includes people. Employees must be knowledgeable of what they are doing, why they are doing it, and the appropriate and honest answers to potential consumer or bystander questions. They must also have pride in their work and employer. Employee training is essential.

Additional steps that can facilitate a positive public image regarding pesticides include:

Join and become involved in local civic groups and neighborhood organizations. Area clean-ups and recycling campaigns can be especially appropriate.

Become proactive in local and state politics.

Develop "fact sheets" to be handed out to clients prior to a pesticide application explaining the product to be used and any associated hazards or instructions. Several professional societies have taken an early lead in providing information for use by local firms. Safety of the products and positive aspects should be promoted, but do not be overbearing. Print the information sheets on recycled paper.

Join and participate in non extremist environmental and conservation groups such as The Nature Conservancy, The Audubon Society, or Ducks Unlimited. Illustrate genuine concern for the environment and efforts to improve it. As someone once said, the Green Industry are truly environmentalists; we just happen to be the calm ones.

Stay current with new pesticide regulations and products or non-chemical alternatives. Select the least toxic alternative to effectively do the job. Investigate and try non-chemical controls where possible.

Join and support national, regional, and local professional societies.

Never become belligerent or argue with those with whom you want to make a point. Learn how to calmly and rationally express your views. Learn the facts; do not spout unsubstantiated claims or half-truths.

Recognize that some pesticides have resulted in problems and that not every operator is an honest and true professional. Most notorious past problems have been the result of applicator error.

Learn to respect the ideas and feelings of others. Everyone has the right to express an opinion in this country, even if it is wrong.

Bibliography

Agnew, M. and N. Christians. *The Mathematics of Turfgrass Management.* Lawrence, KS. Golf Course Superintendents Association of America.

Anonymous. 1981. *Quick Calibration Guide for Spraying.* Spraying Guide 197. Spraying Systems Co., Wheaton, IL.

Anonymous. 1984. Which sprayer is right for you? *Landscape Contractor,* 25(7):13–22.

Bohmont, B. L. 1983. *The New Pesticide Users Guide.* Reston Publishing Co., Inc., Reston, VA.

Brandenburg, R. L. 1990. When 'Chemophobia' strikes. *Landscape Management,* 29(3):66–68.

Buckingham, F. 1981. Choosing the right sprayer for the job. *Grounds Maintenance,* 16(9):30–35.

Buckingham, F. 1982. Spreaders for granular material. *Grounds Maintenance,* 17(11):26–30.

Evans, P. 1981. Calibrating hand sprayers. *Grounds Maintenance,* 16:96–100.

Gaussoin, R. 1991. Granular application equipment. *Northern Turf Management,* 2(10):25, 29.

Gaussoin, R. E. 1991. Water, pesticides and conservation. *Landscape Management,* 30(10):8–10.

Gaussoin, R. E. 1992. Spray adjuvants. *Grounds Maintenance,* 27(4):30–32, 106.

Gaussoin, R., F. Baxendale, J. Watkins and S. Hygnstrom. 1993. *Pesticide Selection Guide for Nebraska Professional Turf Managers.* Cooperative Extension Publication No. EC93-1588. Univ. of Nebraska, Lincoln, NE.

Grisso, R. D. and R. E. Gaussoin. 1993. Spray application equipment. *Grounds Maintenance,* 28(4):84–90.

Hoehm, C. 1993. Pesticides: Ruled by fact or fear? *Lawn & Landscape Maintenance,* 14(3):32–36.

Marer, P. J. 1988. *The Safe and Effective use of Pesticides.* Publication 3324. University of California, Division of Agriculture and Natural Resources, Oakland, CA.

Pluenneke, R. H. 1982. Controlling hard-to-get-at weeds with wiper applicators. *Grounds Maintenance,* 17(5):18–26, 30.

Wilkinson, J. F. 1990. Be prepared for the next pesticide crisis. *Grounds Maintenance,* 25(2):10, 106.

Chapter 14
Leaf Removal

Removal of leaves and debris from turf and landscape areas in the fall is a major task. Nearly 80 percent of the responding landscape management contractors in a 1992 industry survey offered fall cleanup services. Leaves will smother turf, clog storm sewers, kill flowers, and are unsightly. They can also consume a significant portion of the fall maintenance budget. To make leaf removal efficient, develop a leaf removal plan, acquire the necessary equipment, and have a suitable disposal site. Consider the volume of leaves; the amount of time, labor, and equipment available or needed; and budget constraints.

Where there are many trees, especially a variety of species, leaf collection may

Photo 14–1. Removing leaves each fall requires labor and planning. Seed pods and leaves will also require removal at various times during the year. In sub-tropical and tropical areas leaves, seed pods, and spent flowers must be removed and disposed of year round.

start in early September and run into December. More leaves must often be gathered in the spring. Oaks, especially young trees, hold many of their leaves into winter and early spring, and accumulation of new leaves from other areas inevitably occurs. Pine needles are more difficult to pick up than leaves, according to managers in the Southeast.

Equipment

Assigning lucky employees with hand rakes and push brooms to clean up leaves, and other fall debris is inefficient and usually impractical on a large commercial scale. Machines do these tasks much faster and more economically, whether the area in question is a small flower bed or a large property. The goal is to select the right equipment for the sites and operation.

Several factors enter into equipment selection. Obviously, economics must be considered. To reduce equipment investment, select machines that can do more than one job. Grass catchers can collect clippings, remove thatch, and gather leaves in the fall. Hand-held and back-pack blowers are used for sweeping clippings and debris all year. Many turf vacuums also work on hard surfaces. Match equipment type and size to the area, volume of leaves and debris on site, and the time available. Consider the predominant weather during the leaf removal period and available labor.

For open lawn areas or those with relatively few trees, grass catchers mounted on lawn mowers may be the most efficient equipment. In addition to mower-mounted units, large independent catchers can be pulled by riding mowers. Heavy accumulations are usually best handled by sweepers, blowers, or vacuums.

Courtyards, steps, flower and shrub beds, fence rows, and areas with limited equipment access can be cleared by hand-carried, back-pack, or wheeled blowers or vacuum units. Hand raking also remains an alternative for these areas. Leaves in areas adjoining wooded areas can be blown and scattered back among the trees.

Grass Catchers

Grass catchers for commercial mowers have changed during the past few years and there are dramatic differences among brands. The cutting action of the blades reduces leaf volume and packs them into the bag or hopper. There are differences in bag or hopper size for mowers that are essentially the same type and size. The effort required for bag removal and bag durability also vary. Look for bags that resist snagging, tearing, and mildew. Even though larger containers may reduce stops and save time, some personnel may have difficulty in handling extremely large bags or hoppers.

Photo 14–2. Mowers that bag or collect clippings can remove leaves from grass areas quickly.

To save time and reduce unproductive travel, keep a truck or trailer close to the mowing area to permit quick dumping of leaves and clippings.

Vacuum Collectors

More material can be collected in the same time and with fewer stops for unloading by using vacuum collectors on riding or small tractor mowers. Pull-behind or rear-mounted units are powered by a separate engine or by the PTO. Engines range from four to eight horsepower. Vacuum capacity varies from 8 to 45 bushels. The vacuum suction helps collect heavy clippings and thick or moist leaves better than mowers with grass catchers. The force of the air packs the material firmly.

The suction hose of many vacuum units can be disconnected and replaced with a flexible hose from 8 to 20 feet long. This

Photo 14–3. Vacuum collectors remove leaves and other debris from turfgrass and paved areas.

Photo 14–4. Power sweepers make leaf and debris collection fast and efficient in open areas. Leaves along buildings and enclosed areas can be windrowed for collection with the power equipment.

permits easy clean up of hard-to-reach window wells, flower and shrub beds, and areas next to fences and buildings.

Sweepers

Turf sweepers use stiff bristles to brush grass clippings, leaves, and debris into easily emptied baskets. Some sweepers are ground-driven; others are engine powered. Sweeping width varies from 30 inches with larger units available.

Sweepers do not shred leaves or pack them tightly as mowers or vacuum collectors. This means that sweepers with the same capacity as a grass catcher or vacuum must be emptied more frequently when covering the same size area. However, they are less expensive.

Photo 14–5. Hand-held power blowers make quick work of removing leaves from turf.

Photo 14–6. Power blowers remove leaves and debris from paved areas. Select units with adequate power and with adjustable air stream. Photograph courtesy of James Robbins.

Photo 14–7. A mounted power blower concentrating leaves for easy pickup. Photograph courtesy of James Robbins.

Blowers

Blowers are relatively new entrants into the landscape maintenance, but have found a place with almost every firm. According to several manufacturers, the sales of blowers for debris removal are growing faster than any other type of equipment. Blowers include hand-carried, back-pack, and pushed or self-propelled walk behind models.

Air speed and volume blowers can be adjusted to gently remove paper or fallen leaves from delicate flowers or to remove empty bottles, rocks, and trash from bleachers or driveways. Blowers are used to remove light snow and grass clippings from steps, sidewalks, and around parked cars; and to dry damp surfaces.

Leaves in beds are simply blown into adjoining turf areas for collection. In larger areas or for heavier leaf accumulation, blowers are be used to windrow or pile leaves for later pickup.

When considering a back-pack or hand-carried model, look for a unit that is designed for long hours of heavy use. Most electric and small blowers built for intermittent home use are not constructed for commercial operations. Adjustable air speed and volume add flexibility.

Vacuums

Vacuums are available in various sizes, including truck mounted units, and can dramatically speed leaf removal. Leaves are chopped by passing through the vacuum impellers so the volume is reduced. Some manufacturers offer blower/vacuum conversions.

Disposal Sites

Most municipalities banned burning of leaves several years ago. Suitable disposal sites are becoming difficult to find. According to some estimates, landscape waste accounts for 18 to 20 percent of all municipal solid wastes. A 1991 survey showed that yard waste composed 30 percent of all landfill material in Alabama and 47 percent of Arizona landfill waste. Approximately 75 percent of landscape waste is grass clippings. The remaining 25 percent is fall-collected leaves. State and local restrictions on disposal of landscape wastes are developing rapidly. In 1989 there were seven, primarily East Coast states with such restrictions in place or in the process of implementation. By 1991 fourteen states and the District of Columbia had passed legislation banning green waste from landfills or requiring yard waste to be recycled. These include Alabama, Connecticut, Florida, Illinois, Iowa, Massachusetts, Michigan, Minnesota, Missouri, New Jersey, North Carolina, Pennsylvania, and Wisconsin. Other states are contemplating similar legislation or have established percentage goals for recycling to reduce the waste stream.

Many companies and municipalities are disposing of the leaves and green waste by composting. Collected leaves are piled into

Photo 14–8. A vacuum truck. The vacuum unit is mounted on the rear of the truck. A flexible hose allows removal of leaves from plant beds and many other difficult areas of the landscape. Photograph courtesy of James Robbins.

Photo 14–9. An industrial sized trash compactor used to reduce the volume of green wasted collected by a landscape maintenance company.

windrows or stacks around six to eight feet high and 10 to 12 feet wide and allowed to compost naturally. Composting areas should be adequate in size. One New Jersey community of 30,000 uses a three and one-half acre site. Consider the adjoining residential areas, prevailing winds, topography, and drainage when selecting leaf storage and composting areas. Most areas require some type of permits or licenses for compost operations.

Some composters add collected grass clippings but these are not plentiful during leaf collection. Grass clippings supply nitrogen necessary for composting. Commercial fertilizer or manure can also be added to promote faster composting if desired. Small amounts of lime counteract the acidity resulting from fertilizer additions. Microorganisms necessary for decomposition can be added by the addition of a compost starter or by simply adding or layering soil or old compost into the green waste pile. Using manure in composting usually requires additional standards and permits.

Photo 4-10. Composting green waste has become a profitable business for many firms. Many resorts and other in-house maintained sites have found composting the clippings and yard waste they generate an environmentally and economically friendly method of disposal. Photograph courtesy of James Robbins.

Adequate moisture is necessary for good composting. If the pile is too dry, microorganisms are killed. If it is too wet, decomposition becomes anaerobic and odor results. In most localities, natural rainfall is adequate if speed is not of the essence. Leaf compost piles should be turned every six to eight weeks (six times per year). Composting is essentially complete in about a year. Aggressive operations turn compost piles every 10 to 20 days, provide supplementary water, and produce a finished product in 60 to 90 days.

The compost can be used or sold as mulch or soil amendment. Shredded and screened composted material is salable to nurseries, contractors, or to the public. Some cities allowing citizens to pick up free compost have discovered it to be a good public relations effort. Sales to landscape contractors or nurseries may pay for the cost of handling and composting the green waste.

Bibliography

Alexander R. and R. Tyler. 1992. Using compost successfully. *Lawn & Landscape Maintenance*, 13(11):23–34.

Anonymous. 1991. Recycling, compost efforts gaining nationwide. *Lawn & Landscape Maintenance*, 12(4):24–26, 92.

Buckingham, F. 1984. Leaves and debris: Have a blast and give 'em a clean sweep. *Grounds Maintenance*, 19(8):22–28, 58.

Buckingham, F. 1985. Leaves—after they fall. *Grounds Maintenance*, 20(10):18–22, 68–70.

Comery, W. R. 1989. Leaves—from trash to cash. *Grounds Maintenance*, 24(9):20–22.

Evans, J. A. 1992. Turning autumn leaves into cold hard cash. *Lawn & Landscape Management*, 13(7):32–35.

Fletcher, R. A. 1992. Composting landscape waste. *Journal of Arboriculture*, 18(3):112–114.

Gibson, H. 1989. Leaf removal. *Grounds Maintenance*, 24(9):12–16.

Gibson, H. 1992. Leaf removal strategies. *Landscape and Irrigation*, 16(10):8–12.

Mecklenburg, R. A. 1993. Compost cues. *American Nurseryman*, 177(4):63–71.

Wilkinson, J. F. 1989. Composting yard waste. *Grounds Maintenance*, 24(9):10.

Zahirsky, K. 1992. Landfill ban alternative-composting. *Davey Technical Journal*, 9(6):3–4.

Chapter 15
Snow Removal

Snow removal is an important part of many landscape management businesses, especially in the North and Northeast. Interest in removing snow as a sideline has increased from the snow belt to Dixie. One arborist in Honolulu, The Tree People, offers snow removal free to all of his clients. Snow removal is frequently mandated by clients as part of a full-service management program. The work extends the use of key employees and equipment and provides cash flow during the off-season. Plowing snow also keeps the company visible in the winter months.

Some companies service only their general maintenance clients, while others actively seek new business. Snow removal is a profitable part of many enterprises. However, many experienced contractors caution that snow removal should not be counted on as a significant portion of the company's profit base. Snow removal contracts may only pay the overhead, at best.

A relatively new publication, *Snow Fighter's Quarterly,* is available from the Snowplowers Association of America, Lansing, MI (800-367-7569). It provides communication and shares ideas among snow removal professionals.

Marketing and pricing strategies

The two biggest months for marketing and pursuing snow removal contracts is July and August. Focus marketing to the firm's market niche and client base. Personal contact and direct mail seem to be the most effective marketing tactics. Some contractors report success with talk radio stations ads. Some municipal and state governments are privatizing snow removal to protect their shrinking budgets.

There are several alternatives for pricing and bidding snow removal services, but all are complicated by nature. Contractors charge per plowing, per hour, per season, per month, or per square foot basis as part of a contract or per incident. Per plowing is the most common pricing method. Per hour charges are effective if special equipment such as front-end loaders or power brooms are required. Additional charges are made for salting and clearing sidewalks. Regardless of the pricing method, the condition of the site and obstacles must be considered. Ideally two people should estimate the same site and compare notes to insure accuracy.

Adjustments to normal hourly charges for labor and equipment are in order when removing snow. Maintenance and fuel costs of trucks, tractors, and other vehicles are greater during snow removal. Vehicles are operated for long periods in lower gear ranges. Trucks used for extensive winter operations frequently require heavier front axles and sometimes double batteries. Consider the cost and maintenance of blades and other equipment specific for winter use. Two-way radios are a necessity for efficiency and safety.

Most employees removing snow require premium pay. A number of contractors pay premium shifts for pre-6:00 a.m. and post-6:00 p.m., or for weekend snow removal.

Good records determine actual cost per unit or per hour. Records of the time required to service each client during certain conditions enable the manager to prepare an accurate bid for next year's contract. Similar records of mileage, fuel, and maintenance costs will provide a true picture of operating costs during this "off-season."

Contracts

Determine the site's requirements *with* the client. Some clients anticipate that the contractor will be there to catch each snowflake as it falls. Expectations and needs of clients differ. Develop a clear understanding and include everything discussed in the contract.

Clients prefer a guarantee by the contractor to plow every snow (greater than a specified depth) during the season for a set price. This type of contract is easy for the client to budget but the unpredictability of nature makes it risky for the contractor. For instance, three to five, greater-than-two-inch depth snows occur annually in the Kansas City area. If the contractor plans and bids for five such snows and there are only two, then he/she has made relatively easy money. However, what if there are eight such snows and three are over a foot in depth? The contractor may well lose money on the endeavor.

A workable fee schedule can be established based on the area involved and a set charge for a specified number of snows. If it is necessary to plow the site more than the pre-arranged number of times, then the client is charged a set and agreed upon fee per incident. This arrangement can be budgeted by the client and will likely be less costly in the long run. The contractor can now recover his/her actual costs for removals over the contracted amount, rather that hiding potential losses in a one-price annual agreement.

Many contractors prefer to have a mix of fixed, time and materials, and per-occurrence snowplowing contracts. This provides payment during light snow seasons and allows for making substantial money during heavy snow winters.

It is essential not to sell 100 percent of the firm's capability. Good management dictates a reserve of employees and equipment to cover breakdowns, absenteeism, illness, and unforeseen difficulties. Most contractors try to schedule at around 80 percent of their capacity.

What determines a snowfall and when plowing will begin? A usual contractual starting point is one-inch of snow on the ground with more falling. Some clients are not concerned with snows less than two inches in depth. Several contractors break down fees according to the depth of snow, such as one to two inches, two to four inches, four to six inches, and over six inches. Each is billed accordingly.

Determine where the snow will be piled or whether it will be removed from the site. Is space available to pile snow until it melts? Long-term snow piles in parking lots eliminate parking spaces and are unsightly. Melting snow running across traffic areas may re-freeze at night, creating hazardous walking and driving conditions. This may increase the client's and the contractor's liability. Removing snow from the site adds labor and equipment costs if peripheral areas or road ditches are unavailable. A plan for removal, if required, and a place to dump the snow are prerequisites.

Who determines how frequently salt or deicer is applied? Is the property automatically salted? Clarify the difference in results, activity, and cost of different deicers. Verify the client's preference of deicers.

As with any contract, the specifics must be agreed upon and written so both parties understand and remember them. Communication with the client includes explaining the time and equipment necessary for the services, before an agreement is signed. Try to list the necessary equipment. Customers better appreciate the cost of services when they fully understand what is involved.

Other facets to address in the contract are removal of ice and snow from walks, sand and salting streets, and snow removal from or protection of trees and shrubs. Also note any costs for extra equipment like

Photo 15-1. Determine where snow will be piled before a storm and have a clear understanding with the client. Too often snow is piled on planting beds crushing plants below.

front-end loaders and dump trucks. Include a disclaimer holding the firm harmless for injuries on the property. "*The client agrees to hold the firm harmless for any and all liability due to slips and falls on the contracted property.*"

Establish a reasonable payment schedule. A few companies require an initial payment as a "start-up" fee or "Autumn Retainer." This provides cash flow in late fall.

Retainers

Some clients prefer to engage the contractor on a retainer. A *retainer* guarantees the client exclusive use of certain pieces of equipment on his/her property until the snow is cleared. Shopping malls frequently place contractors on retainer to ensure the parking lots are cleared. Equipment is sometimes parked on-site so it can be rapidly mobilized.

Insurance

The contracting firm is liable for much or all of damage to the site and plants due to removal operations. Advise the company's insurance carrier of snow removal operations. Carry a minimum of $1 million liability insurance and more in high traffic areas. Discuss limitations of the firm's liability with the client and include these in the contract. Encourage employees to report damage immediately, regardless of the cause.

Insuring equipment can be complicated. If an item, such as a snow blade, is scheduled on the vehicle policy then it is covered only when it is physically attached to the truck. Removable equipment should be insured on the contractor's equipment schedule to protect it during the summer.

Consider the additional liabilities created by snow removal. Snowplowing is typically accomplished during the worst possible weather in the middle of the night. It is conducted by employees who may have worked all day or by sub-contractors over whom there is little control.

Hiring sub-contractors to plow means relinquishing a degree of control. Subcontractors may be included under the firm's insurance coverage with a proportional increase in premiums. A better plan is to require sub-contractors to carry sufficient liability coverage. This protects the firm. Keep a certificate of insurance of all subcontractors on file. Also, make sure the subcontractors pay workman's compensation insurance, otherwise you may be required to pay the premiums for his/her employees.

Equipment

Most firms adapt summer vehicles, commonly trucks, tractors, skip loaders, and front-end loaders, for winter use to avoid additional equipment costs and to stretch their investment. Two-wheel drive trucks are preferred by some contractors. Load the bed with at least 500 pounds of ballast to increase traction. Be sure a set of chains are available. Four-wheel drive vehicles are frequently recommended and useful for problem areas, such as ramps or steep drives. They seldom require chains.

When purchasing a general-duty truck that will also see snow duty consider opting for an automatic transmission cooler or heavy-duty clutch. Heavy-duty front suspensions are recommended for improved plowing and dry-road handling. For winter

Photo 15-2. Adapting summer equipment to snow removal provides greater return on investment and saves money. While trucks and loaders are the most frequently used large equipment, many smaller units can also be adapted. Blades and power brooms are available for mowers of various sizes. These machines are easily maneuverable for removing snow from walk. Photograph courtesy of Excel Corporation, Hesston, KS.

starting and night work, use a heavy-duty battery and alternator; some trucks are equipped with double batteries for plowing. For high-speed, straight-line plowing, choose a long wheelbase. Shorter wheelbases, however, aid maneuverability. Select all-season radial or bias-ply tires.

Two-way radios serve as communications between the operators and the base. The driver can report problems, break-downs, or anything else that impedes progress. The manager can monitor progress and redirect crews as necessary.

Many types, styles, and brands of blades are available. The most efficient snow blade is curved so the snow continually rolls over the blade surface instead of being pushed into a large pile ahead of the blade. High density polyethylene liners for snow blades save fuel, according to their manufacturers. Coat snow blades with light oil during the summer and between snows to prevent rust. Lights and hydraulics are needed. Purchase the toughest, most durable equipment and accessories possible.

Snow blowers are expensive but offer advantages. They disperse snow over a

Photo 15-3. The most common snow blade is designed so that the snow rolls off the blade and away from the line of motion.

greater distance or onto grassed areas. Blowers, blades, and power broom attachments are available for many utility vehicles, lawn and garden tractors, utility tractors, skip loaders, and mowers. Adapting existing equipment saves capital and provides greater return on investment. Plastic or plastic-and-canvas cabs or enclosures protect operators from the cold and blowing snow. They can be installed on small riding and walk-behind units.

Keep snow blower chutes well oiled to permit easier rotation and prevent water from freezing in the joints. Snow flow can be improved by special paints or sprays if desired. Farm supply stores stock extra-slick paint used by farmers to improve the flow of wet grain from wagon boxes. These paints may improve performance of older snow removal equipment.

Comparison shop before investing in specialized snow removal equipment and make sure the equipment fits the needs. Match equipment to the area; don't send a six-foot blade to clear a four-foot walk or twenty four-foot street.

Photo 15-4. A mower with a power brush and heated cab for operator comfort and safety.

Photo 15-5. Power brooms efficiently remove light or dry snow from walks or drives.

There is an incredible variety of snow-blowers, snow-throwers, and other equipment available. Power brooms, for instance, do a nice job removing light or dry snows from walks and enclosed areas. They can be adapted to summer cleaning operations. Power brooms have trouble, however, removing heavy or packed snows; students on college campuses refer to them as "ice polishers." Think safety. Avoid the temptation to remove safety equipment and deadman controls.

Sand and salt spreaders add to the scope of services a contractor can deliver. Units that mount in a pickup bed make salting and sanding of private streets and parking lots realistically efficient for the smaller operator. Spreaders are especially useful in regions that receive ice with/or instead of snow.

Scheduling

Preparation for snow removal must begin in advance of the first predicted snowfall. Equipment should be tuned and winterized. Check batteries and replace if necessary; be sure to have gasoline anti-freeze available.

Photo 15-6. Sand and salt spreaders expand the winter services that a landscape management firm may offer. Spreaders are essential if the contract calls for caring for streets or large parking lots. Smaller spreads are adaptable to pick ups.

Snow stakes are seldom seen in the Midwest but are part of the winter landscape in the snow belt. Snow stakes mark boundaries and objects that could damage equipment or impede the operation, such as fire hydrants, planting beds, irrigation heads, and curbs. They may be worth considering to improve removal operations, especially on first-time sites.

Determine in advance which employees will handle which accounts. Assigning a worker to handle the same account year after year increases efficiency and reduces call-backs.

Schedule a dry run on a rainy day before the snow season. A practice run allows employees to become familiar with the sites and routes and to iron out problems. Develop maps of the property showing the section to be plowed first, locations for piling snow, obstacles, breaks in the pavement, manhole covers, curbs, and other points of caution. Indicate areas that are to be shoveled and which will be plowed. Include any special instructions from the client or supervisor. Keep copies in the vehicles and on file in the office. Should an operator be delayed or become ill, another crew member can take his/her place with enough information about the site to avoid unnecessary trouble.

When a snowfall is expected listen to the late weather report and check local conditions periodically during the night. This unenviable duty can be shared among the supervisors and managers and may require more than one night owl if contracts are spread over a wide area. An awareness of the actual conditions means that crews and equipment can be dispatched accordingly.

Because of starting problems in cold weather, keep snow equipment inside heated buildings, if possible. Some equipment representatives caution that moving snow with warm equipment causes some of the snow to melt and freeze on the surface. This increases plugging of blowers and pileup on blades. A compromise is to keep equipment inside for easier starting but allow the machines to cool outdoors several minutes before clearing snow. Metal surfaces cool rapidly and the melting/freezing problem is eliminated.

Understand the client's needs and priorities. Factories will need to be plowed before 8:00 a.m. Retail store lots have to be cleared before 9:00 a.m. Apartment and residential plowing usually remain more flexible and areas with weekend or infrequent use, such as churches, may be plowed last. Obviously, areas such as fire lanes must be identified and kept open. Try to diversify the size and type of accounts serviced, according to starting times of the client.

Many contractors prefer to remove snow several times during heavy storms, instead of waiting for the storm to abate. Smaller amounts are easier to remove and the workload is spread over a longer period. Piling snow on the windward side of parking lots or use area increases later drifting and multiplies removal efforts and costs.

Back-up crews are essential. They provide efficiency and maintain job quality. It is also a good idea to have a mechanic on call or available. He/she can make on-site repairs and serve as a back-up driver, if necessary. Several contractors keep relief drivers "on call;" however, remember to include the cost of this on call person when calculating overhead.

Deicing materials

The most common material used to thaw ice on walks and roadways is *rock salt* (sodium chloride [NaCl]), alone, or mixed with sand or cinders. Salt damages some surfaces and plants. Continued use of salt over a long period can contaminate ground water and destroy the structure of the soil. *Calcium chloride* and other "non-sodium based" deicing chemicals are preferable but usually more expensive. Calcium chloride melts ice faster than rock salt and is effective at temperatures as low as $-20°F$. It is less damaging to plants, but there are no de-icers that are totally safe for plants.

Table 15–1. Characteristics of some deicing materials used in landscape management.

Deicing material	Damage to concrete	Effect on plants	Effect on metals	Relative cost
Ammonium nitrate	heavy	slight	slight	moderate
Calcium chloride	slight	some	very corrosive	moderate
Calcium magnesium acetate	none	none	non corrosive	very high
Potassium chloride	none to slight	none to slight	none to slight	moderate
Sodium chloride	some	damaging	corrosive	low
Urea	none	slight	slight	moderate

Mixing de-icing agents with an abrasive such as sand, cinders, or ash increase their effectiveness. The mixture reduces the amount of salt or melting material needed and adds the "grittiness" of the abrasive for traction and increased melting.

Urea is used for deicing at airports because it is non-corrosive to metals. Urea, alone or mixed with sand, is sometimes used on sidewalks and can substitute for salt around plants. Greater amounts of urea are required to obtain melting equal to sodium or calcium chlorides. Excessive amounts of urea or other fertilizers will damage plants and turfgrass.

Calcium magnesium acetate (CMA) was identified in the 1970s by the Federal Highway Administration as the only effective deicer to meet a standard of low corrosion and environmental safety. It is no more corrosive than tap water and biodegrades. CMA is effective to 20°F and is used at the same rates as salt. If CMA is applied to road surfaces early in a storm, it reduces snow packing and bonding of ice to the pavement. The downside for CMA is economics. Its costs around $600 per ton, compared to $20 to $30 for salt. CMA is finding a market for critical areas where corrosion from salt or other deicers cannot be tolerated.

Apply de-icing materials carefully. Do not use them to melt snow. Spread the mixture of abrasive and de-icer after plowing or shoveling, and after the threat of more snow is past.

Salt damage to plants

Damage to plants occurs from splashing or drift of salt spray from traffic, or from contamination of the soil. Salt spray results in death of buds and twigs of deciduous plants and browning of needles of evergreens. Excessive salt in the soil acts more slowly, and damage may not show up for several years. Symptoms include an initial bluish- green cast to the foliage, marginal burn of leaves or needles, and reduction of growth and vigor. Symptoms are more evident in late summer or during drought stress. They can be confused with symptoms resulting from damage due to insects, diseases, nutrient imbalance, or chemical mis-application.

Photo 15-7. Too often planting beds serve as snow storage areas. Serious injury results if the snow is laden with salt and from the weight of the snow. Salt damage can build up over several years without proper management.

Salt injury to plants increases with the amount of vehicle traffic, the amount and number of salt applications, proximity to the roadway or application area, speed of the traffic, location of plants downwind or in drainage patterns away from the source, and with plant species. Injury can be avoided or reduced by using non-salt de-icing materials. Do not pile or store snow on plant beds or turf. Antidesiccants and antitranspirants have been recommended for protecting foliage and reducing drying of plant tissue. These materials have been shown to be ineffective, however, and in some cases resulted in increased plant damage. Plants or trees that are subject to injury can be protected from salt injury with barriers of plastic or burlap. Avoid planting in high salt drift zones along highways and use resistant plants in problem areas. Aerial and soil salt tolerance of several temperate landscape plants is listed in Appendix 11 and 12.

292

Soil additives, such as organic matter, activated charcoal, and gypsum have been used to improve the structure of soils damaged by salt application. Incorporation is necessary for organic material and activated charcoal and greatly improves the effectiveness of gypsum.

Bibliography

Anonymous. 1979. Snow removal. *Landscape Contractor*, 20(11):17–18.

Anonymous. 1980. Calcium chloride controls dust, melts ice. *Grounds Maintenance*, 15(9):54.

Anonymous. 1983. Snow removal: is it for you? *Landscape Contractor*, 24(11):8–9.

Anonymous. 1986. Is snow removal a necessary service for landscape contractors? *Landscape Contractor*, 27(1):40–41.

Anonymous. 1991. De-icing agents can reduce time, effort of snow removal. *Landscape Contractor*, 32(9):16–18.

Anonymous. 1991. Good contracts a requirement for snow removal. *Landscape Contractor*, 32(12):14–15.

Anonymous. 1992. Chemical deicer comparison chart. *Landscape Contractor*, 33(1):42.

Buckingham, F. 1983. Streamlining snow removal. *Grounds Maintenance*, 18(10):10–12, 16, 50.

Buckingham, F. 1986. Plan now for a better snow-removal season. *Grounds Maintenance*, 21(7):48, 52, 54.

Dirr, M. and J. Biedermann. 1980. Amelioration of salt damage to cotoneaster by gypsum. *Journal of Arboriculture*, 6(4):108–110.

Evans, J. A. 1991. The cold war. *Lawn & Landscape Maintenance*, 12(10):42–44.

Gibson, H. 1989. Tactics for snow removal. *Grounds Maintenance*, 24(11):10–14, 16.

Gibson, H. 1990. Deicing agents. *Grounds Maintenance*, 25(11):42–44, 59.

Greenstein, S. 1990. Snow removal: Proper planning can lead to a successful venture. *Landscape Contractor*, 31(9):12–15.

Hall, R. 1993. Snow removal. *Landscape Management*, 32(8):8.

Hasselkus, E. and R. Rideout. 1979. *Salt Injury to Plants*. Cooperative Extension Service Bulletin A2970, University of Wisconsin, Madison, WI.

Hayhurst, H. 1993. Marketing your snow removal services. *Landscape Contractor*, 34(9):10–11.

Hayhurst, H. 1993. Contracting snow removal. *Landscape Contractor*, 34(9):15–16.

Henretty, D. 1993. Snow removal: Making your winter more profitable. *Landscape Contractor*, 34(9):21–22.

Hensley, D. 1982. Snow removal contracts. *Kansas Nursery Notes*, (3):9–10.

King, J. 1989. Snow removal requires professionalism and the right equipment. *Landscape Contractor*, 30(12):8–9.

Leatzow, J. 1983. Insurance for snow removal contracting. *Landscape Contractor*, 24(11):13.

Steele, B. 1992. To plow or not to plow. *Landscape Contractor*, 32(9):12–13.

Steele, B. 1992. Avoid plowing pitfalls with sufficient insurance. *Landscape Contractor*, 32(9):12–13.

Stevens, R. H. 1993. New snow removal technology. *Landscape Contractor*, 34(9):17–20.

Wandtke, E. 1992. To plow or not to plow. *Landscape Management*, 31(210):38.

Wenzel, C. 1979. How to turn snowflakes into cold cash. *Landscape Contractor*, 20(10):6–7.

Appendix 1: Important references useful to landscape managers.

This is by no means a list of every book or reference a grounds manager may wish to acquire or use. Many excellent books enter the market each year. Update your library as new editions are published.

BUSINESS

Arboriculture and the Law. 1992. V. D. Merollo and M. J. Valentine. International Society of Arboriculture, Savoy, IL
Discusses potential liability and obligations facing the arborist.

Grounds Maintenance Estimating Guidelines. 1990. Professional Grounds Management Society. Cockeysville, MD
Methods, forms, and information for developing individualized estimates.

Grounds Maintenance Management Guidelines. 1988. Professional Grounds Management Society. Cockeysville, MD
Maintenance standards, contract specifications, and other information for the professional.

Grounds Management Forms and Job Descriptions Guide. 1989. Professional Grounds Management Society. Cockeysville, MD
As the title describes.

Guide to Developing a Landscape Maintenance Business. 1985. Associated Landscape Contractors of America. Falls Church, VA
General business information for organizing and operating a landscape management firm. Chapters written by professionals in the field.

Landscape Management Supervisory Training Manual. 1991. Professional Grounds Management Society. Hunt Valley, MD
Good publication for new or experienced supervisors. Discusses personnel problems and motivation.

Landscape Maintenance Contracting. No date. P. C. Nilsson. Nilsson Associates, Southington, CT
Management consultant discusses basics of contracting maintenance services.

Manual of Plant Appraisers. 1986. Council of Tree and Landscape Appraisers. Washington, DC
Methods and problems of plant loss appraisal.

Manual of Site Management. 1978. Environmental Design Press, Reston, VA
Information on business and other aspects of the industry from practicing professionals and experts in their field. A new edition is forthcoming.

Taking Over Foremanship. 1986. National Landscape Association, Washington, DC
Helps new managers develop people and supervisory skills.

HERBACEOUS PLANTS

Herbaceous Perennial Plants - A Treatise on Their Identification, Culture, and Garden Attributes.
1989. Alan M. Armitage. Varsity Press, Inc., Athens, GA
Characteristics and culture of herbaceous species.

Manual of Herbaceous Ornamental Plants. 1988. 3rd edition. S. M. Still. Stipes Publishing.
Champaign, IL
General information for the professional and student.

PLANT PESTS AND PESTICIDES

Compendium of Turfgrass Diseases. 1983. R. Smiley. American Phytopathological Society, Ithaca,
NY
Addresses disease and non-infectious problems of turf.

Complete Guide to Pest Control With and Without Chemicals. 1988. G. Ware. Thompson
Publications, Fresno, CA
Addresses intelligent methods of resolving landscape pest problems.

Diseases and Disorders of Ornamental Palms. 1991. A. R. Chase and T. K. Broschat, Editors. ARS
Press. St. Paul, MN
Excellent discussion and pictorial review of biotic and abiotic disorders of palms.

Disease and Pests of Ornamental Plants. 1978. 5th Edition. P. P. Pirone. John Wiley and Sons, NY
Comprehensive book of insects and diseases of trees and shrubs.

Diseases of Trees of the Great Plains. 1986. J. W. Riffle and W. Peterson. USDA Forest Service
General Technical Report RM-129. Rocky Mountain Forest and Range Experiment Station, Fort
Collins, CO
Information and photographs on tree disorders.

Diseases of Shade Trees. 1989. T. A. Tatter. Academic Press, Inc. San Diego, CA
Very useful in identification and control of tree diseases.

Fundamentals of Pesticides. 1986. G. Ware. Thompson Publications, Fresno, CA
Fundamental chemistry, mode of action, and safety of various pesticides.

How to Control Plant Diseases in the Home and Garden. 1966. M. C. Shurtleff, Iowa State Univ.
Press, Ames, IA
One of my favorites for diseases of herbaceous and woody plants, includes ornamentals, fruits and
vegetables.

Management of Turfgrass Diseases. 1994. J. Vargas. CRC Press, Boca Raton, FL
Newest edition of the industry standard that discusses cause and control of turf diseases.

The Standard Pesticide User's Guide. 1990. B. L. Bohmont. Prentice-Hall, Englewood Cliffs, NJ
Information on safe and effective pesticide use.

Turfgrass Insects of the U.S. and Canada. 1987. H. Tashiro. Cornell Univ. Press. Ithaca, NY
Insect problems and control in warm and cool season turf.

Turfgrass Pests. 1989. A. D. Ali and C. L. Elmore. Cooperative Extension, University of CA, Davis, CA
Guide to identification and control of turfgrass pests and problems for California and southern grasses.

Westcott's Plant Disease Handbook. 1990. 5th Edition. C. Westcott, revised by R. K. Horst. Van Nostrand Reinhold, New York, NY
A guide to diagnosis and control of diseases affecting ornamental and food plants.

WOODY LANDSCAPE PLANTS

Betrock's Guide to Florida Landscape Plants. 1991. T. Broschat and A. W. Meerow. Betrock Information System, Cooper City, FL
Description, information, and photographs of common tropical and sub-tropical landscape species.

Betrock's Reference Guide to Landscape Palms. 1991. A. W. Meerow. Betrock Information System. Cooper City, FL
Descriptions, photographs, and information on landscape palms.

Landscape Plants for Eastern North America. 1983. H. L. Flint. John Wiley. New York, NY
For professionals and students of the Green Industry. Information on adaptation, and limitations of many ornamental trees and shrubs.

Manual of Woody Landscape Plants. 4th Edition. 1990. Michael A. Dirr. Stipes Publishing Co., Champaign, IL
The bible of woody landscape plant information.

INTERIOR LANDSCAPES

Guide to Interior Landscape Specifications. 1988. Interior Plantscape Division of Associated Landscape Contractors of America. Falls Church, VA
General information for preparing and bidding specifications.

Interior Landscaping. 1983. T. Furuta. Reston Publishing, Reston, VA
Aspects of interior design and management.

Interior Plantscapes. 1987. G. Manaker. Prentice-Hall, Englewood Cliffs, NJ
An introduction to interior landscaping.

TREE AND SHRUB CARE

Arboriculture Integrated Management of Trees, Shrubs, and Vines in the Landscape. 2nd Edition. 1992. R. W. Harris. Prentice-Hall, Inc., Englewood Cliffs, NJ
In-depth technical information of care of trees and landscape plants.

Plants in the Landscape. 2nd Edition. 1990. Philip L. Carpenter and T. D. Walker. W. H. Freeman. New York, NY
Contemporary principles, practices, and inter-relations of landscape design, contracting, and management.

Tree Maintenance. 1988. 6th edition. P. P. Pirone, J. R. Hartman, M. A. Sall, and T. P. Pirone. Oxford University Press, NY
A standard for the arborist and tree care professional. Latest edition has been updated and expanded including section on pests.

Western Fertilizer Handbook. 1990. Interstate Publishers, Danville, IL
Tables and basic information on plant nutrition, soils, and fertilizers. Useful nation-wide, not just in the "West."

TURFGRASS MANAGEMENT

Florida Lawn Handbook. 1991. L. B. McCarthy, R. J. Black, and K. C. Ruppert, Editors. Environmental Horticulture Department, University of Florida, Gainesville, FL
An Extension publication with cultural and pest control information for southern turfgrass species.

Integrated Management Guide for Nebraska Turfgrass. 1993. F. Baxendale and R. Gaussoin. University of Nebraska Cooperative Extension, Lincoln, NE
Comprehensive turfgrass management guide emphasizing IPM for the Great Plains region.

Southern Turfgrasses: Their Management and Use. R. L. Duble. 1989. Texscape, Inc., College Station, TX
Dedicated to culture of the southern turfgrasses. A good reference for the professional or student.

Turfgrass Ecology and Management. 1993. T. K. Danneberger. G.I.E. Inc., Cleveland, OH
Excellent ecological reference for intermediate or advanced students.

Turf Irrigation Manual. 1978. J. A. Watkins. Telsco Industries, Dallas, TX
The bible of irrigation.

Turf Management Digest. 1993. W. E. Knoop, Editor. Argus Agronomics. Clarksdale, MS
An annual publication with management and establishment information for cool and warm season turfgrass.

Turf Management for Golf Courses. 1982. J. Beard. Burgess Press. Minneapolis, MN
Specialized for management of golf courses.

Turf Managers Handbook. 1987. W. H. Daniel and R. P. Freeborg. Harvest Publishing Co., Cleveland, OH
Reference for the professional or advanced student.

Turfgrass Management. 1985. 3rd Edition. A. J. Turgeon. Reston Publishing, Reston, VA
Text for the intermediate student.

Turfgrass: Science and Culture. 1973. J. B. Beard. Prentice-Hall, Inc., Englewood Cliffs, NJ
Standard text for intermediate and advanced students.

Appendix 2: Magazines and trade publications of interest to landscape management professionals.

American Nurseryman, 77 W. Washington, Suite 2100, Chicago, IL 60602.

Arbor Age, P.O. Box 2180, Cathedral City, CA 92235.

Arborist News, ISA, P.O. Box GG, Savoy, IL 61874.

Golf Course Management, 1421 Research Park Drive, Lawrence, KS 66049.

Golf and Sports Turf, P.O. Box 8420, Van Nuys, CA 91409.

Greenhouse Grower, 37733 Euclid Ave., Willoughby, OH 44094.

Greenhouse Manager, 120 St. Louis Ave., Fort Worth, TX 76104.

Grounds Maintenance, P.O. Box 12901, Overland Park, KS 66282.

In-Site, 24380 N. Highway 45, Vernon Hills, IL 60061.

Interior Landscape Industry, 77 W. Washington, Suite 2100, Chicago, IL 60602.

Interiorscape, 3023 Eastland Blvd., Clearwater, FL 34621.

Irrigation Journal, 68-860 Perez Rd., Suite J, Cathedral City, CA 92234.

Landscape and Irrigation, 68-860 Perez Rd., Suite J, Cathedral City, CA 92234.

The Landscape Contractor, Illinois Landscape Contractors Association, 2200 S. Main, Suite 304, Lombard, IL 60148.

Landscape Design, 68-860 Perez Rd., Suite J, Cathedral City, CA 92234.

Landscape Management, 7500 Old Oak Blvd., Cleveland, OH 44130.

Lawn & Landscape Maintenance, 4012 Bridge Ave., Cleveland, OH 44113.

Hawaii Landscape, 1085 S. Beretania, Suite 203, Honolulu, HI 96814.

Northern Turfgrass Management, P.O. Box 1420, Clarksdale, MS 38614.

Nursery Manager, 120 St. Louis Ave., Fort Worth, TX 76104.

Pro, The Business Management Resource for Lawn Maintenance Professionals, 1233 Janesville Ave., Fort Atkinson, WI 53538.

Southern Golf, 3023 Eastland Blvd., Suite 103, Clearwater, FL 34621.

Southern Turfgrass Management, P.O. Box 1420, Clarksdale, MS 38614.

SportsTurf, 68-860 Perez Rd., Suite J, Cathedral City, CA 92234.

Tree Care Industry, National Arborist Association, P.O. Box 1094, Amherst, NH 03031.

Urban Forests, P.O. Box 2000, Washington, DC 20013.

Western Turfgrass Management, P.O. Box 1420, Clarksdale, MS 38614.

Appendix 3: Professional associations and societies serving landscape management industries.

The following professional associations, societies, or groups serve the landscape management industry or a discrete portion of it. This is by no means an all inclusive list and omits the many local and regional organizations. Professional landscape managers should join and be active in these and other professional organizations.

American Association of Botanical Gardens and Arboreta, Inc., P.O. Box 206, Swarthmore, PA 19081, (215) 328-9145.

American Association of Nurserymen, 1250 I St. NW, Suite 500, Washington, DC 20005, (202) 789-2900.

American Cemetery Association, 3 Skyline Place, Suite 1111, 5201 Leesburg Pike, Falls Church, VA 22041, (703) 379-5838.

American Landscape Maintenance Association, P.O. Box 22318, Hollywood, FL, (305) 925-7996.

American Society of Consulting Arborists, 5130 W. 101st. Circle, Westminster, CO 80030, (303) 466-2722.

American Society of Irrigation Consultants, 4 Union Square, Suite C, Union City, CA 94587, (415) 471-9244.

Associated Landscape Contractors of America, 12200 Sunrise Valley Dr., Suite 150, Reston, VA 22091, (703) 241-4004.

The Association of Higher Education Facilities Officers (APPA), 1446 Duke St., Alexandria, VA 22314, (703) 684-1446.

Composting Council, 114 S. Pitt St., Alexandria, VA 22314, (703) 739-2401.

Council of Tree & Landscape Appraisers, 1250 I St. NW, Suite 504, Washington, DC 20005, (202) 789-2592.

Club Managers Association of America, 1733 King St., Alexandria, VA 22314, (703) 739-9500.

Golf Course Association, 8030 Cedar Ave., Suite 228, Minneapolis, MN 55425, (612) 854-8482.

Golf Course Builders of America, 4361 Northlake Blvd., P.O. Box 31868, Palm Beach Gardens, FL 33420, (407) 694-2977.

Golf Course Superintendents Association of America, 1421 Research Park Drive, Lawrence, KS 66049, (800) 472-7878.

The Irrigation Association, 8260 Willow Oaks Corporation Dr., Suite 120, Fairfax, VA 22031, (703) 573-1913.

International Society of Arboriculture, P.O. Box GG, Savoy, IL 61874, (217) 328-2032.

International Turfgrass Society, Crop and Soils, Environmental Science, VPI-SU, Blacksburg, VA 24061, (703) 231-9796.

Landscape Industry Council of Hawaii, 1085 S. Beretania, Suite 203, Honolulu, HI 96814, (808) 545-1533.

Landscape Maintenance Association, Inc., P.O. Box 728, Largo, FL 34649.

Municipal Arborists and Urban Foresters Society, P.O. Box 1255, Freehold, NJ 07728, (201) 431-7903.

National Arborist Association, P.O. Box, Amherst, NH 03031, 1150 South Highway One, Jupiter, FL 33477.

National Institute on Park and Grounds Management, P.O. Box 1936, Appleton, WI 54913, (414) 733-2301.

National Landscape Association, 1250 I St. NW, Suite 500, Washington, DC 20005, (202) 789-2900.

National Recreation and Park Association, 3101 Park Center Dr., Alexandria, VA 22302, (703) 820-4940.

National Roadside Vegetation Management Association, 309 Center Hill Rd., Centerville, DE 19807, (302) 665-9993.

PlantAmnesty, 906 N.W. 87th St., Seattle, WA 98117.

Professional Grounds Management Society, 1042 Ridgland Rd., Suite 4, Cockeysville, MD 21030, (301) 667-1833.

(The) Professional Lawn Care Association of America, 1000 Johnson Ferry Rd. NE, Suite C-135, Marietta, GA 30068, (404) 977-5222.

Professional Lawn Care Association of Mid-America, P.O. Box 35184, Kansas City, MO 64134, (816) 765-7616.

Professional Plant Growers Association, P.O. Box 27517, Lansing, MI 48909, (517) 694-7700.

Public Golf Course Management Association, 830 Cedar Ave. South, Suite 228, Minneapolis MN 55425, (612) 854-7272.

Responsible Industry for Sound Environment, 1155 15th NW, Suite 900, Washington DC, 20005.

Society of Municipal Arborists, 7000 Olive Blvd., University City, MO 63130, (314) 862-1711.

Sports Turf Managers Association, 401 N. Michigan Ave., Upland, Chicago, IL 60611, (312) 644-6610.

Appendix 4: Addresses for soil testing services and Cooperative Extension publication distribution offices throughout the US and Canada. Compiled by Dr. Roch Gaussoin, Extension Turfgrass Specialist, University of Nebraska, Lincoln, NE.

STATE	SOIL TESTING	PUBLICATIONS OFFICE
ALABAMA	Soil Testing Laboratory Auburn University Auburn University, AL 36849	Head, Administrative Services Alabama Cooperative Extension Service Auburn University Auburn, AL 36380

ALASKA	Palmer Plant & Soils Analysis
	   Laboratory
	Agricultural & Forestry Experiment
	   Station
	University of Alaska
	533 East Fireweed
	Palmer, AK 99645
		School of Agriculture & Land
		   Resources Management
		Agricultural Experiment Station
		University of Alaska
		Fairbanks, AK 99701

ARIZONA	Soil, Water & Plant Testing Laboratory University of Arizona Agricultural Science Building Room 431 Tucson, AZ 85721	Cooperative Extension Service University of Arizona Tucson, AZ 85721
ARKANSAS	Soil Testing Laboratory Cooperative Extension Service 1201 McAlmont Box 391 Little Rock, AR 72203	Cooperative Extension Service Extension Publications Specialist University of Arkansas 1201 McAlmont, Box 391 Little Rock, AR 72203
CALIFORNIA	Soil testing is not provided by the state. Many commercial labs available.	ANR Publications University of California 6701 San Pablo Avenue Oakland, CA 94608-1239
COLORADO	Soil Testing Laboratory Colorado State University Fort Collins, CO 80523	Extension-Experiment Station Publications Office Office of University Communications Colorado State University Fort Collins, CO 80523
CONNECTICUT	Agronomy Section College of Agricultural & Natural Resources The University of Connecticut Storrs, CT 06268	Agricultural Publications, U-35 The University of Connecticut Storrs, CT 06268

DELAWARE	Soil Testing Laboratory Plant Science Department Room 150-E TNS University of Delaware Newark, DE 19717-1303	Agricultural Communications Townsend Hall University of Delaware Newark, DE 19717-1303
DISTRICT OF COLUMBIA	United States Department of Agriculture Beltsville, MD 20705 (Washington, D.C. residents)	United States Department of Agriculture Beltsville, MD 20705 (Washington, D.C. residents)
FLORIDA	Soil Testing Laboratory University of Florida Gainesville, FL 32601	Bulletin Room Cooperative Extension Service University of Florida Gainesville, FL 32601
GEORGIA	Soil Testing & Plant Analysis Laboratory 2400 College Station Road Athens, GA 30601	Extension Editor-Publications University of Georgia Athens, GA 30602
HAWAII	Agricultural Diagnostic Service Center University of Hawaii at Manoa 1910 East-West Road, Sherman Lab 134 Honolulu, HI 96822	Cooperative Extension Service College of Tropical Agriculture University of Hawaii Honolulu, HI 96822
IDAHO	Analytical Services Lab College of Agriculture University of Idaho Moscow, ID 83843	Extension Bulletins Agricultural Science Building University of Idaho Moscow, ID 83843
ILLINOIS	Soil testing is not offered by any public agency in Illinois.	Agricultural Publications 47 Mumford Hall 1301 West Gregory Drive Urbana, IL 61801
INDIANA	Plant & Soil Analysis Laboratory Life Science Building Purdue University West Lafayette, IN 47907	Publications Mailing Room 301 South Second Street Lafayette, IN 47905
IOWA	Soil Testing Laboratory Cooperative Extension Service Iowa State University Ames, IA 50010	Publications Distribution Iowa State University Ames, IA 50011
KANSAS	Soil Testing Lab Throckmorton Hall Agronomy Department Kansas State University Manhattan, KS 66506	Distribution Center Umberger Hall Kansas State University Manhattan, KS 66506

KENTUCKY	Soil Testing Laboratory Division of Regulatory Services Scovell Hall Lexington, KY 40546 (eastern Kentucky residents) Soil Testing Laboratory Division of Regulatory Services West Kentucky Research & Education Center Box 469 Princeton, KY 42445 (western Kentucky residents)	Bulletin Room Experiment Station Building University of Kentucky Lexington, KY 40506
LOUISIANA	Soil Testing Laboratory Department of Agronomy Louisiana State University Baton Rouge, LA 70803	Publications Librarian Room 192, Knapp Hall Louisiana State University Baton Rouge, LA 70803
MAINE	Maine Soil Testing Service 25 Deering Hall University of Maine Orono, ME 04473	Cooperative Extension Service University of Maine Orono, ME 04469
MARYLAND	Soil Testing Laboratory University of Maryland College Park, MD 20742	Agricultural Duplication Services University of Maryland College Park, MD 20742
MASSACHUSETTS	Suburban Experiment Station 240 Beaver Street Waltham, MA 02154	Cooperative Extension Service Stockbridge Hall University of Massachusetts Amherst, MA 01003
MICHIGAN	Soil Testing Laboratory Crop & Soil Sciences Department Michigan State University East Lansing, MI 48824	MSU Bulletin Office Box 231 East Lansing, MI 48824
MINNESOTA	Soil Testing Laboratory University of Minnesota St. Paul, MN 55108	Communication Resources/Distribution 3 Coffey Hall University of Minnesota 1420 Eckles Avenue St. Paul, MN 55108
MISSISSIPPI	Soil Testing Box 5405 Mississippi State University Oxford, MS 39762	Information Department Box 5405 Mississippi State University Mississippi State, MS 39762

MISSOURI	Soil Testing Laboratory University of Missouri 27 Mumford Hall Columbia, MO 65211	Extension Publications 222 South Fifth Street University of Missouri Columbia, MO 65211
MONTANA	Soil Testing Laboratory Montana State University 824 Leon Johnson Hall Bozeman, MT 59717	Bulletin Room Cooperative Extension Service Montana State University Bozeman, MT 59717
NEBRASKA	Soil Testing Laboratory University of Nebraska Department of Agronomy Keim Hall, East Campus Lincoln, NE 68583	University of Nebraska Department of Agricultural Communications Lincoln, NE 68583
NEVADA	Nevada Soil & Water Testing Laboratory College of Agriculture University of Nevada Reno, NV 89507	Agricultural Information Office College of Agriculture University of Nevada Reno, NV 89557
NEW HAMPSHIRE	University of New Hampshire Analytical Services Department Durham, NH 03824	Cooperative Extension Service Plant Science Department Nesmith Hall University of New Hampshire Durham, NH 03824
NEW JERSEY	Soil Testing Laboratory Lipman Hall Annex Box 231, Cook College Rutgers University New Brunswick, NJ 08903	Publications Distribution Center Cook College, Dudley Road Rutgers University New Brunswick, NJ 08903
NEW MEXICO	New Mexico State University Soil, Water, & Plant Testing Laboratory Crop & Soil Sciences Department Box 3Q Las Cruces, NM 88003	Bulletin Office Department of Agricultural Information Drawer 3-A1 New Mexico State University Las Cruces, NM 88003
NEW YORK	Agronomy Department 804 Bradfield Hall Cornell University Ithaca, NY 14853	Mailing Room Building 7, Research Park Cornell University Ithaca, NY 14853
NORTH CAROLINA	Agronomic Division North Carolina Department of Agriculture Raleigh, NC 27611	Publications Office Box 7603 North Carolina State University Raleigh, NC 27695-7603

NORTH DAKOTA	Soil Testing Laboratory Waldron Hall North Dakota State University Fargo, ND 58102	Agricultural Communication Bulletin Room Morrill Hall North Dakota State University Fargo, ND 58105
OHIO	Ohio Agricultural Research & Development Center Research Extension Analytical Laboratory Wooster, OH 44691	Cooperative Extension Service Publications Office, Room 4 2120 Fyffe Road Columbus, OH 43210
OKLAHOMA	Soil Testing Laboratory Agronomy Department Oklahoma State University Stillwater, OK 74074	Central Mailing Service Oklahoma State University Cooperative Extension Office Stillwater, OK 74074
OREGON	Soil Testing Laboratory Oregon State University Corvallis, OR 97331	Bulletin Mailing Service Industrial Building Oregon State University Corvallis, OR 97331
PENNSYLVANIA	College of Agriculture Pennsylvania State University 201 Agricultural Administration Building University Park, PA 16802	Agricultural Mailing Room Agricultural Administration Building University Park, PA 16802
RHODE ISLAND	Soil Testing Lab Department of Natural Resources Science University of Rhode Island Woodward Hall Kingston, RI 02881	Resource Information Office 10 Woodward Hall University of Rhode Island Kingston, RI 02881-0804
SOUTH CAROLINA	H.P. Cooper Agricultural Service Lab Clemson University Cherry Road Clemson, SC 29631	Department of Agricultural Communications Clemson University Clemson, SC 29631
SOUTH DAKOTA	Soil Testing Laboratory South Dakota State University Brookings, SD 57007	Agricultural Communications Office Ag. Communications Center South Dakota State University Box 2231 Brookings, SD 57007
TENNESSEE	Soil Testing Laboratory University of Tennessee Box 110019 Nashville, TN 37222-0019	Agricultural Extension Service University of Tennessee Box 1071 Knoxville, TN 37901

TEXAS	Soil Testing Laboratory Texas Agricultural Extension Service Texas A&M University College Station, TX 77843	Department of Agricultural Communications Texas Agricultural Extension Service Room 229D, Reed McDonald Bldg (2112) Texas A&M University College Station, TX 77843
UTAH	Soil, Plant & Water Analysis Laboratory UMC 48 Utah State University Logan, UT 84322	Publications UMC 50-B Utah State University Logan, UT 84322
VERMONT	Soil Analysis Agricultural Testing Laboratory University of Vermont Morrill Hall Burlington, VT 05405-0106	The Extension Service University of Vermont Burlington, VT 05401
VIRGINIA	Soil Testing Laboratory Cooperative Extension Service Virginia Polytechnic Institute & State University Blacksburg, VA 24061	Bulletin Room Extension Division Virginia Polytechnic Institute & State University Blacksburg, VA 24061
WASHINGTON	Contact local county extension office	Bulletin Office Cooper Publications Building Cooperative Extension Washington State University Pullman, WA 99164-5912
WEST VIRGINIA	Soil Testing Laboratory Box 6108 Morgantown, WV 26506-6108	Mailing Room Communications Building Evansdale Campus West Virginia University Morgantown, WV 26506
WISCONSIN	Soil & Plant Analysis Laboratory 5711 Mineral Point Road Madison, WI 53705 UWEX Soil & Forage Lab 8396 Yellowstone Drive Marshfield, WI 54449	University of Wisconsin Department of Agricultural Journalism Agricultural Bulletin Building 1535 Observatory Drive Madison, WI 53706
WYOMING	Soil Testing Laboratory Plant Science Department University of Wyoming Laramie, WY 82071	Bulletin Room Box 3313, University Station University of Wyoming Laramie, WY 82071

EASTERN CANADA	Department of Soil Science University of Manitoba Winnipeg, Manitoba Canada R3T 2N2	Contact a research branch office of Agriculture Canada, a provincial agricultural representative or a university plant science department for publications about landscape horticulture.
	Soils & Crop Branch Nova Scotia Agricultural College Truro, Nova Scotia Canada B2N 5E3	
	Agri-Food Laboratories 503 Imperial Road, Unit 1 Guelph, Ontario Canada N1H 6T9	
WESTERN CANADA	Soil Testing Unit British Columbia Department of Agriculture 1873 Small Road Kelowna, British Columbia Canada V1Y 4R2	Publications Office Ministry of Agriculture & Food Parliament Buildings Victoria, British Columbia Canada V8W 2Z7
	Soil & Feed Testing Laboratory Room 905, O.S. Longman Building 6909 116th Street Edmonton, Alberta Canada T6H 4P2	

Appendix 5: Drought resistant or low-water consuming plants.

These and many other plants have a place in Xeriscapes™ or limited water landscapes. These lists have been compiled from several sources. Popularity of many of these plants is increasing as supplies and knowledge of their landscape attributes increase among designers and consumers.

TREES

Latin/common name	Height	Special characteristics
Acer grinnala Amur Maple	15′	Small trees or large shurbs, multi-stemmed, fall color red to orange
Acer glabrum Rocky Mountain Maple	15′	Red winter stems, yellow fall color
Acer grandidentatum Bigtooth Maple tolerance	30′	Red, yellow, and orange fall color, shallow root system, slow growth rate
Ailanthus altissima Tree-of-Heaven	50′	Fall color poor; weak wood; messy
Catalpa ovata Chinese Catalpa	40′	Large clusters of white flowers
Catalpa speciosa Western Catalpa	50′	Large clusters of white flowers
Celtis reticulata Nettled Hackberry	35′	Trees from desert seed sources are more drought tolerant
Cercis occidentalis Western Redbud	20′	Drought-tolerant redbud, purplish-red flowers before leaves
Cupressus arizonica Arizona Cypress	30′	Open branched, straight trunk
Elaeagnus angustifolia Russian Olive	15′	Common plant, silver foliage. Several disease problems
Gleditsia triacanthos var. *inermis* Thornless Honeylocust	40′	Yellow fall color; many cultivars
Gymnocladus dioica Kentucky Coffee Tree	60′	Flowers of female trees are fragrant; seed pods are messy but males seedless
Juniperus deppeana Alligator Juniper	30′	Blue-green foliage, red-brown alligator-patterned bark
Juniperus monosperma One-seed Juniper	30′	Slow-growing, drought-tolerant
Juniperus occidentalis Western Juniper	20′	Single-trunked, pyramidal upright evergreen
Juniperus scopulorum Rocky Mountain Juniper	35′	Upright evergreen, many cultivars available

Juniperus utahensis Utah Juniper	10′	Multi-branched, irregularly shaped
Koelreuteria paniculata Golden-Rain Tree	30′	Panicles of yellow blooms in summer; small, irregular shaped trees
Pinus aristrta Bristle-Cone Pine	30′	Slow-growing, irregularly shaped
Pinus edulis var. *cembroides* Pinyon Pine	30′	Very drought-tolerant, slow-growing
Quercus gambelii Gambel Oak	15′	Red, yellow, orange fall color; variable growth habit
Quercus macrocarpa Bur Oak	70′	Unique bark, stately tree
Robinia neomexicana New Mexico Locust	20′	Fragrant blooms
Sapindus drummondii Western Soapberry	35′	Excellent yellow-gold fall color; yellow fruit
Sophora japonica Japanese Pagoda Tree	50′	Medium-to-fast growing tree for poor soils; whitish flowers
Ulmus parvifolia Lacebark Elm	40′	True Chinese elm with cinnamon, lacey, exfoliating bark
Ulmus pumila Siberian Elm	60′	Vigorous, prolific tree for many conditions; insect and storm damage problems; *many* better plants are available. A dog.
Zelkova serrata Japanese Zelkova	40′	Variable fall color

SHRUBS

Latin/common name	Height	Special characteristics
Agave parryi Parry Agave	2′	Leaf clusters 1′–2.5′ tall, flower stalks 10′–20′
Agave utahensis Utah Agave	8″	Plants clustered, flowering stem 6′–12′ tall, leaves 4″–10″ long
Amelanchier utahensis Utah Serviceberry	10′	Fruit dark bluish-purple, flowers white or pink
Amorpha canescens Lead Plant Amorpha	24″	Small, erect shrub with silvery-canescent leaves; spike-like clusters of purple flowers
Amorpha fruticosa Indigo Bush Amorpha	6′	Flowers purple-violet in long, dense spike-like clusters
Amorpha nana Dwarf Indigo Amorpha	1′	Low, erect shrub; flowers violet in spike-like clusters
Arctostaphylos patula Green-Leaf Manzanita	6′	Leaves leathery, evergreen; flowers small, pink, in dense clusters; red-purple bark

Arctostaphylos pungens Mexican Manzanita	4´	Thick, leathery, evergreen leaves; pink flowers in clusters
Artemisia arbuscula Low Sagebrush	1´	Low spreading evergreen
Artemisia cana Silver Sagebrush	4´	Erect, finely branched, silvery evergreen leaves
Artemisia filifolia Sand Sage	4´	Round, finely branching; thin, silvery-white leaves; evergreen
Artemisia frigida Fringed Sage	12´	Mat forming sagebrush
Atriplex canescens Four Wing Saltbush	5´	Branching freely from base, gray-green leaves, one of most widespread and adaptable western shrubs
Atriplex confertifolia Shadscale Saltbush	2´	Nearly leafless in winter, found on heavy clay or sandy soils, very salt tolerant
Atriplex corrugata Mat Saltbush	4´´	Low shrub. Dense, extremely prostrate, evergreen leaves, extremely salt tolerant
Atriplex cuneata Castle Valley Clover Saltbush	1´	Many-branched, evergreen, light green leaves, very salt tolerant
Berberis fremontii Fremont Barberry	6´	Evergreen, thick and leathery, spiny leaves; yellow flowers, fragrant; erect branches
Berberis haematocarpa Red Barberry	4´	Holly-like, evergreen, blue-green leaves; red berries; fragrant yellow flowers
Ceanothus fendleri Fendler Ceanothus	2´	Dense gray or silky branches; fragrant white flowers
Ceanothus greggii Desert Ceanothus	4´	Rigidly-branched evergreen shrub, fragrant cream-white flowers
Ceanothus ovatus Inland Ceanothus	2´	Fragrant white flowers; dark green leaves
Cercocarpus intricatus Littleleaf Mountain Mahogany	6´	Intricately branched evergreen shrub; high temperature and drought resistant
Cercocarpus ledifolius Curlleaf Mountain Mahogany	8´	Evergreen, leathery leaves; erect branches
Cercocarpus montanus Mountain Mahogany	10´	Gray-green leaves deciduous
Chamaebatiaria millefolium Desertsweet Tansybush	4´	Aromatic shrub; glandular and pubescent, fern-like leaves; fragrant white flowers
Chilopsis linearis Desert Willow	25´	Fragrant, pink and white or purple flowers; deciduous, light green leaves; slender, upright branches
Chrysothamnus greenei Greene Rabbitbrush	8´	Small highly-branched shrub, green branches becoming white and shiny
Chrysothamnus nauseosus albicaulis White Rubber Rabbitbrush	4´	Erect shrub

Coleogyne ramosissima Common Blackbrush	3´	Intricately branched, spinescent shrub; thick leaves; twigs blacken with age
Cowania mexicana Mexican Cliffrose	8´	Shrub or small tree with narrow, rounded crown; leaves evergreen or nearly so, dark green; flowers strongly fragrant
Dasylirion wheeleri Wheeler Sotol	3´	Large plants resembling yucca, leaves to 3´, flowers on 5´–8´ stalk
Ephedra nevadensis Nevada Mormontea	3´	Coarse, erect shrub; evergreen stems
Ephedra torreyana Torrey Mormontea	3´	Stems bluish green; yellow cones
Ephedra viridis Green Mormontea	2´	Bright green, erect stems; broom-like shrub; yellow cones
Fallugia paradoxa Apache-Plume	4´	Much branched, often evergreen; white showy flowers
Fendlera rupicola Cliff Fendlerbush	5´	Much branched shrub; large white flowers
Fendlerella utahensis Utah Fendlerella	1´	Low, much branched; small, white flowers in dense, terminal clusters
Forestiera neomexicana New Mexico Forestiera	6´	Erect, spreading; flowers inconspicuous, privet-like fruit
Forsellesia meionandra Greasebush	2´	Low, spiney, tiny leaves
Fraxinus anomala Single-Leaf Ash	20´	Shrub- or tree-like with rounded crown; single, almost circular, dark green leaves
Greyia brandegei Spineless Hopsage	3´	Tan to rose colored fruit
Greyia spinosa Spiny Hopsage	3´	Much branched; leaves deciduous; white or rose colored fruit
Gutierrezia sarothrae Broom Snakeweed	2´	Deep taproot; numerous stems; slender, erect; erosion stabilizer
Holodiscus dumosus Bush Rock Spirea	6´	Intricately branched from base; flowers are white to pinkish; showy fruit
Mimosa borealis Mimosa	4´	Very thorny; plumes dense globose flowers in Velvetpod clusters; fragrant and pinkish-purple
Nolina microcarpa Sacahuista Bear Grass	3´	Erect to spreading; narrow leaves, resembles large coarse evergreen grass
Nolina texana Texas Bear Grass	3´	Resembles large, coarse evergreen grass
Peraphyllum ramosissimum Common Squawapple	6´	Intricately-branched; light green, smooth leaves with minute pubescence; pale-pink, fragrant flowers; small, yellowish, bitter pome fruit
Philadelphus lewissii Lewis Mock Orange	8´	Heavily branched, white, fragrant, showy flowers

Philadelphus microphyllus Littleleaf Mock Orange	6′	Small, narrow leaves; showy, white, fragrant flowers, rounded crown
Prunus besseyi Sand Cherry	4′	Fragrant white flowers; black, edible fruit
Prunus fasciculata Desert Peachbrush	5′	Low, intricately-branched, cream to white flowers
Ptelea trifoliata Common Hop Tree	20′	Short, interwoven branches; large shrub or small tree; buff colored winged fruit
Purshia glandulosa Desert Bitterbrush	7′	Dense, upright shrub; evergreen, dark green leaves dotted with glands; yellow to cream-colored flowers
Purshia tridentata Antelope Bitterbush	4′	Intricately-branched varying form; yellow flowers; aromatic, thick leaves
Quercus turbinella Shrub Liveoak	25′	Rounded, densely branched shrub; blue-green leaves, spinose-dentate
Rhus glabra Smooth Sumac	6′	Commonly used, spreads by root suckers; rose to scarlet fall color
Rhus trilobata Fragrent Sumac	6′	Dark green foliage; flowers before leaves; Clusters of hairy red fruit, excellent fall color, cultivars available
Rosa woodsii Woods Rose	6′	Prostrate to mounded form; light pink to deep rose flowers
Sambucus mexicana Mexican Elder	25′	Large shrub or small tree; leaves compound, leathery; white flowers; blue-black berries
Sarcobatus vermiculatus Greasewood	9′	Erect, spiny-branched, coarse textured; leaves bright green; root sprouting
Shepherdia rotundifolia Roundleaf Buffalo Berry	4′	Compact, evergreen; leaves silvery above, oval or round; cherrylike, silvery fruit
Tetradymia canescens Gray Horsebrush	3′	Much-branched shrub; gray leaves; flowers golden yellow
Yucca angustissima Fineleaf Yucca	1′	Leaves 12″–18″ long with fiberous margins, 1′–3′ inflorescence
Yucca baccata Datil Yucca	3′	Dark green leaves 20″–30″ long; flowers 2′–3′ tall; large fruit
Yucca brevifolia jaegeriana Joshua Tree	10′	Single-stemmed tree, not branching like common Joshua Tree
Yucca elata Soap Tree Yucca	10′	Slender-leaved; definite trunk

PERENNIAL/GROUNDCOVERS

Latin/common name	Height	Special Characteristics
Achillea filipendulina Tall Yarrow	24″	Seed heads used in dried arrangements

Achillea millefolium Common Yarrow	12″	Aggressive
Achillea tomentosa nana Woolly Yarrow	24″	Groundcover
Aegopodium podagraria Bishop's Weed	12″	Variegated green and white foliage, aggressive, groundcover
Alyssum saxatile Basket of Gold	8″	Early spring bloom
Antennaria spp. Pussy Toes	2″	Evergreen foliage, groundcover
Anthemis tinctoria Golden Marguerite	12″	Fernlike gray foliage
Arctostaphylos uva-ursi Kinnikinick	3″	Evergreen foliage; red fruit
Artemesia schmidtiana Silver Mound	12″	Silvery gray foliage
Ascelpias tuberosa Butterfly Weed	15″	Orange flowers
Centaurea montana Perennial Bachelor Button	18″	Brilliant blue flowers
Cerastinum tomentosum Snow-in-Summer	6″	Aggressive
Ceratostigma plumbaginoides Plumbago	12″	Late summer flower, good fall color, groundcover
Convallaria majalis Lily-of-the-Valley	6″	Aggressive, shade tolerant, groundcover
Coreopsis spp.	24″	Bright yellow flowers, short and tall selections
Cytisus decumbens Creeping Broom	24″	Prostrate
Delosperma nubigenum Hardy Ice Plant	1″	Aggressive, excellent succulent, good winter color, groundcover
Echinacea purpurea Purple Cone Flower	30″	Soft lavender flower
Epilobium angustifolium Fire-weed	30″	Aggressive
Erianthus ravannae Hardy Pampas Grass	10′	Attractive seed heads
Eriogonum umbellatum Sulphur Flower	6″	Bright, green-yellow flowers
Festuca ovina glauca Blue Fescue	8″	Blue-gray foliage
Gaillardia spp. Blanket Flower	18″	Flowers all season

Hemerocallis spp. Daylilies	24″	Variety of colors, sizes
Kniphofia uvaria Red-Hot-Poker	18″	Red spiked flowers
Liatrus spp. Gay Feather	24″	Purple and other colored spiked flowers
Linaria vulgaris Butter-and-Eggs	15″	Aggressive, yellow flowers
Mahonia repens Creeping Holly Grape	18″	Evergreen foliage, groundcover
Miscanthus sinensis Miscanthus grass	48″	Graceful form, aggressive
Molina caerulea Variegated Moor Grass	12″	Aggressive
Monarda didyma Bee Balm	18″	Aggressive
Oenothera spp. Evening Primrose	12″	Aggressive
Papaver orientale Oriental Poppy	24″	Aggressive, good for naturalizing
Phlox subulata Creeping Phlox	4″	Early spring flowers
Physostegia virginiana Obedient Plant	24″	Aggressive, good for naturalizing
Polygonum affine Border Jewell	6″	Groundcover
Polygonum reynoutria Japanese Fleece Flower	12″	Aggressive, groundcover
Potentilla hippiana Silvery Cinquefoil	12″	Groundcover
Potentilla verna Creeping Potentilla	2″	Aggressive
Ranuculus repens Buttercup	6″	Aggressive
Rudbeckia spp. Gloriosa Daisy	24″	Flowers all season
Saponaria ocymoides Rock Soapwort	8″	Aggressive
Sedum spp.	12″	Many forms available
Sempervivum spp. Houseleek	4″	Evergreen foliage
Solidago decumbens Dwarf Goldenrod	8″	Aggressive

Stachys lanata Lamb's Ears	8″	Aggressive, open foliage
Tanacetum densum amani Partridge Feather	8″	Gray foliage
Thermopsis divaricarpa Golden Banner	12″	Yellow flowers
Tradescantia virginiana Spiderwort	15″	Aggressive, partial shade
Veronica repens Creeping Veronica	1″	Aggressive, tight growing
Waldsteinia fragarioides Barren Strawberry	6″	Strawberry-like groundcover
Zinnia grandiflora Paperflower	6″	Long-lasting bloom

Appendix 6: Annuals for landscape color.

The following list was compiled from recommendations by commercial and non-commercial sources in the various regions. These annuals were recommended on regional quality, environmental tolerance, vigor, pest resistance, and landscape effectiveness. This list is by no means complete; it represents merely a starting point.

Common name	Botanic name	Color	Preferred exposure[1]
Northeast (New York)			
Bedding plants			
Shasta Daisy	*Chrysanthemum × superbum*	White	S
Tickseed	*Coreopsis grandiflora*	Yellow	S
Cosmos	*Cosmos sulphureus* 'Sunny Red'	Orange	S
Pinks	*Dianthus* 'Telstar Picotee'	Crimson/White Margin	S, Psh
Globe Amaranth	*Ghomphrena globosa* 'Strawberry Field'	Red	S
Rose Mallow	*Hibiscus moscheutos* 'Disco Belle'	White, Red	S
Polka-dot Plant	*Hypoestes phyllostachys* 'Pink Splash'	Pink	S, Psh, Sh
Balsam	*Impatiens balsamina* 'Blite Orange'	Orange	S, Sh
Crimson Fountain Grass	*Pennisetum setaceum* 'Rubrum'	Rose Pink Flower and Foliage	S
Petunia	*Petunia × hybrida* 'Ultra'	Assorted	S
Hanging Baskets			
Sapphire Flower	*Browallia speciosa* 'Sky Blue'	Light Blue	Psh
Madagascar Periwinkle	*Catharanthus ×* 'Magic Carpet'	Assorted	S, Psh
Fuchsia	*Fuchsia × hybrida* 'Dark Eyes'	Violet, Blue, Pink, Red, White	Psh
English Ivy	*Hedera helix*	Evergreen Foliage	Psh
Ivyleaf Geranium	*Pelargonium peltatum*	Assorted	S
Petunia	*Petunia × hybrida* 'Cascade'	Assorted	S
Cape Grape	*Rhoicissus capensis*	Foliage, Rusty Underside	Sh, Psh
Black-Eyed Susan Vine	*Thunbergia alata* 'Susie'	Yellow	Psh, Sh

Upper Midwest (Illinois)

Bedding Plants

Wax Begonia	*Begonia* × *semperflorens-cultorum*	White, Pink, Red	Sh, S
Madagascar Periwinkle	*Catharanthus roseus*	Assorted	S
Poppy	*Eschscholzia caespitosa* 'Sundew'	Yellow	S
Japanese Humulus	*Humulus japonicus* 'Variegatus'	Foliage, White	S
Feathertop	*Pennisetum villosum*	White	S
Annual Phlox	*Phlox drummondii*	Yellow, Blue, Pink	S
Smartweed	*Polygonum cuspidatum* var. *capitatum*	Pink	S
Blue Sage	*Salvia farinacea*	White, Blue	S
Wishbone Flower	*Torenia fournieri*	Blue	Sh
Garden Verbena	*Verbena rigida*	Pink	S
	V. canadensis		
	V. × *hybrida*		

Hanging Baskets

Pimpernel	*Anagallis moneli* 'Pacific Blue'	Blue	S
Algerian Ivy	*Hedera canariensis* 'Glorede Marengo'	Grey-Green Foliage	Sh, S
Baby Blue Eyes	*Nemophila menziesii*	Blue	S
Ivyleaf Geranium	*Pelargonium peltatum*	Assorted	S
Germander	*Teucrium scorodonia* 'Crispum'	Foliage	S
Black-Eyed Susan Vine	*Thunbergia alata*	Gold/Yellow	S, Sh

Middle South (Tennessee)

Bedding Plants

Floss Flower	*Ageratum houstonianum* 'Blue Danube'	Violet	S
Sweet Alyssum	*Lobularia maritima* 'Wonderland White'	White	S
Madagascar Periwinkle	*Catharanthus* × 'Little Pinkie'	Pink	S
Sweet William	*Dianthus barbatus* 'Telstar Mix'	Red	S
Geranium	*Pelargonium* × *hortorum* 'Ringo Rose'	Pink	S
Globe Amaranth	*Gomphrena globosa* 'Strawberry Fields'	Red	S
Petunia	*Petunia* × *hybrida* 'Polo Salmon'	Salmon	S
African Marigold	*Tagetes erecta* 'Perfection Yellow'	Yellow	S
Garden Verbena	*Verbena* × *hybrida* 'Amethyst'	Blue, Purple	S

Hanging Baskets

Wax Begonia	*Begonia* × *semperflorens-cultorum* 'Pink Avalanche'	Pink, White	S, Sh
Ornamental Pepper	*Capsicum annuum*	Yellow	S
Madagascar Periwinkle	*Catharanthus* × 'Polka Dot'	White with Red Eye	S
Treasure Flower	*Gazania rigens*	Assorted	S
Impatiens	*Impatiens wallerana*	Assorted	Sh

Petunia	*Petunia* × *hybrida* 'Bernese'	Purple	S
Geranium	*Pelargonium* × *hortorum* 'Summer Showers'	Red	S
Moss Rose	*Portulaca grandiflora* 'Wildfire'	Mix Yellow-Orange	S
Creeping Zinnia	*Sanvitalia procumbens* 'Mandarin Orange'	Tangerine	S
Black-eyed Susan Vine	*Thunbergia alata* 'Susie Orange'	Peach	S

Great Plains (Kansas)

Heat Tolerant Annuals

Cockscomb	*Celosia cristata*	Assorted	S
Creeping Zinnia	*Sanvitalia procumbens*	Yellow with Purple	S
Dusty Miller	*Senecio cineraria*	Yellow, Silver Foliage	S
Four O'Clock	*Mirabilis jalapa*	Assorted	S
Firecracker Plant	*Cuphea ignea*	Red with Black and White	S
Globe Amaranth	*Gomphrena globosa*	Assorted	S
Jacob's Coat	*Amaranthus tricolor*	Red, Green, Gold Foliage	S
Madagascar Periwinkle	*Catharanthus roseus*	White, Pink, Mauve	S
Marigold	*Tagetes* spp.	Yellow, Orange, Bronze	S
Mexican Sunflower	*Tithonia rotundifolia*	Reddish Orange	S
Ornamental Pepper	*Capsicum annuum*	Assorted	S
Petunia	*Petunia* × *hybrida*	Assorted	S
Rose Moss	*Portulaca grandiflora*	Assorted	S
Salvia/Sage	*Salvia* spp.	Assorted	S
Snow-on-the-Mountain	*Euphorbia marginata*	Green, White Foliage	S
Verbena	*Verbena* × *hybrida*	Assorted	S
Zinnia	*Zinnia* spp.	Assorted	S

Drought-Tolerant Annuals

Burning Bush	*Kochia scoparia*	Foliage, Green-Red	S
Cockscomb	*Celosia cristata*	Assorted	S
Creeping Zinnia	*Sanvitalia procumbens*	Yellow with Purple	S
Dusty Miller	*Senecio cineraria*	Yellow, Silver Fol.	S
Four O'Clock	*Mirabilis jalapa*	Assorted	S
Gazania	*Gazania rigens*	Assorted	S
Jacob's Coat	*Amaranthus tricolor*	Red, Green, Gold Foliage Madagascar	
Periwinkle	*Catharanthus roseus*	White, Mauve, Pink	S
Mexican Sunflower	*Tithonia rotundifolia*	Reddish-Orange	S
Moss Rose	*Portulaca grandiflora*	Assorted	S
Salvia/Sage	*Salvia* spp.	Assorted	S
Snow-on-the-Mountain	*Euphorbia marginata*	Green, White Foliage	S
Sweet Alyssum	*Lobularia maritima*	Assorted	S

Annuals for Shade

Begonia	*Begonia* × *semperflorens-cultorum*	Pink, White, Red	Sh
Browallia	*Browallia speciosa*	Assorted	Sh
Coleus	*Coleus* × *hybridus*	Foliage Assorted	Sh
Impatiens	*Impatiens wallerana*	Assorted	Sh
Edging Lobelia	*Lobelia erinus*	Assorted	Sh
Nicotiana	*Nicotiana alata*	Assorted	Sh
Pansy	*Viola* × *wittrockiana*	Assorted	Sh
Salvia/Sage	*Salvia* spp.	Assorted	Sh
Wishbone Flower	*Torenia fournieri*	Assorted	Sh

Southern California

Bedding plants

Sweet Alyssum	*Lobularia maritima*	White, Purple, Pink	S
Wax Begonia	*Begonia* × *semperflorens-cultorum*	Assorted	Psh, Sh
Madagascar Periwinkle	*Catharanthus roseus*	Assorted	S
Cockscomb	*Celosia cristata*	Assorted	S
Impatiens	*Impatiens wallerana*	Assorted	Psh
Edging Lobelia	*Lobelia erinus* 'Crystal Palace'	Dark Blue	S, Psh, Sh
Petunia	*Petunia* × *hybrida*	Assorted	S
Moss Rose	*Portulaca grandiflora*	Assorted	S
Pansy	*Viola* × *wittrockiana*	Assorted	S

Hanging Baskets

Orchid Cactus	*Epiphyllum* spp.	Assorted	Psh
Mandevilla	*Mandevilla splendens*	Pink	Psh
Fuchsia	*Fuchsia* spp.	Assorted	Psh
New Guinea Impatiens	*Impatiens* spp.	Assorted	S
Ivyleaf Geranium	*Pelargonium peltatum*	Assorted	S, Psh, Sh
Petunia	*Petunia* × *hybrida*	Assorted	S

Desert Southwest (Arizona)

Bedding plants

Orange Cosmos	*Cosmos sulphureus*	Yellow, Orange	S
Dahlberg Daisy	*Dyssodia tenuiloba*	Yellow	S
California Poppy	*Eschscholzia californica*	Orange	S
Blanket Flower	*Gaillardia pulchella*	Yellow, Orange	S
Lupine	*Lupinus sparsiflorus* *L. succulentus*	Blue	S
California Bluebell	*Phacelia campanularia*	Blue	S, Psh
Flaming Poppy	*Stylomecon heterophylla*	Orange	S

Appendix 7: Herbacious perennials for landscape color.

The following list was compiled from recommendations by commercial and non-commercial sources in the various regions. These perennials were recommended on regional quality, environmental tolerance, vigor, pest resistance, and landscape effectiveness. This list is by no means complete; it represents merely a starting point.

Herbaceous Perennials

Common name	Botanic name	Color	Preferred exposure[1]
Northeast (New York)			
Fern-leaf Yarrow	*Achillea filipendulina*	Yellow	S, Psh
False Spirea	*Astilbe × arendsii*	Pink, Lilac, Red, White	S
Chrysanthemum	*Chrysanthemum nipponicum*	White	S
Queen-of-the-Prairie	*Filipendula rubra*	Pink	S, Psh
Baby's Breath	*Gypsophila paniculata*	White, Pink	S
Plantain Lily	*Hosta sieboldiana*	Blue	Sh
Bee-Balm	*Monarda didyma* 'Cambridge Scarlet'	Red	S, Psh
Nepeta	*Nepeta × faassenii* 'Six Hills Giant'	Light Blue	S, Psh
Stonecrop	*Sedum spectabile*	Pink, Red, White	S
Upper Midwest (Illinois)			
Blue Star Flower	*Amsonia tabernaemontana*	Blue	S
Wild Senna	*Cassia hebecarpa*	Yellow	S, Psh
Rose Turtle-Head	*Chelone obliqua*	Pink	S, Psh
Colewort	*Crambe cordifolia*	White	S
Dropwort	*Filipendula vulgaris* 'Flore Plena'	White	S
Bowman's Root	*Gillenia trifoliata*	White	Psh
Sun Drops	*Oenothera* spp.	Yellow	S
Smartweed	*Polygonum cuspidatum* var. *compactom* 'Crimson Beauty'	Red	S
Meadow-Rue	*Thalictrum* spp. 'Thundercloud'	Lavender	S, Psh
Middle South (Tennessee)			
Common Yarrow	*Achillea millefolium* 'Summer Pastels'	Orange, White, Salmon	S

Shasta Daisy	*Chrysanthemum × superbum* 'Snow Lady'	White	S
Blanket Flower	*Gaillardia grandiflora* 'Goblin'	Red, Yellow	S
Heliopsis	*Heliopsis scabra* 'Summer S'	Gold, Yellow	S
Rose Mallow	*Hibiscus moscheutos* 'Disco Belle Pink'	Pink	S
Common Lavender	*Lavandula angustifolia* 'Munstead'	Blue, Purple	S
Black-eyed Susan	*Rudbeckia hirta* 'Antique Images'	Yellow, Red	S
Salvia/Sage	*Salvia farinacea* 'Victoria'	Dark Blue	S
Rock Soapwort	*Saponaria ocymoides*	Pink	S

South (Atlanta)

Spring Color

Blue Wild Indigo	*Baptisia australis*	Blue	Psh
White Wild Indigo	*Baptisia pendula*	White	Psh
Shasta Daisy	*Chrysanthemum × superbum*	White	S
Mouse Ear Coreopsis	*Coreopsis auriculata* 'Nana'	Yellow	Psh
Allwood Pinks	*Dianthus allwoodii*	Pink	S
Cheddar Pinks	*Dianthus gratianapolitanus* 'Bath's Pink'	Pink	S
Maiden Pinks	*Dianthus deltoides*	Dark Pink	Psh
Japanese Iris	*Iris kaempferi*	Assorted	Psh
Yellow Flag Iris	*Iris pseudacorus*	Yellow, Blue	Psh
Siberian Iris	*Iris sibirica*	White, Purple	S
Roof Iris	*Iris tectorum*	White, Blue	Psh
Phlox	*Phlox amoena; ozarkensis*	Pink	Psh
Creeping Phlox	*Phlox stolonifera*	Blue, White	Psh
Moss Phlox	*Phlox subulata*	Blue, White, Pink	S
Green Lavender Cotton	*Santolina virens*	Yellow	S

Summer Color

Common Yarrow	*Achillea millefolium* 'Cerise Queen'	Red	S
Canna Lily	*Canna* spp.	Assorted	Psh
ThreadLeaf Creopsis	*Coreopsis verticillata* 'Moonbeam'; 'Zagreb'	Yellow	S
Purple Coneflower	*Echinacea purpurea*	Pink with White	S
Russian Sage	*Perovskia atriplicifolia*	Blue	S
Coneflower	*Rudbeckia* 'Goldsturm'	Gold	S
Alpine Speedwell	*Veronica alpina* 'Goodness Grows'	Blue	S
Long-Leaf Veronica	*Veronica longifolia* 'Icicle'	White	S

Late Summer Color

Frikart's Aster	*Aster × frikartii* 'Monch'	Blue	S
Tatarian Daisy	*Aster tartaricus*	Lavender	S
White Boltonia	*Boltonia asteroides* 'Snowbank'	White	S
Hybrid Red Chrysanthemum	*Chrysanthemum rubellum* 'Clara Curtis'	Pink	S
Hardy Ageratum	*Eupatorium coelestinum*	Blue	S, Psh
White Snakeroot	*Eupatorium rugosum*	Cream	S, Psh
Swamp Sunflower	*Helianthus angustifolius*	Yellow	S
Willowleaf Sunflower	*Helianthus salicifolius*	Yellow	S
Russian Sage	*Perovskia atriplicifolia*	Blue	S
Obedient Plant	*Physostegia virginiana* 'Vivid'; 'Alba'	Pink; White	S, Psh
Autumn Joy Sedum	*Sedum ×* 'Autumn Joy'	Pink	S, Psh

Winter Color

Mouse Ear Coreopsis	*Coreopsis auriculata* 'Nana'	Foliage	Psh
American Alumroot	*Heuchera americana*	Foliage	Psh
Hellebore	*Helleborus coriscus*	White, Green	Psh
Lenten Rose	*Helleborus orientalis*	White, Pink	Psh
Spurge	*Pachysandra* spp.	Foliage	Psh
Phlox	*Phlox amoena; ozarkensis*	Foliage	Psh
Creeping Phlox	*Phlox stolonifera*	Foliage	Psh
Moss Phlox	*Phlox subulata*	Foliage	S
Christmas Fern	*Polystichum acrostichoides*	Foliage	Psh
Lavender Cotton	*Santolina* spp.	Foliage	S

Southern California

African-Lily	*Agapanthus* spp.	Blue, White	S
Kaffir Lily	*Clivia* spp.	Orange	Sh, Psh
Day lily	*Hemerocallis* spp.	Assorted	S
Hairy Alumroot	*Heuchera villosa*	Pink	Sh, Psh
Lavender	*Lavandula* spp.	Lavender with Grey Foliage	S
Evening Primrose	*Oenothera californica*	White	S
Geranium	*Pelargonium × domesticum*	Assorted	S
Geranium	*Pelargonium peltatum*	Assorted	S, Psh
Sage/salvia	*Salvia (farinacea, greggii, leucantha, sonomensis)*	Foliage	S

Desert Southwest (Arizona)

Desert Marigold	*Baileya multiradiata*	Yellow	S
Bearded Tongue	*Penstemon eatonii;*	Red	Psh
	parryi; superbus		Sh
Sage/salvia	*Salvia farinacea*	Blue	S
Globe Mallow	*Sphaeralcea ambigua*	Orange	S
Verbena	*Verbena gooddingii*	Lavender	S
Zinnia	*Zinnia grandiflora*	Yellow-Orange	S

Pacific Northwest (Oregon)

Fleabane	*Erigeron* spp.	Assorted	S
Lily	*Lilium* spp.	Assorted	Psh
Bearded Tongue	*Penstemon* spp.	Blue, Pink, White, Yellow	S
Phlox	*Phlox* spp.	Assorted	S
Primrose	*Primula* spp.	Assorted	Sh
Saxifrage	*Saxifraga* spp.	Purple, Pink, Yellow	Psh

[1]Preferred exposure. *S* = Sun; *Sh* = Shade; *Psh* = Partial Shade

Appendix 8: Addresses of State Pesticide Agencies. Compiled by Dr. Roch Gaussoin, Extension Turfgrass Specialist, University of Nebraska, Lincoln, NE.

ALABAMA
Agricultural Chem. & Plant Industry
Department of Agriculture & Industry
Beard Building, P.O. Box 3336
Montgomery, AL 36109

ALASKA
Dept. of Envn. Conservation
P.O. Box 2309
Palmer, AK 99645

ARIZONA
Office of State Chemist
P.O. Box 1586
Mesa, AZ 95201

ARKANSAS
Division of Feeds, Fertilizer &
    Pesticides
State Plant Board
One Natural Resource Drive
Little Rock, AR 72205

CALIFORNIA
Calif. Dept. of Food & Agriculture
Division of Pest Management
1220 N Street, Room A414
Sacramento, CA 95814

COLORADO
Division of Plant Industry
Colo. Dept. of Agriculture
1525 Sherman Street
Denver, CO 80203

CONNECTICUT
Hazardous Materials Management
Dept. of Environmental Protection
State Office Bldg., Capitol Ave.
Hartford, CT 06115

DELAWARE
Delaware State Dept. of Agri
P.O. Drawer D
Dover, DE 19901

DISTRICT OF COLUMBIA
Hazardous Chemical Control
D.C. Government/Bureau Consumer
    Health Services
415 12th St., N.W., Room 301
Washington, DC 20004

FLORIDA
Inspection Division
Dept. of Agriculture
Mayo Building
Tallahassee, FL 32301

GEORGIA
Pesticide Division
Georgia Dept. of Agriculture
Capitol Square
Atlanta, GA 30334

HAWAII
Pesticide Branch
Plant Industry Division
P.O. Box 22159
Honolulu, HI 96822

IDAHO
Pesticide Enforcement
Idaho Dept. of Agriculture
Division of Plant Industries
P.O. Box 790
Boise, ID 83701

INDIANA
Office of Indiana State Chemist
Dept. of Biochemistry
Purdue University
West Lafayette, IN 47907

KANSAS
Weed & Pesticide Division
Kansas State Board of Agriculture
1720 South Topeka Avenue
Topeka, KS 66612

LOUISIANA
Pesticide & Environmental Programs
Box 44153
Capital Station
Baton Rouge, LA 70803

MARYLAND
Maryland Dept. of Agriculture
Parole Plaza Office Bldg.
Annapolis, MD 21401

MICHIGAN
Pesticide Programs
Room 11-Agriculture Hall
Michigan State University
East Lansing, MI 48824

MISSISSIPPI
Division of Plant Industry
Mississippi Dept. of Ag. & Commerce
P.O. Box 5207
Mississippi State, MS 39762

ILLINOIS
Bureau of Plant & Apiary Protect.
Illinois Dept. of Agriculture
Emmerson Bldg., State Fairgrounds
Springfield, IL 67206

IOWA
Iowa Dept. of Agriculture
Wallace Building
Des Moines, IA 50319

KENTUCKY
Division of Pesticides
Capitol Plaza Tower
Frankfort, KY 40601

MAINE
Board of Pesticides Control
Maine Dept. of Agriculture
State House Station #28
Augusta, ME 04333

MASSACHUSETTS
Div. of Food & Drugs
Mass. Dept. of Publ. Health
305 South Street
Jamaica Plain, MA 02130

MINNESOTA
Agronomy Services Div.
State Dept. of Agr.
90 West Plato Boulevard
St. Paul, MN 55107

MISSOURI
Plant Industries Div.
Missouri Dept. of Agr.
P.O. Box 630
Jefferson City, MO 65102

MONTANA
Environmental Management Division
Montana Dept. of Agriculture
Agriculture/Livestock Building
Capitol Section
Helena, MT 59601

NEVADA
Nevada Dept. of Agriculture
350 Capitol Hill Ave.
P.O. Box 11100
Reno, NV 89510

NEW JERSEY
Division of Environmental Quality
CN 027
Trenton, NJ 08625

NEW YORK
Bureau of Pesticide Management
Dept. of Environmental Conservation
50 Wolf Road
Albany, NY 12233

NORTH DAKOTA
North Dakota St. Laboratories Dept.
P.O. Box 937
Bismark, ND 58505

OKLAHOMA
Plant Industry Division
Oklahoma State Dept. of Agriculture
122 State Capitol Building
Oklahoma City, OK 73105

PENNSYLVANIA
Bureau of Plant Industry
Pennsylvania Dept. of Agriculture
2301 North Cameron Street
Harrisburg, PA 17120

NEBRASKA
Bureau of Plant Ind.
Department of Agr.
301 Centennial Mall
Lincoln, NE 68509

NEW HAMPSHIRE
New Hampshire Dept. of Agric.
Pesticide Control Division
85 Manchester Street
Concord, NH 03301

NEW MEXICO
Division of Pesticide Mgmt.
New Mexico Dept. of Agriculture
Box 3AQ
Las Cruces, NM 88003

NORTH CAROLINA
Food & Drug Protection Div.
North Carolina Dept. of Agr.
P.O. Box 27647
Raleigh, NC 27611

OHIO
Division of Plant Industry
Ohio Dept. of Agriculture
8955 East Main Street
Reynoldsburg, OH 43068

OREGON
Plant Industry Division
Oregon Dept. of Agriculture
635 Capitol Street, N.E.
Salem, OR 97310

RHODE ISLAND
Division of Agriculture
Rhode Island Department of
    Environmental Management
83 Park Street
Providence, RI 02903

SOUTH CAROLINA
Regulatory & Public Service Program
Clemson University
Clemson, SC 29631

TENNESSEE
Plant Industries Division
Tennessee Dept. of Agriculture
Box 40627, Melrose Station
Nashville, TN 37204

UTAH
Utah State Ag. Dept.
147 North 200 West
Salt Lake City, UT 84103

VIRGINIA
Div. of Product & Industry Reg.
VA Dept. of Ag. & Consumer Serv.
P.O. Box 1163
Richmond, VA 23209

WEST VIRGINIA
Plant Industry Division
West Virginia Dept. of Agriculture
State Capitol Bldg.
Charleston, WV 25305

WYOMING
Wyoming Dept. of Agriculture
2219 Carey Avenue
Cheyenne, WY 82002

VIRGIN ISLANDS
Dept. of Conservation and
    Cultural Affairs
Div. of Natural Resource Management
P.O. Box 4340
St. Thomas, VI 00801

SOUTH DAKOTA
Division of Ag. Reg. & Inspections
South Dakota Dept. of Agriculture
Anderson Building
Pierre, SD 57501

TEXAS
Ag. & Environmental Sci. Div.
P.O. Box 12847
Austin, TX 78711

VERMONT
Plant Industry Division
Vermont Dept. of Agriculture
116 State St./State Office Bldg.
Montpelier, VT 05602

WASHINGTON
Grain & Chemical Division
Washington State Dept. of Ag.
406 General Admin. Bldg.
Olympia, WA 98504

WISCONSIN
Plant Industry Division
Wisconsin Dept. of Agr.
    Trade & Consumer Protection
801 West Badger Rd., Box 8922
Madison, WI 53708

PUERTO RICO
Analysis & Reg. of Agr. Materials
Division of Laboratory
Dept. of Agric., Box 10163
Santurce, PR 00908

Appendix 9: Sources of MSDS's.

A list of chemical companies that may be contacted to provide Material Safety Data Sheets (MSDS) for their products. Compiled by Dr. Roch Gaussoin, Extension Turfgrass Specialist, University of Nebraska, Lincoln, NE.

Abbott Laboratories
Chem. & Ag. Products Div.
1401 Sheridan Rd.
N. Chicago, IL 60064
(708) 937-5109

American Cyanamid
One Cyanamid Place
Wayne, NJ 07470
(201) 831-3615

American Pelletizing Corp.
P.O. Box 3628
Des Moines, IA 50322
(515) 278-5900

The Andersons
Lawn Fertilizer Div.
P.O. Box 119
Maumee, OH 43537
(419) 893-5050

Aquashade, Inc.
P.O. Box 198
Eldred, NY 12732
(914) 557-8077

BASF Corporation
Agricultural Chemicals
100 Cherry Hill Road
Parsippany, NJ 07054
(201) 316-3052

Bonide Chemical Co., Inc.
2 Wurz Ave.
Yorkville, NY 13495
(315) 736-8231

Burlington Bio-medical and
Scientific Corp.
91 Carolyn Blvd.
Farmingdale, NY 11735-1527
(516) 694-9000

Chevron Chemical Co.
P.O. Box 5047
San Ramon, CA 94583
(415) 842-5712

Ciba-Geigy Corp.
Turf & Ornamentals Products
P.O. Box 18300
Greensboro, NC 27419
(919) 852-6192

W.A. Cleary Chemical Corp.
1049 Somerset St.
Somerset, NJ 08873
(201) 247-8000

Doggett Corporation
Cherry Street
Lebanon, NJ 08833
(201) 236-6335

Dow Elanco & Co.
4040 Vicennes Circle
Indianapolis, IN 46268
(317) 276-2299

Four Star Ag Services, Inc.
110 1/2 E. Wabash
Bluffton, IN 46714
(219) 824-5384

Jonathan Green & Sons, Inc.
Squankum-Yellow Brook Rd.
P.O. Box 326
Farmingdale, NJ 07727

Howard Johnson Enterprises
P.O. Box 2990
Milwaukee, WI 53201
(414) 276-4184

Lesco, Inc.
20005 Lake Rd.
Rocky River, OH 44116
(216) 333-9250

Miller Chemical & Fertilizer
P.O. Box 333
Hanover, PA 17331
(717) 632-8921

Milorganite Div. of MMSD
P.O. Box 3049
Milwaukee, WI 53201
(414) 225-2080

Monsanto Ag. Products Co.
800 N. Lindberg Blvd. M2F
St. Louis, MO 63167
(800) 225-2883

E.I. DuPont de Nemours & Co., Inc.
1007 Market St.
Wilmington, DE 19898
(302) 774-7547

Griffin Corporation
Griffin Ag. Chem. Group
P.O. Box 1847
Valdosta, GA 31603

Hawkeye Chemical Co.
P.O. Box 899
Clinton, IA 52732
(319) 243-5800

Lebanon Total Turf Care
Div. of Lebanon Chemical Corp.
P.O. Box 180
Lebanon, PA 17042
(717) 273-1685

J.J. Mauget Co.
2810 N. Figueroa St.
Los Angeles, CA 90065
(213) 227-1482

Milliken Chemical
P.O. Box 817
Inman, SC 29349
(803) 472-9041

Mobay Corporation
AG Chem Div.
P.O. Box 4913
Kansas City, MO 64120
(816) 242-2000

NOR-AM Chemical Co.
3509 Silverside Rd.
Wilmingotn, DE 19803
(302) 575-2000

PBI-Gordon Corp.
P.O. Box 4090
Kansas City, MO 64101
(816) 421-4070

Rockland Khemical Co., Inc.
P.O. Box 809
West Caldwell, NJ 07007-0809
(201) 575-1322

Sierra Chemical Co.
P.O. Box 4003
Milpitas, CA 95035-2003
(408) 263-8080

O.M. Scott & Sons Co.
1411 Scottslawn Rd.
Marysville, OH 43041
(515) 644-0011

Vigoro Industries (Estech)
Specialty Products Div.
P.O. Box 512
Winter Haven, FL 33882-0512
(813) 294-2567

Rhone-Poulenc Ag Co.
Chipco Group
P.O. Box 12014
Research Triangle Park, NC 27709
(919) 549-2172

Safer, Inc.
189 Wells Ave.
Newton, MA 02159
(617) 964-2990

Sierra Crop Protection Co.
12101 Woodcrest Executive Dr.
St. Louis, MO 63141
(314) 275-7561

Uniroyal Chemical Co., Inc.
Middlebury, CT 06749
(203) 573-3544

Wilt-Pruf Products, Inc.
P.O. Box 469
Essex, CT 06426
(203) 767-7033

Appendix 10: Federal Pesticide Agencies. Compiled by Dr. Roch Gaussoin, Extension Turfgrass Specialist, University of Nebraska, Lincoln, NE.

ENVIRONMENTAL PROTECTION AGENCY

Office of the DAA for Pesticides
Environmental Protection Agency
401 M Street, S.W.
Washington, DC 20460

EPA REGIONAL PESTICIDE OFFICES

EPA Region I
John F. Kennedy Federal Bldg.
Boston, MA 02203

EPA Region II
26 Federal Plaza, Room 907
New York, NY 10007

EPA Region III
6th & Walnut St., Curtis Bldg.
Philadelphia, PA 19106

EPA Region IV
345 Courtland St., N.E., Room 204
Atlanta, GA 30308

EPA Region V
Federal Office Bldg.
230 South Dearborn Street
Chicago, IL 60604

EPA Region VI
1201 Elm Street
1st International Bldg.
Dallas, TX 75270

EPA VII
324 E. 11th Street
Kansas City, MO 64106

EPA VIII
1860 Lincoln St., Suite 900
Denver, CO 80295

EPA Region IX
215 Fremont Street
San Francisco, CA 94105

EPA Region X
1200 6th Avenue
Seattle, WA 98101

Appendix 11: Tolerance of some temperate ornamentals to salt spray.

Tolerance of some temperate landscape plants to aerial spray of salt used in winter snow and ice removal operations.

DECIDUOUS TREES

SENSITIVE	INTERMEDIATE	TOLERANT
Carpinus caroliniana Hornbeam	*Acer ginnala* Amur Maple	*Acer platanoides* American Norway Maple
Celtis occidentalis Hackberry	*A. negundo* Boxelder	*A. saccharinum* Silver Maple
Cercis canadensis Eastern Redbud	*A. rubrum* Red Maple	*Aesculus hippocastanum* European Horsechestnut
Crataegus spp. Hawthorn	*A. saccharum* Sugar Maple	*Ailanthus altissima* Tree of Heaven
Fagus grandifolia American Beech	*Alnus* spp. Alder	*Elaeagnus angustifolia* Russian olive
Liriodendron tulipifera Tuliptree	*Amelanchier* spp. Serviceberry	*Fraxinus americana* White Ash
Malus spp. Crabapple	*Betula* spp. Birch	*Gleditsia triacanthos* var. *inermis* Thornless honeylocust
Prunus serotina Black Cherry	*Catalpa speciosa* Catalpa	*Juglans nigra* Black Walnut
Quercus alba White Oak	*Fraxinus pennsylvania* Green Ash	*Populus* spp. Poplar
Q. palustris Pin Oak	*Quercus macrocarpa* Bur Oak	*Robinia pseudoacacia* Black Locust
Q. rubra Red Oak	*Tilia americana* American Linden	*Sorbus decora* Mountainash
Tilia cordata Littleleaf Linden	*Ulmus americana* American Elm	

SHRUBS

SENSITIVE	INTERMEDIATE	TOLERANT
Berberis thunbergii Japanese Barberry	*Alnus rugosa* Speckled Alder	*Caragana arborescens* Siberian Peashrub
Buxus sempervirens Common Box	*Berberis koreana* Korean Barberry	*Euonymus alata* Winged Euonymus
Chaenomeles speciosa Floweringquince	*Forsythia* × *intermedia* Border Forsythia	*Juniperus chinensis* 'Pfitzerana' Pfitzer Juniper
Cornus spp. Dogwood	*Juniperus horizontalis* Creeping Juniper	*Philadelphus* spp. Mockorange
Corylus spp. Hazelnut	*J.h.* 'Plumosa' Andorra Creeping Juniper	*Rhamnus* spp. Buckthorn
Euonymus europaea European Euonymus	*Liqustrum* spp. Privet	*Rhus aromatica* Fragrant Sumac
Sambucus canadensis American Elder	*Lonicera* spp. Honeysuckle	*R. typhina* Staghorn Sumac
Spiraea spp. Spirea	*Syringa vulgaris* Common Lilac	*Ribes alpinum* Alpine Currant
Symphoricarpos orbiculatus Indiancurrant Coralberry	*Viburnum dentatum* Arrowood Viburnum	*Rosa rugosa* Rugosa rose
Viburnum lantana Wayfaringtree Viburnum	*V. lentago* Nannyberry Viburnum	*Symphoricarpos albus* Snowberry
	V. trilobum American - Cranberrybush Viburnum	*Syringa reticulata* Japanese Tree Lilac
		Tamarix ramosissima Five-stamen Tamarix

CONIFERS

SENSITIVE	INTERMEDIATE	TOLERANT
Abies balsamea Balsam Fir	*Juniperus* spp. Juniper	*Juniperus virginiana* Eastern Redcedar
Metasequoia glyptostroboides Dawn Redwood	*Picea abies* Norway Spruce	*Larix decidua* European Larch
Picea glauca White Spruce	*Pinus ponderosa* Ponderosa Pine	*Picea pungens* Colorado Spruce
Pinus resinosa Red Pine	*Pseudotsuga menziesii* Douglasfir	*Pinus banksiana* Jack Pine
P. strobus Eastern White Pine		*P. nigra* Austrian Pine
P. sylvestris Scotch Pine		
Taxus spp. Yew		
Thuja occidentalis American Arborvitae		
Tsuga canadensis Canada Hemlock		

Appendix 12: Tolerance of some temperate ornamentals to soil salts.

Tolerance of some temperate landscape plants to deicing salt contamination in the soil.

DECIDUOUS TREES

SENSITIVE	INTERMEDIATE	TOLERANT
Carpinus caroliniana American Hornbeam	*Acer platanoides* Norway Maple	*Aesculus hippocastanum* European Horsechestnut
A. rubrum Red Maple	*A. negundo* Boxelder	*Ailanthus altissima* Tree-of-Heaven
A. saccharum Sugar Maple	*A. saccharinum* Silver Maple	*Elaeagnus angustifolia* Russianolive
Fagus grandifolia American Beech	*Cercis canadensis* Eastern Redbud	*Fraxinus americana* White Ash
Alnus spp. Alder	*Betula* spp. Birch	*Gleditsia triacanthos* var. *inermus* Honeylocust
Liriodendron tulipifera Tuliptree	*Malus* spp. Crabapple	*Prunus serotina* Black Cherry
Juglans nigra Black Walnut	*Populus* spp. Poplar	*Quercus alba* White Oak
Tilia cordata Littleleaf Linden		*Robinia pseudoacacia* Black Locust
Tilia americana American Linden		*Quercus rubra* Red Oak
		Quercus macrocarpa Bur Oak

SHRUBS

SENSITIVE	**INTERMEDIATE**	**TOLERANT**
Berberis thunbergii Japanese Barberry	*J.h.* 'Plumosa' Andorra Juniper	*Juniperus chinensis* 'Pfitzerana' Pfitzer Juniper
Alnus rugosa Speckled Alder	*Liqustrum* spp. Privet	
Buxus sempervirens Common Box	*Lonicera* spp. Honeysuckle	
Euonymus alata Winged Euonymus		
Corylus spp. Hazelnut		
Euonymus europaea European Euonymus		
Spiraea spp. Spirea		
Viburnum dentatum Arrowood Viburnum		
Viburnum lantana Wayfaringtree Viburnum		
Viburnum lentago Nannyberry Viburnum		
Viburnum trilobum American Cranberrybush Viburnum		

336

CONIFERS

SENSITIVE	**INTERMEDIATE**	**TOLERANT**
Picea abies Norway Spruce	*Abies balsamea* Balsam Fir	*Juniperus virginiana* Eastern Redcedar
Larix decidua European Larch	*Picea glauca* White Spruce	
Picea pungens Colorado Spruce	*Pinus ponderosa* Ponderosa Pine	
Pinus resinosa Red Pine	*Thuja occidentalis* American Arborvitae	
Pseudotsuga menziesii Douglasfir		
Pinus strobus Eastern White Pine		
Tsuga canadensis Canada Hemlock		

Index

About the Author

Associate Professor and Extension Landscape Specialist in the Department of Horticulture, University of Hawaii since 1992.

Taught courses in landscape design, landscape contracting, and landscape management at Kansas State University for 11 years. Presently teaches a course in tropical landscape horticulture.

Research programs include landscape installation and management technology and problems.

Extension experience with the green industry in Missouri, Indiana, Kentucky, Kansas, and Hawaii. Advisor to the Landscape Industry Council of Hawaii.

Published 39 scientific articles and over 160 trade and popular articles in trade magazines such as *American Nurseryman, Nursery Manager, Hawaii Landscape,* and *Grounds Maintenance.*

Professional experience in designing, installing, and maintaining landscapes. Superintendent of Purdue Horticulture Park for 3 years.

B.S., University of Missouri; M.S. and Ph.D. from Purdue University with Dr. Philip Carpenter.